Once Upon A Time
in Naples

By JOHN LUDDEN

The Parrs Wood Press
Manchester

First Published 2005

THE PARRS WOOD PRESS
St Wilfrid's Enterprise Centre
Royce Road, Manchester, M15 5BJ
www.parrswoodpress.com

© John Ludden 2005

ISBN: 1 903158 68 0

Printed and bound by Newton Printing Ltd of London
www.newtonprinting.com

For our little boy Matthew, who we love
more than all the stars in the sky.

ACKNOWLEDGEMENTS

I would like to thank the following people for their help during the writing of *Once upon a time in Naples*. Foremost amongst them is my wife Christine, who has had to contend with Diego in our lives for much longer than was healthy. Cheers darling, I promise no more epics... for now! My Mum, Dad, brother Paul, Gran, Grandad and mother-in-law Rita, friends, Chris Searles, Paul Rothwell and Rachael Moores - without their constant encouragement this book would never have been completed.

Gerry Kelly, Sherlock Holmes author extraordinaire, whose early proof-reading only helped to confirm my long-term suspicions that I can't spell. Mario Giaquinto (Vivadiego.com), who watched Maradona regularly during his glory years in Naples and proved priceless in helping me research those heady times. *Graze*, Mario. Andy Searle at The Parrs Wood Press for making my dreams of this book seeing the light of day come true. And, finally, my little boy Matthew, whose arrival on the scene slowed down considerably my writing output but ultimately proved only an inspiration to me. A little star!

Thanks all.

As for Diego Maradona, I wish him only happy days ahead, hopefully playing with his grandchildren, for there has never been or will be a player likehim.

John Ludden
CFIELDSOFFIRE@aol.com
May 2005

CONTENTS

INTRODUCTION

VESUVIUS ERUPTS

Once upon a time.

The volcano was rumbling, its ancient slumber stirred. In 64AD, the notorious Roman Emperor Nero travelled deep into the south of Italy to bestow upon the citizens of Naples his royal presence. In any part of the Empire such a visit from the Emperor would have been the cause of huge festivities and excitement, but not in Naples. Neapolitans saw through the madman from Rome who claimed nonsensically to be related to the Gods. Nero was on his way to their city to partake in the annual music festival. He was not, as the legends relate, an atrocious fiddler, but an awful singer, whose screeching voice and idiotic lyrics reduced even his most fawning admirer to fervid looks of incredulity. Nero's frightful renditions of the Roman classics were endured through gritted teeth, only to be wildly applauded at their finish. For no one was allowed to leave the auditorium whilst the Emperor was performing. To do so risked instant death. None dared chance the wrath of a man whose mood swings ranged from mildly psychotic to wholly demented.

Forced into having to indulge their master's every whim, Nero's all-obeying entourage arranged for him to make his first public performance in Naples. Much to their great annoyance a crowd of Neapolitans quietly going about their daily business were rounded up and taken to the theatre where their Emperor was staging his one-man show. Once inside they were barred from leaving. Midway through Nero's pathetic performance the building began to shake violently. For several seconds panic reigned as the Neapolitans feared their volcano had finally blown its top and let loose in all hell and thunder. Astonishingly, through the ensuing chaos Nero continued to sing, appearing totally oblivious to any danger. Come the end of a soul-destroying, ear-screeching encore, the entire theatre house applauded wildly, and with a fleeting wave of the royal hand Nero vacated the stage. His huge ego satisfied, the Emperor returned home. Only moments after the last person had left the theatre, the roof collapsed. Elsewhere in Naples the tremor was hardly felt. The hall was the only building badly damaged. The superstitious Neapolitans wagged their finger in the direction of their Emperor. Could it really have been Nero's terrible wailing that caused Vesuvius to stir?

But the Emperor's ultimate ambition was to enter the singing contest at the Olympic games. Rome's finest fulfilled his crazed ambition for glory when he triumphed amidst stage-managed, mass scenes of adoration in Greece. Victory for the Emperor appeared a certainty when Nero with typical self-interest invented a royal decree barring others from taking part in the singing competition. He also triumphed spectacularly in the chariot races when despite falling many times off his vehicle, other competitors kindly stopped to let him back on. For they dared not risk overtaking him. A man who murdered his own mother would surely have had no problem in executing a few measly Olympians?

As for the people of Naples they cursed the Emperor for the rousing, of what they referred to as their 'Fire Mountain'. Once awoken it was feared only a matter of time before disaster struck. And so they waited, watched, and prayed. Fourteen years lapsed before hell in all its fury came raining down upon them. For shortly after 1pm on 18th August 79AD, Vesuvius erupted spewing death and destruction on all who dwelt in her foreboding shadow. A whole side of the mountain was torn away for a length of two kilometres, lashing tongues of red fire soared violently in all directions. Billowing clouds of black ash soared upwards, stealing the daylight, obscuring the afternoon sun. The surrounding cities of Pompeii and Herculaneum disappeared beneath a torrent of boiling rocks and poisonous gases. The death toll was horrific. Naples felt the deadly wrath of Vesuvius but survived the ghastly horrors that engulfed its tragic neighbours. Five thousand people died in Pompeii alone. Many still stand, frozen in death masks, such was the ferocity and swiftness of their untimely end, to this day the shock and horror recognisable on their faces.

By this time Nero had made the defining career decision of committing suicide to gain a new audience. After being informed that the Roman Senate had finally grown weary of his insane behaviour, and issued an order that he be arrested and flogged to death, the Emperor decided to vacate this mortal coil to torment the next world with his unbearable singing. His dying words, *'Qualis artifex pereo'* ('What an artist the world loses in me'), were greeted with joy and great disdain in Naples. For the Neapolitans were left in no doubt whom to blame for what happened. This Roman despot had travelled to their city uninvited and unwanted. The carnage this evoked defied belief. From that moment on their lives became forever linked with the huge brooding menace that soared above them. Invested with the knowledge that hell may return at any waking hour the people of Naples began to live for the day. For the price of a song an eternity of impending doom hung over those who decided to chance all on the changing moods of Vesuvius. It began a fitful sleep, occasionally disturbed from its slumber, but never fully opening its eyes. The centuries passed, and the fear she might erupt was only ever a moment away. But not even the mighty volcano could have shook Naples more than the arrival into their clan, on 5th July 1984, of *El Pibe De Oro*, Golden boy! Diego Armando Maradona.

CHAPTER 1

IN THE DAYS BEFORE

Sunday 8th October 1983. The beleaguered President of SSC Napoli, Corrado Ferlaino, bore the haunted expression of a man being forced to witness his own funeral. A stone-faced Ferlaino watched in dismay as a rampant AS Roma ventured south to inflict an embarrassing 3-1 defeat on his hapless Napoli side. After a horrendous start to the season, increasing pressure grew on the President from tifosi (supporters) to stand down. Even before the game began against Roma a small plane had flown low over the San Paolo stadium dropping thousands of leaflets, telling him in no uncertain fashion to go. The blind loyalty of the Napoli following meant them capable of anything. Fires were lit on the terraces as mass brawling erupted between frustrated tifosi and police. Tear gas filled the air. Naples was a city where, after family, football was life. One love, SSC Napoli mattered, and any thought not giving their all for the cause were considered fair game. It was a fraught-looking Ferlaino who tried in vain to ignore the insults hurled in his direction.

Two days later whilst playing host to a small select band of still loyal journalists, the President heard them clearly when a crude, homemade device exploded outside his villa. At the same time another went off at the San Paolo, injuring no one, but ripping through a wall, badly damaging the ticket office. The *tifosi* had begun a sustained terror campaign of threats and intimidation. The message to Corrado Ferlaino reached deafening proportions and one he could no longer afford to ignore. It was either step aside, or prove your worth to the city of your birth. Ferlaino had been at the helm of this runaway train of a football club for close on fourteen years, suffering constantly the wrath of a blood clan who claimed he cared more about a personal bank balance than the well being of their beloved team. Accusations raged that the President had abused club finances to fund other suspicious business activities. In the past he could afford to ride the storm, for there was always another season. Not anymore, the fanatical hardcore of Napoli *tifosi* had finally lost patience. Time had run out. It was *capolinea* (end of the line).

In an effort to appease his many critics the President brought back former popular coach Rino Marchesi to steady the ship and ultimately save them, albeit by a single point, from being relegated. But Corrado Ferlaino knew this was not enough to rescue him from the mob. Somewhere in Naples a gallows awaited. Something extraordinary was needed to regain the trust of the Neapolitans. Nothing short of a miracle would suffice. Ferlaino's eyes drifted south, across the ocean to Spain and Barcelona. Whispers had reached him of an extraordinary talented young footballer who was willing to come and save his neck. In a last throw of the dice the President went public to promise his city and its rebellious clans a prize beyond their wildest dreams. In an audacious swoop Corrado Ferlaino vowed to bring Naples the great Diego Maradona.

Bought for a then world record of $7.3 million from Argentinian champions Boca Juniors, Maradona had struggled desperately to settle in the chic, sophisticated surroundings of the Catalan capital. The kid from the back streets of Buenos Aires slums was looked down upon as a *Sudaca*, an insulting term for a dark-skinned South American. During a troubled two-year spell at Barcelona, Diego Maradona showed only brief, if illuminating scraps of his true worth as illness and injuries dogged him endlessly. A severe bout of hepatitis brought on partly by his crazed antics off the pitch hardly helped his cause, sidelining him for three months.

As if cursed, there was also the infamous incident when Maradona fell victim to one of the most outrageous fouls ever witnessed in Spain. On 24th September 1983 at the Nou Camp in Barcelona, a horrific scything lunge from behind by the aptly nicknamed 'Basque Butcher', Andoni Goicoechea, meant two screws having to be inserted into his left ankle. For this heinous tackle the Butcher received a mere eighteen-day ban, whilst Maradona was ruled out for four months and his career placed in serious jeopardy. This appalling injury sadly proved the most enduring memory of Diego Maradona's dismal stay in Catalonia. As for Goicoechea, he earned everlasting notoriety as the man who so nearly crippled Maradona. To this day he keeps the boot in a showcase at home as a sordid remainder of his notoriety. Hardly an inscription to die for.

Revenge showed itself in the aftermath of a Spanish cup final defeat against Andoni Goicoechea's, Bilbao, when a kung-fu kicking Diego Maradona led his teammates into a free-for-all pitch battle. Maradona's target clear for all to see as he launched himself at the Butcher. Watching on grim-faced was guest of honour King Juan Carlos of Spain and millions live on television. For the Barcelona hierarchy it was all highly embarrassing. They could not stomach anymore this troublemaker dragging their proud name through the mud. When disturbing reports reached the President Jose Luis Nunez of him indulging in cocaine-fuelled orgies with Barcelona's ladies of the night, the Catalan giants let it be known privately to the Neapolitans that for the right price Maradona was theirs. Nunez had spies watching his most valuable asset. He knew all his gripes and vices and had grown to despise this foreigner and his peasant entourage, whose blatant disrespect and flouting disregard for his beloved club could not be tolerated as Barca's motto was '*Mas que un club*' ('More than just a club'). No *Sudaca* from the backstreet slums of Buenos Aires would be allowed to stain Barcelona's colours, especially when not proving value for money.

It was ironic this all occurred as Diego Maradona starred in a Spanish television advertisement for an anti-drugs campaign. Set on a beach surrounded by a crowd of fresh-faced youngsters, a grinning Diego Armando appeared the epitome of clean living as he declared to the camera, 'Enjoy life, drugs kill.' The incoming Barca manager Terry Venables was asked his opinion of what should be done by Nunez. Much as Venables had looked forward to working with whom he considered the best player in the world, after hearing lurid tales of Maradona's debauched lifestyle the Englishman realised he would be better off rid. Catalonia was not big enough for them both. Short, terse and to the point, 'Sell him,' declared Venables. Diego Maradona had outstayed his welcome amongst the Catalans, for even genius has a price, and when it came with such a curse even more so. Barca's Vice-President Juan Gaspart was ordered by Nunez to begin proceedings and oversee the transfer.

Napoli's legendary General Manager and most favourite son, Antonio Juliano, was the man entrusted by his President to bring Maradona home to Naples. Juliano was a Neapolitan living legend who hailed from the tough backstreets of the notorious Forcella district of the city. During a fifteen-year career he gave all for the club and wholly earned the respect of the Napoli *tifosi*, who lovingly christened him *Our Totonno*. Without Juliano it is doubtful whether the transfer of Maradona would have happened. Corrado Ferlaino's final instructions to his number two and close friend on departing for Barcelona bordered more on a cry for help as he implored Juliano not to return without Maradona. His was a pivotal role in clearing the way of obstacles by massaging hugely inflated Catalan egos, and ensuring with his Neapolitan streetwise wisdom that those whose palms needed crossing with silver were taken care of. When tempers frayed and threats raged it was Juliano who calmed the waters.

Respected by one side, deeply loved by another, Totonno earned the eternal gratitude of all Neapolitans as his diplomatic skills paved the way for a deal to be brokered. For above all this was a man who recognised and appreciated genius. Antonio Juliano understood that footballers like Diego

Maradona were worth their weight in gold. His city for so long the poor relations to the fat cats in the north had been handed a God-given opportunity to fight back. It could not afford to be wasted. Whatever the fee it would be cheap at twice the price. For this kid who moved as if no one was ever in his way was truly special. Juan Gaspart placed a new world record of $13 million on the bargaining table. Take or leave it?

Gaspart had little time for the Neapolitans whom he considered mere peasants. He enjoyed watching them squirm. At first Ferlaino baulked at paying such an astronomical fee. He ordered Juliano home, it was not meant to be. Such a sum was simply beyond them. Totonno refused and argued endlessly for doing so. After being harassed, harangued and ultimately convinced by his fellow Neapolitan that they were actually getting a bargain, the President agreed reluctantly to trust Juliano's judgement and pay the king's ransom. Juliano found himself increasingly drawn to Maradona. Both hailed from similar backgrounds of hardened poverty. A friendship quickly developed and the Italian managed to convince the Argentinian that in time he would become a living God in Naples. And be well paid doing so.

An idol to the Napoli *tifosi*. For if ever a player was born to galvanise the fanatical southern hordes into action against the footballing aristocracy of Turin and Milan it was he. The player himself was keen to push the transfer through, for his finances lay in ruins. Maradona's long-time friend and appointed business manager, twenty-six-year-old Jorge Cyterszpiler, had slipped up disastrously on the numbers. In short they were broke: no money was left in the bank. Gambling and losing heavily on a series of inept, commercial enterprises, he had left them all but bankrupt. The $3 million earned during a two-year spell in Spain had gone. Cyterszpiler's pitiable attempts to make Maradona Productions a viable venture proved calamitous. This allied to Diego's extravagant lifestyle and huge entourage of family, friends and fixers left them deep in the mire. Indeed it had plunged such depths that Maradona was forced to borrow cash off Barca coach at the time, former Argentinian national manager Cesar Menotti, to bale him out. It was only Cysterszpiler's close relationship with his boss that saved him from getting the boot. The player would earn close to $6.5 million from the transfer to Naples. Maradona could hardly let such a sum go begging. Signing for the Neapolitans became a financial necessity, it could not be allowed to fall through.

During the initial negotiations President Nunez appeared to be on the verge of a change of heart. Maybe he had been a little hasty in dumping his most prized asset? Sensing trouble Maradona moved fast, informing Barca officials that he had no intentions of ever kicking a ball again in the Nou Camp and would do all in his power to make life as difficult as possible for them. Knowing this was no idle threat the Catalans reluctantly caved in and waived their rights to this jagged thorn in their side. It was adios Barcelona: Napoli had their man, or so it appeared. Even before the ink was dry on the contract Naples was celebrating the signing of Maradona. Never ones to let a good business opportunity pass them by, the Neapolitans cashed in. Traders dealt in bootleg tapes of songs extolling the beauty of all things Diego. The smiling face of their new boy was stitched onto banners and flags of SSC Napoli, sold on every street corner along the Spaccanapoli. A slashing, winding, ribbon road that stabs through the heart of the city.

Corrado Ferlaino could afford to smile again. Life was good. But, sadly, as ever with all things Naples, there remained one last twist. With television stations across the southern Peninsula breaking into normal programming to announce Diego Maradona's signing, the Barcelona supremo made his move. With nothing to lose he sent word; 'Bleed Napoli dry.' Knowing well how desperate the Neapolitans were to have Maradona, the Catalan envoy went for broke. In a blatant act of gamesmanship Barca demanded a further $600,000 or the deal was off. On being informed, Corrado Ferlaino had the look of man facing a firing squad without a blindfold. After pledging to his birth city that Maradona's signature was theirs, he now faced up to the reality that he was being made a fool of. The President exploded in rage. Clearly this *straniero* (foreigner) had no idea who he was dealing with. For Ferlaino was a man that had made his fortunes in the murky world of the Neapolitan construction business. It was not wise to treat someone like he with such blatant disrespect.

It was an open secret across Naples that the Napoli Supremo held dark links with a criminal organisation that stretched its poisonous hold over the south and deep into the heart of the region's capital. Ferlaino had done a pact with the Devil, the Neapolitan version of the Sicilian Mafia, the Camorra, derived from the Spanish *'Buscar Camorra'* ('To look for trouble'). Many who knew of such things claimed they were even more ruthless in conducting matters than their more famous Sicilian cousins. *Camorra* activities ranged from corruption, bribery, drug trafficking, smuggling and murder. They also took an unhealthy interest in the exploits of their local football club, for amongst the vast legions of Napoli *tifosi* there were many who plied an illegal trade working for the city's Godfathers. With loyalty unquestionable and ruthlessness unnerving, they were *Camorra* foot soldiers that dealt in blood. Ferlaino understood only too well they would not take kindly to losing out on such a wonderful talent, for rumours were strong at the time it was mob money that made up a hefty slice of the transfer fee. If the Argentinian went elsewhere someone would pay a heavy price. *Lo Camorra* did not suffer such disappointments lightly.

Membership to this ungodly world could only be earned by the committing of a murder for the cause. Unlike the Mafia, which was controlled by five leading families, it was an uneasy alliance of sixty bloodthirsty clans from the region of Campania. These would heed and fall in line with whoever was most ruthless at any given period. Since the seventeenth century, this sinister brotherhood of crime that originated in the city's prisons secretly ruled over the poverty-stricken heartlands of the Mezzogiorno, the Italian South, and nowhere were they more prevalent than in Naples itself. Their hold over the southern capital was like an invisible cord that strangled the life out of anything or anyone who dared to defy them. All that was required when the need arose was a simple tug on the strings and the victim would be made to dance.

A local shopkeeper would rather hand over ten per cent of his hard earned money to a *Camorristi* henchman, known as a *guappo*, than pay taxes to a state that he neither respects or does anything for him. With *Camorra* you paid *tangente* (protection money) and were allowed to do business. Simple but effective. In Naples they were the absolute law, whose rules and regulations differed from the norm but had to be strictly adhered to. Perversely they called themselves the 'friends of the poor'. But there was no Robin Hood romanticism attached to the *Camorra*. If any ever dared to cross them the consequences would be severe. Many a time the simple fishermen of Naples would find in their nets a catch they hardly expected.

The Catalans ruse, apart from infuriating Ferlaino, shocked him to the core, for there was also the fearful notion of Maradona being stolen away at the last by other interested parties. Worrying rumours had swept Naples that representatives of the hated Juventus were in town ready to step in, if given the slightest hint of the deal collapsing. Whether true or false they sent cold shivers down the spine of the Napoli President. The world would not have been a big enough place to hide if he failed Naples and allowed Maradona to slip his grasp and into the arms of Juve. La Vecchia Signora, the old lady of Italian *calcio* (football), was the epitome of true evil for Napoli followers. Already in Turin was the great number ten, French playmaker Michel Platini. With the Argentinian alongside him? To even consider such was unthinkable for any Neapolitan. Losing Maradona at this late stage was not an option. Such a huge loss of face against Gianni Agnelli's Fiat-bankrolled giants could never be lived down. In the Napoli trophy room there was only one trophy worthy of note. The Cup of the Alps was an obscure competition now resigned to the dimming pages of history books. The supporters of SSC Napoli deserved more, for they and their fathers and grandfathers before them had already suffered too much.

A despairing Ferlaino was on the brink. The President was cornered, there was no more money. He had bankrolled both his and Napoli's entire future on this one deal. The consequences of it collapsing around his ears could not be contemplated. There was one card left to play, but it resembled neither an ace nor a joker. In desperation, and in an act totally unprecedented elsewhere, Corrado Ferlaino went for broke and appealed direct to the citizens of Naples for the extra cash. It was a dangerous ploy and one that could easily have seen him hounded out of the city. The scenario of him being frog-marched by a Neapolitan lynch mob to the summit of Mount Vesuvius and thrown into its abyss could not be ruled out.

But luckily for Ferlaino the response to his desperate plea for help defied belief. The word spread quickly of the President's plight. In the crumbling tenements of the Quartieri Spagnoli (Spanish Quarter) that stretched from the legendary Via Santa Lucia to the over-hanging hills of Pizzofalcone, the collections began. This decaying, winding den of intrigue and blind alleys that spilt messily downwards to the seaport was home to the true hardcore of Napoli *tifosi*, and a place feared by strangers and Carabinieri alike. So named after the invading Spanish army who billeted there in the seventeenth century, it remained forever sheltered from the sunlight by the endless sheets of flapping washing lines that lay festooned across the cobbled alleys. A world in the shade, a law apart.

In the ravaged slums of the Forcella district, a *Camorra* stronghold of the fearsome Giuliano clan for two decades, people gave all they could afford and more. Across the city long queues gathered outside the Bank of Naples offices, desperate to help. For the thought of seeing Maradona in the despised black and white stripes of Juve was unbearable. It would rip open their hearts. Despite the dislike for their club President it could not be allowed to happen. In less than a day the amount was raised as Neapolitans rallied round. *Camorra guappos* helped to collect the cash. No matter how small their donation people were determined to contribute. In a place plagued by crippling unemployment and wretched crime the sheer magnitude of this generosity shocked outsiders. But such was the craving to have Diego Maradona amongst them, families went without food, women pawned their best jewellery, children sold their favourite toys. The more fanatical would have sold their soul to the Devil himself if it meant seeing the Argentinian in a Napoli shirt. A miracle occurred in Naples and the begging bowl was filled. It would not be the last. Maradona dare not let them down.

But there was still to be one final shake of the snake's tail before the transfer could be completed. The deadline to register the Argentinian for the forthcoming season had been missed by a whisker. Already President Ferlaino had sent into the Italian Football Association headquarters in Milan a letter listing the names of players Napoli had signed up. Due to all the last minute drama Maradona was not amongst them. However Corrado Ferlaino refused to let such a minor problem scupper his plans. A call was made and come the moment of the letter being opened, Maradona's name was miraculously included. A remarkable feat considering the rules and regulations of the Italian FA stipulated such changes were not allowed. That a security guard, charged with looking after the property swore he saw nothing untoward, came as no shock to all those who understood how Neapolitans excelled in making such problems disappear. In Naples there were those whose influence touched Kings and Presidents. They were hardly going to let the petty rules of a northern bias FA prevent them signing Diego Maradona. Not exactly a miracle, but a darn fine trick nonetheless!

And so late on the evening of 30th June 1984, aboard President Ferlaino's luxurious yacht moored off the beautifully lit-up island of Capri, Diego Maradona soothed Napoli nerves by finally putting pen to paper. Corrado Ferlaino welcomed Maradona in typical Italian tradition by kissing him on both cheeks. Their embrace appeared to those unknowing of a father embracing his long-lost son. But In this city such an act held a hidden meaning: 'Do not ever cross me.' As the champagne corks popped, Napoli *tifosi* prepared for the biggest parties in their history, for Diego Maradona was coming to town! In the days before there had been nothing but sadness and despair. But now a new era dawned. A sweet Neapolitan moon shone bright. In Naples life was about to become interesting.

CHAPTER 2

THE CORONATION

It was a most wonderful day for the crowning of a king. Whoever said dreams don't come true could not have been in Naples at 6.30pm on Sunday 5th July 1984. A day now etched into the rich tapestry of Neapolitan folklore. 'L'uomo della provvidenza' ('a gift from the Gods'). Like an angel descending from heaven the helicopter carrying Diego Maradona to his new kingdom soared high above Vesuvius before swooping low over the city. On board an excited but nervous Maradona gazed down at the sprawling, winding mess of Naples that seemed to stretch forever below him. Her poverty-stricken neighbourhoods dominated by family clans and street gangs, but united on this historic day to pay homage to the greatest footballer in the world.

Three hundred years after the crucifixion of Christ a lone Bishop arrived in Naples to aid Christians against the persecution of Rome. Gennaro hailed from the nearby town of Benevento and came armed only with a staff carved into the shape of a cross. His appearance outraged the Roman Governor Timotheus, who issued an immediate decree for the Bishop's arrest and execution. Timotheus would make an example to the troublesome Neapolitans who chose to worship a long-dead criminal rather than the imperial Emperor of Rome. The one known as Gennaro was seized by Roman legionnaires and taken to a molten furnace that blazed away eternally at the foot of Mount Vesuvius. Forced at sword point by the Centurion in command to walk to his death, San Gennaro trod warily into the furnace, only for the flames to die down before him and flitter out. Feeling afraid the shocked Roman commander sent word back to his Governor of the strange event that had occurred.

Timotheus acted fast, for these were dangerous times. Rome had suffered enough the antics of these Disciples who claimed to follow in the shoes of the long-dead mystical fisherman from Galilee in troubled Palestine. Who even three centuries after being nailed to a cross held the power to strike blind fear into the heart of the greatest empire the world had

19

ever seen. Word spread like wildfire across Naples of the weird happenings at Vesuvius. A second execution was ordered, this time at the arena in Pozzuoli on the edge of the city. Thousands rushed to watch as Roman soldiers began to form a wall of steel to keep out the vast throngs who came mainly out of curiosity to catch a glimpse of the ill-fated Bishop. On Timotheus's command the lions prowled into the ring. Gennaro walked bravely to face a savage end in the jaws of the roaring beasts, but, to the wonder of all, a miracle again took place, and as the Romans watched on open-mouthed the lions lay meekly down before him.

The Neapolitans cheered, the arena was cleared and a red-faced Timotheus seethed with anger. This was not Jerusalem; Naples lay only a short distance from Rome. As the audience pleaded for the Bishop's life the Governor decided to end this nonsense. He called for the axeman. Gennaro would be beheaded on the guillotine. Suddenly Timotheus cried in terror, as from a clear blue sky he was struck blind by a thunderbolt. The frightened masses screamed at this divine retribution. As the Governor fell to his knees in despair, the Bishop whispered a short prayer for this Roman to be granted his sight back. Immediately Timotheus could see again. The crowd roared for a pardon but in a fit of rage and embarrassment he ignored their pleas and ordered the axeman to end Gennaro's life.

To gasps of horror amongst the watching hordes the ghastly sentence was carried out and the axe came down. An eerie silence settled over all. Finally satisfied, the Governor gave instructions for the arena to be cleared and the body left to rot. Later that night a gang of Neapolitans sneaked back over the walls to remove the severed head of the Bishop. An old lady dried Gennaro's blood and filled two small vials. Little did the Romans understand what their evil deeds had done, for in killing the man they succeeded only in giving birth to his legend. For it was said San Gennaro never really died, his spirit remained to watch over the city of Naples in her many hours of need. Neapolitans have always claimed their Patron has saved their necks on countless occasions. His has been an arduous and thankless task.

Many years later, '*Di Miracolo in Miracolo*!' ('The miracle of miracles!'). Three times a year in Naples Cathedral a modern day miracle occurs. The Archbishop raises high the clotted blood of San Gennaro and prays for it to liquefy live before a hushed congregation of hundreds and a television audience of millions across Italy. It is said that if the miracle fails to occur, impending disaster will strike the region. As the ceremony reaches its climax, nearby on a stone in Pozzuoli, where San Gennaro was beheaded, a spot of blood takes on a brighter hue. At such a moment the miracle is deemed to have successfully taken place and the city of Naples gives thanks and breathes a heavy sigh of relief. In moments of dire need, and there have been many over the decades for the troubled football club of SSC Napoli, their *tifosi*, in a last throw of the dice, took to praying en masse on the terraces to their Patron saint. Cries of '*San Gennaro, aiutaci tu!*' ('San Gennaro please help us!') echoed countless times across the San Paolo stadium. On a memorable summer's day in 1984 their prayers were finally answered.

At first just a bright speck on the southern blue horizon, the helicopter began its descent and closed in on the San Paolo. The home of SSC Napoli was a cauldron of rampant hysteria. 70,000 fanatical *tifosi* converged on the Stadium to worship their new messiah, each content to be charged a thousand liras for the privilege of watching the Argentinian superstar set foot on their hallowed turf for the first time. Many Neapolitans from Italy and across the world had partaken in what was nothing short of a religious pilgrimage to be present on this fateful day for the city of their birth. They just had to see it with their own eyes! 'Maradona is a romantic. He plays well only when he feels loved, and he has come to the right place,' said one Naples historian. As the bay basked in the warm glow of the late evening sunshine, Naples prepared to say a heartfelt '*Buenos sera*' to Diego Armando Maradona.

He entered the arena from deep within the bowels of the stadium. Dressed in white T-shirt and tracksuit pants, this twenty-four-year-old with the handsome fresh-faced good looks and thick mop of black hair appeared the epitome of Neapolitan cool. So like any other native of this fair city who roared down the alleys and streets of Naples on their Vespas at death-defying speed. Maradona was handed a Napoli scarf that he placed with tender care around his neck. Then, taking a deep breath, Diego made the sign of the cross and headed up a small stairway that led onto the pitch into blinding sunlight and legend.

The word was out on Maradona from the age of eight years old. After making his debut for Cebollitas, the adopted youth club of first division side Argentinos Juniors, rumours spread of a magical boy who made the ball sing. Hundreds came to watch, bewitched by fantastic tales of young Diego in action. A scout for Argentinos, Francisco Cornejo, once claimed that 'Diego must have come from another planet,' such was his ability to do whatever he wanted with a football. Soon the touchlines at every Cebollitas match brimmed full of football scouts and supporters unable to believe their own eyes at what they were witnessing. People came from all over Buenos Aires to catch a glimpse of this extraordinarily talented youngster. Even at such a tender age the people of Argentina hailed Maradona with a true religious zeal. A dash of magic dust led to the birth of a kid who with the ball at his feet waltzed with angels.

At ten Maradona entertained a full house at an Argentinos Junior home match by juggling a ball for the entire interval. When the time arrived for the second half to recommence, the entire stadium rose to its feet applauding and chanting, '*Que se quede, que se quede!*' ('Let him stay on, let him stay on!'). Unable to resist, the young Diego persisted on, and to the delight of the crowd and the utter astonishment of the two teams who waited to re-start the second half, continued to provide his adoring audience with an audacious encore. He would later say, 'It felt like I touched heaven with my hands that day.' This was not so much a rising star but a blazing comet. Bidding a tearful adios to Argentinos the big clubs came calling and a $1 million deal saw Maradona join his boyhood heroes, the famed Boca Juniors, where he continued to forge a growing reputation. Formed by Italian and Irish immigrant in 1905 Boca prided themselves in being the team of the working classes. The vast majority of their followers hailed from the poor downtrodden neighbourhoods of Buenos Aires docklands. Here the similarities with Naples were many, indeed most of their supporters were only one or two generations removed from Southern Italy. Maradona's mother was of Italian descent whose parents risked the dangers of an unknown continent to escape the despairing poverty of early 20th century Naples to find a better life.

They also, like the Neapolitans, loved nothing more than putting one over those who considered themselves their superiors. The city's other major club, River Plate, were every Boca Juniors supporter's sworn enemy from birth. The murderous rivalry between the sets of fans made the Italian North/South divide appear like two nuns bickering over a sewing needle. River Plate was seen as the choice of the upper classes, the snobbish and the bourgeois. A national institution. When the two clashed either at the home of Boca, La Bombonera, or the proud residence of River, El Monumental stadium, all of Argentina anticipated fireworks. The *Superclasico* rarely disappointed as these giants of Argentinian football went for each other's throat with a blazing ferocity dipped in the dangerous waters of tradition and class.

It was during such blood-curdling contests that Diego Maradona experienced for the first time the immeasurable hatred that such a simple game generated amongst the masses. He would endure taunts from the River crowds regarding his father's Indian heritage and his childhood of pitiful poverty spent in the wastelands of Villa Fiorito, a breeding ground for assassins, pimps, priests and footballers. Maradona excelled in such hell-hole, intimidatory atmospheres and even though the Argentinian in his years at Naples was subjected to torrents of abuse at most away grounds, it hardly compared to the tribal warfare on the bloodstained terraces whenever Boca and River Plate went head to head. A huge-money transfer to Europe proved inevitable as word reached across the globe of Argentina's finest. Barcelona jumped first and paid out a world record fee for this remarkable kid who was already being hailed as the heir apparent to the great Brazilian Pelé. The journey to the stars had begun. But already there were whispers. Some told tales of Doctor's needles, others spoke of steroids. Diego Armando Maradona appeared too good to be true.

Well aware of Maradona's imminent arrival in the Southern Peninsula, the day before saw the infamous Italian paparazzi lay siege to Naples international airport. All exits appeared to have been covered but, with typical Neapolitan ingenuity, an escape plan was hatched and Diego was smuggled through the press melee before being whisked off at breakneck pace to the harbour. It had been arranged for a speedboat to take him to the nearby isle of Capri. But even there photographers and camera crews lay in wait, desperate to be first to capture an image or a simple soundbite of conversations with the elusive Argentinian. To help evade the chasing pack Napoli employed Diego lookalikes to put journalists off the scent. As news filtered back to Naples that the great man had been spotted on the island a great rush of journalists hurried over on the ferry or paid local fishermen to take them the short distance. As confusion reigned Maradona was then sneaked back to the mainland by hydrofoil and taken to a secret location in the city, out of harm's way, enjoying the intrigue. The scenes back on the island as hard-bitten newsmen realised that they had been duped were priceless. For the moment it was all a game, cat and mouse. Sadly it would not always remain so.

To watch Maradona as he hurtled past opponents' challenges with alarming ease was to witness the ultimate craftsman at the peak of his powers. The tools, a bewildering sleight of foot, unnerving balance and a power unknown for someone so diminutive in size. Diego Maradona's upper body strength in his midriff and thigh muscles gave a fearsome advantage as defenders bounced off him. Lightning pace, speed of thought and dribbling ability allowed Maradona God's granted extra second to cause havoc in opponents' penalty boxes. In South America it was known as the *Gambeta*, a slalom-like dribble at top speed, a talent reserved for those only truly blessed. As a child it came naturally, like devouring ice cream. As a footballer Diego Armando was without doubt heaven sent, his miracles clear to see on the pitch. When on form Maradona was impossible to handle; whether by fair means or other, he could not be brought to earth. Previously it had been widely regarded that the two best players ever to emerge from South America were Alfredo di Stefano and Pelé. But such was the genius of Maradona, even in his early twenties he was being hailed as better than these two great icons. For Diego Armando Maradona, the world was his, he simply had to go out and grab it.

Wild scenes of delirium broke out on the bouncing, dancing terraces as Maradona came into view. For a second he appeared to stagger, as if blinded by the thousands of camera flashes exploding in his face. But swiftly he recovered to make his way towards a centre circle covered beneath a huge flag that read, '*Grazie Napoli, Grazie Ferlaino*'. Stood waiting to greet him was the Kingmaker, a beaming Corrado Ferlaino who threw both arms around the Argentinian in a huge bearhug. The President listened incredulously as the crowds chanted his name. How fickle the line between love and hate, for only a short time before they would have preferred him dead. Maradona blew a thousand kisses to his adoring audience. Rockets blasted high into the crystal blue heavens, crackers sputtered and spat, homemade fireworks thundered with the ferocity of an awakened Vesuvius. A song rang out: 'All the city are celebrating, our sad seasons are over. Now that we have bought Maradona, the donkey is a lion. Maradona, Maradona, Ole Ole!'

The San Paolo lay covered in a thick, hazy mist of smoke as a city trembled in expectation. The Neapolitans' inherited trait from their ancestors for a love of explosions shone through in an astonishing display of pyrotechnics. In the wide-reaching shadows of a fading sun Maradona disappeared amidst a raging foray of photographers and pressmen. Madness appeared to reign on the pitch as security guards and Carabinieri surrounded the new arrival to shelter him from hordes of over-enthusiastic well-wishers. Across Naples the winding steeped-alleyways that housed the rebel heart of the Neapolitan *tifosi* lay drenched blue and white. Paint-peeled doorways and balconies strewn with washing lines were anointed in Napoli colours. There thousands gathered to watch on televisions. Banners flown high echoed the feelings of an entire city. One read, '*Mo che arriva Diego Armando Tutto il Mondo Sta Tremando*'('Now that Diego arrives here, all the world is shaking with fear'). Away in the distance the noise and furore rose high from the stadium and echoed joyfully across the bay. This city, whose great beauty drew a dark contrast to its everyday reality hailed a young man whose arrival amongst them was being heralded as the second coming of San Gennaro.

Thousands of balloons drifted high into the Neapolitan sky, off in the direction of the volcano. Maradona was handed a microphone in the centre circle. He induced his adoring public to even further levels of hysteria when he announced, '*Buenos sera Napolitani. Sono molto felice di esserscon voi.*' ('Good afternoon Neapolitans, I am happy to be with you.') Smiling wide, he began to juggle a football thrown to him before lashing it far and high. A huddle of ball boys began a chase for the ultimate memento. The crowd went mad! Naples was his and he was Naples. Clutching hold of a Napoli scarf around his neck Maradona set off on a lap of honour. He would later be quoted that 'the whole day blew my mind.' The 5th of July 1984 was nothing less than a Coronation.

On arrival from Barcelona Diego Maradona acted out his role as wide-eyed footballer to perfection on discovering that everything was not as it should be with his newfound Neapolitan friends. Maradona knew only too well his real paymasters stayed hidden in the shadows. The smell of the streets never left those who had experienced its realities. During the press conference where he sat in front of a crammed auditorium alongside Cysterszpiler, Corrado Ferlaino and interpreter, French journalist Alain Chaillou was handed the dubious honour of asking the first question from the floor. A shocked audience was reduced to a momentary silence when the foolhardy, brave or just plain stupid Chaillou asked Maradona 'if he was aware that a substantial amount of his transfer fee had been funded by the *Camorra*'. Suddenly all hell let loose. Before the Argentinian had a chance to answer through a worried-looking interpreter, bedlam erupted. Ferlaino hurled a pile of papers in the shocked Frenchman's direction and demanded an instant apology for the slur upon his city. As he suffered the outraged President's wrath, Chaillou suddenly found himself ripped from his seat and escorted out of the room by two burly Napoli security guards/henchmen. They gently informed him that it would be wise to leave Naples, such was the disrespect his question had caused. The Frenchman did not need to be told twice and was soon on the first plane back to France.

Diego Armando Maradona, this young man born and raised on the outskirts of Buenos Aires in the ramshackle slums of Villa Fiorito, who had been granted by God a gift so rare and wonderful was offered the keys to a kingdom. That its crown held pointed thorns seemed irrelevant on that day of wine and roses. But sadly in time they would prick. For seven, memorable, crazy years, Neapolitans would indulge themselves in Maradona's sorcery as he led their quest for that elusive *Scudetto*. In doing so he would ignite a Southern revival and scare the living daylights out of the North. So many moments of wonder, head down with the ball glued as if rigid to his left boot. Charging alone, frightened defences retreating, petrified, all to the delight of the masses as their hero roars down upon them. And then the acceleration, the swift turn, lightning burst, whiplash drive. Goooaaaal! Maradona wheels away in celebration over to the deepest throng of writhing Southern *tifosi*, all engulfed in ecstasy. He makes the Sign of the Cross and raises an arm in salute. Milan, Juventus, Northerners all, the times they were changing!

A feverish bout of Maradona-mania engulfed the bay of Naples. A city was hooked, in this mad Neapolitan outpost where old men sit and gossip at traffic lights waiting eagerly for the next accident. Whose patron saint comes alive three times a year. Where the Devil and the ancient art of Voodoo are equally worshipped as Christ and the Holy Mother. A city closer to the shores of Africa than its own far Northern borders. Maradona's time beneath the volcano would prove a wild, passionate love affair that reached the heights of footballing ecstasy, only to finish in dark, mortal despair.

San Gennaro watched from high and prayed for a happy ending, but, alas, in the last city before Africa begins such things rarely came to pass. For when Maradona first dropped from the sky, it was not the politicians of Rome who ran the south, it lay instead in the ferocious murderous grip of the *Camorra*, as Napoli's new number ten would in time discover to his cost. But, for a while he would as he had as a child, waltz with the angels, never knowing that all along he was dancing in the Devil's shade. Little more than a puppet dangling on a gangster's string... *Benvenuti in Napoli*, Welcome to Naples!

CHAPTER 3

LAVATEVI

The banner was draped for full effect over the advertising billboards on the bottom tier at the curva sud (the south end). Painted blue and yellow, the battle-hardened colours of the Veronese, it read 'Lavatevi' ('have a wash'). A poisoned arrow fired into the heart of the Neapolitan. Simple, short and crude. Tinged with contempt, etched in disdain. Once a year the so-called Africans from the south went rampaging to Verona. Defiant and always in their thousands, the ragged hordes of SSC Napoli sang their war songs on the foreign terraces of the Stadio Comunale Bentegodi. Unloved, unwanted, pitied, and despised, to the Neapolitans it all mattered little. For had these arrogant Northerners not heard? Maradona had come to Naples!

As Neapolitans clung on tight to the dying embers of their sweet summer of 1984, Diego Maradona set about making himself at home. In an extremely rare stroke of cute business acumen, his agent Jorge Cysterszspiler scored great success with club President Ferlaino in agreeing for Napoli to foot the bill for his client's temporary accommodation in the city's finest hotel. Maradona and his unlikely tribe/ensemble of family blood relatives, fixers, business associates and hangers-on landed like a bad smell at the doors of the Hotel Royal. Needless to say that all chits run up by the indulging Argentinians found their way to despairing Napoli officials. As the swirling clouds turned black over Vesuvius and darkness drew a veil over the Southern Peninsula, so the partying began. Sheltered from the prying eyes of outsiders and feeling safe and secure in a city only too willing to grant his every wish, the newly crowned King Diego Maradona succumbed to temptation.

He and his posse cruised Naples most notorious nightspots. Maradona partied with the *abbient* (Naples underworld) and indulged in the more dark excesses of southern hospitality, enjoying the company of Naples' most beautiful women. They found the young Diego with the easy smile, sense of humour, dancing black eyes and large wads of cash, irresistible. His long-standing girlfriend Claudia Villafane appeared for public consumption only as the Argentinian enjoyed the full hospitality of his adopted city. The truth as ever lay hidden in the spicy gossip of downtown Naples, in the sidestreet café bars of the Forcella where Maradona's previous night-time antics were discussed, dissected, admired or frowned upon. Even before a ball was kicked in anger Diego Maradona risked becoming the heady stuff of Neapolitan legend.

House rules: President Corrado Ferlaino had one unspoken rule for his young superstar. Fully aware of Maradona's outlandish lifestyle and certain habits, Ferlaino allowed for a little dallying. However, he was adamant that from the Thursday onwards the player had to be clean of drugs and drink. After being forced to run a gauntlet of snobbery and antagonism in Barcelona, the hot, alluring, sensual, atmosphere of Naples nightlife provided a perfect antidote for the young Argentinian. One of Maradona's huge entourage and alleged personal trainer/cheer leader, Victor Galindez, summed it up to perfection when he claimed, 'We escaped the hell of Barcelona and arrived in the heaven of Naples.'

The Neapolitans' fascination with this young man who fell from the sky promising to make their wildest dreams come true knew no bounds and they quickly took him to their hearts. The painful memories of Catalonia were forgotten as Diego Armando found kindred spirits who danced, sung, laughed and cavorted as if every night was their last. 'To Vesuvius,' went the toast, 'one day he will get us all.' At Barcelona Maradona used cocaine to block out obscene shooting pain from his crippling ankle injury and to help fight the boredom of many a bleak month spent recuperating. In Naples the temptation to dabble once more proved overwhelming, only this time at the joy of being back amongst people like him. Live for today, as tomorrow is just a distant dream. For a time the sheer relief at being unshackled from Catalan chains made Maradona feel he was in paradise. And for a while it would prove to be so but, as in life, nothing lasts forever.

The forty-seven-year-old Rino Marchesi was a man of refined tastes. He enjoyed the finer things in life. A luxurious Cuban cigar, classical music, a civilized game of chess. All were a brief respite from his main purpose in life, which on and off since 1981 had been to manage the Neapolitan soap opera that was SSC Napoli. A short spell at Inter Milan was curtailed to see him lured back south. Though the pressures of such a job were enormous, Marchesi relished the dream that, just maybe, he could awaken the slumbering giant and bring success to the football-mad Neapolitans. Napoli was a club that did nothing by half, but sadly like the city she represented appeared eternally to be in a state of turmoil, the next disaster never more than a stone's throw away. But the signing of Maradona upped the stakes dramatically. Sixty-seven-thousand season tickets had been sold and the President made it known both publicly and in private conversations with Marchesi that the under-achieving was over. The time had come for *Lo Scudetto*, the Serie A title, to come South. The city of Naples demanded an instant return on their huge investment. Both financially and in spirit the signing of Maradona was viewed as a last throw of the dice. It was do or die. Sallustro, Altafini, Juliano, Sivori. These blue-shirted ghosts of the past still echoed in quiet moments across the playing surface of the San Paolo. How the *tifosi* ached for success.

Marchesi relished the rare opportunity of working with a talent such as Diego Maradona, but he was also a realist. Ferlaino's bold gamble in landing the much-lauded Argentinian meant expectations soared beyond the crystal blue Neapolitan heavens. For also arriving under the volcano alongside him were a tenacious, classy Italian midfielder from Inter Milan, Salvatore Bagni, and fellow countryman, the experienced winger Daniel Bertoni. Naples so feared to dream, there had been too many false dawns. The signing of Maradona may have roused the south but the odds still appeared stacked heavily on the side of the northern giants. In Turin, the home of accursed champions Juventus, and elsewhere in Milan and Rome they were hardly quaking in their boots. Rino Marchesi was not expecting to pick up his pension in Naples.

Maradona sent Neapolitan hopes soaring for the forthcoming league campaign as he excelled in the early rounds of the Italian Cup, *Coppa Italia*, with a hatful of goals and scintillating performances. These included a flashing free kick against Arrezzo and an astonishing overhead strike against lowly Pescara that he executed with stunning technique as he lay flat on his back. Even an opposing defender couldn't help but applaud Maradona's moment of magic. But the true test of his calibre lay amidst the furore, passion and dark intrigue of the Italian championship. At the San Paolo and in the hostile footballing arenas of the North, Diego Maradona would attempt to cement his reputation as the finest footballer in the world.

Let the games begin: It was on the eve of 16th September 1984 that the grand northern city of Verona fell into a fitful sleep with one wary eye left half open. Verona was amongst the most elegant, prosperous cities in all Italy, especially famous for providing the setting for Shakespeare's *Romeo and Juliet*. In 1984 it again played host to pure theatre when Diego Maradona made his Serie A debut for SSC Napoli against Hellas Verona. The Neapolitans ventured into enemy territory in huge numbers to support their team. By train, coach and car they came, their war songs resonating tales of bitterness and revenge. The troubled residents of this noble city that sat proudly in the shadows of the majestic Dolomite Mountains dreaded the sight of these wretched southerners descending like a herd of savages upon their precious, ancient, cobbled pathways. Not since Hannibal had they turned their noses up such. Back then, whilst the legendary barbarian and his elephants were rampaging throughout the north, far south in Naples, Neapolitans would taunt their own Roman garrisons with the immortal line, 'Hannibal is at the gates!'

The coach of Hellas Verona was wily tactician Osvaldo Bagnoli, who with great meticulous care had created a formidable side that would take the Italian championship by storm. The heartbeat of Hellas was undoubtedly the barnstorming 6' 6" German powerhouse Hans Peter Briegel. Bagnoli's masterplan based itself almost entirely on Briegel's immense physical presence and accurate long passing, providing the bullets for a devastating forward partnership of lethal Danish hitman Preben Elkjaer and his Italian sidekick Giuseppe Galderisi. Ready and primed to perfection Verona were set to ignite. Napoli would never know what hit them.

Like most northern *tifosi* the Veronese loved to indulge themselves by heaping scorn on the heads of their despised visitors from the toe of Italy. Mockingly referred to in cities north of Rome as the 'Black South', the southerners sundrenched dark skin in comparison to the pale white faces of the damp north saw them subjected to monkey chants and incessant choruses of 'Seig Heil' throughout any match between the two. The hardcore of the Verona support came together under the sinister umbrella of a notorious ultra-right wing mob of hooligans, Brigate Gialloblu. But the Neapolitans themselves were hardly shrinking violets and carried a fearsome reputation that came well deserved and battle-earned. Treated with utter contempt wherever they travelled outside Naples the Napoli *tifosi* chose to cock up their noses and swap curses and insults with their northern counterparts. For whenever they ventured up country the atmosphere inside stadiums simmered with an electrifying undercurrent of tension. The foul arid stench of pure hatred stalked the air.

The most fanatical of Napoli *tifosi* was undoubtedly the CUCB, Commando Ultra Curva B. Established in 1972 by the legendary Neapolitan figure of Gennaro Montuori, their numbers hailed from all corners of Naples. Petty insular squabbles were forgotten as the street gangs united under one banner to take on all who dared to chance their arm against them. Montuori was amongst the first to organise large-scale away trips, safety in numbers being one of the CUCB's most important reasons for coming into being, for any trip outside Naples' borders, either to the battlegrounds of the north or equally embittered southern rivals carried a resemblance of bad blood. It became essential that whatever their differences, once in enemy territory they stuck together, for in every town and city across Italy the local youths awaited with glee the arrival of the loathsome Neapolitans.

Whilst a *Carabinieri* helicopter buzzed menacingly overhead, baton-waving local police used heavy-handed tactics to shove the visitors into the ground like a herd of cattle. Maradona took to the pitch with his teammates for the pre-match warm up and looked visibly shaken at the hail of abuse being meted out to him by the home supporters. So this was Italy? The Argentinian applauded the corner of the stadium draped in blue where his own adoring followers stood. Both teams made their entrance into the Comunale Bentegodi. To a deafening welcome the Verona Ultras took up their war anthem, '*Chi noi siamo?*' ('Who are we?') '*Chi noi siamo, Brigate, Brigate Giaboblu!!*' The Brigate had rolled a blue and yellow banner over the advertising hoarding on the bottom tier where they stood, grouped behind the goal in the *curva sud* proclaiming '*Benvenuti in Italia*' (Welcome to Italy). Alongside it, the infamous '*Lavatevi*'. That cut deep. In time the Veronese would pay dear for such insults. The waving of 100,000 lira notes at the Neapolitans was also a cause of great amusement amongst Verona's finest. The bowl-shaped Bentegodi roared in appreciation of such wit. The chants and songs swept down from the terraces. Amongst the hundreds of Hellas flags there lay sprinkled a sizeable amount of Nazi Swastikas. A clash of cultures, the Mezzogiorno, badlands of the South versus the rich fat cats of the so-called White North. So much for Shakespeare's 'City of Gentlemen'.

The new Neapolitan empire appeared made from sand as they crumbled disastrously against a rampant Hellas Verona. In what was a torrid opening game Napoli were thrashed 3-1 and lucky not to be beaten by many more. Both Maradona and Bertoni were isolated from the off as they found themselves treated to some rough treatment by Verona defenders who took turns and great delight in kicking them up in the air. Up the other end Hellas cut through with alarming ease. Inspired by the thundering runs of Hans Peter Briegel the home side won convincingly. A first half goal from the German was doubled when Galderisi combined with Elkjaer to make it 2-0 on the hour. Matters went from bad to worse for Napoli when their veteran defender and longest-serving player, Giuseppe Bruscolotti was sent off in frustration as his team was overrun. This mean-faced son of Naples did not take kindly to seeing his beloved club humiliated and reacted so. They might go down but it would not be without a fight.

For a brief period in the second half, with Diego Maradona showing some wonderfully incisive touches, the Neapolitans rallied. Maradona single-handedly took on the home defence but, amidst relentless attention from Verona hatchet-men who felt nothing in scything him to the floor at every opportunity, his threat waned. Hopes were raised momentarily that a point could be salvaged when Daniel Bertoni lashed one back to halve the deficit, but any chance of a revival was dashed fifteen minutes from time when Hellas sealed a deserved victory, with a third goal scored by Italian international midfielder Antonio di Gennaro. A season in which the Veronese would surprise all and win their first ever *Scudetto* began in impressive manner. As for the Neapolitans? Different season, same old story. Results elsewhere saw them cast adrift at the bottom of the table. '*Lavatevi*'? How they laughed.

The following week felt like an eternity for all connected with SSC Napoli as they ached to banish the nightmare of what befell them in Verona. Maradona got ready to tread the boards for the first time in his hometown theatre house against Sampdoria. It was opening night at the San Paolo and expectations were as high as the infamous volcano that soared above them. You could not get a ticket for your life. The moment Neapolitans had prayed for arrived on the hour when in a fiercely fought encounter Napoli were awarded a penalty. Seventy thousand hushed as Diego Maradona stepped forward to take responsibility for the kick. As Naples held its breath Maradona coolly converted a cheeky chip-shot past Bordon in the Sampdoria goal. Bordon screamed in frustration at being humiliated by the audacity of the Argentinian, whose wonderful technique made him appear foolish.

The arena erupted! Homemade firecrackers exploded, rockets crashed and roared impressively, if rather worryingly, high into the Naples sky. Thousands danced for joy on the packed terraces. Maradona raced away and fell to his knees near the corner flag, his teammates falling upon him as a mad melee ensued. Photographers and club officials rushed on the pitch in wild celebration. Sadly for the Neapolitans the men from Genoa refused to lie down and on seventy-three minutes ruined the party when centre-forward Daniel Salsano shot past the Napoli keeper Luciano Castellini to take a point back north. 1-1.

The final whistle saw the stadium empty swiftly. It had been an inauspicious start for Marchesi's team and they badly needed a win. The verdict amongst the Napoli *tifosi* regarding Maradona was mixed. In both opening matches he had found himself firmly shackled. Serie A bristled with top class defenders who though masters of their art, tended to err dangerously on the side of brutality, if not downright thuggery. The hatchet men across the land sharpened their studs and encircled his name on the team sheet. There would be no easy rides for Diego Armando. Quickly he decided that he had little option but to wear two pairs of shinpads, for his card had been well and truly marked.

The following week disaster befell the Neapolitans with utter humiliation in Turin. Inspired by the incisive passing of Austrian midfield schemer Walter Schachner, and the attacking flair of exuberant bushy-haired Brazilian fullback Junior, a 3-0 scoreline did Torino little justice for the quality of their play. The Stadio Comunale, shared with hated city rivals Juventus erupted in the first minute when the electric-heeled home forward, Italian international Aldo Serena caught the Neapolitans cold. It proved a wake-up call sadly ignored by the men from the South as a massacre ensued in all but the scoreline. *La Granata* (The Clarets), much to the delight of their supporters, ran riot. At the final whistle Rino Marchesi's men appeared shell-shocked. What began as a season full of hope had quickly deteriorated into a shambles. President Ferlaino watched on in exasperated fashion as his expensively put together team trooped sullenly off the pitch. The disastrous events in Turin proved only the beginning of the nightmare for Neapolitans, as from that wretched Sunday afternoon up until the Christmas break Napoli won only two games to lie deeply entrenched in a relegation dogfight alongside Lazio, Udinese, Ascoli and Cremonese. *Spaventoso* (abysmal).

There had been few highlights for Diego Maradona in the first four months; a first goal in open play at the San Paolo against Como when in typical fashion he scythed through the middle to strike a tremendous shot that screamed high into the goal to electrify the terraces; a masterpiece of opportunistic skill in Rome against Lazio where he struck like a cobra to earn a vital point. These had been tantalising glimpses of genius that caused even the most rabid of northern *tifosi* to gasp in admiration and whisper a silent prayer to the heavens that one day Maradona would wear their team's colours. A drop of the shoulders and three opposing defenders would be left in a bedraggled heap. But by far the disappointments outweighed such moments; precious as they were, the Neapolitans needed more.

A soul-destroying 2-0 defeat against the infernal Juventus in which they were totally outclassed caused dismay in Naples. The wonderfully artistic Frenchman Michel Platini sealed the win to raise the roof off the Comunale by stroking home a decisive second goal. A banner by the Juve *tifosi* taunted, 'Vesuvius, we are counting on you'. This only rubbed salt in the wounds of the disgruntled visitors who travelled home feeling their dream was as far away as ever. The gloom continued when they lost to Internazionale of Milan at the hostile San Siro. Inter's winner was a last-gasp effort by striker Allesandro Altobelli that cut deep to leave the despondent Napoli players at the mercy of a gloating Milan crowd rejoicing at their misfortune. The banner that waved 'Maradona, suck on a banana' displayed a lesser-known side of a city normally cited for its class and style.

Ferlaino acted. He organized a *ritiro* (retreat) in which both players and coaching staff were ordered to attend and express their opinions on where things were going wrong. The town of Vietri lay delicately poised on the spinechilling, steep cliffs of the breathtaking Amalfi coast. It is noted worldwide for the skill of its ceramic craftsmen and it was here that SSC Napoli retreated to in their hour of need. The coming together seemed to have the desired effect on all and the bonding session ended positively in a flurry of bear hugs and shouts of '*Forza Napoli!*' The shutdown at Christmas handed the club a chance to regroup, for all Neapolitans were under no illusions that unless performances drastically improved SSC Napoli was in grave danger of being relegated. There was only one Christmas wish in Naples that year, survival.

To escape the rising tension Diego Maradona packed his bags for a short vacation and headed home to Buenos Aires. The depth of feeling and goodwill shown Maradona in Naples had overwhelmed him and it showed no signs of easing up during the struggling campaign. But even the most torrid of love affairs needed time to cool and come back down to earth. Maradona had some serious thinking to do. His head had been turned by the attentions lavished upon him but to repay such generosity and loyalty he had to recharge his batteries and get away. For despite rumours to the contrary in Naples, he was only human. The Neapolitans were dreadfully worried, a sad total of nine points was all they would take into the New Year. The normally festive, joyful Christmas period would instead be an anxious time for the city of Naples as it pondered the coming months. As ever, that most illustrious of prizes, the *Scudetto*, appeared an impossible dream, indeed relegation to Serie B looked a more likely scenario. The jury was out: the situation was grave. The time had come for the king of Naples to dig Napoli out of its self-made God-forsaken hole at the bottom of the table and prove to his subjects he was worthy of the crown bestowed upon him.

Maradona returned early in the New Year refreshed and in dogged frame of mind to prove his many doubters wrong. The Neapolitans' league campaign restarted on 6th January with a match at the San Paolo against fellow strugglers Udinese. Udinese had enjoyed a fine season the previous year when against all expectations they finished sixth in Serie A. Blessed with a potent striking duo of Brazilians, Edinho and the man nicknamed the 'White Pelé', Zico, Udinese arrived in the Southern capital determined to beat Napoli in their own backyard and place Marchesi's side under intolerable pressure by dumping them into the bottom three. Level with the Neapolitans on points but lagging behind on goal difference, it was billed as a clash neither side could afford to lose. Udinese entered into the seething atmosphere of the San Paolo wearing their traditional black and white stripes. This served only to irritate the hell out of the already fraught Napoli *tifosi*, the ghost of Juve forever in their midst.

Played in driving rain, sleet and a cold bitter wind that cut deep into the bones of everyone present, a classic game of football ensued. On this holy day of the blessed feast of the Epiphany, the under-pressure Rino Marchesi raged towards the heavens when in only the twelfth minute his team conceded a penalty that Edinho gleefully converted. The rain-soaked Napoli coach must have heard the sound of knives being sharpened all around him as the small but enthusiastic band of Udinese followers celebrated. The Neapolitans rallied and to the delight of the home supporters Diego Maradona equalised ten minutes later, also from the penalty spot. With both teams going hell for leather Daniel Bertoni shot Napoli in front only for Udinese to draw level a minute before the break. Maradona was in thrilling form, time and again he bore down on the Udinese rearguard only to be thwarted at the last. As Naples shivered in the midst of a January blizzard Diego Maradona warmed his people's hearts with a bravura performance.

Half-time came, went and still the battle raged. Fifteen minutes from the end Maradona scored again from the spot and when Bertoni grabbed his second moments later the game appeared won. With the massed blue-clad hordes of the CUCB indulging in their victory songs, Udinese lashed back one final time when Billini crashed home to create a grandstand finish. To the relief of President Ferlaino, a stressed-out Marchesi and hordes of whistling Neapolitans, the referee finally ended the match and the city of Naples sighed a collective gasp. Diego Maradona leapt across the advertising billboards that surrounded the pitch and went across to acknowledge the Neapolitans for their ferocious backing in what had been an enthralling encounter. Maradona had given a wonderful display that bewitched his adoring following and made them realise how fortunate they were to have someone of his ilk. On this form he appeared unplayable and worth every penny of the king's ransom paid. From that day on Napoli lost only two games in the league. The blessed feast of the Epiphany celebrated Jesus Christ rising from the dead. On Sunday 6th January 1985, Diego Maradona lit the flames to spark the fires that ignited a football revolution. The badlands of the South were once more ablaze. The charge for the *Scudetto* was on.

As the blizzard increased in blind fury across the Southern Peninsula and snow fell heavily onto the steep slopes of Mount Vesuvius, a city paid homage to its king. When offstage and away from the San Paolo, Maradona's behaviour in the nightclubs and seedy fleshpots of Naples was so shocking as to even disturb Neapolitan streetwise morals. A steamy affair with a local television presenter while Claudia was visiting family in Argentina became public knowledge. Much to Jorge Cysterzspiler's concern it was leaked to the press and all hell let loose in Naples. One more cross against his name. It was a leggy Californian born blond called Heather Parisi who kept him warm during that January, one of the coldest months ever recorded in Italy. And true to form she would surprise no one by later kissing and telling her story to the infamous Italian gossip magazine *Oggi* for a sizeable fee. But despite all it would be his God-given genius with a ball that made Maradona invulnerable to criticism. Diego Armando was having the time of his young life and while he cast magic spells on the football field no one would be allowed to ruin his fun, no one. Maradona danced between the raindrops. He was untouchable.

CHAPTER 4

BADLANDS

Alas for Neapolitans their bedraggled, much put upon, but always beloved football team, SSC Napoli, struggled miserably through the years against the mighty Northern powers. In what felt like an eternal procession of funeral marches the teams of Juventus and Milan turned up each season in Naples to beat them with soul-destroying ease. In doing so they laid down the law, for a football pitch was as good a place as any to keep the Southern Terroni (lowlifes) in their place. Despite the endless bouts of heartache and failure the Neapolitans refused to give up on their team. The worse they were treated, the more they yearned for success. It was a relationship that bore all the hallmarks of a doomed love affair. Love, hate and love again. Amore: and it has always been so.

The grand old story of SSC Napoli begins in the early years of the last century. The flourishing seaport of Naples was enjoying a boom, attracting huge foreign investment. Amongst them was Cunard Liners, whom in 1903 transferred one of their top mechanics to the Southern Peninsula. The Englishman James Poths arrived in Naples, carrying a suitcase in one hand and a football under the arm. He had been an avid, amateur footballer, who made up for what he lacked in skill with sheer enthusiasm. Poths was simply mad about the game and wasted little time extolling his passion to the locals. However in Southern Italy, football remained at that time still practically unknown. Nobody played, it was only in the far north of Turin, Milan and Genoa that the game of association football was taken seriously as a sport. But this failed to deter the enthusiastic Poths who saw himself as a footballing missionary. He, along with his newfound, friend, a Neapolitan engineer called Emilio Anatra, managed to scrape together a side to play the crews of visiting ships. Poths and Anatra very grandly christened their team Naples Cricket and Football Club, and a show of hands saw them vote to play in strips of light and dark blue striped shirts. So began a long enduring love affair between a city and its team.

Their first match took place against eleven sailors of the visiting British liner, Arabik, and proved a great success with Naples winning 3-2. The victory was shown to be even more impressive considering the crew of the Arabik had only recently beaten Genoa, who were considered by far the best club side in Italy. News of this shock result spread like wildfire and to Poth's utter amazement a most unlikely invitation dropped on his desk from the Sicilian royal family. The King himself wished for them to partake in a prestigious tournament on his island. Delighted to accept, off went Poths and his band of merry men to Sicily, where they beat the hosts 2-1 and returned triumphantly to Naples with the impressive-looking trophy.

However there would be no welcoming reception put on by the locals who, due to the insistence of James Poth picking only Englishmen for his team, had simply disowned them. The Neapolitans were outraged at the arrogance of this foreigner who took the name of their city and yet refused to play any of its citizens. How could Poth's men possibly represent Naples when the players were constantly sailing off elsewhere? It wasn't right, there was only one option. Another team was born, US Internazionale came into being. They, of course, to prove a point, built their side around Neapolitans and a great rivalry, bitter and fierce, swiftly developed between the two. Neither took prisoners when the two clashed. Many foreign sailors left the port of Naples nursing a black eye or a broken bone.

Finally in 1920 both clubs came to their senses, shook hands and merged to become Internaples. But it was not until 23rd August 1926, in a famous meeting at the restaurant D'Angelo in Naples, that they became Associazione Calcio Napoli, enrolling in the Italian Southern division. A prominent local businessman called Giorgio Ascarelli was nominated as club President and they were up and running. Chosen as club emblem was a proud galloping black horse. But their first season turned swiftly into humiliating failure with only a single point earned in a lone draw against Genoa. Altogether a shambolic tally of 69 goals conceded to 7 scored had all Naples shamefaced with embarrassment. Indeed the Neapolitans themselves changed the symbol of their club to a sad, downtrodden, if somewhat loveable donkey christened *O Ciuccio*. An enduring image that returned many times, even to this day in haunting them.

But all was not doom and gloom, for in its midst Napoli possessed a treasured gem of a footballer. A Neapolitan legend long before Diego Maradona fell from the sky making dreams come true. The child prodigy, Attila Sallustro, made his debut at the unbelievably tender age of twelve. Born the son of Paraguayan immigrants, but raised in the poverty-stricken backstreets of Naples, the attractions of this unique youngster saw Napoli performing to packed houses both home and away. Sallustro's talents were such that even though the Neapolitans were thrashed by all in their fledgling opening year, relegation was avoided due to the Italian Football Association realising they could ill afford to lose such valuable income. Instead they voted in an incredulous ruling preventing Napoli from going down, thus keeping Atilla Sallustro and his pulling power within their grasp.

To Naples' great relief the same decision was repeated the following year when again they found themselves beaten out of sight on an almost weekly basis. Amazingly, such was Sallustro's love of the game he declined wages to play. Being a true gentleman he saw the game as merely a hobby and refused point blank a salary. However after one particularly impressive season, a determined President Ascarelli insisted Sallustro accept his offer of a luxurious new car on behalf of the club. Grudgingly he accepted. With his strutting manner and film star good looks, the player was also a popular figure amongst the ladies of Naples, who would giggle with delight and clap politely whenever their hero received the ball. This remarkable character went on to have a glittering career with SSC Napoli, becoming all-time top scorer with 137 goals in 259 games. Even in the city today his name is spoken in hushed tones of awe. Atillo Sallustro, a true legend of Naples.

Napoli's finest moments in those early formative years came under the much-travelled Englishman, Willy Garbutt. In 1933 and 34 the former Arsenal player led the football-mad Neapolitans to two consecutive third-place spots, behind Inter Milan and Juventus. But this apart, Napoli's trophy cabinet stayed bare. *Lo Scudetto*, (championship shield) remained north in Turin, for they had the money, best players and, it appeared, most disturbingly, when the need arose, the referees also. There were many times when supposedly impartial referees caused outrage in the south with highly controversial decisions against Napoli that defied belief. This also caused great unrest amongst the supporters, constantly spilling over into disturbing scenes of crowd violence and unrest. Against such unmatchable odds the hopes of Neapolitans wrestling the title away from two such formidable foes appeared astronomical.

But on 15th March 1936 hopes soared in Naples when shipping tycoon Achille Lauro became club President. Lauro vowed to end their barren run and bring success to the passionate followers of SSC Napoli. Born in nearby Sorrento, Achillo Lauro inherited his first ships in 1912. In time he built up a sizeable fleet of freighters and cruise liners that were to make him rich beyond his dreams. Lauro was also a man of huge ego and political ambition. He used the role of Napoli supremo as a stepping stone to becoming Mayor of Naples. But his burning desire to bring south for the first time the Holy Grail of the championship trophy was real. Sadly any plan became scuppered by the cataclysmic outbreak of World War Two. As the Southern Peninsula became drenched in blood, thoughts turned to matters other than football. Living and dying.

Naples 1941: Benito Mussolini, *Il Duce*, believed he had a splendid idea. The pompous despot had grown increasingly annoyed at the Neapolitans' total lack of regard for him and his rabid Fascist black shirts. Their annoying habit of drawing Charlie Chaplin moustaches on his wonderful self on the many posters that adorned the city walls caused the great one to lose his temper. Hardly known for his sense of humour the mad dictator decided they must be taught a painful lesson. He issued a decree for the city's air raid sirens to be randomly switched on even when there was no threat of bombs falling. Finally, on 4th December 1942, the ominous drone of American B-24 liberators flying from their base in Egypt was heard over Naples as they came in low over the Tyrrhenian Sea to hit the city. As the sirens wailed many Neapolitans were confused as to whether the alarm was genuine and did not go to the underground shelters, thus sealing their fate. On hearing of this a smug Mussolini declared, 'A good dose of terror will turn the people of Naples into true Italians.'

Such cruel acts of folly caused blind panic and fury amongst a people who had already suffered terribly from relentless allied air attacks. It was rumoured American intention was to bomb the crater of Vesuvius triggering an eruption that would devastate the region. Also Mussolini's infamous comments that 'it gratified him when Naples was bombed', hardly endeared him to the citizens of this much put-upon city. As his pipe dream of a new Roman empire crumbled into dust the allies landed at Salerno and headed up to Naples. The Americans and British forces found themselves aided by *Camorra* fugitives who played an integral role in the Neapolitan uprising of 1944, *Quattro Giornate*. In a ferocious four-day battle they helped to organise resistance, handing out guns and ammunition as the city rose in fury to kick out the last remaining German forces. As the Nazis retreated northwards the chasing American and British forces entered the southern capital. On 1st October 1944 Allied forces liberated Naples to find nothing short of hell on earth. The burnt smell of charred wood forever lingering in the air, starvation and disease rife, as a once proud city and its people appeared broken. Ravaged by incessant Allied bombing and Nazi revenge, Naples lay dying. Dirty, hungry children begged and pleaded with Allied troops. The cries of '*biscotti*' and '*sigarette*' were everywhere as soldiers found dreadful scenes of starvation, horror and neglect. No other city in Italy suffered the wanton devastation than that which was wrought on Naples.

But the war did end and in 1952 Achillo Lauro's lifetime ambition of becoming Mayor was finally realised. Now one of the most powerful figures in all Italy, *Il Commandante*, as he had became known (much to his delight), set about winning his electorate over by announcing plans for a spectacular new home for SSC Napoli. In such a moment the San Paolo stadium was born, and on 19th November 1959 it became a reality. A fond if rather overdue *arrivederci* was said to the rundown, though still highly evocative arena of their former ground in the city region of Vomero. Surprisingly it was arch enemies Juventus who were invited south by Lauro to provide the opposition for the stadium's grand inauguration. In front of a full house a goalless draw saw honour served on both sides, as just for a day the two adversaries declared a ceasefire.

Finally on 21st June 1962, SSC Napoli could boast of silverware when the *Coppa d'Italia* (Italian Cup) was won in Rome. Thousands had travelled up from the south to celebrate this historic 2-1 victory for their club over little Spal in the Eternal city. For the first time Europe beckoned with a place in the European Cup Winners' Cup secured. On being handed an opening tie against lowly Welsh non-league side Bangor City in the preliminary rounds, Neapolitans gleefully rubbed their hands. For most had never even heard of Wales, never mind Bangor and their football team! That soon changed, for on 5th September 1962, on an unforgettable evening at Farror Road with a capacity 8,000 crowd roaring their team on, Napoli slid shame-faced to defeat. Unbelievably a side of part-timers, lying sixth in the Cheshire League, inflicted upon their supposed vastly superior and highly illustrious opponents a 2-0 loss.

A Bangor team playing in a typically British long ball style totally overwhelmed the Italians, who simply collapsed under the incessant pressure. Two goals were scant reward for the rampaging men from Gwynedd who also twice hit the bar and created numerous other opportunities to score. Led by their manager, ex-Everton and Wales star Tommy Jones, Bangor became the first Welsh side ever to win in Europe. Back in Italy this result was greeted with a mixture of incredulity and anger. These much lauded, highly-paid superstars were left in no doubt by their fanatical support that nothing more than a massacre in the return would save their necks. In Naples such a threat had to be heeded.

Three weeks later Bangor City's first ever flight to the continent so nearly ended in tragedy when lightning struck their plane, forcing it to make an emergency landing in Switzerland. After such a harrowing experience, the rotten fruit and urine bags hurled at them from the San Paolo terraces paled into insignificance. Inspired by 80,000 rabid *tifosi* screaming for Welsh blood,

Bangor ignored the abuse and in bravura fashion took the game to Napoli on their own patch. Tommy Jones's brave side crashed into tackles and gave everything in a gallant effort to attempt the impossible. But as the game wore on class finally began to tell and on thirty minutes *Azzurri* international Mariani struck a low shot from the edge of the penalty area that beat City goalkeeper Len Davies. Suddenly Welsh fire waned and Neapolitan passions erupted. Bristling with newfound confidence, Napoli's pass and move game mesmerised the Bangor defenders. A terrible error by the normally reliable Davies let in the electrifying forward Ronzon to level the tie and delight an enraptured San Paolo. A second half promised only further carnage for a home team seeking revenge.

But yet again Bangor showed wonderful spirit as they found hidden depths of courage to take on the Neapolitans. A heart-stopping display by this remarkable ensemble of factory workers, electricians and plumbers pinned back the shell-shocked Italians and ten minutes from time they received their just reward. A long throw-in from Bangor defender Ken Birch caused confusion in the penalty area. Waiting to pounce was City winger Jimmy McAllister who fired past a despairing Pontel in the Napoli goal, silencing not just a stadium, but also an entire city. Knowing full well they faced a real prospect of being lynched on the pitch, Napoli tried one last time to save themselves. With the City defence wilting, a dramatic lifeline was grabbed when their speedy winger Pornella kept his cool to make it 3-3 on aggregate. Naples heaved a heavy sigh of relief, for it had been a close call.

Unlike today, away goals never counted for double, and the tie went to a play-off match. The venue chosen, much to Neapolitan chagrin was the home of Arsenal Football Club, Highbury. Napoli officials argued vehemently, but with a woeful lack of British geography, that London was practically a home game for Bangor City! They demanded to play elsewhere in either France or Spain. Meanwhile as the argument raged, the Welsh became increasingly irritated at being regarded as English by their opponents! Despite fierce Italian objections, the footballing authorities decided to overrule and the game went ahead. On Wednesday 10th October 1962, fifteen coachloads of Bangor supporters added their own particular brand of passion to the 21,895 present at Highbury. Finally, third time round, the Napoli players showed their true style and though the Welshmen fought tenaciously, the gulf between the sides became apparent. On thirty-six minutes, after many close shaves, the sublime Argentinian Rosa let fly a wonderful twenty-yard shot that screamed past a helpless Len Davies. But Davies had little need to feel guilty, for if it had not been for him the scoreline could easily have resembled a rout. That Bangor remained just one down at half-time was itself a minor miracle, and due solely to their heroic keeper.

The second period saw little respite for the Welsh minnows as the Italians swarmed all over them. Opportunities arrived only to be wasted, some through sheer bad finishing, others foiled by the magnificent Davies. With time running down and the Neapolitans settling for 1-0, it just had to happen! Bangor centre half Brian Ellis headed down for the darting Jimmy McAllister to fire his second goal in three games against Napoli. This famous old ground, sensing a most unlikely upset, exploded. Sadly for Tommy Jones, his wonderfully courageous team were utterly spent of energy and seven minutes from time Rosa struck to score his second of the night and win the tie. The Neapolitans were through, but only after the most frightful scare. Bangor City returned to European anonymity, but with their place in Welsh footballing folklore secure. It had been an epic journey and a truly monumental effort. As for SSC Napoli, their short-lived adventures in the Cup Winners' Cup ended in the next round when OFK Belgrade knocked them out. That same season the Neapolitans also suffered the ignominy of relegation from Serie A. In Naples the song remained the same.

Come 1965 and Napoli supremo Achillo Lauro had grown increasingly frustrated at his clubs constant under-achieving. Armed with his own money, Lauro went for broke and signed two of the great players from the north. This self-styled original 'King Of Naples' drew a line in the sand, a gesture of defiance. He offered two of Napoli's sworn enemies, AC Milan and Juventus, a king's ransom to part with their star South American wizards, the Brazilian centre forward Jose Altafini and Argentinian winger Omar Enrique Sivori. Altafini had performed only a cameo role in Brazil's legendary 1958 World Cup-winning side in Sweden, but his talent had already been noted. The Milan scouts moved swift to ensure the prodigious youngster became their property. The twenty-year-old Brazilian loved to go by the nickname of *Mazzola*, so called after the majestic playmaker of AC's fierce local rivals. However, on signing for Inter it was explained to him in no uncertain terms that the name had to go! Jose Altafini proved a marvellous signing, scoring freely and never more so than during AC Milan's 1963 victorious European Cup campaign, hitting a record fourteen goals. Included amongst these were two special strikes at Wembley stadium in a 3-1 victory over Eusebio's famed Benfica.

As for the astonishingly sublime, if somewhat temperamental Omar Sivori? He went to Naples after falling foul of Juve's Paraguayan disciplinarian coach, Heriberto Herrera. The hard-nosed Herrera was not for Sivori, who saw himself as a free spirit. He was labelled *El Cabezon*, 'Bighead', by Italians for a tendency to enjoy making opposing defenders appear ridiculous with his magical ball skills. Sivori would run past opponents exclaiming, 'Congratulations, you have just been beaten by the best player in the world!' Never one to hide his true feelings, the fiery Argentinian hardly helped his cause when on one memorable occasion, he beat an opponent on the wing, noticed Herrera on the touchline, and smashed the ball into his midriff, bringing tears to his eyes! As Herrera screamed abuse at him the smiling Sivori milked the moment, for he knew his glittering career with Juventus was at an end. It was time for a new challenge. A worthy 150 goals in eight seasons for the *Bianconeri*, in which he shared a magnificent partnership with the great John Charles, and being voted the 1961 European Player of the Year, meant Omar Sivori would be forever remembered as a true Juve legend. But now it was over, and *El Cabezon* went south.

The price for both players was incredibly high and Lauro helped subsidise the transfers by handing Gianni Agnelli a lucrative contract to fit out his fleet of ships. Despite a close friendship with Agnelli he knew well that the intense feelings in Naples against Juventus meant he had to appear that any dealings with Turin's royal family was akin to a pact with the devil. There also was an agreement with AC Milan not to sell Jose Altafini to any of their rivals for a period of at least three years. Lauro shook hands with the Milan hierarchy on this, but was severely tested when Juve immediately proposed a double your money offer to buy the Brazilian. However, not wishing to cause a civil war, and hardly relishing the idea of being hung from the highest tree by irate Neapolitans, the Napoli supremo declined.

The bold capture of these exceptional footballers electrified the southern *tifosi*. It was seen as a wonderful coup by all of Naples. Both men were born entertainers who quickly became idols on the terraces of the San Paolo. More so Omar Sivori, who with socks rolled down to the ankles enchanted the Neapolitan crowds with his alluring wizardry and theatrical gestures. Sivori mirrored in style and attitude another Argentinian who followed in his exalted footsteps many years later. Although Sivori's time in the blue of Naples would be haunted with endless injuries, he still earned a place in Neapolitan folklore, such was his artistry and showmanship. Also arriving in the southern capital to aid Neapolitans in their championship quest was the highly regarded goalkeeper Dino Zoff. Signed from lowly Mantova, the young Zoff was destined in time to become the greatest number one in Italy's history, culminating in 1982 when at the grand old age of forty he lifted the World Cup for the *Azzurri*. Zoff proved a formidable barrier at the back for Napoli before his eventual departure to Juventus.

Sadly the title continued to elude and frustrations spilled over onto the terraces. Outbreaks of violence became increasingly common and there were many incidents at the San Paolo and elsewhere that shamed the club.

One of the worse took place at home against Palermo when an incensed Napoli *tifosi* had to be restrained by water cannons from lynching a referee who had particularly annoyed them. The poor official was only rescued when a helicopter landed on the pitch and lifted him to safety. The Napoli crowds greeted his great escape with mocking applause. Trouble also flared in matches against Genoa and Bologna where full-scale riots broke out on the stands. Pitch invasions and scenes of mass brawling forced the authorities to act and the Southerners were fined extraordinary heavy sums and ordered to play home matches away from Naples. SSC Napoli's God-given gift for self-destruction meant there appeared not a single chink of light in what had been a long, dark tunnel stretching back decades. Neapolitans prayed for a miracle.

Far away in a dustbowl, ramshackle slum of Argentinian capital Buenos Aires, a young boy played alone. He was entertaining himself by juggling a small orange from his left to right foot, before flicking it upon a shoulder, then onto his head, before starting all over again! All was achieved with a snake charmer's ease. Dreaming of great adventures, a five-year-old Diego Armando Maradona played on and on, and....

In 1967 the Neapolitans were drawn against unfancied English side Burnley in the Fairs Cup. Even today in this rural Lancashire town the occasion is recalled with a shudder and infamously referred to as 'The Battle of Naples'. For Neapolitans it was simply another night when emotions were roused and tempers frayed. With a confidence bordering towards cockiness Napoli journeyed to England for the first leg minus many of their star players. The Napoli hierarchy appeared to have learned little from their nightmarish experience against Bangor City, for many in Naples scoffed they had never heard of the Lancastrians. Again the two games that followed changed all. The South American heroes Altafini and Sivori were notable absences, although their omissions were said to have been down to injuries.

Both had succeeded setting Naples ablaze with their talents, and Argentinian maestro Sivori had just recently been awarded an engraved gold medal by his grateful adopted city for scoring the winning goal against fierce rivals Roma, the Romans being one of many clubs that the Neapolitan *tifosi* tended to have problems with! Napoli coach Enrico Zuppardi raised eyebrows amongst the English press when asked what he knew of his opponents. Zuppardi's reply entered Burnley footballing folklore when he declared, 'Harris, Lochhead, Irvine and Turf Moor are all new names to me, but I am

45

sure they are all first-rate players.' The Napoli head-man watched on quizzically as hard-bitten newspapermen fell to the floor in fits of laughter, Turf Moor obviously being the name of Burnley FC's ground!

The Italians abandoned their usual free-flowing style and switched to the dreary, defensive system of *catencaccio*. Still fuming from his embarrassing 'Turf Moor' gaff, Zuppardi had the sole intention of securing a 0-0 draw and finishing off the English in Naples. But he reckoned without a Burnley team that had been dangerously under-estimated. With the home ground packed to the rafters and the blurry haze of the floodlights illuminating the black Lancashire sky, Burnley thrashed the cocky Neapolitans 3-0. In a typically tempestuous confrontation between sides of these two nations, each kicked, mauled and punched. Neither became intimidated, instead their only thoughts appeared to get even as a fierce battle raged.

The bloodcurdling Napoli centre half Dino Panzanato was sent off for sticking the boot into forward Andy Lochhead as he lay forlorn on the ground. Revenge was mercilessly swift by the Burnley players as they sought out Panzanato seeking retribution. Anarchy reigned: chaos ensued on the pitch as bodies from both sides became involved in pushing and slanging matches. Punches were thrown as infamously short Neapolitan tempers snapped. Finally with officials, policemen and managers on the field, order was temporarily restored. The two Captains were hailed towards the beleaguered referee and warned the game would be abandoned if the melee continued. To make matters worse Dino Panzanato then refused to leave the field. It was only through the intervention of his coach Zuppardi, who coaxed him off the pitch, that the game was allowed to resume. Lochhead had the last laugh when he drove home a late third to set Turf Moor ablaze and set up a firecracker of a second leg. The final whistle blew and the embarrassed Napoli players went home vowing revenge would be theirs, under the all-watchful eye of Mount Vesuvius.

On 8th February 1967 Burnley entered into the bear pit of the San Paolo. A fiercely partisan crowd of sixty-thousand Neapolitans greeted them in inimitable style by hurling abuse and anything else they could get their hands on from behind a six-foot perimeter moat that encircled this impressive footballing arena. It wasn't just the English who ducked, everyone cowered! Napoli brought out the big guns. Omar Sivori and Jose Altafini returned from injury to help bury the English. Also back in the starting line-up was local hero and wonderfully talented midfielder Antonio Juliano. Another name in the team was Ottavio Bianchi. Later as manager, Bianchi was destined for great deeds with Napoli. But that remained still a generation away. That moment in time his gifts were needed as a player. Left with no choice, Enrico

Zuppardi had decided to throw caution to the wind. From the first minute to the last it would be all-out attack. Neapolitans gathered in their hordes expecting the three-goal deficit to be washed away in a blue tidal wave. Woe betide if they were left disappointed?

In what proved to be the game of his life Burnley goalkeeper Harry Thompson produced a heroic display to keep the Italians at bay. In the first minute Jose Altafini showed his class by letting fly from fully thirty yards, only to see his blinding shot crash loud against the crossbar. A massacre appeared likely as the wizardry, pace and movement of the Napoli forwards had their opponents constantly on the back foot. But despite being hugely outclassed the Lancastrians refused to yield. Sivori led the frantic onslaught as he weaved his magic, but time and again the magnificent Thompson was at hand to foil them. Fantastic last-gasp saves from Altafini, Bianchi and Juliano caused Neapolitans to shake their heads and ponder if they would ever beat him. Five minutes before half-time Naples erupted when they were awarded a penalty. As Jose Altafini struck it towards the left-hand corner, Thompson leapt miraculously across his goalline to push the ball away. Altafini pounded the floor in disgust, for he never missed. Remarkably, only four days previous he had scored a sensational hat-trick of spot-kicks in the league.

The game wore on and still Burnley held out. As the locals grew increasingly restless fires started on the terraces of the San Paolo. Twenty minutes remained when Jose Altafini was forced to leave the battle after a clash of heads. With blood seeping from a forehead wound, the home supporters showed little mercy and the Brazilian's unfortunate exit was met with a hail of coins and cushions hurled in his direction. In Naples even heroes had to dive for cover when all went awry. As the clock ticked down and the home side realised the cause was lost, tempers erupted. Omar Sivori got away with murder when he elbowed the Burnley player Dave Merrington in full view of the referee, only then for the official to prefer not to see it. Wise move, for the Naples air had turned a disturbingly misty red inside the San Paolo.

Come the final whistle and though jubilant, the intimidating atmosphere meant English celebrations were sober and subdued. It was no time to gloat when only a surrounding moat and a vastly outnumbered, half-hearted handful of policemen and soldiers stood between them and a possible murky fate. The Italian players prowled around, menacing, eager to pick a fight. They were in no mood to accept defeat and go quiet. Burnley's finest Harry Thompson went to shake Napoli's Alberto Orlando's hand, only to be spat at in the face and floored by an Orlando right hook. As the unfortunate goalkeeper lay distraught, other home players took out their frustrations on the felled Thompson. The Burnley reserve keeper Adam Blacklaw charged across the turf and immediately laid into his teammate's assailants. Blacklaw was a rugged, tough Scot who could handle himself. In a fury he grabbed one Neapolitan and hurled him down a set of stone steps. In no time he was surrounded by a herd of irate Italians howling for blood. Not fancying the overwhelming odds, Blacklaw ran off and fortunately survived to tell the tale.

Outside the stadium a Neapolitan lynch mob had gathered to vent their anger at the Burnley coach. It was only when police fired shots above their heads that the crowds dispersed into the night, going home glumly to their beds. Even then no chances were taken as the embarrassed authorities attempted to make amends to their visitors. To the utter astonishment of the English, a military convoy armed with enough firepower to kickstart a revolution roared up outside the San Paolo. Nine army jeeps, all equipped with machine guns, and an armoured tank was provided to escort them to the city airport. Not even the most hardened follower of SSC Napoli would have attempted to take on such a force! Bruised but elated, the pride of Lancashire finally bade a bloodied *arrivederci* to Naples. On returning to Burnley the headlines in the local paper summed up their fiery encounter with the Neapolitans. It read, 'See Naples and die!'

Three years later they were at it again! This time it was against poor unsuspecting Swindon Town in the inaugural Anglo-Italian Cup final held in the San Paolo. On Thursday 28th May 1970, 55,000 watched first in dismay, and then growing anger as the English underdogs ran Napoli ragged, roaring into a three-goal lead. Finally after seventy-nine minutes it all proved too much to bear as once again that legendary Neapolitan short fuse ignited and riots broke out on the terraces. Fires were started, seats were ripped up and thrown onto the pitch. The Swindon players watched in amazement as a full-scale battle ensued between the war-weary, baton-wielding police and supporters. All a long way from the sleepy picturesque settings of their hometown. As mayhem erupted all around the referee was left with little option but to abandon the game and award the trophy to Swindon. Not surprisingly the presentation took place well out of sight of the rioters who seemed intent on razing the San Paolo to the ground!

That same year controversy erupted once more when with Napoli closing in on their first title, sinister events occurred at the San Siro in Milan that caused cries of corruption in Naples. Neapolitan folklore came to regard it as the *Scipo of Saint Siro* (a bag snatch at the San Siro). It was an all-or-nothing clash against Inter with the winner likely to clinch the title. With the Southerners leading 1-0 at half-time through their Brazilian talisman Jose Altafini, the game turned on its head in the second period when the home side were awarded an imaginary penalty that defied belief by referee Sergio Gonnella. Napoli stopper Dino Panzanato was once more in the forefront of battle as he was alleged to have fouled Inter great Sandro Mazzola. The resulting spot-kick was slammed home by another Milan legend, centre forward Roberto Boninsegna, to set up a tense finish. Bonninsegna had not yet finished with the Neapolitans and in the closing moments he stabbed home a gut-churning winner to break their hearts. Following the final whistle an outraged Panzanato had to be physically restrained by his teammates from attacking Gonnella who was swiftly ushered away out of harm's way. For the Southerners it all stank to high heaven. What was the point, how do you defeat an enemy that never took to the field and yet still retained the power to influence? *Spudoramente* (shameless). Their spirit shattered, SSC Napoli ultimately finished in third place with Inter taking the championship and neighbours AC grabbing runners-up. And it hardly got any better.

Stricken by mounting debt the Napoli President Corrado Ferlaino was forced to cash in on some of his major assets and to the absolute horror of Naples, a reluctant Ferlaino sold off the family jewels to Juventus. Jose Altafini and Dino Zoff moved north to Turin in a deal that allowed the club to stay afloat. Decades of over-spending had finally seen Napoli hoisted by their own petard. It was the eternal struggle. Forever at the races, but never backing the winner. In typical Neapolitan street theatre fashion both Zoff and more significantly Altafini returned to haunt them in an infamous final encore. Basking in the twilight of a glorious career, Jose Altafini enjoyed a sumptuous golden summer in Turin. In the 1972-73 season it was his 200th league goal in the last match of the campaign that clinched yet another *Scudetto* for *La Vecchia Signora*. He also would have one last role to play in the eternally tragic history of SSC Napoli. Cast as chief villain in the despised colours of their most bitter rivals, the Brazilian would deliver the ultimate *coup de grace* to his one-time love. For time immemorial, until their volcano decided otherwise, Jose Altafini's name would be spat out with venom in Naples. He would become known as *Core Ngrato* (the ungrateful heart).

Towards the end of the 1974-75 season SSC Napoli and Juve were involved in one of the tightest finishes ever to an Italian championship. The title had all but come down to one match played in the Agnelli's personal kingdom of Turin. The atmosphere inside Stadio Comunale was electric. In a show of amazing loyalty and sheer defiance the Napoli *tifosi* had infiltrated around the ground to vastly outnumber the home supporters. With many thousands of Neapolitans living in Turin and employed by Agnelli's Fiat Company, tickets were easily snapped up. The Comunale was draped blue and white. It appeared as if all of Naples had descended upon Turin to make sure their team did not again fail them and finally see that damned *Scudetto* won. Many years later this scenario would again appear, only with a happy ending. In a rousing encounter the *Bianconeri* drew first blood on nineteen minutes when *Azzurri* winger Franco Causio struck to give Juve a half-time lead.

Once more the title looked set for Turin. But then with thirty minutes remaining SSC Napoli's beloved captain, Antonio Juliano, smashed home an equaliser and bedlam erupted in the Comunale. Juliano had set up a grandstand finale. The championship became a shootout, nothing less, next goal wins! The Neapolitans roared forward, immortality beckoned. With the home team looking spent and Napoli creating chances at will, only the magnificent efforts of goalkeeper Zoff, a one-time Southern idol prevented a massacre. At last the title appeared Naples-bound. But as the minutes ticked down and the *Bianconeri* held on by the skin of their imperial teeth, many in the Stadio Comunale sensed it was not to be Napoli's day. As Neapolitans held their breath and prayed for a goal, fate once more transpired against them. High above San Gennaro looked away, his hands tied, it was happening again. It was decreed that one of their own, Jose Altafini, would deliver the knockout punch. Altafini latched onto a clearance on the edge of the Napoli goal and without feeling or remorse for his former love smashed home to leave them cursing their old flame. There was no time to come back, the final whistle blew and the sound of crying was heard back in Naples. The following season saw a little consolation gained with a comforting, 4-0 thrashing of Hellas Verona to win *Lo Coppa Italia* for a second time. But overall it mattered little, for the Southern hordes lay grieving. Jose Altafini had not only broken their hearts, he had come indecently close to destroying their spirit. But still the faith was kept in Naples. Mocked, abused and derided as mere barbarians and a sore on the face of all Italy, the followers of SSC Napoli licked their wounds, dusted themselves down, sang their songs and prepared to fight another day. Their time would come.

Great players came and went. One of the best was legendary Dutch master Rudi Krol. He arrived in 1980 and under Krol's leadership, inspired by his immaculate fifty-yard passes sprayed delightfully around the field, Napoli earned a much needed third-place spot. However even this achievement was dulled by Juventus winning the title in Naples on the penultimate Sunday of the season, when to half of Turin's delight the Neapolitans were forced to play host to the gloating celebrations of the Grand Old Lady. To make matters worse the 1-0 victory came courtesy of an own goal! Many present in the San Paolo that day swore as the ball crossed the line, Vesuvius itself let loose a groan of bitter disappointment. Naples wept, how many tears did a city have to shed? The years rolled on and still the trophy cabinet lay bereft of *Lo*

Scudetto. History decreed that a club with such resources and a fanbase such as SSC Napoli, the third largest city in Italy, would one day triumph. But when? *Sempre domani* (Always tomorrow.) Love, hate and love again: *Amore*! It was four years before Maradona.

CHAPTER 5

'EL PIBE DE ORO'

The Naples nights came laced with lurid tales of debauchery and decadence that would have satisfied the Borgias. In the Hotel Royal, women flowed as freely as the alcohol and the white powder. An entire floor was given over to Diego Maradona and friends and each night it rocked in true orgiastic style. Anything went, staff stayed tight-lipped at what they witnessed for they recognised the faces of some of those who kept Maradona company deep into the witching hour. A hotel once renowned for its hospitality and clientele was turned overnight into a den of ill repute. So it was with great delight that the dignified figure of the Royal's Maitre De, Ettore Bosse, received word from Napoli officials that his most famous guest was moving out. The sighs of relief could be heard all across Naples!

The district of Posillipo, perched high on the top of sea-ravaged cliffs, offers its residents enchanting views of the bay and Mount Vesuvius. It was home to the more affluent members of Neapolitan society, both legal and otherwise. Judges and politicians lived alongside corrupt government officials and drug barons. The smell of freshly-laundered cash lingered amidst the sweet aroma of exotic flower bowls and lemon groves. Sprinklers drenched immaculate green cut lawns, giving fresh life beneath a scorching Southern sun: clean money. The great, good and the downright scandalous. Neighbours deemed fit for this dubious king with a crown of thorns. Posillipo would play host for seven years to Maradona and his band of self-loading freeloaders as they attempted to drink Naples dry.

At first Maradona turned up his nose at the luxurious two-floor apartment given to him by Napoli, claiming that he would only vacate the Royal if accommodation similar to the mansion he had inherited in Spain became available. In Catalonia the lurid tales of drink and drug-fuelled orgies that took place there had already catapulted into the realms of Barcelona legend. Something of similar size and stature was desired by Maradona. But when it was explained to him that this was impossible due to the overcrowding in Naples and the sheer lack of space, he mellowed and grudgingly moved himself and his clan uptown to Posillipo.

'EL PIBE DE ORO'

On 23rd November 1980, to the abject horror of all Naples, the miracle of San Gennaro failed to transpire. Many feared this an omen for impending disaster. While the rest of Italy laughed and dismissed such nonsense as Neapolitan witchcraft, the ground exploded and 5,000 people were killed in a fearsome earthquake. The area was devastated, billions of lira and medical aid poured into the South but the *Camorra* ripped off most in an array of cunning and malicious schemes. No sooner indeed had the re-housing projects began than the lead engineer in charge was shot and and left for dead for refusing to accept a pay-off. All the while the homeless were left with no option but to pay the *Camorra* protection money for the ramshackle dwellings they were forced to live in. Naples was rocked on its heels as the earth trembled along the coastline. For most Neapolitans these tragic events came as no surprise. Sadly no one heeded San Gennaro's warning and death and chaos descended upon the region.

Four years on and thousands of people in the surrounding areas still lived in tents and makeshift homes, as there was no room in the already overpopulated city. It would have harmed Maradona's reputation if his petulance became public knowledge. Aware of how important it was for Diego's image to remain untarnished, Jorge Cysterzspiler persuaded him it made more sense to go quietly. And so the king had a new home: the court jesters turned up the ghetto blaster, the neighbours pretended not to mind and life for Diego Armando carried on in its own inimitable way. But all this apart, when the time arose to adorn the light blue of SSC Napoli, Maradona did so in a way that exhilarated and charmed the footballing soul. He became known as *El Pibe De Oro* (Golden boy). There were times in the San Paolo and beyond when for a brief second time itself appeared to stand still as Maradona cast a sorcerer's spell over his captive audience. He became every Neapolitan's brother, every girlfriend's lover. An infatuation that was healthy for the heart, wonderful for the ego but ultimately deadly for the soul. For something so intense could eventually end only one way. In tears. Maradona in time would face the surreal prospect of becoming a living Saint.

The week following the epic victory against Udinese and courtesy of Maradona, the Neapolitans staged a smash and grab raid in Florence, home of the great South Americans Daniel Passarella of Argentina and the Brazilian Socrates. On an ice rink of a surface at the Stadio Artemio Franchi, with bright specks of snow melting under a winter sun, the *Viola* of Fiorentina were beaten by a fantastic effort on forty-nine minutes from the Argentinian as he played a clever wall-pass with striker Luigi Caffarelli before firing his club well clear of the relegation zone. Caffarelli was one of many Napoli players who began to shine in the wake of Maradona's sudden surge into top gear. His clever link- play with the dancing feet of the Argentinian bursting deep from midfield was becoming an integral part of Napoli's play.

It proved to be the only goal and the *tifosi* of Fiorentina, the *Collettivo Autonomo Viola*, seething at losing to the Southern scum acted in typical fashion by attempting a full-scale assault against the gloating Neapolitans at full-time. Strangely both shared some common ground, an unholy, rabid hatred of Juventus. But when at each other's throats across the battlegrounds of Serie A, this mattered little as they sought ways to outwit the *Carabinieri* and ignite World War Three on the streets of Florence. Unlike the Neapolitans, whose loathing for the Old Lady stretched back decades and came etched with social and political reasons, the Fiorentina following hated Juve for entirely footballing matters.

Two years previous all of Florence was convinced that sinister tactics had been employed and someone at Juve's behest had bribed officials to rob them of the championship on the last day of the season. A penalty by Liam Brady gifted Juventus the *Scudetto* after Fiorentina saw a goal controversially ruled out. It was one if allowed that would have handed them the title. But it was not to be and the Florence skyline was lit up crimson red for three nights as riots erupted across the city. At the time such scenarios occurred with disturbing frequency in Italy. A dark hand, meddling, fixing. Many were caught taking poisoned gold, amongst the most famous Paolo Rossi, whose goals led the *Azzurri* to victory in the 1982 World Cup. History now recalls that during the Eighties match fixing was rife in Serie A, and nowhere more than in the South. In time SSC Napoli would also appear to suffer the same torment as what befell Fiorentina.

In the month of February the Neapolitans began a steady climb up the table. Respectable draws were earned with league leaders Verona and away to the impressive Sampdoria in Genoa. In both matches Napoli held their own and after extracting revenge against Torino in Naples with goals from Maradona and Caffarelli, European qualification became a distinct possibility. Following an away draw on the lakes of Como, earned with yet another Maradona penalty, the Neapolitans prepared to play host to struggling Lazio. It was in this game that their number ten showed the full extent of what he was truly capable of when the mood arose, an occasion so memorable that those lucky enough to attend would never tire of boring their children with the fantastic tale of when *El Pibe de Oro* put the Romans of Lazio to the sword in the glorious amphitheatre of the San Paolo.

It had been ten years since the legendary Welsh-born Giorgio Chinaglia led Lazio to their only *Scudetto* triumph to set half of Rome ablaze. Since winning the championshiop, this club that once boasted Benito Mussolini amongst its most fervid supporters had suffered the indignities of match fixing scandals, relegation and years of mediocrity. So it was no great surprise that again they found themselves involved in a battle royal at the foot of the table to avoid Serie B. It had proved a traumatic campaign for the *Biancocelesti* (the whites and skies). The light blues had begun poorly and slowly as the months passed, collapsed like a pack of cards to turn into a horrible rabble. In a desperate gamble to turn the grim tide they hired legendary veteran Argentinian manager Juan Carlos Lorenzo.

The controversial sixty-four-year-old Lorenzo was in his third spell as coach of Lazio and a reputation for win at all cost tactics went before him. This man, who would stoop to any level to see his team achieve victory, prepared for one last throw in Serie A. During a career which stretched back four decades and included a period managing his country in the 1966 World Cup finals (Antonio Rattin and all) Lorenzo earned everlasting notoriety when he led Argentinian champions Estudiantes to unprecedented success, culminating in winning the World Club Championship in successive years against Celtic and Manchester United. The chaos, violence and thuggery involved in both clashes saw Lorenzo's ruthless doctrine castigated and reviled but in an age where the result was everything, he became a wanted man and Lazio lured him to Rome.

There he earned the eternal gratitude of the Roman *tifosi* by regularly beating hated cross-city rivals Roma and qualifying for Europe for the first time. But after a series of embarrassing altercations against English sides Arsenal and Ipswich in the UEFA Cup, where Lorenzo wound his team up to such an extent that they attacked the Arsenal players in a restaurant following a game in Rome, he was reluctantly forced to bid *arrivederci* to the ancient Capital. Now, sadly for the Lazio cause, Juan Carlos Lorenzo's fire had waned and the man who took his seat on the bench in the San Paolo was a mere shadow of the fanatical character whose teams had once terrorised the world.

The Roman *tifosi* had prayed that someone with such a vast wealth of experience would help them pull off a miraculous escape, but sadly Lorenzo was a man handed the keys to a car after it had already crashed. His arrival failed miserably to inspire and by the time Lazio arrived in Naples, plans were already underfoot for his replacement. The relegation trapdoor was looming and a disgraceful surrender at home to Udinese where they were thrashed 4-1 saw the supporters turn savagely. Defeat by the Neapolitans and the ringing of the death knell would be heard loud two hundred miles away in Rome.

Rino Marchesi did not relish the idea of twisting the dagger any further into the bleeding, open wounds of his beloved former club. Marchesi had played for five years with Lazio and they still held a special place in his heart. However, his adopted Neapolitans who waited with bated breath for a raging Maradona to send the Romans home weeping did not share such feelings. For them the only decent thing to come out of Rome was the Autostrada winding its way back south. Neapolitans had grown weary of self-righteous, crusading politicians crying crocodile tears for their city, for Rome represented everything they detested, an arrogant, aloof central government that washed its hands of Naples and all her ailments. Overcrowding, spiralling crime rate and a poverty level unsurpassed anywhere in the Western world. All mattered little, for Romans eyed the *Mezzogiorno* with nothing but contempt.

There was an old adage in Naples, '*Ajutat'ca dio t'ajut*' ('God helps those who help themselves'). Where Neapolitans saw themselves as resourceful and relying on their streetwise wits to survive, elsewhere they were seen as lazy, foul, unkempt, lacking in morals and having no respect for authority. Well aware the *Camorra* held sway and called the shots in the murky waters of Neapolitan politics, Rome's hierarchy were always suspicious and reluctant to sanction financial aid to a city deemed unruleable and so openly abused. The uncollected tax revenue from Naples alone ran into billions. Extortion rackets strangled the life out of any business that dared to chance a dream. A law unto themselves, a culture apart. A place whose heart and soul lay shackled in the cruel and ruthless chains of the underworld. The *Mezzogiorno* was best left alone to rot.

Such attitudes by outsiders tarring all Neapolitans with the same brush infuriated the vast majority who wished only to earn an honest living. Hammering the living daylights out of Lazio and banging another nail into their relegation coffin would, in a small way, offer sweet revenge. For despite all the grandeur of Rome - the Coliseum, the Vatican, St Peter's Basilica, the Spanish steps, the Sistine Chapel - Napoli possessed their own wonder, Maradona! The *Biancocelesti* entered into the lion's den. A city expected, they were handed a typically warm Neapolitan greeting with 86,000 *tifosi* screaming abuse, demanding Roman blood. Vesuvius rumbled in gruesome expectation. The teams broke away for a brief warm-up before battle commenced. Juan Carlos Lorenzo, a man who had seen it all in his many years, feared the worse and crossed himself, praying for the day to go well. But no one was listening. Lazio's descent into hell began.

In a storming first half Napoli threw everything they had at the besieged Lazio defence. Fernando Orsi in the visitors' goal was peppered with shots as the home side carried the game to them. The noise from the crowd soared high towards the heavens whenever Diego Maradona received possession. He appeared to ignite jet fuel as he tricked, jinked and weaved past hapless

Lazio defenders. The haunted expression of Lorenzo on the touchline told its own story as the bewildering Maradona twisted the rearguard of Calisti, Filisetti, Vianello and Padovino first one way then another. The stadium swayed, ebbed and rocked with delight as their favourite son wreaked mayhem. Each foray by Napoli into the Romans' half came tinged with memories past, of slurs and chants suffered, flags that waved 'Cholera' in their faces after the earthquake of 1980. Who was laughing now?

Half-time came and swiftly disappeared with the Neapolitan *tifosi* dancing throughout, singing the name of their hero. The siege was relentless and finally a breakthrough occurred when a terrible backpass by the centre-half Vianello was read by Maradona who took the ball in his stride before lashing a viscous strike past Orsi into the top corner of the net. The white shirts dropped to their knees. A brave stand had been broken, as had their spirit for a fight. With the travelling Lazio supporters fearing the worse it duly happened when an own goal by Filesetti left Orsi helpless to double Napoli's lead. The Rome-born goalkeeper pounded the Neapolitan earth, the game was up. Juan Carlos Lorenzo stood motionless as bedlam erupted around him, his mind was already back home in Argentina. But before he departed Italian shores a fellow countryman was about to hand him a going away present that he would never forget.

On eighty-four minutes Diego Maradona scored a goal that would live forever in the memories of all present on that long gone Sunday afternoon. From forty yards Maradona smashed a dramatic half-volley past a disbelieving Orsi. As the ball screamed into the net delirium broke out on the terraces. Around the stadium people danced uncontrollably in the aisles. The San Paolo was in a state of hysteria. Maradona disappeared beneath a heap of bodies smothering him with thanks. Players, club officials, ballboys, even a beaming Napoli policeman joined in! But the goalfest wasn't over. *Pibe De Oro* had not yet finished with the traumatised Romans.

Three minutes from time the hat-trick was completed when Maradona scored again. This time a curling effort direct from a corner that once more Fernando Orsi failed miserably on. The magical little Argentinian had dipped back into his box of tricks to end a depressing and humiliating day for Lazio. 4-0, and so much for a thousand years of history and all the grandeur of Rome! All that glittered that day in Naples was gold, Maradona!

The Argentinian ended his first season on Italian soil with an impressive third place in the *Classifica Marcatori* (goalscoring charts), finishing only behind the great Michel Platini and Allesandro Altobelli with an outstanding tally of fourteen goals. A reputation that had become tarnished after his brief nightmare sojourn in Barcelona was enhanced. Naples was seen to have got itself a bargain. To the delight of their followers Napoli finished a respectable eighth position and could hold their heads high. Further highlights included another rampaging performance in the San Paolo, this time a revenge mission against Inter Milan, two goals from Daniel Bertoni inspiring them to a sparkling 3-1 victory.

Towards the final weeks Juventus went south and were lucky to escape with a draw. Neapolitan honour had been duly served. The last game saw Fiorentina beaten 1-0 in Naples and a wonderful ovation for the team at the full-time whistle. Diego Armando Maradona had dragged SSC Napoli kicking and screaming out of the relegation mire and into midtable safety. A seed of hope had been planted under heavenly blue Neapolitan skies and was already beginning to flower. For once life under the volcano was good. As for the championship, that darned elusive *Scudetto*, it was a case of '*L'anna prossimo?*' ('Maybe next year?').

CHAPTER 6

IRREVERSIBLE SUNRISE

Under a jet black Neapolitan sky that glistened with stars and a striking full moon, the port of Naples entered the midnight shift. Lit by torchlight, scurrying figures whose faces lay masked hurried towards the waiting ships. Freight lorries sat empty on the quayside: their owners nervous, fretting, and eager to be loaded and away. As a city slept the Camorra went to work. Contraband smuggled from far and near. From Sicily, their good friends in Palermo, Africa, and the Balkans. Drugs, cigarettes, alcohol, Rolex watches, even human cargo to be used for prostitution and labour was unloaded down plank-ways to be whisked away under the dead of night. Nearby, port officials and night watchmen played cards, their palms already crossed with silver. Armed lookouts along the seafront kept a wary eye for Carabinieri patrols, their Uzi machine pistols hidden from sight. For this is business, Camorra style: the midnight shift.

Princes of the Forcella: Don Vittorio Giuliano was the Father and founding member of a family dynasty that ruled secretly over the Forcella district of the city for twenty years. His was a clan united by blood that dealt in blood. As a child in post-World War Two Naples, Vittorio had little choice but to mature fast through his tender years in order to survive as a *Scugnizzi* (street kid). Vittorio would run errands for the neighborhood *Camorristi*. He listened enthralled as the old time *guappos* related tall tales of legendary characters of the Neapolitan underworld (some fantasy, others frighteningly real) who never answered to anyone except God and San Gennaro. Young Giuliano dreamt that one day men would talk of him in such hushed tones of awe.

As a teenager Vittorio formed his own street gang and quickly earned for himself a fine reputation as a good earner. Rich pickings could be found in the city's seaport, and here Giuliano excelled. A little planning, greasing of palms and soon he and his gang were making a small fortune from smuggled contraband, mostly cigarettes, robbed from visiting ships. But at nineteen, Vittorio Giuliano's luck ran out when after insulting a policeman in public he found himself behind bars. It was hardly a serious offence, but with Giuliano's activities well known it proved a perfect opportunity to get him off the streets. It was a mistake and one that the Neapolitan authorities would come to regret, for during his time in jail this young hood from the slums of the Forcella saw his ambitions soar.

Up to that time Giuliano had only been playing at being a gangster, but once forcibly enrolled into Naples university of life, he was given the finest education possible. On release Vittorio gathered around him men he could trust as he began expanding his business interests to the gambling, prostitution and protection rackets. A move into the murderous, if lucrative heroin and marijuana drugs market, handed them the necessary funds to secure their future by paying off those who had vowed to bring them to justice. No one or nothing was allowed to stand in Giuliano's way as he carved up the Forcella to make it his own. Rival gangs in the districts faced the option of coming under the wing of this new kid on the block or being wiped out. Those who chose to fight were shown no mercy as the name of Vittorio Giuliano became feared and respected not only in the surrounding area but also across the entire region of Campania.

The wise Don Vittorio married the daughter of a local bigshot who bore him many sons. This delighted Giuliano, for in a place like the Forcella, where danger and death lurked round every corner, he needed blood clan. In Naples almost anything could be bought except blind loyalty. Such a rarity came only through family. Luigi, Carmine, Guglielmo and Rafaele would all follow in their father's footsteps. Come the Eighties and with Don Vittorio in semi-retirement, his offspring prospered to carry on the family business. Ruling their kingdom with a disturbing concoction of a kind hand and senseless brutality, they resembled a Neapolitan institution and were as close to royalty that Naples could muster.

Sitting next to the city's main railway station, the Forcella was more Third World than European in appearance. It came as an immediate eye opener for quizzical tourists who foolishly contrived to discover for themselves, the 'Real Naples'. Known locally as the Kasbah, it was first established as a main base for the flourishing Neapolitan black market during the Allied wartime occupation. To the present day anything for the right price could be bought. Women, drugs, both legal and otherwise. Treasured art, borrowed and stolen! Rare antiques. Never a question asked. An unwritten rule was always that the Giuliano clan received a cut of anything sold. The consequences for those few foolish enough to ignore was severe.

An utter contempt for the authorities was such, that any attempt made to bring them to heel was met with the deadly hail of Kalashnikov bullets and a barrage of kidnappings, car bombs and pay-offs. The Forcella was off bounds to the authorities, for it simply wasn't worth the price in blood that would be spilled. Many thousands of Napoli football *tifosi* supplemented measly incomes by hiring their services to the Giulianos. These ranged from petty jobs such as peddling contraband, drug trafficking, arson, and, when the call came from above, the ultimate act. For those brave enough to take on *Lo Camorra*, the threat of assassination became a constant companion. Sure as a southern wind blows, it was inevitable that whenever their guard was dropped, they would be hit. Shopkeeper, salesman, lawyer, politician, it mattered little. If a Don so desired, they were deemed dead men walking.

Jorge Cysterzspiler stood once more on the edge of financial ruin. A series of amateurish, half-baked commercial enterprises to promote his client's name in Barcelona saw his reputation as some manipulative whizz-kid in tatters. More importantly Cysterzspiler realised his job hung by the most slender of threads. The twenty-six-year-old knew their time in Italy had to prove worthwhile off the pitch. He simply had to turn Maradona Productions into a profitable organisation and be seen doing so. Make some real cash to keep the boss happy. Diego's blind assumption that money grew on trees meant many a sleepless night tossing and turning for the Argentinian. Whilst Maradona lived it up with his love of Naples nightlife, a twenty-plus entourage, Ferrari, Rolls Royce, Porsche, luxury yacht plus an insatiable appetite for women and cocaine, Jorge Cysterzspiler sweated buckets looking for the next paycheck.

Theirs was a friendship formed when both were teenagers. Where Maradona caused palpitations in grown men's hearts everytime he stepped onto a football pitch, Cysterzspiler was a rather sad figure of fun, an overweight youth, forever miserable and cursed with a straggling limp, a sad legacy of a childhood ravaged by polio. Such misfortunes saw him lapse into a dark period of depression. It was only when a concerned family friend persuaded Jorge to accompany him to a nearby football match that his true vocation in life called. Playing that day was a frail-looking fifteen-year-old from the back of beyond called Diego Maradona. After finding the courage to introduce himself to the young Diego, an enduring friendship between the two began. The raggedy kid from the dustbowl shacks of Villa Fiorito, and the middle class Jewish boy from one of the more leafy suburban areas of uptown Buenos Aires.

Many a night Maradona escaped the hardships of Fiorito to stay over at his newfound friend's house. There they would talk until the early hours about hopes for the future, share their dreams. An unlikely double act, but close nonetheless. Both shared a wish to be the best in their field. After securing for himself a business degree Jorge Cysterzspiler was asked by Diego Maradona to become his manager in all matters financial. A touched Cysterzspiler said yes whole-heartedly to his *amigo* and together their journey to the stars began. Maradona trusted his friend implicitly with not just his hard-earned dollars, but more importantly the financial security of his family. At first this was deemed by Cysterzspiler as a privilege, but as time went by and Diego started to act like the spoilt kid in the playground, wanting all the best toys, it developed into a heavy burden.

He, as much as anyone, was blinded by Maradona's genius and sadly it blurred him from the harsh realities that the books always had to balance. Fortunately the transfer to Naples enabled Cysterzspiler the perfect opportunity to grab hold tight of the reins, have a long think and ensure the money started to roll in. This once dumpy kid who everybody laughed at, or worse pitied, was ready to make his own mark in the wonderful, weird world of Maradona. Jorge coveted dollar bills like Diego loved a ball. He was determined to impress by showing true business acumen and wring every last lira out of Neapolitan pockets. Flood Naples high streets with Diego Maradona products, sit back and watch the money come rolling in. Unfortunately, much to the Argentinian's distress, somebody would beat him to it!

Carmine Giuliano was thirty-two years old and a *Camorra*, Prince of the City, when Diego Maradona streaked like a bolt of lightning into his midst. His nickname of *Il Lione* (The Lion) was well deserved. Although Giuliano appeared just like any other young Neapolitan with his wavy black hair and demonstrative swagger, the eyes gave light to his true character. Dangerous, all seeing, mysterious, downright frightening. The signing of the legendary Argentinian was viewed as an ideal opportunity for rich picking by *Lo Camorra*. As Diegomania erupted across Naples, *Il Lione* marshalled together his army of marketeers, hustlers and street vendors. With Neapolitans keen to be parted from their cash for anything with the player's name emblazoned upon it, the gangs cleaned up. For as blessed Diego Maradona was with his talents, so the *Camorra* were equally gifted in their field. Keen also to lure Maradona into their inner circle, the brother's Giuliano devised a plan. It was one deemed simple but effective. They would laud him with kind words, reverence and a respect reserved only for a king. It was time to throw a party.

At seeing Neapolitan peddlers on every street corner selling all types of unlicensed Maradona-themed goods, Jorge Cysterzspiler became driven to despair. An indignant Cysterzspiler fumed. He rather foolishly began threatening to sue whoever was behind the unofficial merchandising campaign. Naples had become awash with Diego-related hats, cup, scarves, flags, T-shirts, posters and bedsheets. At the city's heart in the Bassi (Naples' most poverty-stricken slum area), entire families worked day and night in airless tiny one-room flats to cope with the mass demand. But no one complained for business had never been better. There was food on the table, nothing else mattered. There appeared only one individual in the entire city unhappy with proceedings. However, Cysterzspiler's public hard stance softened quite dramatically when representatives of *Lo Camorra* paid him a visit to 'recommend' that it would be in his best interest to stop making threats, for such arrogance from an outsider would not be tolerated. It was politely and very clearly explained to the perspiring Jorge Cysterzspiler that 'The poor people of Naples should be allowed to make a living.' In short, keep your mouth shut!

Frightened for his life, Cysterzspiler swiftly changed tack. He was smart enough to realise that although the message was delivered in a calm and friendly manner, the next time would not be so amicable. In this place, like no other, business was conducted in a manner that could not be taught in any school or university. The Argentinian thanked God he had not upset them more. For twenty-six was no age to meet your maker and he hardly relished the idea of being throttled, with his body hurled over the side of a fishing boat into the bay of Naples, as food for the fishes. Jorge Cysterzspiler had been handed an unforgettable lesson in the ways of his adopted city. It was one he learned well. Who was he to rock the boat? Especially when he could end up in one!

Theirs was an invitation dreaded, but never declined. A fleeting view through a half-opened door, at a world and its people, for whom normal rules did not apply. In the early weeks of January 1986, on a bitter, cold January morning, two young emissaries from the clan Giuliano went to the Napoli training complex in Soccavo on the city's edge. Known with typically biting, ironic Neapolitan humour as the Paradise Centre, it was hardly worthy of a side with ambitions to win Serie A. Quite simply it was a disgrace. Run down to the point of antiquated, the centre was a constant source of bitterness amongst the players. As ever at Soccavo, security was tight as hundreds of Neapolitan *tifosi* milled around, desperate to catch a glimpse of their hero. The *Camorra* messengers appeared like any other of the supporters gathered at the main gates. But these two were different, for after a whispered conversation with a huddle of burly Napoli security guards, they were ushered through to be granted an audience with the normally untouchable Diego Maradona.

The Argentininan was approached with great courtesy and informed they were there on behalf of Carmine Giuliano to invite him to a party being held in his honour. The message was conveyed in the hushed tones of a servant speaking to his king. It was explained that Maradona's presence would be deeply appreciated by Don Carmine and his brothers who wished to extend the hand of friendship. How could he possibly refuse? Though aware of their notorious reputation and how they earned a living, Maradona felt no qualms in gratefully accepting, for he and the brothers had met many times on his countless sojourns in Naples' fleshpots and drinking holes. The opportunity to attend was viewed by the player as an ideal chance to mix with those who were just like him. Men who had dragged themselves kicking and screaming from a lifetime of poverty to earn money, power and, ultimately, respect. Men who had refused point blank to accept the hand fate dealt them. To rage against God's will.

That the Giulianos chose to live their life outside establishment rules saw Maradona's admiration for them increase no end. The brothers had come from nothing to Princes of the City. The Forcella was their's, no argument. A kingdom within. A childhood spent in the shattered wastelands of Villa Fiorito, where only a heaven sent gift for football helped Diego Maradona escape, saw him recognize kindred spirits, blood brothers in the Giulianos. He would later say of those early days in Argentina, 'If you had money for food you ate, and if you didn't, you didn't.' Unknown to most and shrouded in the swirling fog of Naples politics, it was alleged *Camorra* money was instrumental in bringing Maradona from Barcelona. Only those skilled in the ways of Neapolitan intrigue knew the truth. For the substantial investment the gangs expected much in return, not least the opportunity to be seen in his company and to bask in Maradona's illustrious shadow. To impress women and dazzle friends. Like a dangling puppet on a string, *El Pibe De Oro* was made to dance for their amusement.

The gleaming array of Jaguars, Porsches and Ferraris littering the parking area of the palatial villa chosen to host that sumptuous occasion hinted heavily at the glittering guest list. Politicians, actors, rock stars, judges, even respected men of the cloth, the church's finest, mixed openly with a fearful cast of characters who served the Giulianos in any number of ways. From the loyal foot-soldiers patrolling the surrounding ground, armed with machine pistols and Alsation dogs at their heel, to the lawyers, who robbed more with one briefcase than mere *guappo's* could ever dream of aspiring to with their guns and knives. The beautiful people came out to play. Vintage champagne served in crystal glasses, the finest caviar from the Baltic Sea. *Pesce Spada* (swordfish), *Arogasta* (lobster), all freshly caught. Endless lines of cocaine on a silver platter. It was a display of wealth and arrogance that dared the authorities to come and take them on. Lavish, extravagant, shocking, outrageous. Even in this mad, live for today city, nobody ever threw a party like the Giulianos.

With regal pomp and gangster's swagger, Diego Maradona made a dramatic entrance. Feeling every eye in the building upon him, the king of Naples breezed through the front door, lapping up the adulation. This was his kind of world: Don Carmine Giuliano stepped forward out of the crowd to welcome his guest of honour into the fold. He kissed Maradona on both cheeks before embracing the smiling Argentinian to great applause. Carmine raised his glass calling for a toast. He ushered a photographer to capture the moment for posterity, wrapping an arm around Maradona as he did so. A flash went off and the cameraman quickly checked the snap was good before disappearing through a waiting exit into the Naples night. They had him.

As the evening wore on the dance floor filled with a dazzling concoction of drug and alcohol-fuelled, Versace-clad revellers dripping with jewellery. The dazzling neon rays illuminated diamond-studded shirts, sparkling gold bracelets and chains of the partygoers, as they appeared determined to dance through the night, until the sun rose once more over Vesuvius the next morning. Away from the madding crowds the Giulianos attended to family business. There were those present who came seeking justice. A daughter's dishonour cleansed on the end of a fishhook. The brothers gave equal concern to all matters, either large or small, for they considered themselves the true law in the kingdom of Forcella.

Diego Maradona partied long and hard as any. His glass constantly refilled before he ever had the chance to finish it, the white powder forever nearby if the desire arose. There was never a need to seek female companionship, for they sought him in droves. Like a preening alley cat that had the cream, Maradona took his pick. Throughout the night endless photographs were taken of the footballer with the brothers and other dubious family acquaintances. At the time it appeared all harmless fun, high spirits, but when the bad times came and Diego Armando refused to perform when his strings were tugged they would return to haunt him. Though early in his time in Naples, what happened that night set in motion momentous events from which, ultimately, there could be no turning back. As morning came and revellers staggered to their cars, home to bed, bright specks of sunlight appeared to cast large shadows over the steep slopes of the volcano. An Irreversible Sunrise had broken for Maradona. He was well and truly hooked.

CHAPTER 7

CROWN OF THORNS

In times gone by, on a path laden knee deep with flowers, the triumphant Roman General took the tumultuous acclaim of thousands who lined the roads of ancient Rome, to honour and welcome him home. Senate law forbade the parade of an army through the city gates, so the General, all-splendid in a uniform of purple toga lined with gold and silver braid and etched with scenes of the victorious battle, entered in a single chariot with just a lone slave known as a lictore for company. The lictore had one purpose only: in order to prevent his master from thinking he was in any way Godlike, he would whisper constantly into his ear the words, 'Remember thou art only a mortal.' Holding high an ivory scepter that lay sculptured into an eagle's head the General acknowledged the baying crowds who paid homage to the conquering hero. 'Remember thou art only a mortal,' uttered the slave time and again. The General looked proudly on, the words hardly registering. 'Remember thou art only a mortal, remember thou art only a mortal, remember, remember...'

When the Pope met Diego. They watered down the Communion wine, told the Vatican nuns to stay in their rooms and placed a NO ENTRY sign on the Confessional box, for there were simply not enough hours in the day! As San Gennaro prayed from high for his boy not to embarrass him, Diego Maradona set off to Rome to meet the Pope. Maradona had received a Papal invitation for a private audience with his Holiness, Pope John Paul II, who himself was renowned as a goalkeeper of some standing and repute in his younger days in pre-World War Two Poland. Maradona journeyed to the Eternal city with his mother and girlfriend, all excited at this opportunity to meet face to face with the Holy Father. They arrived at the Vatican to face a blazing charge of cameramen, journalists and photographers who were all eager to capture for posterity the moment the leader of the Southern barbarians entered onto the blessed grounds of St Peter's Square.

All of Naples watched live on television as their favourite son was ushered through the paparazzi hysteria for a private meeting with the man given the arduous task of following in the shoes of the Fisherman. Dressed in a jet-black leather jacket with smart white shirt and black tie, Maradona caused Neapolitan hearts to burst with pride as he ventured beyond the Swiss Guard and into the sacred inner sanctums of the Vatican. Naples regarded him as one of their own. This was as much an honour for them as for him. On meeting his Holiness Maradona smiled politely, but appeared visibly nervous throughout, his laughing eyes trying desperately to conceal secrets that would have made even the Borgias, those infamous past residents of the Vatican, blush with red-faced embarrassment.

Pope John Paul towered above Maradona as they engaged in polite conversation. The Pope's amiable patter, friendly manner and disarming smile took pity on the clearly ill-at-ease footballer who appeared to expect at any time someone to jump from behind a curtain and denounce him as a fraud. Diego's mother watched with quiet pride and no little awe. How could she possibly have known that when she held her firstborn son in her arms all those years ago that he would grow up to be such a man. Dona Dalma Salvadora Franco Maradona felt her eyes well up with tears. As for his girlfriend, Claudia, she smiled serenely as her boyfriend was lauded with plaudits for a clean living lifestyle and for being an inspiration to all young men.

Diego shook the hand of the Holy Father and accepted a set of blessed Rosary beads as a gift. He himself appeared close to tears. It was all a fine example of how effective the Maradona publicity machine operated and how the truth was hidden and tampered with to suit a particular image. The Vatican had been duped, or if they knew the truth showed no intention of revealing it. For it suited them also to have the greatest footballer in the world parading his faith every time he scored a goal by making the sign of the cross and giving thanks to the lord almighty for divine assistance. What better publicity could there have possibly been?

'*Ciao Corrado!*' In the summer of 85 with an entire city ready to wage war on his command, Diego Maradona went in search of Napoli supremo Corrado Ferlaino eager to pick a fight. A successful second half of the season in which he carried SSC Napoli almost single-handedly out of the relegation zone and into midtable safety meant he felt confident that demands for the forthcoming campaign would be heeded. After all, what was a mere President when compared to a king? Ferlaino was relaxing in his office when suddenly the door swung open and in waltzed Diego Maradona. The dumbstruck President sat open-mouthed as the Argentinian sat himself down, treated himself to one of Ferlaino's Cuban cigars, and greeted him with a cheery 'Ciao Corrado, we have got to talk!'

Maradona began: he made it clear that unless Ferlaino made a heavy investment in team rebuilding, he was off! He put the fear of God into his supremo by wickedly suggesting he would seriously consider offers from elsewhere. Milan and Turin being just two of the places thrown into the one-way conversation that caused the President to shift uneasy in his seat and wonder why the hell he had ever brought the troublesome Argentinian to Naples. A perturbed Ferlaino listened with growing fury as he found himself being lectured on how he should get rid of the players whom the fans booed and replace them with better. Flabbergasted by Maradona's crazed assertion that it was he and not himself who ruled the roost over the city's football club, Ferlaino felt his blood pressure steadily rising as Naples' favourite son lectured him on how to do his job. His piece said, Diego Armando swaggered off, leaving behind a shaking, ashen-faced Corrado Ferlaino, speechless and seething with rage. Ferlaino watched from his window as Maradona's sleek black Ferrari sped away into the city. Although regarded by his fellow Neapolitans as heaven sent, the President remained convinced this cocky Argentinian upstart had horns.

He was of the old school, that players were seen and never heard. Mere servants of the club, not this fellow. Maradona had rewritten the rule book. President Ferlaino had bought himself a heapload of trouble and there was little he could do about it. Corrado bit his tongue for he knew that given enough rope Maradona would almost inevitably hang himself. Only then, when the love affair was over, would revenge be had. As the lynch mob gathered at the gallows and the noose was tightened around the player's neck, the President would have no qualms about kicking away the chair.

Rino Marchesi was proved correct in assuming his stay in Naples would not be long-term. His contract in the Neapolitan hotseat was not renewed and replacing him was the coach of Como, hard-nosed disciplinarian Ottavio Bianchi. Marchesi joined the long list of coaches who had tried and failed to bring success to the Neapolitan hordes. A good man, he would later surface two years on as manager of arch enemies Juventus as the two clubs fought to the death in their struggle for the championship. In came the stern Germanic features of forty-four-year-old Brescia-born Bianchi, who as a former Napoli player understood the pressures that went with such a role. His time in the pale blue of Napoli coincided with one of the Neapolitans' rare flirtations with success in the 1960s, when twice they challenged for the title. He saw at first hand the expectations and hopes of a city that lived and breathed *calcio*. The slightest hint of glory and the people of Naples would be awoken with a passion fierce enough to rouse Vesuvius. Ottavio Bianchi had little doubt that if he succeeded then the city would ignite.

Bianchi carried with him from the Northern lakes of Como the well-deserved nickname of the 'Iron Sergeant'. A deep-thinking man, he had devised a masterplan to win SSC Napoli *Lo Scudetto* and earn for himself an everlasting place in the hearts of all Neapolitans. Marchesi's game plan failed because it relied almost completely on the genius of Maradona, but not Bianchi's. He realised substantially more than just the dancing feet of *Pibe De Oro*, was required if the dream was to be made real. For though no one doubted Maradona's role as the undisputed shining light of Napoli, even the brightest of stars needed a supporting cast of proven quality to perform to their true measure. Given time Bianchi would make this so. Four months previous in March, at a secret location in the enemy territory of a plush Milan hotel, Corrado Ferlaino met secretly with Bianchi to secure his services.

In a cloak and dagger operation designed to keep the Italian press at arm's length, Ferlaino thrashed out a deal with Ottavio Bianchi to prise him away from his beautiful villa on the banks of Lake Como and plunge him into the mad, passionate hotbed of Naples. Bianchi did not come cheap, amongst his vast wage demands was a guarantee that he be allowed a free hand in the transfer market. He handed Ferlaino a list of players he required for the forthcoming season. After taking a deep breath the President assured Bianchi he would do all in his power to acquire them, and indeed proved true to his word. Class acts such as the talented sweeper Allessandro Renica from Sampdoria and the explosive centre forward Bruno Giordano from relegated Lazio were lured to Naples. And, most surprisingly, from Serie A champions Hellas Verona, experienced goalkeeper Claudia Garella was persuaded to leave behind the sumptuous surroundings of Verona to play his football in the Southern Peninsula.

Renica had impressed the previous seasons in Sampdoria's two clashes with Napoli. As for the exciting Giordano, his was a somewhat tainted background after he found himself caught up in the betting rigging scandals that rocked Italian football in the early Eighties. Bruno Giordano was banned for two years with no appeal, whereas others such as Paolo Rossi were shown leniency, thus being allowed to partake in the 1982 World Cup finals with dramatic consequences. Claudio Garella was needed to replace Napoli's keeper and long-time servant between the posts, Luigi Castellini. Garella had played in all of Verona's matches during their title-winning season and his performances had been instrumental in their success. The rivalry between the two cities was poisonous and Ferlaino's success in tempting the formidable Garella to move south was hailed as a momentous signing and one in the eye for the hated Veronese. The President had his man. Ottavio Bianchi offered Corrado Ferlaino his hand, promising to see him soon in Naples. Little did

Ferlaino realise how much he had gained on that miserable, damp, rainy Milan afternoon in winning the services of this humourless, balding, if superbly tactically astute Northerner. For given time Bianchi would grant every Neapolitan on this planet from New York to Rio their heart's desire.

Something was badly wrong in the royal court of King Diego. It had become obvious to all in the player's entourage that his behaviour and general demeanour to those around him was of someone suffering wild delusions of self-grandeur. The public persona paraded by Maradona of a family-loving, God-fearing individual who lived only to bring joy to the people of Naples was in serious danger of being derailed by the man himself. The arrogant trait acquired by Maradona of referring to himself in the third instance and the petulant manner in which he treated those closest to him infuriated family and friends who tended to suffer the worst of his bad moods.

One who felt the wrath of this petulant king with a crown of thorns more than any was his long-time girlfriend Claudia Villafane. At first a reluctance to believe the stories and rumours about Diego stemmed from the simple fact that he was the love of her young life, but as she experienced up close Maradona's metamorphism from mere mortal to Neapolitan idol she finally admitted defeat. Exhausted and humiliated by her partner's many indiscretions, Claudia fled Naples and returned home to Argentina nursing a broken heart, their stormy ten-year relationship seemingly at an end. The mist had cleared on the looking glass and what she saw filled her with horror. A man she despised had replaced the boy she once loved. Still not satisfied and appearing hellbent on ridding himself of all those closest to him, Maradona struck again.

For Jorge Cysterzspiler, Lady Luck would again conspire against him. The 1986 World Cup Finals were to be held in Mexico and the head of Maradona Productions had flown to its capital to open negotiations with a host of media and advertising companies, all busy falling over themselves to sign up the greatest player in the world to promote their various products. All were prepared to pay handsomely to have Maradona's name and face emblazoned alongside their logos and on billboards. Cysterzspiler was swamped with agents desperate to gain his client's service. Free from the restraints of Naples and its all-demanding Godfathers, the Argentinian felt certain his horrific run of bad luck was finally over. Jorge Cysterzspiler was on to a winner. Diego was gold dust not only on the pitch, but commercially off it he was equally so. Maradona Productions had hit the jackpot. Then came the earthquake.

On Thursday 19th September 1985 at a little after 7.15am a devastating earthquake hit Mexico City. The loss of life was overwhelming as thousands perished under the rubble and carnage of fallen buildings. Cysterzspiler was

70

in his hotel bed when all around shook. The irony was not lost on him as he thought it typical of his luck that he should spend every waking hour under the murky eye of the brooding hulk of the most menacing volcano on the planet, only to find himself in the midst of a frightening natural disaster the minute he leaves its shadow! As chaos reigned in the city and rescue squads fought desperately to free those trapped under the huge mass of debris, all communication to Mexico City was down. Finally after a long delay the phone lines were patched up and Cysterzspiler received a call from Naples that changed his life forever. The words hit him like a bolt of lightning careering wildly into a falling tree. To his infernal horror Maradona had sacked him.

To court Diego Maradona's attention, a Chinese whisper propped up with equal measures of half-truths and exaggerations was used to bring down Jorge Cysterzspiler from his esteemed position at Maradona's side. Acting on the back of mischievous, secondhand Neapolitan rumours that came laced with jealousy, he turned on one of his most trusted and oldest friends. Without trial or jury Cysterzspiler was given the axe and cast adrift. The so-called crime, an alleged business transaction in which he was accused of personally profiting from, so ripping off his boss in the process. True or false, it was irrelevant, the verdict upon him had been passed.

On returning to Naples a seething Cysterzspiler immediately sought out Maradona to demand an explanation. In a furious encounter the player refused to listen to his manager's pleas of innocence. Acting the part of betrayed friend, the King of Naples produced a bravura performance of bitterness, anger and tears that matched anything he ever produced on a football pitch. For in Maradona's eyes Jorge Cysterzspiler had committed the ultimate sin, he had betrayed his trust. There could be only one punishment, he was out. It was time for new blood.

As the thorns in his crown cut the skin Diego Maradona needed more than anything a calming influence in his life, a steady hand. Unfortunately, breezing into Naples International Airport with a wink and a smile for the impressed air hostesses was the larger than life thirty-eight-year-old fellow charismatic Argentinian Guillermo Coppola. Coppola's appetite for making money was matched only by an insatiable lust for good wine and bad women. In no time he made a huge impression on Maradona, who came to regard him as a world-wise older brother. He was a man of wonderfully dry sardonic humour and endless charm, equally at ease in any company, either kings or peasants. Coppola liked to think that he cut a *bella figura*, a beautiful figure. His appearance was that of a handsome old-time Latino gigolo making his living in the seedy tango dance halls of 1950s Buenos Aires.

An awe-inspiring reputation for making money from dust was first established in Argentina where he negotiated for a host of the country's top players, driving a hard bargain and ultimately succeeding. Offers of employment poured in not just from the football world but also from major banking financial institutions that recognised such precious talents. But despite approaches asking him to name his price, Coppola was not tempted. For his 'work hard, play harder' attitude to life made the offer to go and manage Maradona in Naples utterly irresistible. It was a God-given opportunity to indulge his three favourite pastimes in a place that was heaven on earth for such as he.

But before pleasure came business and Coppola wasted little time ingratiating himself with his new paymaster as he strove to make Maradona further fortunes. The wily Coppola negotiated a lucrative deal with a local television company for the player's own weekly show. But more importantly he began to test the water with Napoli for a further extension to Maradona's present contract to be worth a king's ransom. Maradona Productions was shut down and in its place, rising phoenix-like from the ashes, rose DIARMA with Guillermo Coppola at the helm. Diego Maradona may have solved his money problems but, unknowingly in Coppola, he had bought himself a heapload of trouble.

As for a grieving Cysterzspiler, he packed his bags and returned home to Argentina. That he would later be proved innocent of any misdemeanour mattered little. Maradona had already begun to commit the grievous error of bowing to his own image. Unlike the conquering Roman Generals of old, Diego Armando Maradona did not have the luxury of a slave to remind him of his mere mortality. Instead he surrounded himself with freeloaders and sycophants who only ever told him what he, Maradona, wished to hear, the roars of the adoring Napoli *tifosi* ringing incessantly in his ears: chanting 'Diego, Diego, Diego!' The Argentinian risked losing sight of who he was and where he came from. The crown of thorns had already begun to prick. 'Remember thou art only a mortal.'

CHAPTER 8

A LOATHING SUPREME

Maradona hit it and the San Paolo exploded! At 5.27, on Sunday 3rd November 1985, Diego Armando Maradona finally cast off a twelve-year-old curse over his adopted city of Naples. As the ball crashed into the net the roar from across the terraces told its own story, for the games between SSC Napoli and Juventus were never just simple football matches, they came laced with bitter memories of battles past and supposed injustices. Struck with vengeance and a devil's swerve, El Pibe De Oro's shot set Naples alight. 'La Vecchia Signora' were down. For the first time in twelve seasons Juventus faced defeat on Neapolitan soil. There was eighteen minutes left to play.

On 1st November 1897 all Neapolitans awoke to find their worse nightmare become real. Two students from the Massimo D'Azeglio Grammar School for young men in Turin, brothers Eugenio and Enrico Canfari, had decided to start a football team. Being grand gentlemen they desired a name worthy of their good selves. They chose *Juventus*, the Latin word for youthful energy, strength and vigour. From small acorns, so began a hundred years and still counting of *La Vecchia Signora*, the dear Old Lady of Italian football. Six years passed and in 1903 on a business trip to Nottingham, England, a Juve committee member was so taken by the colours of Notts County that he bought up an entire kit of black/white striped shirts and took them home to Turin. Two years later, wearing their newly-adopted strip the first national title was won. It would be the first of many. On 24th July 1923 the modern birth of Juventus took place when the ludicrously wealthy Agnelli family took majority control of the club and began what would be an enduring tale of success, controversy and intrigue. With the financial muscle of the lucrative family business, Fiat, put to good use, Juve soared in both power and size. They came to be viewed as the team of the establishment, with supporters not just in Turin but across all Italy. A national institution. Helped by referees, always appearing to get the breaks. Hated, adored but never ignored. But nowhere were they more despised than Naples.

The first clash between the two took place in Naples on 21st November 1926. Juventus won 3-0 and four months later, when the return game was played in Turin, it proved lambs to the slaughter as the home side smashed eight goals past the beleaguered Neapolitans. So it began. Mischievous rumour-mongers told tall tales of the Agnelli clan using their almighty influences in higher circles to court favours for their club. In Naples this was regarded as fact and in a city that lay forever stricken by poverty and crime, an unhealthy concoction of bitterness and jealousy developed throughout the years towards the affluence of the North, and in particular the flourishing Turin. The animosity tended to show itself most vividly whenever the two cities met on a football pitch, and with the Neapolitans' frustration maddened by their team's inability to snatch the championship away from the northern powers of Turin and also Milan, these games between the haves and have nots, produced bouts of mass violence a generation before the English believed they had cornered the market in football hooliganism. The supporters of SSC Napoli and Juventus had been at each others' throats for decades.

The 1985-86 season dawned and in typical fashion Diego Maradona wasted little time falling foul of new coach Ottavio Bianchi. His reputation as a strict disciplinarian who ruled with a rod of iron and not one to suffer fools cut no ice with Maradona who refused to bow to no man. The Argentinian took great delight in telling all at the time, 'You could not beat a smile out of Bianchi with a stick!' The training ground at Soccavo proved a battlefield as Naples' finest took an instant dislike to his new boss and all at the football club watched and waited to see how the man who had acquired the nickname of the 'Iron Sergeant' would deal with this prickly stone in his shoe. From the off Bianchi was determined to make an impression and in an early meeting with the Napoli players he laid down his rules by instigating a fierce fitness regime that bore more of a resemblance to the Foreign Legion. Bianchi understood his immediate impact had to be substantial and decided from the off to go for broke and tackle his most troubled but prized asset with all guns blazing. Ottavio Bianchi's first clash with Diego Armando Maradona became instantly the stuff of Napoli legend.

A sullen Maradona was pulled aside by his new boss and ordered to partake in a special exercise. It involved the Argentinian sitting on the floor and having to sweep away with either foot a ball thrown at him by Bianchi. Maradona was having none of it, he argued it was the opposition's job to try and bring him to earth, no one else's. The Argentinian refused point blank to go along. Ottavio Bianchi warned the player that if he did not do so they would have problems all year. Maradona simply laughed in his face, remarking, 'Right, and you will have to go!' Hardly wishing to commit career suicide Bianchi shrewdly backed down. After conversing with his President on how to deal with the troublesome Argentinian, Bianchi realised that Ferlaino himself was nervous on taking on a player who in Naples yielded an all-ensuing power that extended beyond a mere football pitch. He decided to let the matter ride, for the moment.

But it could have been different. In that same summer Bianchi tried desperately to prise away from Juventus legendary midfielder Marco Tardelli, and the explosive Polish forward Zbigniew Boniek. If successful he may well have held a good enough hand to triumph in his battle of wills with Diego Armando, but they simply scoffed at their southern cousin's motley attempts to buy two of Turin's ageing but still superbly talented stalwarts. They had shown in the past a willingness to do business with Napoli but only when it suited their needs. Tardelli and Boniek would be sold, but not to the Neapolitans. It would never be allowed to happen, *La Vecchia Signora* laughed their heads off at the sheer cheek of Naples. Had they forgotten their place in the greater scheme of things? Surely history had taught them they could be seen, maybe heard, but never treated serious.

The arrogance and self-styled aristocratic stance of Juventus meant they would rather give both players away than sell them south. The deep contempt in which the southern capital was held in Turin could only be measured in the depths of hate that engulfed encounters between the two cities. Juve had won the title an extraordinary sixteen times, to Napoli's none. The signing of Maradona disturbed but hardly caused shockwaves in Turin. For the Juve *tifosi* remained convinced they still held the ace card in French midfield maestro Michel Platini. The Gallic genius held few equals on the playing fields of Serie A, and a majestic showing in the 1984 European Championship when Platini as Captain led France to victory on home soil, made it hard to disagree that he was indeed the world's best. Except that is in Naples, for they would rather argue the world was flat!

SSC Napoli was still deemed by all teams north of Rome as the sad inadequate joker in the pack. How many times had they promised only to ultimately disappoint? Juventus, over their dead bodies, would never find it in their hearts to help them out of their trough, for they enjoyed nothing more them watching them kick, splash, splutter and ultimately drown. As for Diego Maradona's spat with Ottavio Bianchi, a serious rift was quickly averted. There was enough spitefulness directed towards Napoli's direction from elsewhere, they could ill afford friction within. A show of unity was called for. Both characters knew that if the dream of *Lo Scudetto* was ever to be realised, all Neapolitan ships had to sail in the same direction. Finally a deal was grudgingly struck between the two. Neither would rock the boat. On 8th September 1985, to the delight and relief of all Napoli *tifosi* the time came once more to get the ball out.

The Neapolitan crusade to capture and bring south that elusive championship resumed and as ever the footballing Gods showed a wicked sense of humour by handing Ottavio Bianchi an opening match against his former club, the team from the northern Lakes, Como. In a hard fought contest Napoli sneaked home 2-1. Goals from new boy Bruno Giordano and Naples' other Argentinian Daniel Bertoni gave Bianchi's men the points. This kickstarted a seven-match unbeaten run that saw the Neapolitans enjoy one of their best ever beginnings to a Serie A campaign. Amongst these was a truly ruthless 5-0 dismantling of reigning champions, the much-despised Hellas Verona at the San Paolo. It was a consummate performance by SSC Napoli and for one player in particular, Diego Maradona, it repaid Verona with interest for the humiliating drubbing suffered in the opening game of the season past. '*Lavatevi*' was washed away in a shower of goals.

With Maradona hurtling into top gear after what had been by his immeasurably high standards a stuttering start, and a superb showing by the increasingly impressive Giordano up front, Neapolitans watched in awe as their team produced a display of attacking prowess not witnessed in Naples for many a year. Maradona had failed to shine during Napoli's early good run. His troublesome left ankle, a torturous memento of the Argentinian's lamentable time in Barcelona caused him terrible agony. Only the frightful temporary cure of a dreaded cortisone injection enabled Maradona to play on although, even then, this only dulled the pain and come the aftermath of the contest, away from the roars and adulation of the terraces, he suffered intolerably.

Still Maradona contributed to the Neapolitan cause with a crucial penalty at home to Roma that earned his club a point. But it was during the match against Hellas Verona that the king of Naples truly made them pay for crimes past! Verona had endured a painful beginning to their reign. Osvaldo Bagnoli's much-lauded team had failed to recapture the form that saw them sweep aside the old order and capture the title. Also others had begun to look upon them in a new light as champions, and theirs became a much sought after scalp. The Veronese won only two of their first seven games, struggling in ninth position. The momentous events in Naples on 7th October 1985 saw them hit rock bottom as the Neapolitans cut loose in bloodthirsty, rampaging manner.

A first-half strike from Bruno Giordano was scant reward for the home team's total dominance. It was only in the second with Diego Maradona wreaking mayhem that the goals began to flow. Playing just behind Giordano and Daniel Bertoni, Maradona proved impossible to handle for the Verona defenders as he came at them from deep. Ottavio Bianchi watched on from the dug-out with his usual hangdog expression. If he was happy with proceedings Bianchi refused to show it. But as Napoli's number ten constantly tore the

Northerners to ribbons time and again with his devastating attacking spurts, a slight smile appeared to cross even the Iron Sergeant's lips.

Three minutes after half-time the superb Salvatore Bagni broke from midfield to add a second and open the floodgates. On the hour Maradona proceeded to bring the house down when from thirty-five yards he crashed home a ferocious half-volley that dipped with great venom past the Verona keeper Giuliani. On seeing the ball hit the net the San Paolo became a madhouse! Maradona set off in celebration to be swamped by jubilant teammates. The bloodfest was in full flow with another goal making it 3-0. Ten minutes remained and, with their yellow shirts stained with humiliation and wanting just to get the hell out of Naples, further agony was heaped upon the Verona players with two late goals from Daniel Bertoni and Eraldo Pecci. SSC Napoli was a team on a mission. Revenge had proved a dish served sweet and best, Neapolitan style! This 5-0 massacre of the champions moved Bianchi's men to within four points of leaders Juventus. The race was on. The times they were definitely changing: but not just yet in Turin. For some things it appeared, were carved from stone.

As if fired by jet fuel, Juve had raced out of the traps, threatening to disappear over the horizon with a frightening opening sequence of seven straight wins. Their team was an impressive concoction of the finest that world and Italian football had to offer. *La Vecchia Signora* never did anything by half. Only the best was ever considered good enough by the Agnellis to represent them, and they came no better than Giovanni Trapattoni. The forty-five-year-old Trapattoni enjoyed a fine playing career as a talented ball playing left sided midfielder for AC Milan and Italy. He was hailed as being the only player capable of man-marking the great Brazilian Pelé by honest means. A famous 3-0 win for the *Azzurri* against the mighty Brazilians at the San Siro, when he had the dazzling South American under lock and key for the entire ninety minutes, earned Trapattoni huge praise both in Italy and in Brazil, where his tough if fair handling of their hero saw him lauded with plaudits. However, anything achieved on the field would be dwarfed by his future staggering exploits in management.

Il Trap, as he became known, had been in Turin since 1977 and during that period enjoyed unparalleled success. The Sardinian-born Trapattoni moulded his teams with the typical Italian philosophy of *Catenaccio* defence laced with swift counter-attacking football. In his eight-year reign Juventus had won four national titles, a European Cup Winners' Cup, UEFA Cup, and a runners-up place in the European Cup final. Indeed, the bulk of Italy's 1982 triumphant World Cup-winning side came from Trapattoni's side, with the majority featuring in the 3-1 final victory over West Germany at the Santiago Bernabeu in Madrid. Dino Zoff, Marco Tardelli, Antonio Cabrini, Claudio Gentile, Gaetano Scirea, Paolo Rossi. The names read like a who's who of Italian football.

Come 1985 and Juventus remained a formidable force. The veteran goalkeeping legend Zoff had finally lost his battle with Father Time and retired, but the backbone of the team remained in place. In attack they had been reinforced immeasurably by the fantastic pace and skill of Danish winger Michael Laudrup. In midfield Michel Platini remained to add that beguiling touch, which only those truly blessed possessed. As an artist paints pictures on his canvas board with the swish of a brush, so Platini played his football. With the wily, all-domineering defender Gaetano Scirea sweeping and organising at the rear, Juve appeared unbeatable. In Turin there was already early talk of going through the entire season unbeaten. But they had not counted on Maradona. The Old Lady was due in Naples for a much-anticipated showdown.

Sunday 3rd November 1985. Unlike the Roman Emperor Nero, who back in 64AD had swaggered into Naples to the blaze of trumpets and accompanied by an extravagant parade of exotic dancers and acrobats, the footballers of Juventus entered the city in a considerably less eye-catching manner. Hardly wishing to antagonise a local population who would have had no qualms whatsoever in ripping their Northern, arrogant, pompous heads off, the Juve team coach arrived early at the San Paolo stadium to avoid their customary reception of howling Napoli *tifosi* baying for Turin blood.

Juventus travelled deep into what they considered bandit country to defend a proud twelve-year unbeaten record against a side they refused to even contemplate as serious rivals. To do so would in their eyes hand the Neapolitans undue recognition, for they saw them as nothing more than thieves, scum and vagabonds. Their banners told of 'Mafioso', the songs of 'Cholera' and 'You're the scum of all Italia'. It was all deadly, spiteful, racist and cruel. The brave, foolhardy, and sheer lunatic fringe of the Juve *tifosi* who risked life and limb to travel south and support their team in Naples did so with an escort that would have done justice to a visiting American President. A *Carabinieri* helicopter flew above their coaches, possibly wary of a Neapolitan air assault! The authorities would have put nothing past the Napoli hardcore hooligans in their eagerness to get at their most bitter enemy, for theirs was a loathing supreme.

Nothing was ever too much trouble for the Neapolitans in their eagerness to make their enemy from the North feel unwelcome, even to the point of the ballboys, all young apprentices of Napoli, receiving instructions (out of earshot) to make life difficult as possible for the Juventus players. If the home side was winning they were told to take their time returning the ball back onto the pitch. Juventus were not just playing against eleven players for SSC Napoli that day, an entire city was plotting to take the *Bianconeri* down. Unlike all others who felt a bond with his football club in Naples that day, Giovanni Trapattoni wished to return to Turin with more than just his neck intact he desperately desired the points. For twelve seasons *La Juve* had gone to Naples to leave unbeaten and unbowed, if at times a little battle scarred. They had received a hammer blow to their fierce pride in losing the championship title to Hellas Verona the year before and Trapattoni was determined to win it back and return the *Scudetto* to its rightful home in Turin. A win over the Neapolitans would go a long way in achieving that goal. *Il Trap* was confident his iron-tight defence would prove unyielding against potentially the most lethal attacking force in all of Italy.

A victory for Juventus would leave Napoli trailing in their wake by eight points. Not to mention the dramatic effect on morale in suffering another defeat against their most hated foe. The week previous the Neapolitans unbeaten record had crashed in Turin against Torino when a wonderfully struck free-kick from Maradona came too late to save them going down 2-1. A second loss against that city's other side would have been calamitous. As kick off grew near a draw was being widely touted inside the San Paolo by those who considered the fact that both sides simply could not afford to lose, a game of cat and mouse was predicted. Could the much-vaunted Juventus rearguard contain the on-fire Maradona? Would Platini produce a piece of magic and steal the points? Was Giordano truly good enough to outwit the canny Scirea? All of Italy waited to watch live on television as the two tribes of Naples and Turin prepared once more to lock horns. A sense of history, raging hatred and a treacherous rain-lashed surface. Naples on the edge. Throw in Maradona, Platini and you had a cast worth dying for. It proved a contest worthy of such an occasion.

Twelve years of pent-up frustration came pouring out in a first half that saw Napoli launch a blistering all-out assault on the Juve defence. Inspired by thousands of screaming, crazed Neapolitans, Diego Maradona led the charge, but unlike most in this passionate red-hot city this particular 'Old Lady' kept her virtue intact against the incessant advances of *Pibe De Oro*. On a soaked surface covered in pools of water, Maradona was still able to lift his followers to heady heights of dizziness as he electrified the stadium with every touch. But the *Bianconeri* held firm. Gaetano Scirea was magnificent deploying his defensive forces with the tactical genius of a five star General, and as the contest entered its final quarter a draw appeared the likely outcome. Then it happened. The tricky footwork of Daniel Bertoni saw him burst into the Juve area only to be brought crashing. As the crowd howled for a penalty the referee instead awarded an indirect free-kick for obstruction twelve yards out from goal. The indignation and disgust that poured down from all corners of the stadium eased when Diego Maradona stepped forward to take control. A city held its breath as midfielder Pecci tapped the ball sideways for Maradona to curl a stunning shot past the keeper Stefano Tacconi into the net. Hit with vengeance and a devil's swerve! From an angle that appeared impossible this adopted Son of Naples, a street-wise rascal had hoodwinked the great and the good of Turin.

Mayhem reigned in Naples! Off soared Diego to accept the acclaim of his adoring *tifosi* as the San Paolo bathed in a glorious lather of joy and excitement. No one ever played a crowd like Diego Armando as he appeared close to tears with the emotion of the moment. His was the ultimate performance in time of ecstasy. Through a cloak of darkness a small chink of light shone. On the other side lay redemption, the lifting of the curse. Twelve years! His battleplan in tatters, Trapattoni screamed instructions from the touchline to his players, urging them forward. Now it was the Neapolitans' turn to hold what they had.

Juventus swept forward in desperation, Michel Platini and Michael Laudrup suddenly coming alive on being released from shackling defensive duties to play their normal game. Many in the stadium could hardly bare to watch as the visitors staged a last gasp fightback to save the day. Tempers inevitably flared and Brio of Juve along with Napoli's Bagni were both dismissed for fighting. The seconds ticked down and with the crowd whistling, baying and pleading for the referee to end their torment, he finally called time. *La Vecchia Signora* had been taken. Carnival time descended upon Naples. The Juve players made a hasty retreat from the celebrations that were erupting in a mad frenzy around them, sick to the stomach with the thought at losing to the Southerners.

The dark clouds that enveloped the Gulf of Naples since first light finally cleared, and a dot of blue sky broke through. An eye to the heavens. Even San Gennaro wished to view his city in its moment of joy. Car horns blazed triumphantly across the bay. The Napoli *tifosi* took to the road to show their delight at beating Juventus. Trucks filled with flag-waving supporters set off across the Peninsula to share their triumph with those who could not be present. In Naples hundreds of Vespas sped along the seafront past the historic ancient fortress of Castel dell'Ovo, roaring out Maradona's name. Down every alleyway and crumbling tenement of the Forcella and the Spanish Quarter, Neapolitans indulged in that rare event for their club, a victory celebration over Juventus. The spell had been broken.

One totally underwhelmed by events unfolding around him was Ottavio Bianchi, who remained as ever stone-faced. Bianchi was shrewd enough to realise the setback which befell Juve on the day, and the jeering of gloating Neapolitans that accompanied Trapattoni's men as they made an inglorious exit from the San Paolo would ultimately serve only in spurring them on to win back the Serie A title. Naples may well have won a famous battle but the war was far from over. *La Vecchia Signora* would bite back with a vengeance. As for Diego

Armando, he was off into the night. The sultry, arousing air of downtown Naples, where devils and fallen angels offered great temptations, proved irresistible to Maradona. His every whim, desire and fantasy could be realised. A city sat for eternity on death row, its fate, forever hanging on the moods of a bad-tempered Mount Vesuvius, had long since lost any inhibitions. Live for today, for tomorrow is a distant dream. They were dancing in the streets and alleys of the Forcella, for Diego Maradona had lain to rest the curse of Turin. Anything was now deemed possible.

THE TANGO OF MARADONA:
Napoli tifosi OLE!

*You dance tango between Maradona's legs,
then you get drunk and the people call you stupid.
But please stay at home with your crooked legs,
because after the tango there is also the Tarantella.
If you are tired and you want to try some more,
call the police to stop him, but
don't care, don't call them, because he can go round them as well.
Our money is ready for the season ticket,
and all the people are ready to buy it,
we are well trained and used to sacrifices,
but please don't poison our Sundays.
Please, I recommend you don't be a failure, because this time we would be
very sad.
You are a 'Scugnizzo', like all these people who live for football and have
nothing else.
This is the song of Diego Armando Maradona!
We paid a lot of money for him, it is true,
but the people are happy.
Because where can we ever find another like him?'*

CHAPTER 9

CRISTINA

Amore. In his short time in the bay of Naples Maradona had surged through the willing female population of this city with the same ease that he scythed past the tightest Serie A defence. The crazed notion that he had become romantically attached to a local 20-year-old Neapolitan girl called Cristina Sinagra was genuinely thought absurd to those amongst his entourage who had witnessed at first hand his night-time antics. For ever since his long-time girlfriend Claudia had fled Naples in tears to return to Argentina, Maradona had not so much played the field as sowed his wild oats with all the gusto of a young stallion on heat: he was simply insatiable! And how they flocked. Diego's goal against Juventus had elevated him above seventh heaven. He had turned water to wine. There were those in the city who thought him a God. Others who saw him off-stage knew better. Beware of false idols.

A week on and still drunk on euphoria after their historic victory over Juventus, the massed legions of Napoli *tifosi* descended on Milan for what was yet another do-or-die clash with an age-old adversary, the aristocrats of Internazionale. Inter was a formidable side that bristled with world stars. The wonderful poise and technique of West German centre forward Karl-Heinz Rummenigge, the fleet-footed *Azzurri* striker Allesandro Altobelli and sublime Irish midfield maestro Liam Brady were the pick of an attacking crop. *La Grande Inter!* The followers of the *Neazzurri* (blue and black stripes) held those from Naples in lower regard than the dirt on their designer shoes. The twice-yearly sojourn by the Southerners to Milan was greeted with the same amount of warmth and enthusiasm that would have been shown a plague of rats. The Milanese looked upon Neapolitans as barbarians, lacking in true Italian virtue and character. That Naples was closer to the shores of Africa than to their own city handed the Inter *tifosi* ample ammunition to launch a hail of verbal slings and arrows at the Southern invaders. Their banners aimed low; 'Clean the steps before leaving!', another saying 'Soap and water, wash yourselves!' The Neapolitans replied in typically whimsical fashion, 'Milan, Turin, is this Italy? It is better being Africans!'

CRISTINA

The appearance of the two teams to do battle was barely visible as coloured smoke bombs enveloped the San Siro stadium. This, with a freezing Milan fog which had settled itself on the pitch, meant the early stages of the contest could hardly be witnessed by any on the terraces. But nothing much was missed as both began with caution. After a drab opening period the stalemate was broken four minutes into the second half when a long, hopeful cross into the Inter penalty area by Bruno Giordano was met by Diego Maradona, who out-foxed two defenders, chested the ball down and with unerring accuracy slashed a left-foot drive past goalkeeper Walter Zenga into the bottom left-hand corner. Maradona ran with arms outstretched to the thousands of Napoli followers who had prayed during the arduous trip north to witness such a moment. A Neapolitan God in football boots slaying his city's many enemies.

Emotions overflowed both on the field and off when a bottle thrown from the terraces laid low Napoli's goalkeeper Garella. As tempers frayed the red mist came down and a horrendous tackle by Milanese defender Mandolini broke the leg of Neapolitan midfielder Ruben Buriani. Such was the severity of the foul Buriani never again played top class football. As the battle raged matters worsened when Giuseppe Bruscolotti and Allesandro Altobelli squared up to each other and came to blows. A besieged referee was left with no option but to send both off. Finally the sides reverted to playing football and fifteen minutes from time, with Inter fighting desperately for an equaliser to save face, pressure told when the magical left foot of Liam Brady grabbed a point from the penalty spot. The game finished 1-1 with honours shared. With each starting the day four points behind Juventus there really was only one winner, for in Turin the *Bianconeri* had resumed business as normal with a 3-1 victory over Roma. Inter and SSC Napoli had simply cut each other's throats.

The following week at the San Paolo an early wonder strike from Diego Maradona against Udinese looked set to spark a Neapolitan massacre. *Pibe De Oro* executed a wickedly bending free-kick from the far touchline into the top corner when all others on the pitch expected him to simply cross it into a crowded penalty box. A repeat showing of the 5-0 Verona performance looked on the cards but it failed to materialise as a strange malaise settled over the home side. Maradona found himself under siege every time he received the ball as Udinese defenders lined up to kick lumps out of him. The Argentinian was scythed down with relish and disturbing regularity. It appeared a vendetta as the foul count mounted steadily throughout the first period. With a referee seemingly blind to what was occurring, Napoli's number ten finally cracked and went looking for revenge.

Five minutes into the second half Maradona saw red and exacted justice. After being scythed down one too many times from behind the Argentinian sprang up from the floor and headbutted his worst tormentor Antonio Crismanini. With Crismanini collapsing theatrically, rolling around on the turf like he had been shot, there was little option for the referee who, after such a blatant show of retaliation by Maradona, was forced to order the leading man off the stage in his own theatre house. As frustrations mounted in the San Paolo the inevitable duly occurred when Udinese snatched a soft late equaliser ten minutes from time. The final whistle brought only muted boos, somehow it was all so predictable. In Naples nothing is ever as it seems, in time a disturbing epitaph reared its ugly head.

In the summer of 1986 while conducting a drugs investigation, Turin police listened in on a recorded tapped phone call between Napoli's general secretary Iallo Allodi and his counterpart at Udinese, Cordi. What they heard astounded them. The conversations centred round the above match between their two clubs in Naples on Sunday 10th November 1985. They spoke of an agreement to ensure the game finished a draw and that Udinese players would be assigned to wind up Maradona and get him sent off. Allodi was already a notorious figure in Italian football and had earned a dark reputation as the ultimate fixer. His speciality was rumoured to be the gift of a gold watch for any referee willing to do business and allegedly his past paymasters at Inter Milan and Juventus offered whatever necessary to gain an advantage. When all became public Allodi obviously denied such damning allegations, only to duly resign! His parting line was, 'I have always been a clean man.' The evidence proved overwhelmingly otherwise. A sorry tale.

Seven days later Napoli travelled across the deep boot of the South to the Adriatic coast where they took on lowly Bari at the San Nicola stadium. Two goals by Bruno Giordano handed the Neapolitans a 2-1 victory helping them forget the unfortunate setback against Udinese. They followed up with a fine 2-0 victory in Naples against AC Milan. Strikes from the lethal Giordano and a second from the wonderfully combative Salvatore Bagni proved sufficient to send the *rossoneri* (red and blacks) back north with their tails planted firmly between their legs. But the news from the Stadio Comunale that a Michel Platini effort had won the points against Sampdoria to keep Juventus well clear left them feeling deflated. One small step for Naples, two giant steps for Turin. So it continued until the Christmas break when hostilities ceased momentarily for Yuletide season. The *Bianconeri* were six points ahead of Napoli and Inter. They were chasing the wind. Like one of Agnelli's finest Ferrari sports cars, *La Vecchia Signora* stood revved, purring and set to disappear over the horizon. Again.

The many who basked in Diego Maradona's shadow, feeding off the scraps, enjoying the high life, watched in awe and a little jealously at the footballer's incredible popularity with the young ladies of the south. There were times when his living quarters resembled an Arab sheik's harem as huddles of starry-eyed girls, some lusting, others ambitious would be brought before the king of Naples so he could take his pick. Those not chosen would be led tearfully away. But such was Diego Armando's rapacious appetite their time would come again. So it was with genuine, open-mouthed disbelief that his inner sanctum greeted the sight of Cupid's arrow striking him in the heart.

Maradona knew Cristina Sinagra through sister Maria, who lived below him in the ground floor flat of his apartment in Posilippo. Maria feared greatly for her kid brother as she watched him go through life as if blindfolded on a high wire, staggering and without a safety net to break his fall. She saw in Cristina someone who just might be capable of bringing him down from the tightrope and away from the madcap circus that surrounded his every move. This softly-spoken girl from the backstreets of Naples would in time earn the approval of the most powerful member of the clan Maradona. His mother. Being accepted by Tota was an accolade reserved for only a chosen few outside the blood family.

Almost immediately the two sparked and what began as a purely platonic relationship swiftly developed into something more. Diego fell in love with Cristina because she represented everything opposite to the world he lived in. Innocent, honest and pure. She made him feel safe, cleansed almost, appealing to a side of him that many close feared had gone forever, the happy-go-lucky young kid from the rundown shacks of Villa Fiorito playing football from dawn till dusk. The lad who adored his mother and lived in awe of his honest hardworking father, Diego Senior. The world Maradona came to inherit, though filled with earthly goods, was devoid of the one thing money could never buy, genuine friendship. The path to the crown of thorns came littered with crooks, con-men and two-bit hustlers who all drank from the well of *Pibe De Oro's* talent.

More pretty than strikingly beautiful Cristina's entry into the epic saga of Diego's life was a much-needed breath of fresh air. She was not after him for anything, and that to a man who had lived his young life surrounded by sycophants and hangers-on meant so much. And so the king of Naples retired from public life to spend nights in with his new girl. Theirs were simple needs, a pizza and a video. But, just when all seemed peaceful and the nightclub owners of Naples were enjoying the relative calm, a thunderbolt struck Maradona when Cristina announced she was pregnant.

Suddenly all was dark, swiftly as love came, so it vanished. Maradona felt betrayed, the stirrings of paranoia again gripped his every thought. The crown of thorns pricked once more and Diego Armando disappeared into the Neapolitan night. The word that their hero was back amongst them spread like wildfire across the city. With his strutting Versace-clad posse dressed to kill, acting up like they owned the world, never mind Naples, Maradona cruised the bay looking for action. A disc jockey would announce their entry, '*Benvenuti Diego Maradooona!*' The air would electrify, hearts would miss a beat. To the sensual, pounding rhythm of the Salsa drum Pibe De Oro would take to the dance floor to strut his stuff. Every girl in the club tried to catch his eye. With the wicked grin of a prowling alley cat stalking its prey, Maradona would simply smile at a bevy of willing Neapolitan beauties, for that was all it required. His entourage slapped high fives, the boss was back!

Cristina Sinagra's desperate pleas to Diego Maradona for him to acknowledge the pregnancy fell on deaf ears. His only response was in telling her to get rid and have an abortion. A beleaguered Cristina found herself being frozen out by people she had once considered family. Personal opinions counted for nothing as the clan closed ranks around their boy. She was forced to leave the Maradona household and return home in floods of tears and shame-faced to her parents. Cristina had every intention of having the baby, for her to consider otherwise was unthinkable. Diego Maradona's abject denial of his responsibilities as a father would return to immeasurably haunt him as around the city rumours flew of his indiscretion against one of their own.

In a place so densely populated no one was ever out of earshot, out of reach. Behind every wall, in every doorway and half-open window, nothing was missed. What began as the distant echo of a faraway wind grew to resemble a raging hurricane as Naples debated furiously the actions of their king. There was a saying, '*I figli so 'figli*'(Children are children'). Nothing was more precious to Neapolitans than their young, for the footballer to act in this uncaring manner was seen as an insult to all those who came to regard him as heaven sent, a saviour to lead Naples in its eternal struggle against the North. The treasure of San Gennaro, a gift from the Gods. But it was no winged horse that soared over Vesuvius taking Maradona to his Coronation at the church of San Paolo. It was a simple helicopter. He had stepped over a line that Lords, Princes and even Kings had reason to fear crossing. Naples possessed the capacity to spit out its heroes with the same ease it embraced them. For the first time doubts were cast about the true character of Diego Armando Maradona. The natives were restless, there was unease beneath the volcano. '*Qualche divinita?*' ('Some divinity?').

The more fanatical of the Napoli *tifosi* considered such talk as treachery, heresy even. The idle chatter of madmen. In their eyes Diego could do as he pleased, it was his city, his people. To even hint at the suggestion of their king being forced to abdicate from his crown was met with derision. For the young from the districts of the Forcella, Spanish quarter, Fuorigrotta, Sanita and San Giovanni, all breeding grounds of the Napoli hardcore following, Maradona was their life. Ravaging unemployment, drugs and heart bleeding, devastating poverty, *Lo Camorra*. A miserable weekly existence only made palatable by the mouth-watering thought of watching *Pibe De Oro* rip to shreds their northern tormentors every Sunday afternoon. These were Diego Maradona's foot soldiers, loyalty unquestionable, driven by blinded faith. Dare any who tried to take their king away from them. '*Lo potenza della speranza*'('The power of hope'). This was what Maradona gave to those who struggled to survive in one of the most dangerous cities in the world. Lose that and they had nothing.

As a madman pursues a fleeing butterfly so Ottavio Bianchi's team continued their obsessive, incessant pursuit of leaders Juventus. Naples was allowed to dream when in the opening month of the New Year Juve managed to scrape together only a measly three points. But this brief flicker of hope was extinguished when Napoli themselves hit an iceberg and slipped even further behind when a run of four games in which only two points were won proved disastrous. An embarrassing 1-0 defeat at home to Pisa followed by a 2-0 loss in the Olympic Stadium against Roma saw the gap rise to nine points. Their cause was hardly served when Bruno Giordano broke his collarbone in a road accident. Giordano's prowess in front of goal was badly missed as he was sidelined for several weeks. Vital matches that had to be won suddenly began to be drawn. But most importantly Diego Maradona's increasing jaunts back to Buenos Aires in preparation for the forthcoming 1986 World Cup Finals in Mexico left him jaded and a shadow of his true self. Napoli's once rapier cutting edge had been blunted. As Maradona's form fell away, so did the Neapolitan title hopes.

The great honour of being chosen to lead his nation into battle rested heavily on Maradona. It was a responsibility he did not take lightly. Naples was in his heart but Argentina was blood. The national coach Carlos Bilardo had gone public with the comment, 'My team is Diego Maradona and ten others.' Such talk only increased the intense pressure that was heaped onto his shoulders. Everybody wanted a piece of *Pibe De Oro*. The manner of the humiliating defeat by Brazil four years previous that ended their reign as world champions left an indelible mark on the Argentinian psyche. The

Brazilians had indulged themselves with great delight in twisting the dagger deep and the sending off of Diego Maradona for a rash over-the-top lunge only added to the pain. The sight of the twenty-one-year-old trooping off, head down in tears proved an abiding memory of a match infamous in Argentinian history. Its people ached for a shot at redemption, and no one more than Maradona.

As the challenge from the south faded Juventus pulled smoothly away from the chasing pack. The *Bianconeri* looked set to triumph once more. With the *Scudetto* gone the fight for European qualification began and on 23rd February SSC Napoli ventured way up north to champions Verona, where in a stirring encounter they fought back from 2-0 down to earn a courageous draw. Maradona appeared inspired. Stung by criticism of his recent performances he took on Verona single-handed. Looking back to his smouldering, magical best the Argentinian led a rip-roaring second half showing by the Neapolitans. It was his penalty hit with nonchalant ease that halved the deficit. And, with time ticking away, *Pibe De Oro* headed in a scrambled equalizer that sent the travelling hordes of Napoli *tifosi* into a frenzy. The *Brigate Gialloblu* stood in grim silence as they watched the wretched Southerners dance with delight on their terraces. For them it had been a horrendous season and as Maradona ran across and blew kisses to the one corner of the Bentegodi stadium bathed blue and white, it finally plunged the depths.

Torino went south and were given short shrift with a 3-1 drubbing for their troubles. Goals from Bagni and Cafferelli helped them on their way as Naples bade farewell with many a two-fingered salute. La Granata left Naples and returned to Turin the colour of their shirts. The much-anticipated grudge, return match with Juventus in Turin finished in a 1-1 draw. In a game littered with nerves and petty fouls Napoli led at half time through an own goal by Juve defender Brio, only for the home side to hit back early in the second with an equaliser from fellow stopper Favero. Trapattoni's team had looked decidedly edgy as the finishing line drew near. Then, on 16th March, as Napoli beat Internazionale at the San Paolo, in a grueling contest settled only by a single penalty from a newly bearded Maradona, the real story unfolded in the eternal city where at the Olympic stadium Juve were thrashed 3-0 by closest rivals Roma. *La Vecchia Signora* was rocking. The Old Lady was beginning to show her age.

Suddenly with just five games remaining the difference in points at the top of the table had been reduced to just two. But alas for third placed Napoli their seven points deficit left them needing a miracle of San Gennaro proportions to take the title. The chase for the championship lay between the

'Gialiorossi,'(' Red and yellow') of Rome and the *Bianconeri*. Naples, as ever, was again left to lick its wounds and dream what might have been. This was confirmed a week later when a 2-0 defeat at Udinese mathematically ended their chances. Two finely taken goals by the Italian striker Andres Carnevale finished off Napoli once and for all. Bianchi watched on, resigned to defeat but admiring the skills, pace and strength of the young curly haired Udinese centre forward as he cut a swathe through his defence. As a full house of 40,000 at the Stadio Friuli wallowed in the Southerner's misery Bianchi made a note of the name. Carnevale. There was something very Neapolitan about it!

In the end Turin got to stage a victory party but only after Roma had given them the fright of their imperial lives. Juventus would also go on to lift the European cup for the first time but tragically it would be stained with the blood of Heysel as supporters of both Juve and Liverpool dragged themselves into the gutter in horrific manner. As for Naples a place in the UEFA cup was earned in bravura style as their team wound up the season with four straight victories. The highlight was a much-deserved 2-1 victory against AC Milan in the San Siro with a winning goal scored by Maradona that bore glorious echoes of events to follow in Mexico. A pass from Giordano was snatched upon by the Argentinian on the edge of the Milan box, and in the midst of half a second Maradona dummied, sidestepped three defenders, before hitting a thunderous low drive into the net. His work for the season with Naples was done, Argentina called.

CHAPTER 10

DRUM ROLL

'El sueno del pibe' ('The boy's dream'). There exists early black and white footage of a twelve-year-old Diego Maradona being interviewed by a Buenos Aires television station. Even at such a tender age the young Diego's prodigious talent was evident to all and he had become something of a local celebrity. On a gravelly, garbage-strewn, dusty Fiorito surface with decrepit old freight trains clattering past on a nearby railway, Maradona produced an exquisite display of ball juggling for the benefit of the camera. Once done he was asked his hopes and dreams for the future. His reply was prophetic as he declared his wish 'to play in the World Cup and be a champion for my team'. The manner in which it was said sent a cold shiver down the spines of all who listened. For something sparkled in this special kid's eyes.

Argentina's glory: In 1978 Argentina was under the stomping, jackbooted heel of a murderous military dictatorship that reacted to criticism like a jackal rips the throat of a rabbit. A motley gang of senior Army officers led by General Jorge Videla had seized power to engage in an unholy reign of terror over the nation. That FIFA felt justified in awarding such a despotic regime the eleventh World Cup Finals caused outrage amongst Human Rights organisations like Amnesty International. Amnesty were at the forefront of a determined campaign to reveal the true horror of what became known as the 'Dirty War'. Not since Hitler's Nazis had there been such a sustained show of state sponsored brutality inflicted upon a civilian population. Senor Videla and his henchmen were a bunch of bloodthirsty, bullying two-bit gangsters interested only in lining their pockets. Their neatly pressed uniforms with gold braid sparkling and rows of unearned medals pinned upon fat bellies failed to hide the fact that in reality they were nothing but thugs.

But such was their frightening hold over the population no one dared speak out. A visit in the dead of night by the feared secret police, torture and a bullet in the head was the Junta's method of dealing with those who dared to question them. To illustrate the savagery that went on, a much-favoured method of execution was to tie people's hands behind their backs and throw them out of helicopters from high above into the murky depths of the River Plate. Over ten thousand innocents disappeared (murdered) during this horrifying period of modern Argentinian history. Teachers, journalists, doctors, priests, trade unionists, no one was safe. A cloak of evil descended over the land as night and day army helicopters hovered menacingly over the shantytowns, forever watching. The opportunity to host the *Mundial* was snatched upon with both hands by the regime, for the propaganda advantages to show themselves in a good light off the back of such a prestigious competition was huge. In Argentina there was nothing like football to dull the painful hardships of everyday life, if only for a month.

The man handed the unenviable task of making every Argentinean dream come true was the forty-year-old Cesar Luis Menotti. Nicknamed '*El Flaco*' ('the thin one'), the chainsmoking Menotti had the engaging appearance of an ageing hippy with his long straggling hair and a gaunt almost tortured expression. But this only hid an extraordinary sharp football brain. In South America Menotti was regarded as being the only man capable of taking the Argentinians to the Promised Land. He believed in a style of play that suited the traditional gifts of the Argentine footballer, *La Nuestra*, a short passing game performed with great finesse and subtlety of touch. For decades those who believed winning was all that mattered, at any price hijacked Argentinian football. How victory was achieved proved irrelevant, as teams packed their defences in preference to a more attractive adventurous play favoured by the purist. On coming into the job as national coach Menotti vowed to bring back *La Nuestra*, which for too long had been played only in the hearts of footballing romantics. In front of their own people at the *Mundial* of 1978, *El Flaco's* swashbuckling team attacked with style and panache as they took on the world with all guns blazing.

That his politics differed wholly from the Fascist puppets that ruled Argentina was inconsequential when it came to matters on the pitch. Even the Generals understood the importance of letting Menotti have a free hand for as long as the tournament ran its course. If matters went well and the trophy was won he could be excused for anything. Failure and any criticism of themselves or the state would be remembered. This free-thinking liberal, who detested Galtieri's toy soldier Mafia, knew the consequences of defeat for himself and his team. But would victory be achieved with an extraordinary precocious slip of a kid from the poverty-stricken, rat-infested hellhole of Villa Fiorito in his line-up?

On the evening of Sunday 22nd February 1977, a sixteen-year-old Diego Armando Maradona made his international debut for Argentina against Hungary at the La Bombonera stadium in Buenos Aires. An hour gone and with a rampant home team 5-1 up, Menotti decided the time was right to unleash *El Cebollito* on the already beleaguered Hungarians. To the incessant pounding of a thousand drums resonating across the terraces, a familiar war chant began. After just eleven matches played for Argentinos Juniors, on went Maradona to a reception more worthy of a conquering hero than some untried teenager who had yet to prove anything. 'Maradoona, Maradoona, Maradoona,' boomed out. What began as a drizzle turned into a thunderstorm.

During the short time he was on Diego Maradona electrified La Bombonera with typically incisive attacking spurts. But there was also the odd misplaced pass and the unwanted fierce clattering challenges of Hungarian defenders who had no wish to be further humiliated by this fleet-footed, cocky, bushy haired little brat. Watching on intently Cesar Menotti saw enough to realise that although Maradona undoubtedly possessed the skill and technique to perform at the highest level, he remained dubious as to whether the youngster was mentally prepared for the cut throat battlefields of World Cup competition. Also, the young maestro was still developing. If selected he would have been targeted by opponents who would have slashed and hacked him mercilessly at every opportunity. After a period of soul searching Menotti decided not to take the risk, for if picked Maradona's career could well have been finished before it ever got started. He was out.

On being informed the youngster burst into tears. Showing the immaturity that had so worried the national coach, Diego Maradona stated that Menotti had betrayed him and that he would never again play for one of his teams. In the same interview an irate Maradona also declared his intention to retire from international football. This at seventeen! Happily he changed his mind the next day and the following week smashed a hat-trick for Argentinos Juniors. Diego Armando would have his day in the sun, but in 1978 he would along with the rest of his country folk watch from afar as amidst a blur of blue and white ticker tape, fantastic football and suspicious refereeing, Cesar Menotti's exuberant Argentinian team captured the trophy for the first time to spark unparalleled celebrations.

On Saturday 2nd June 1979 Argentina played a friendly international against Scotland at Hampden Park. This famous old stadium was packed to the rafters as the Scots came to admire the famed 1978 World Cup winners of Mario Kempes, Leapoldo Luque and Daniel Passarella. But it was to be a little-known eighteen-year-old tearaway called Diego Maradona that stole the show with a beguiling display. Gasps of admiration mixed with spontaneous applause swept down from the terraces as Maradona slipped past tackles with the slightest of effort to torture the home side. Playing for Scotland that day was Ipswich Town midfielder John Wark. Even today the memory remains vivid of his close encounter with the sensational, rising Argentinian superstar.

Wark recalls fondly of, 'Bouncing off Maradona, on the rare occasions I managed to get near! I had never seen anyone like him. Diego was lightning fast, skilful and unbelievably strong. And yet so young! He was simply frightening.'

The knowledgeable Glasgow crowd took this special young player to their hearts with a passion not seen since the great Alfredo Di Stefano and Ferenc Puskas entered Scottish footballing folklore, back in the legendary 1960 European Cup final, when Real Madrid thrashed Eintracht Frankfurt 7-3. It was during a comprehensive 3-1 win for the world champions that Maradona scored his first international goal. On seventy minutes there was a typical piece of bewildering footwork when the youngster took on and beat a host of Scottish defenders with alarming ease before shooting past the keeper George Woods. Man and boy at Hampden stood to applaud such a magnificent effort. What they failed to recognise was for this remarkable teenager it really was nothing unusual.

That same summer an irresistible Diego Maradona led Argentina to victory in the World Youth Championships held in Japan. Inspired at being made Captain, a proud Maradona had the normally reserved Japanese crowds leaping out of their seats in sheer excitement with a host of spellbinding performances. Sweeping all before them the extravagantly talented Argentinians stormed to the final in Tokyo where a capacity 63,000 watched enthralled as Maradona teased, toyed and ultimately destroyed the reigning champions of the Soviet Union. A 3-1 scoreline crowned the South Americans and to the delight of the home supporters Diego Maradona produced a magnificent free-kick that brought the house down. A fitting finale. He had confirmed his position as the finest young talent on the planet. Was he human? Some had their doubts. Three years on and Cesar Menotti's faith in his boy had grown to such an extent that he was now the first name on the team sheet. Both physically and mentally Menotti considered Maradona ready for the high octane, no holds barred arena of World Cup competition. Sadly the best made plans...

Espana 82: A World Cup won in controversial circumstances at home was lost in equally dramatic fashion on Spanish soil. Only on arriving in Spain did they realise how much their own government had lied to them regarding the pointless war fought many miles away on a God-forsaken bunch of small islands in the South Atlantic. The sinking of an Argentinian battlecruiser, General Belgrano, by a Royal Navy nuclear submarine initiated a horrific chain of events that quickly escalated out of control. With a job lot of Exocet missiles bought at a Paris Arms Fair proving value for money, Argentina lashed back and when HMS Sheffield exploded in a red flash on BBC and

ITV television, a savage dose of reality suddenly hit home in the United Kingdom. This was a war: a line in the sand was drawn. The velvet glove of diplomacy came off and a ruthless campaign was fought to clear the Falklands of all unwanted visitors.

The superbly trained British forces made short work of the mostly conscript Argentinian soldiers and only the Solomon-like decision of their Commander-in-Chief avoided a possible bloodbath, General Mario Benjamin Menendez ordering an unconditional surrender of all his forces. Menendez would not allow his raw recruits to be massacred for what was a hopeléss cause. Sat in tearstained disbelief, Argentina's footballers watched open-mouthed as Spanish television reported the truth as to what befell their countrymen in the Malvinas. Such had been the Junta's terrifying influence over the Argentinian media, Menotti's men had arrived in Spain convinced the war was going to plan. What had began in triumph back on 2nd April 1982, when Videla's successor General Leapoldo Galtieri announced that the Malvinas was back in Argentinian hands, ended sixty days later when British troops raised the Union Jack over Port Stanley. In between had been senseless slaughter as hundreds died to satisfy political egos on both sides.

Against such a dreadful background of bloodshed and despair, it came as little surprise that the opening ceremonial match in Barcelona at the Nou Camp ended in disaster as Argentina slid miserably to a shock 1-0 defeat against Belgium. It was Diego Maradona in the closing stages that came closest to saving face for his nation when he lashed a vicious free-kick against the Belgian bar, only to see the ball drop onto the goalline and cleared. The final whistle saw Maradona stomp angrily off the field, blazing mad at the loss and his own below-par performance. The refusal to swap shirts with any of the Belgian players provoked cat-calls from the neutral Catalans in the crowd that watched on rather apprehensively at the petulance of this Argentinian for who their club had just splashed out a king's ransom. It was hardly love at first sight.

This result proved a wake-up call for Cesar Menotti's Argentina, they could ill afford to drop another point. That the South Americans managed to scrape through the first round was thanks mainly to the dazzling skills and determination of Diego Armando who although suffering the effects of a niggling hamstring pull, still produced enough moments of magic to ensure his country qualified out of the group. A two-goal blast against Hungary in the second match when a 4-1 win eased Argentinian nerves provided a fleeting glimpse for a worldwide audience of just what all the fuss was about. Menotti showered praise upon his young starlet claiming 'that at just twenty-one years of age he is already a miracle'.

It would be an epic three-way duel of gladiatorial proportions with the last one standing proclaimed the victor. The second phase produced an all-star cast as Maradona, Zico, Socrates, Paolo Rossi and a host of others battled for top billing. Argentina, Italy and Brazil all gunned for one semi-final spot. The pressure to win the opening game was intense and on 29th June 1982 at the Sarria Stadium in Barcelona the Argentinians and Italians stepped first into the ring. Here Diego Maradona met his worse nightmare and the most inaptly named defender of all time, Claudio Gentile. The *Azzurri* coach Enzo Bearzot had earmarked for the ferocious Libyan-born Gentile the unenviable task of man-marking the snakecharming ball skills of Maradona. Though raised in Naples, it was Atalanta that had picked up this raw kid for next to nothing and, after being sold on to Juventus, Gentile was turned into one of the most accomplished defenders of the modern era. But there was more, a dark side. Claudio Gentile would hack down his grandmother if the cause required, for he was a hatchet man of the highest order. So it was that when Bearzot gave him instructions to rein in the leash on Argentina's finest, Gentile warmed to his role with a truly worrying relish.

Though a genuinely good man, Enzo Bearzot was a pragmatic and realist when it came to matters regarding the so-called beautiful game. Such idealism was for dreamers, this was the World Cup and all that mattered come the final whistle was the result. There was no honour in defeat, just defeat. Claudio Gentile was instructed to stop Diego Maradona by any means. No player in the world bore the destructive qualities necessary for such an awesome task more than he. Come the match and Gentile's performance of cruel near-controlled aggression against Maradona proved disturbingly memorable.

For the full ninety minutes the Argentinian felt the Italian's breath on his neck. Ably abetted by fellow defenders Antonio Cabrini and Gaetano Scirea, Gentile never let his man breathe. A television camera placed solely on this battle of wills captured for posterity the full ferocity of World Cup competition as Maradona found himself caged. After the match a raging Diego claimed, 'Gentile should have been a butcher, not a footballer.' For weeks after he would stare in the mirror and see Claudio Gentile's face over his shoulder. A frightening ghost, an assassin of the streets. A hit, a job well done. Bumped, shoved, clattered and mauled, Maradona was placed under lock and key by the Italians who won 2-1 to set up an all-or-nothing clash against the Brazilians in which they so spectacularly triumphed with an incredible Rossi hat-trick. In 1986 fate decreed that Argentina and Italy meet again and Bearzot was once more faced with the awesome prospect of shackling *Pibe De Oro*. By then the kid had become a man and the Drum Roll had began its countdown to greatness.

Cesar Menotti's fading team finally relinquished their crown with a scowl and little honour in a harrowing 3-1 defeat against Brazil. It was a match recalled not only for the superb quality of Samba football, but more so the shabby dismissal of Diego Maradona who, unable to stand his country humiliated by their most hated foes, lashed out in frustration at the unfortunate Brazilian substitute Batista in the dying moments. Argentinians still talk about the mad gleam in Batista's eye as he entered the fray to wind-up Maradona. By that time the contest was over and the Brazilians had delighted in handing Argentina a thrashing. Those who had claimed that the young Argentinian was ready to take the great Pelé's crown stepped back into the shadows. But, by hook or by crook, Diego Armando Maradona was determined that one day he would knock him off his lofty, imperial, Brazilian perch. One day.

CHAPTER 11

MEXICAN DAZE

On landing in Mexico, Diego Maradona found himself pursued relentlessly by the world's media as his every word, move and gesture was analysed and dissected across the globe. It resembled a circus, but with no clowns or jugglers, no knife throwers, no acrobats. Just a stockily-built little footballer with a crowd winning smile and blessed with the ability to make the finest defender appear a drunken fool. To make grown men lose sleep and catch their breath. To the beat of the drum roll and trapped in the flashing, blinding haze of the worldwide spotlight Maradona prepared to prove himself worthy to stand alongside the legends of the past. Di Stefano, Puskas, Eusebio, Cruyff and Pelé. All great names, illustrious and famed. Given time Diego Armando would not just join such esteemed ranks, he would leave them in his wake. Naples would prove just a kingdom fortress, for there remained an empire in waiting for the kid from Villa Fiorito.

Matters took on a turn for the manic when word from Naples reached Diego Maradona that a seven-month pregnant Cristina Singrita, surrounded by lawyers, family and friends, had held a press conference to declare the footballer as the father of her child. Hell hath no fury like a Neapolitan female scorned as Cristina demanded Maradona underwent blood tests to prove once and for all he was responsible. Acting like a cornered alley cat, Diego Armando lashed out and denied all. But the damage was done and unable to believe their good fortune, the Italian press went for the kill. Any opportunity to hammer the Argentinian was taken with bloodcurdling relish. The headlines screamed out moral outrage. Once more and without really trying too hard Maradona became public enemy number one in his adopted homeland.

In a vain attempt to escape the rising football fever that had gripped Mexico City, the Argentinians based themselves on the outskirts of the capital in the seemingly peaceful surroundings of the suburbs. But such was the charismatic pull of their Captain, the South Americans found themselves under daily siege by an army of media and supporters that turned them into virtual prisoners at the training facilities of team Club America. Press conferences resembled wild scenes of bedlam and hysteria as a mad flurry of cameras, microphones and tape recorders were endlessly thrust within inches of the player's face. They flew like bullets; 'Diego, are you the father? Diego, do you love Cristina? Diego how is your ankle? Diego, look this way! Diego, Diego, Diego, Diegoooo!!' It was a madhouse.

Thrown in with world champions Italy, Bulgaria and South Korea for the opening rounds, Maradona showed explosive form as the Argentinians began with a 3-1 victory against the Koreans. Though not on the scoresheet he was instrumental in all three goals, running amok amongst his terrified opponents. Having no answers, the men from the Orient resorted in attempting to kick lumps out of him, but this was easier said than done as Maradona, dynamic, cunning and firing on all cylinders, sped away from flailing tackles and last gasps lunges. Despite the Captain's fine form the critics were scathing in their comments regarding the alleged average quality of his teammates.

Maradona reacted furiously in a post-match interview and spat out that he hoped 'everyone would pay him and his side more respect when they get to the final.' Watching on worryingly was Enzo Bearzot. Given half an inch the Argentinian maestro would undoubtedly wreak similar havoc against the Italians if his threat weren't curtailed. But how do you down a missile that appeared impregnable to all known defences? With Gentile retired, Bearzot had only one player in his squad blessed with the capability and know-how to stem such danger. He required an edge, someone on the inside. In a controversial move that sparked shockwaves across all of Italy, Enzo Bearzot announced that the dubious honour of curbing the threat of Diego Maradona had gone to teammate and close friend at Napoli, Salvatore Bagni.

The ancient mistrust of all things Neapolitan surfaced with frenzy as the northern-based media began a great flurry of debate. Many of them were uneasy with Bearzot's choice of player to jail Maradona. It was well documented they shared a friendship off the pitch. Salvatore Bagni's arrival from Inter Milan coincided with the Argentinian touching ground in Naples. From the beginning they hit it off. During matches the highly competitive Bagni took it upon himself to play the role of Diego Maradona's bodyguard. As the hired assassins of Serie A went for the kill he offered protection and when necessary fierce retribution.

It was claimed that this adopted Southern *Terroni* would not show the necessary heart and aggression for such a difficult task. The proud blue shirt of the *Azzurri* demanded nothing less than total loyalty, a willingness to stop Maradona at any costs. In the end the doubters in Milan, Turin and all cities north of Rome were proved wrong as Salvatore Bagni went for his Napoli teammate with unrestrained passion and fire. A fascinating duel between the two ensued with Maradona finding himself hunted and harassed repeatedly throughout the contest. No quarter was given or asked as each gave their all in an enthralling one-to-one encounter. The Argentinian escaped only once from the clutches of his Italian shadow but it was sufficient for him to grab an equaliser after Inter's Altobelli had put the world champions in front from the penalty spot.

It was typical Maradona as he hit a sweet left foot volley low past *Azzurri* goalkeeper Galli to secure a point. The game ended in a 1-1 draw and the final whistle saw the two players embrace warmly and share a quiet joke. There remained criticism in the Italian press that Bagni had gone easy on the Argentinian, but considering Diego Armando finished the match limping and with his shirt in tatters, the evidence proved otherwise. The Neapolitan blood brothers had given all and more for their respective countries. In Naples there was great satisfaction at the outcome. Honour had been served, their lads had not let them down. The end result also suited both nations as it all but secured qualification for the last sixteen. Next was a date with age-old foes Uruguay.

The Uruguayans have a word: '*Garra*'. Roughly translated it means 'to stand strong, be a man'. In their impressive World Cup history this small nation of three million had repeatedly battled above their weight against overwhelming odds to triumph. Twice world champions, Uruguay achieved their greatest ever result in 1950 when true *Garra* was shown to clinch the trophy in front of 200,000 fanatical Brazilian supporters in the footballing cathedral of the Maracana. The host nation was left grief-stricken as legendary Uruguayan Captain Obdulio Varela led his countrymen to an astonishing 2-1 win over Brazil, a result that left the Brazilians crestfallen and plunged the country into a state of national mourning. A victory over Maradona's Argentina would be exalted equally so.

Following an honourable 1-1 draw against West Germany in their opening group game, the Mexican skies collapsed on Uruguay when they fell victim to an emerging Danish side that thrashed them 6-1. Three goals from Verona hitman Preben Elkjaer and a strike from Juve's devastating forward Michael Laudrup helped to provoke unmerciful criticism back home for beleaguered coach Omar Borras. As emotions ran high his family were forced into hiding and given twenty-four-hour armed protection by the authorities. Borras was deemed the luckiest man alive when results elsewhere saw only a point required against Scotland in their final game to secure qualification for the next round. That Uruguay's fate still lay in their own hands after what befell them against a rampaging Denmark meant they could ill afford to waste such a God-given chance of redemption. The Uruguayans stretched the mythical *Garra* to its limits. With a brutality more suited to a brawling street gang they acted like crazed madmen in their desperation to ensure progress. Omar Borras wound up his team to the extent that the South Americans hacked, mauled, spat and intimidated in order to grab their point.

The mood was set after just fifty-five seconds when defender Jose Batista scythed down Scottish midfielder Gordon Strachan from behind to leave him writhing in agony on the turf. Acting with indecent haste the Spanish referee Joel Quiniou flashed a red card from his pocket and sent the startled Batista off the field. At first it appeared Quiniou had simply pulled out the wrong colour, but not wanting to be seen foolish decided instead to dismiss the player and in doing so create a new record for the competition. This proved only to further incite the Uruguayans and one of the darker chapters in World Cup history gloomily unfolded. In a strip of all white Uruguay performed more like devils than angels as their squalid showing dragged their country's proud name into the gutter. The Scotland manager Alex Ferguson stomped, raged and ranted on the touchline at the antics of his opponents and the Scots' own inept play and apparent lack of courage to overcome such tactics.

Some of the Uruguayan mischief-making defied belief as they hurled water bags at the referee and his officials at half-time on leaving the pitch. Needing to win in order to qualify, an insipid Scotland surrendered meekly to go out with a whimper. Only the manager showed traditional Scottish fire as he tore into Omar Borras on the touchline as he urged his men to waste time. Afterwards a straight-faced Borras with a shrug of his shoulders commented that he 'could not see what all the fuss was about'. On hearing this Ferguson gave full vent to his feelings at the post-match press conference when in typical unrestrained manner he declared, 'If Borras sits there defending his team, he is lying, cheating and uttering a load of rubbish. I can't even wish him luck.' FIFA acted swiftly. Uruguay were fined 25,000 Swiss francs and threatened with expulsion if they dared misbehave again. As for Borras, he was barred from the touchline for one game and banished to the stand for the showdown against Argentina.

This latter day battle of the River Plate took place sixty miles southwest of the capital in the picturesque city of Puebla. Set against a wonderful mountain backdrop in a beautiful tree-lined valley gorge, Puebla was referred to by native Mexicans as the 'City of Angels'. In ancient times the Aztecs thought this land sacred and touched by their many Gods. Here on 16th July 1986 at the Cuauhtemoc stadium a modern day idol sprinkled his gold dust upon such blessed soil. Argentinian cheers soared towards the heavens as Diego Maradona appeared hellbent in taking on the Uruguayans single-handed.

With the hatchet men from Montevideo out only on bail and their every tackle scrutinized they were forced to clean up their act. A stage was provided for *Pibe De Oro* to exhibit his full repertoire of skills while being free from the worry of being kicked senseless. Playing on the shoulders of Argentina's two attackers, his room mate Pedro Pasculi and the tall, elegant Jorge Valdano, Maradona ignited from deep leaving Uruguayan defenders scattered in his wake. From high in the Directors' Box Omar Borras screamed instructions through a walkie-talkie to his bench, but it was to no avail as the Argentinian Captain sliced through his team at will, causing panic. It came as little surprise that three minutes before the interval Argentina took a well deserved lead when a move started by a jinking Maradona dribble ended with Pasculi firing home from twelve yards past Uruguayan goalkeeper Alves to delight their supporters. With Italian referee Luigi Agnolin keeping a terse eye on every Uruguay challenge, their thirst for battle waned as they appeared only intent in trying to avoid an embarrassing scoreline.

But this was a scenario that couldn't last for the weight of history between two such historically bitter adversaries meant that old habits died hard. Twenty-five minutes remained when the skies above Puebla suddenly turned a deathly black. Without any due warning a terrifying electrical storm erupted. As the heaven sobbed, jagged streaks of lightning ripped through the night-time sky, a brief prelude to a roaring thunder that shook the surrounding mountains. It appeared to act as a wake-up call for the Uruguayans, who having played with unnatural calm finally decided they would not go down without a fight and damn the consequences. The gloves came off and battle commenced in all its fury in the City of Angels.

Grown weary of being made to look ridiculous by the alluring sorcery of the opposing number ten, the Uruguayan defenders resorted to type and went in search of Argentinian blood, one in particularly. On a treacherous swamp of a surface the tackles flew in on Diego Maradona, but with an unerring capacity to conjure Houdini-like escape routes out of seemingly impossible situations, Maradona showed remarkable courage as he refused to curtail his dynamic bursts into enemy territory. The more they kicked, the more he appeared determined to ensure that those from across the River were taught a lesson they never forgot.

Hurtling over legs, skating across a rain splattered, drenched pitch, twisting, exploding past defenders, the ball obeying his every command as it appeared tied by invisible string to his dancing feet. A masterclass from the greatest player in the world. With the referee blowing to end the game the Uruguayans finally brought Maradona to earth, but quickly he was lifted up by adoring teammates and embraced in a bearhug by Carlos Bilardo. In

101

Argentina they had begun dancing in the streets. The revellers roared out his name, an unofficial National Anthem, 'Maradooona!' A war cry adopted in Naples, but born in Buenos Aires. He was their boy! Uruguay would go home missed by no one; as for the Argentinians, their reward for victory was huge as another monumental encounter lay ahead: The Pirates from the Malvinas, England.

In Naples there exists a little-known card game called *Scopa*. It is played by men of questionable values who care little how they win. At *Scopa's* dark heart lay rule number one: 'Always try and glimpse your opponent's hand.' To triumph it is expected to lie and cheat, but always watch your back, cover your hand. Armed with this archetypal Neapolitan tactic Diego Maradona prepared mentally for the biggest match of his life so far. To beat the English by fair means or other, it mattered little, for the bitter humiliation suffered in the South Atlantic left Argentina in mourning. Maradona was viewed in his country as the one man capable of restoring national pride by slaying the bullying British bulldog.

A Falklands War Part Two scenario was stirred up by rabid tabloid hysteria in both nations as a dangerous patriotic fervour took hold. Maradona was referred to in the Buenos Aires-based newspaper *Cronica* as 'our Exocet', while its English equivalent *The Sun* proclaimed 'It's war Senors' and the *Daily Mirror* called to 'Bring on the Argies!'. As kick-off grew close a simmering, powderkeg, hostile atmosphere left a bad taste in the mouth as old images of the conflict were dredged up on television and replayed constantly. With both sets of supporters not of the ilk to walk away from confrontation, the Mexican police prepared for the worst. In the pre-match press conferences the managers Bobby Robson and Carlos Bilardo spent more time fending off questions that had absolutely nothing to do with football, but each knew deep down what was at stake. Sometimes football really is just a game.

Maradona refused also to be drawn. 'I am here,' he exclaimed a thousand times, 'to play football. Look mate,' he exclaimed wearily to an English journalist from *The Times*, who questioned him repeatedly on the thorny issue of revenge, 'when we go on the pitch it is the game of football that matters and not who won the war.' Fine words from the Captain as he tried to defuse a potentially explosive situation. But it was only akin to taking a pin out of a grenade and covering the fuse with your thumb. No matter what was claimed in public, there remained a hidden agenda for both sides. Former England manager Ron Greenwood was asked his opinion on the best way to stop Maradona. Greenwood replied, 'First you pull out a handgun!' Hopefully he was joking! The quarter-final took place in the legendary surroundings of the Azteca stadium in Mexico City and huge security measures were taken to ensure a bloodbath did not occur on the terraces. The 'Rule Britannia' hordes of Saint George and the notorious Argentinian hooligans *Barras Bravas* would have needed little prompting if the opportunity arose to go for each other's throats.

Bobby Robson's battleplan focused almost completely on blotting out the threat of Diego Maradona. Robson knew that any attempt to simply man-mark the Argentinian was doomed to failure for such was his explosive form there was not a player on the planet capable of dulling the threat for ninety minutes. Instead England would attempt to block him out by numbers, crowd him, cut off his air. Plans were made, tactics discussed, the battlelines were drawn. But little did the Three Lions realise the full extent of what they would be up against. *El Pibe De Oro* would surprise them all, for he would be playing to an entirely different set of rules: *Scopa*.

High noon on Sunday 22nd June 1986. A staggering crowd of 114,580 gathered at the Azteca to witness this titanic struggle between two sides that, judging by the looks etched on their faces, understood the magnitude of what was at stake. The Mexicans in the stadium threw in their lot alongside the South Americans with a rampant enthusiasm as they chanted the name of Argentina's number ten with unreserved passion. As the two teams stood for their respective National Anthems, Diego Maradona glared down the line of players and gave the white shirts of England what could best be described as a murderous look of disdain. The intent was clear to all who witnessed the moment. The kid from Villa Fiorito was up for this match like no other in his career.

To thunderous applause the teams broke for a brief warm up before battle commenced, England in traditional white, Argentina in a change strip of dark blue shirts. Both Captains were called to the halfway line by Tunisian referee Ali Ben Nasser for ceremonial duties. Diego Maradona and England's thirty-six-year-old veteran goalkeeper Peter Shilton exchanged the slightest of handshakes, which was polite but nothing more. A touching of gloves: two heavyweight champions seconds before the first bell. Shilton and Maradona attempted to stare each other down. The Englishman all seriousness, the Argentinian wearing a worrying half-smile, like he had already read the script. With the stadium close to emotional meltdown the game began.

'*Trompe l'oeil*' (Tricks and deceptions'). After a turgid opening period with both teams appearing overcome by the sheer enormity of the occasion, events exploded wildly into life on fifty-one minutes. A badly misjudged hooked clearance by English midfielder Steve Hodge succeeded only in sending the ball spinning back into his own penalty area. Sensing the danger

103

Peter Shilton rushed out to clear, only to be challenged by a jumping Maradona who with a mischievous flick of the wrist erupted into infamy. Blessed with all the cocky charm of the finest streetwise Neapolitan hustler, Argentina's number ten struck to steal a goal. A sleight of hand invisible to most punched the ball over the head of England's goalkeeper to set ablaze this magnificent footballing arena.

Shilton's momentary expression of quizzical disbelief bore comparison with a man who had just seen his wallet snatched. In order to stoop low the Argentinian had leapt high to infuriate the hated English with an infamous stroke of gamesmanship, forever immortalised in World Cup folklore as the 'Hand Of God'. A likely story, for it was no divine intervention on the football pitch that day, just a twenty-five-year-old footballer called Diego Armando Maradona, sporting a knowing grin after succeeding in getting away with the biggest scam of his young life. In Naples they danced with joy, for it was clear they had taught him well. As Maradona ran off to soak up the adulation of the crowd he glanced nervously over his shoulder at the referee and the melee that ensued. His close friend Jorge Valdano ran over to embrace him and with a finger over his mouth gestured sssshhh to his compadre, as if suggesting 'Don't push it Diego!'. High in the stand Maradona spotted his Father and gave a clenched fist salute. Argentina led. All hell had broken loose in Mexico City.

The referee appeared oblivious to protests as he waved away shell-shocked English players. A furious Shilton ran after Ali Ben Nasser, pointing to his hand, but he appeared unmoved. A disgusted Bobby Robson pleaded with officials on the touchline but was shown short shrift. Nasser never again refereed another international football match. Before matters could calm down Diego Maradona struck once more, this time with the greatest goal ever scored in World Cup football. Racked by a sense of injustice and disbelief, England simply did not see him coming as he received the ball just inside his own half and took off on a mazy, weaving run towards their penalty area. A flurry of white shirts pounced, only to be left trailing in the Argentinian's wake as he hurtled clear over the halfway line and into the history books.

Across Argentina and in the back alley café bars of Naples they watched mesmerised. Surely their boy could not beat them all? *El Pibe De Oro* dribbled at high pace past panicking, retreating English defenders and bore down on a waiting Peter Shilton. The crowd in the Azteca rose as one to their feet in mounting excitement. A final desperate challenge by Terry Butcher appeared to have put Maradona off balance, only for him to throw Shilton a dummy at the last and switch the ball to his other foot before finishing coolly with a flashing, low shot into the net. The Azteca exploded in disbelief and delight. The sly and the sordid equally applauded as the beauty and the brilliant, by those who revered this stocky little figure with Godlike status. You simply could not make it up!

Stung by the bittersweet circumstances of Diego Maradona's first and the sheer bloody genius of his second, England staged a rip-roaring effort to get back in the game. On the brink of elimination and with nothing to lose Bobby Robson threw caution to the wind. Off came midfielders Peter Reid and Trevor Steven, both victims of Maradona's whirlwind, to be replaced by two young, gifted, if unpredictable wingers in Chris Waddle and John Barnes. In a heart-stopping final half hour Barnes in particularly almost saved the day for the Three Lions as he terrorised the Argentinian rearguard with his electric pace and guile. When in the mood and firing on all cylinders, the enigmatic Jamaican-born forward possessed the talent to take apart the finest defence.

Nine minutes remained to play when a typically devastating run and cross from the Watford man was met by Gary Lineker who swooped from close range to smash a header past Argentina's keeper Nino Pumpido. With the South Americans hanging on by the skin of their teeth and praying for the final whistle, John Barnes again soared down the left flank and hit an inch-perfect ball for Lineker who failed by a whisker to force it over the line. Finally the full time whistle sounded and Argentinian players went in search of their Captain. Later in the sanctity of the dressing room, Diego Maradona led the celebrations as he wrapped himself in his country's flag and along with his teammates sang a boisterous rendition of the National Anthem. Nobody bothered to mention the Malvinas... They didn't have to.

Late in the game England centre half Terry Butcher had motioned to Maradona if he had punched the ball over Shilton. With a wry smile the Argentinian Captain simply pointed to his head. Questioned afterwards Maradona caused outrage amongst the English journalists when he claimed with straight face and all mock innocence it was not he but indeed 'The Hand Of God' who soared high over Peter Shilton to score the first goal. With a wicked glint in his eye the Argentinian told one reporter, who repeatedly tried to force him to admit his indiscretion, 'To go and cry in a church'. Seemingly enjoying himself torturing the Gringo newspaper hacks, a teasing Maradona finally admitted with an ironic smile and slight shrug of the shoulders that it was 'a little bit of the hand of God, a little of the head of Maradona'. How they raged: suddenly as was his wont, and again without trying too hard *El Pibe De Oro* earned an entire new audience to despise him. Not that Maradona cared, for despite all that was aired publicly the victory in the Azteca was indeed payback time for what occurred in the South Atlantic. A war without guns and bullets, but a war nonetheless. A semi-final date with unfancied Belgium lay in waiting and after beating England the Argentinians feared no one, for destiny and if you were to believe their Captain, God himself, was in their line-up! Against such odds the Belgians did not have a prayer. And so it proved.

Just three days on from the victory over England, the blue and white hoops of Argentina stepped out again into the vast cauldron of the Azteca stadium to take on the blood-red shirts of Belgium, the dark horses of the tournament. An impressive run to the latter stages saw the Belgians collect the scalps of highly-fancied Spain and a USSR team that was seen by many as the best in the competition. A mixture of experience in players such as Eric Gerets and Jan Ceulemans, added to a dash of youth in the wonderfully talented Enzo Scifo meant they could not be taken lightly. The hugely partisan audience of 110,420 that had gathered once more in the Azteca came with the intention of seeing the Europeans put to the sword by their hero. Though they would rage against the light for close to an hour and show huge heart Belgium's fate was never in doubt, for truly great players have a moment in history when it is clearly their time. The 1986 World Cup finals were without question Diego Maradona's.

Ever the showman, Maradona produced a few party tricks in the opening moments to keep his adoring following happy, but mostly the first half was spent probing, plotting and searching for a weakness in the opposition's rearguard. Superbly organised by the wily old coach, Guy Thys, the Belgians dug in. Theirs was a gameplan simple but crude, to hold out for a hundred and eighty minutes and win the match on penalties. It was akin to throwing a party on a railway line. Sooner or later *El Pibe De Oro* would get them. On the eve of the semi-final Belgium goalkeeper Jean-Marie Pfaff claimed, 'Maradona wasn't all that special.' For the first fifty-one minutes Pfaff might have appeared to have a valid point as the Argentinian number ten bore the look of a player disinterested and lacking in determination. Neapolitan deception! *Trompe l oeil*. Then, as against England, when all seemed peaceful the train appeared at breakneck speed to splatter all on the track as Diego Armando Maradona awoke from apparent slumber to break Belgian hearts. Showtime! It was time to go to work.

Just when Belgium had dared to dream, Maradona tore menacingly into their penalty area to clip a gloriously low cross-shot past the fingers of a despairing Jean-Marie Pfaff to ignite scenes of jubilation across the Azteca. The unerring technique and precision needed to score such a goal took the breath away of all who witnessed this moment of sublime ingenuity by the little Argentinian. With their battleplan in tatters and looking bereft of spark and the necessary guile required to claw their way back against such a formidable team as Argentina, Guy Thys' men appeared resigned to the inevitable. It duly occurred twelve minutes later when *Pibe De Oro* finally put them out of their misery with a touch of magic that bore easy comparison with his previous *tour de force* against the English.

Picking up the ball midway inside the Belgian half Diego Maradona found himself shadowed by a blazing shower of red shirts. All eyes both on the pitch and off fell upon him. A drop of the shoulder and two, three, four defenders were left for dead. Exploding into top gear Maradona scythed through a heap of bodies and roared onwards into the penalty area. Once more the Azteca came to its feet: he was at it again! Still surrounded by a seemingly impenetrable mass of red and forced wide of the goal, Maradona produced from nowhere an astonishing left foot shot that screamed past a bemused Pfaff and into the net, before wheeling away in triumph. A Mexican daze! Amongst the cheering crowds was England manager Bobby Robson who, although still smarting from the Hand Of God incident, typically stood up and applauded Maradona's exquisite piece of artistry. Shortly after, the hat-trick was almost completed when he went through again, only this time to fire inches wide of the far post. On surviving this particular Diego close encounter, Jean-Marie Pfaff glared daggers at his tormentor before breaking out in a huge smile. It was no disgrace to be beaten by such as he. Pfaff's pre-match comments that Maradona was 'nothing special' had returned to immeasurably haunt him. The full-time whistle saw Jean-Marie Pfaff go in search of his destroyer only to embrace him like a long-lost brother and wish him all the best for the final. Diego Maradona appeared genuinely touched by Pfaff's sporting gesture and the two men left the pitch arm-in-arm, deep in conversation. It was, after all, away from the madness, just a game. A World Cup final awaited Argentina, their opponents a team who loved nothing better than to spoil a party.

CHAPTER 12

KING OF THE WORLD

Diego Armando Maradona was many things to all men. A cheat and chancer, maker of dreams, Devil and God. With the ball at his feet he possessed the magic to lift entire stadiums off their seats to gasp in wonder and adoration. There were those who loved and admired, others who loathed and raged, screaming venom at the mere mention of his name. Maradona! Opinion varied wildly. How do you measure greatness in a man and a footballer? The 1986 World Cup Finals hardly supplied answers, instead they only added to the myth and mystique. King of the world or streetwise hustler made good? With the greatest prize of all at stake the time came for Diego Maradona to show his true hand.

Argentina's opponents would be a West German team managed by the legendary Franz Beckenbauer, (Der Kaiser) that had proved to be typically efficient, if hardly spectacular during their crab-like crawl to the final. Some spoke of cannon fodder for Maradona to savage at will. Others were more wary, for history dictated that they never lay down for anyone. Better teams than Argentina had been put in their place by these resilient, never-say-die Germans over many decades of World Cup competition. Great players such as Puskas and Cruyff had been ambushed at the last. Would the same fate befall Maradona?

As ever with the Germans their football was dour, functional but extremely effective as they came out of the first round with sufficient points but few new friends. Behind the scenes chaos reigned. Franz Beckenbauer was left with little option but to send the reserve goalkeeper Ulli Stein home after he scathingly referred to him as 'Humpty Dumpty'! Not content with insulting his coach, Stein also tore into his teammates by claiming they 'played like a bunch of cucumbers' in warm-up matches. Matters hardly improved as the tournament began when a German tabloid alleged stories of prostitutes being seen leaving the players' hotel rooms.

There was also the problem of a bitter fall-out between two of their most experienced stars, centre-forward Karl-Heinz Rummenigge and goalkeeper

Harald Schumacher. Both had newspaper columns back home and could not resist the temptation to let fly in the other's direction whenever the opportunity allowed. Embarrassed and outraged by the team's antics Beckenbauer exploded with rage when West Germany failed to live up to expectations in their opening two first-round games. Words such as 'stupid' and 'garbage' were used to describe their showing against Uruguay and Scotland. That they managed to qualify out of the group surprised even their manager who was forced into a public apology by the German FA after his uncharacteristic outburst. In his entire illustrious career Der Kaiser had never faced such a daunting challenge as in attempting to drag these maddeningly frustrating Germans to the pinnacle of world football, a side packed full of talent but laced with niggling injuries and personal hatreds that threatened at any time to send them reeling.

Come the knockout phase only a last minute free-kick from one of their few impressive players Lothar Matthaus saw off unlucky Morocco. Then in the quarter-finals a drab affair against host nation Mexico was settled miserably by a penalty shootout, in which the Mexicans totally lost their bottle and missed four of five attempts, thus sending their people into mourning and handing the game to the Germans. The semi-final in Guadalajara pitted them against the exhuberant but sadly, ageing French Musketeers of Platini, Tigana, Fernandez and Giresse, billed as a re-match of their classic duel in Seville during the last World Cup, when West Germany came from 3-1 down in extra-time to finally, as ever, win on penalties. This time round it proved much more comfortable for Beckenbauer's dogged warriors. After a truly exhausting epic contest against Brazil, France were already a spent force and, to the bitter disappointment of the watching neutrals, an Andreas Brehme free-kick, allied to a last minute breakaway from centre forward Rudi Voller, put paid to the French to secure a fifth World Cup final appearance.

It spoke volumes for German mentality that despite nowhere near the class of former great sides, sheer guts and determination enabled them to claw a path to within ninety minutes of becoming World champions for a third time. Preparation to deal with Diego Maradona hinged on paranoia after witnessing his momentous exploits against England and Belgium. For the coach he remained the last major obstacle that stood between him becoming the first ever to win the trophy both as player and manager. 'He is the best player in the World Cup, the best in the world. We will do our best to put him out of the game, but it is almost impossible.' Though respective of all the Argentinian forwards, none put the fear of God into Beckenbauer like Maradona, so much that he sacrificed his best player in attempting to make the game a ten-a-side contest.

Der Kaiser placed his trust in the twenty-five-year old Bayern Munich dynamo Lothar Matthaus. Here was the archetypal German midfielder, fast, strong, shoot with either foot, fine technique, intelligent and well disciplined. But most importantly, to take on the malevolent cunning and guile of Maradona, the Bayern man needed nerves of steel. Lothar Matthaus possessed this in abundance. By attaching himself limpet-like to the Argentinian, Matthaus hoped to snub him out like a cigarette butt. It would be a battle royal and to the winner would go the thirteenth World Cup.

Unknown to the outside world Maradona finished every game in searing agony as his accursed left ankle inflamed wildly during the fury of battle on the pitch. Only the ominous sharp prick of the cortisone needle enabled him to withstand the pain, as knowledgeable defenders knew exactly where to hit. The manager Carlos Bilardo had little sympathy with his Captain, for he graduated from the Argentinian school of thought that winning was all that mattered. During his career as a player with the infamous Estudiantes side of the late Sixties Bilardo built a reputation as a notorious hard man who took no prisoners, most memorably assaulting Manchester United's Nobby Stiles with an outrageous headbutt as the Argentinians roughed up Matt Busby's European champions with a vengeance to win the 1968 World Club Championship.

Carlos Bilardo was ruthless in his all-consuming desire to attain legendary status as the man who won back the World Cup. To do so it was imperative the Captain was on the field. There was nothing he would not stoop to in order to make this so, for without his coveted number ten the cause was hopeléss. Argentina needed Diego Maradona like a flower needed rain. Without him they would wilt and die under the blazing Mexican sun. Maradona's own passion and determination to play and lead his nation to glory meant he was his own worst enemy, for dark tales surfaced that whatever he was given to continue performing might have drastic consequences in later years. In his case the term 'dying to play' could well have been frightfully apt.

In Buenos Aires thousands of posters on every street corner declared unequivocally, 'MARADONA PRESIDENTE!'. A local priest from Villa Fiorito, Monsignor Jorge Caseretto, claimed he had received a message from God saying that 'the Almighty himself was a Maradona fan and that everything was arranged. They would prevail over the Germans.' As exclusives go it took some beating. As for the Neapolitans, once the *Azzurri* had been eliminated all of Naples immediately shifted allegiances towards Argentina and rallied behind their king. On the eve of the final Diego Maradona spoke well in praising Beckenbauer's men; 'They play like a real team, they never give up and it would be ignorant not to have the greatest respect for them.'

And so at the Azteca Stadium on Sunday 29th June 1986, Argentina and West Germany fought out a thrilling climax to what had been a truly absorbing and dramatic Mexican fiesta of football. In the history of the World Cup no player had ever dominated an entire tournament like Maradona. His goals and all-round performances had overshadowed all. Only West Germany stood between him and a place amongst the game's immortals. Only the Germans, a familiar tale. But not this time. Drawn to the wonder of Diego Maradona like a dragonfly to light, the Mexicans firmly nailed their colours behind fellow Latinos, Argentina. A local banner hailed, 'Maradona, why was you not born in Mexico?' Huge swathes of blue and white gathered joyfully with their green and red clad hosts to decorate the spectacular, wide-open terraces of the glorious Azteca as both sets of supporters joined forces to roar Maradona's team over the finishing line. With genius there were simply no borders. Neither ocean nor deserts could separate as *El Pibe De Oro* united football lovers across the globe. Except maybe Brazil, and, of course… England!

With the Argentinians in traditional hoops and West Germany in change shirts of green, the game began. In a ploy no doubt planned in the dressing room beforehand, Argentina launched a callous pre-emptive strike against Lothar Matthaus in an attempt to break loose the chains on their Captain. The opening moments saw the hunter become the hunted as defender Giusti tracked down the German midfielder to stamp viciously on his ankle. A furious Matthaus was fortunate to escape serious injury and on twenty-three minutes extracted sweet revenge by slicing down Maradona from behind for which he was booked. From the resulting free-kick played high into the German penalty area, Harald Schumacher could only watch in horror as he failed to punch clear and Argentinian centre-half Jose Luis Brown soared high to thunder his header into the net.

A stalemate took hold as a disappointing first half ensued. Argentina was content to just sit back and hit on the break. Their opponents appeared hesitant to open up, dreading that the South Americans would strike out and score again. Maradona worked tirelessly for the cause, his footballing brain forever scheming to entice German attention upon him and release fellow teammates to do damage. Finally, as the second period began, Beckenbauer's men realised they were in a World Cup final and started to chase the game. But then the almost inevitable occurred nine minutes after the interval when a clearance from an Andreas Brehme corner saw the Argentinians fly like the wind on the counter attack. A typically breathtaking twist and turn by

Maradona, followed by a clever pass to Hector Enrique had the Germans racing back in panic. Enrique placed an exquisite through-ball that was latched onto by Jorge Valdano, who sped clear into the penalty area and with great assurance swept the ball low past the advancing Schumacher to surely clinch the World Cup for Argentina.

Valdano disappeared beneath a blue and white mountain of joy as all the players and those on the Argentinian bench raced onto the pitch in celebration. A sense of hysteria took hold. Maradona sank to his knees and raised his hands in prayer. The Germans were on the floor. A grim-faced Franz Beckenbauer bore the look of a man resigned to defeat as he stood arms folded on the touchline, watching the cavorting of the South Americans. Carlos Bilardo gestured wildly at his players to keep their concentration for the game was not yet won. As the clock ticked down the Azteca was already partying. The small scatterings of German support lay silent, steadying themselves for the inevitable.

West Germany rallied, Lothar Matthaus was released from marking duties on Maradona with orders to push forward. Fifteen minutes from time the mood changed dramatically in the Azteca when from a corner Rudi Voller flicked on for Rummenigge, who slid in to grab a goal back. Sensing blood, Der Kaiser's men threw everything they had left at a backpedaling Argentina. As against England, from appearing to be coasting, they found themselves fighting for their lives in the closing stages. With Bilardo close to a heart attack on the touchline and their Captain unable to break the siege, it just had to happen. Another German corner, and with millions watching around the world in total disbelief Rudi Voller broke Argentinian hearts as he stooped low to head home the equaliser. 2-2: Argentina looked to have blown it. The old adage of never underestimating the Germans had again proved true. Extra-time loomed. As a child Diego Maradona had once proclaimed that his greatest wish was 'to play in the world cup and be a champion for my team.' That dream in no short time had been reduced to tatters as West Germany launched their barnstorming comeback.

As Argentina stood on the brink of disaster this irascible magical little street urchin, who plied his trade in Naples but whose heart lay ensconced in Buenos Aires, produced one last stroke of wizardry to save the day. Six minutes remained when Maradona in centre midfield found in his box of tricks a parting gift to Mexico '86. In the blink of an eye and surrounded by green shirts, he played the most outrageous volleyed pass to send twenty-two-year-old Nantes midfielder Jose Burruchaga racing through to fire unbelievingly past a despairing Harold Schumacher. 3-2! The Germans fell to their knees, this time there was no way back. One punch too many: it was as cruel as it was beautiful.

The thirteenth World Cup final ended and Carlos Bilardo was a man possessed as he sprinted onto the field to embrace his Captain. Every photographer and camera focused on one man, Diego Armando Maradona. He and his team were champions of the World. On receiving the trophy a beaming Maradona was hoisted shoulder-high by his adoring countrymen and carried around the stadium. A nation's honour had been satisfied, now all that remained was the keeping of a promise made to a city and its people that had adopted him as one of their own. Diego Maradona had shown that he possessed the power to make dreams come true. The time had come to end Neapolitan misery and finally win that elusive *Scudetto*. He had unfinished business in Naples.

CHAPTER 13

CAPITANO

Giuseppe Bruscolotti was a man born with the blue blood of Naples flowing through his veins. Signed from neighbouring Sorrento back in 1972, Bruscolotti had shared the pain of the tifosi time and again as Napoli fell at the last hurdle. He had played in the infamous Core Ngrato match when former hero Jose Altafini broke Neapolitan hearts. Nobody ever gave or suffered more than he for the cause. That fateful day when Bruscolotti was made Captain saw the tough, fierce-tackling defender shed tears, such was his passion for the club. So it was with heavy heart and grand sense of duty that this Napoli legend Giuseppe Bruscolotti passed on his mantle of leader to Diego Maradona in exchange for 'the promise of the Scudetto'. Maradona embraced Bruscolotti and with the handing over of a baton, dipped in the hopes and broken dreams of past generations, the Argentinian took the precious armband vowing not to let Naples and this proud warrior down. He would prove true to his word.

Over the ages Neapolitan folk ballads have echoed across oceans and continents. Known as the *Canzoni*, these haunting melodies tugged at the heartstrings as they told tales of love lost and found, of a yearning for the old country. Made famous by the legendary Italian Tenor, Neapolitan-born Enrico Caruso, classics such as *Funiculi-Funicula*, *Return to Sorrento* and the incomparable *O Sole Mio* helped romanticise Naples as a city like no other. But perhaps the greatest *Canzoni* of them all was performed at the San Paolo footballing cathedral by a massed chorus of thousands back in the mid-Eighties. 'Oh Mama, Mama, Mama, oh Mama, Mama, do you know why my heart beats so fast? Because I have seen Maradona, I have seen Maradona, and Mama, Mama, Mama, I'm in love!'

A perfectionist like the genius Caruso may have baulked at the lyrics but as a native of Naples he could not have argued with the passion in which they were sung, for something remarkable was stirring under the volcano. With Diego Maradona at the peak of his powers a rare and fearful sense of optimism had taken a grip. The Napoli *tifosi* knew well it was now or never for the *Scudetto*. Reinforcements in attack had been provided in the fast and lethal forward Andres Carnevale, who so impressed as the two sides met late in the previous season when he scored twice in a 2-0 win for Udinese. Recruits were also sought to add fire and guile in midfield. From Avellino came the tenacious Fernando De Napoli, whilst in a shrewd show of business acumen Ottavio Bianchi secured from Triestina in Serie B the ball-playing skills of Francesco Romano. With these two alongside Salvatore Bagni to help fire the bullets, Naples now possessed a team to rival any in Serie A.

All that remained for coach Ottavio Bianchi and the Napoli faithful was to get their Captain back in one piece, firing on all cylinders. Special prayers were offered to San Gennaro to keep a wary eye on *El Pibe De Oro*. Save him from temptation, bad luck, dangerous women, but mostly, from himself. In Naples huge pride was taken from Diego Maradona's incredulous performances, but also there were worries about his state of mind now he had reached the ultimate pinnacle of his career. Ability was never in question, it was whether he possessed the necessary strength of character to carry on producing miracles in the colours of SSC Napoli? After his history-making adventures in Mexico, Maradona returned to Argentina for a holiday before travelling onto Naples. But little did he know what awaited him on home soil, for after landing at Buenos Aires he was greeted in truly hysterical manner as the entire city turned out to welcome home the conquering hero. A triumphant motor cavalcade paraded Argentina's favourite son through the streets with thousands lining the pavements waving flags, chanting the name of their beloved Diego. He was taken to the Presidential Palace at Casa Rosada, where on a balcony with Argentine President Raul Alfonsin in a showering blur of a sky thick with blue and white confetti, a delighted Diego Maradona proudly showed off the World Cup trophy to his blood people. The kid from the back alleys of Villa Fiorito had come a long way.

Back in the arms of the man she loved was Claudia Villafane. A reconciliation had occurred and much to Claudia's joy Diego Maradona was back in her life with a promise to behave and settle down. That Cristina Sinagra was due at any time to give birth to the Argentinian's baby was not lost on Claudia, who appeared to waste little time in getting pregnant. Domestic bliss for Diego Armando was not yet on his agenda as the partying in the wake of Argentina's momentous victory continued at full hilt. Taking a much needed sabbatical, Maradona retired to his parents house where in a rare moment of tranquillity two young local boys found the courage to chance their arm and knock on the door to ask if he would join them for a kickabout. Unable to resist, Maradona led them into his Mother's garden where he spent an hour enjoying what he did best, making dreams come true. The lads stood mesmerised as their idol all but made the ball stand up and beg, a tall tale they could relate to their grandchildren.

On Sunday 14th September 1986 the Neapolitans trekked north to begin their Serie A campaign against newly-promoted Brescia. It took the new *Capitano* just forty-one minutes of the opening 1986-87 season to confirm that SSC Napoli's all-obsessive, burning desire to win the championship was close to being realised. With his back to goal Diego Maradona took a prodded pass from Salvatore Bagni exquisitely on his chest and tore with malicious intent towards the penalty area. In almost nonchalant manner he slipped past two defenders before taking aim and slamming a terrific drive past the keeper. The Brescia players stood transfixed; whatever had swarmed amongst them was surely not human? Those who had dared to doubt hung their heads in shame. Maradona soared towards his adoring followers, punching the air, thanking the Almighty. Pure theatre. A seething Northern crowd sat outraged but secretly admiring this barbarian king from the South. The final whistle brought great scenes of rejoicing amongst the Neapolitans that had infiltrated all around the ground. The journey home to Naples would be long but one bathed in the magical memory of Diego Maradona's winner. The omens were good; it promised to be, in the words of another famous singer of Italian extraction, Francis Alberto Sinatra, a very good year!

On the eve of Napoli's opening home fixture against Udinese, Diego Maradona received word that, although expected, still shocked him to the core. Cristina Sinagra had given birth to a bouncing baby boy and just to ensure there was no misunderstanding, she went live on Neapolitan television to announce, 'I will name him after his father. Diego Armando.' To call the child this in Naples was akin to naming him Jesus Christ. Cristina appointed one of Naples' most respected lawyers, Enrico Trucillo, to go after Maradona. This he did with a vengeance for even before the cord had been cut on the child, Trucillo issued a paternity suit against the alleged father. Enrico Trucillo had forged an entire career as a protector and fierce advocate of the underdog's cause. He was also said to possess an enormous ego. The opportunity to bring Diego Maradona to heel was one Trucillo would relish.

When challenged, Maradona was again adamant the baby was not his. With the media circus giving the story colossal coverage on television, radio and newspapers, there was nowhere to hide. His apartment in Posilippo became a prison as the lens of the paparazzi descended en masse to the player's door. Up trees, on roofs, above in helicopters, the cameras clicked and flashed, his every move watched. Across Italy this sensational storyline of a King denying his own blood caused huge controversy. It was a scenario greeted with delight by those who loved nothing more than sticking the knife

116

into Diego Maradona. The next day Maradona played one of his worst matches to date for the Neapolitans as Udinese held them to a 1-1 draw. A thunderous twenty-five-yard strike by Fernando Di Napoli proved the only highlight of an insipid performance by the home side. From the beginning, on appearing from the tunnel Maradona looked reluctant to even set foot on the pitch. His mind elsewhere, the normally incisive passing of *El Pibe De Oro* lacked its normal penetration and accuracy. Also missing was the terrifying, electric spurts forward. There was simply no spark. The Argentinian appeared lost, afraid of his own shadow. Suddenly, in front of a capacity crowd at the San Paolo, Diego Maradona looked to have been swallowed up by the life he had created for himself, the pressure and expectations catching up with him when he felt at his most vulnerable.

The Napoli *tifosi* watched horrified as Maradona struggled to find form. They roared his name, sang the songs, but all to no avail. Diego Armando knew he had been given a son, but with Claudia expecting also, his thoughts were in turmoil. The King's lot was not a happy one. Diego Maradona's one escape from the madness that followed his every move was out on the football field, where his only worry was opposing defenders wishing to kick him senseless. This was a minor irritancy in comparison to what the Argentinian was forced to endure off pitch. If he lost this he had nothing. After the match a depressed looking Maradona was smuggled out of a side door by his entourage who hustled him through the media wolves that stood ready to devour him. But there was no getaway, for as he sped off into downtown Naples with Claudia alongside in a jet black Ferrari, the jackals followed. He might lose them for a while, but in the end Maradona's scent proved overwhelming. They would always find him.

To add insult to injury, further heartache followed in the manner of an ignominious exit from the UEFA cup in Southern France at the hands of unfancied Toulouse. A lone goal from new boy Carnevale was cancelled out by the French on home ground when a similar scoreline led to a penalty shootout after extra-time. Ironically it was two of Naples most favourite sons that failed to convert the spot-kicks as Napoli went down 4-3. First Bagni, and then of all people Diego Maradona, to the utter bewilderment of his teammates and more so himself, saw his weak shot hit the post. The sad sight of their Capitano in floods of tears and inconsolable meant no *tifosi* could possibly point a finger of blame upon him. Indeed his popularity increased to even higher levels of adulation. Whatever cynicism had been cited regarding Maradona's complete devotion to Naples disappeared. He was truly one of their own, a gift from the Gods. A treasure of San Gennaro.

For an interview to the RAI Italian television station in the immediate, miserable aftermath of defeat, a visibly emotional Diego Maradona thanked the Napoli fans for their unyielding support. This was not Maradona simply playing to the gantry, he desperately wanted to repay their loyalty. There had been a banner amongst the Neapolitans that read *'Diego, Il no di noi'* ('Diego, you are one of us'). It reminded the player of the blood oath he had swore to the young *tifosi* whose lives he had so indelibly touched in many ways. It was a debt that Diego Armando Maradona intended to honour. In a short time time *El Pibe De Oro* would have them dancing like dervishes in the backstreets of Naples.

Stung by their embarrassing loss at the hands of Toulouse, Napoli's title charge took on an almost frenzied quality. Diego Maradona was ablaze, the reborn enthusiasm evident in every exaggerated gesture and mannerism. Soaked in Neapolitan passion, he cast his diminutive but captivating presence over Serie A. They embarked on an unbeaten eight-match run that included four goals for Maradona. Two were vital winners at Sampdoria and Roma. A penalty finished with ridiculous, cocky ease secured a hard fought 2-1 victory at the Luigi Ferraris stadium in Genoa. The abiding memory of the game was an instance on the touchline, when on a rain-drenched swamp of a surface Diego Maradona teased, mocked and beat every Sampdoria player who had the temerity to try and take the ball off him.

In Roma's Olympic Stadium Maradona's classic piece of control and astute finishing a minute after half time from a scything through pass by Bruno Giordano earned them the points. Before the game began the Argentinian performed a remarkable display of ball juggling in the centre circle that caused gasps from the terraces. *El Pibe De Oro* showing off in the capital! It proved a bitterly fought contest played out against a spectacular, dramatic backdrop of Roma red/yellow and Naples blue. As ever when in Rome the Neapolitans had to earn the right for every tackle, pass and goal scored. This result shot Napoli to the top of Serie A, but unfortunately the joy was tarnished by having to share their lofty position with an unwelcome old foe. A reluctant Juventus shifted their imperious backsides to allow the great unwashed room upon the pedestal. A showdown waited in a city and stadium that was nothing short of hell on earth for all Neapolitans. On the 9th November 1986 all roads led to Turin.

La Vecchia Signora were under new management. Giovanni Trapattoni's dramatic decision to divorce the Old Lady and upstake to Inter Milan opened the door for former Napoli coach Rino Marchesi. The affable Marchesi had glimpsed both sides of the coin. He understood the history, emotions and sheer hatred that existed in confrontations between these two giants of the

Italian league. The black/white stripes of the mighty Northern Industrial heartland of Turin versus the sky blue of the downtrodden, irascible, troublesome but always proud Southern capital of Naples. In an unprecedented show of mass support the Napoli hordes converged on the Stadio Comunale. With the vast amount of Neapolitans employed in the city working for Agnelli's Fiat, ferocious backing was always guaranteed. But the epic events of 9th November would echo through eternity as the Southerners descended like an invading army onto their most hated foes. The gigantic housing estate of the Mirafiori, built in close duration to the grey, foreboding car plants housed the tens of thousands who plied their trade for the Agnelli family. It bore the look of a little Naples, as those who lived there chose to show their true colours and follow the heart as the dream of *Scudetto* began to grow ever increasingly real.

The scheming Agnellis' original ploy for their workers to spend all week toiling for a motley sum of lira, only to then hand back the cash to support the family's hobby horse Juventus, thus self-servicing the monster, fell short when it came to the exiled Southern Brethren. For though far from under the shadow of great Grandfather Vesuvius, the passion never left. The Agnellis might have owned the bodies, but for those who kept the faith, they were damned if he would ever wrestle away their souls. What price a mere paycheck in comparison to watching Diego Maradona lifting the most coveted of all trophies? The opportunity had arisen to not just glimpse a shooting star but to ride aboard till its journey's end. There was something in the air!

Well before first light broke over Mount Vesuvius, the blue-clad *tifosi* of the Bulldogs, Fedayn, Blue Tigers and the massed ranks of the CUCB were en route to Turin. Fifteen thousand made their wary way north by car, coach and train to swell the numbers of their Neapolitan brothers already ensconced behind enemy lines. It was an outrageous twenty-nine years previous, on 24th November 1957, that SSC Napoli last won in the league on Juventus territory, a 3-1 victory cancelling out a goal by the *Bianconeri*'s much celebrated Welshman John Charles, '*Il Giganta Buono*' (the gentle giant). Many of those from the South who went to witness with their own eyes Diego Maradona end this witchcraft over their team would not even have been born on that long gone day. The time had come to lift the curse.

With three-quarters of the Stadio Comunale bathed in the blue/white of Naples, the away side attacked from the kick off. Ably supported by his trusty, swashbuckling Lieutenants, Giordano, Carnevale and Bagni, *El Pibe De Oro* led the charge on Turin's finest. Roared on by their astonishing following, the first half belonged almost exclusively to Napoli as they dominated possession.

Juventus were forced to retreat and defend, but yet, for the away side, it still remained worryingly scoreless. Five minutes after the interval normal service between these two embittered adversaries appeared to be resumed when keeper Claudio Garella could only push away Juve defender Antonio Cabrini's shot, and from six yards the deadly left foot of Michael Laudrup followed up to lash the ball into the net. It was a goal totally against the run of play and a savage kick in the teeth for the visitors. A sickening sense of reality washed over the Neapolitans. How dare they chance to dream? How dare they?

An inherited, fatalistic outlook on life that sprouted from waking up each day in the menacing shade of Vesuvius meant they half expected disaster to strike. Not so much paranoid, but more resigned to inevitable failure. But little could anyone have known what was set to unfold, for stirred by an overwhelming sense of indignation inflicted upon them, not just that day but in years gone by, Ottavio Bianchi's men set about Juventus with unreserved venom. Though no way to treat a lady, *La Vecchia Signora* found herself trampled on as Maradona inspired Napoli to not just take her honour, but more importantly the points.

And so the Neapolitans attacked, driven, sick of failure, determined to rid themselves and their city of this ancient thorn in their sides. Since James Poths and Emilio Anatra took up the mantle many decades ago, SSC Napoli had witnessed some wonderful players, but none held more passion and desire for the cause as those who finally put paid to the curse of the dreaded *Bianconeri* on that November afternoon. On seventy-two minutes Bruno Giordano let fly a crashing twenty-five-yard drive that was tipped magnificently over the bar by Juve goalkeeper Steffano Tacconi. As the clock ticked down the incessant pressure told at last when Tacconi, after making an array of breathtaking saves to keep the Neapolitans out, was finally beaten.

A richly deserved equaliser arrived from a Francesco Romano corner, as the unlikely figure of centre-half Morenio Ferrario stabbed home a shot a from eight yards. Greeted with more relief than joy by the Napoli faithful, they would at least take pride in a point. A minute later from a Maradona corner, Allesandro Renica flicked on for Bruno Giordano to smash a thunderous, arching volley at the far post past Tacconi, and into the realms of Southern legend. Bedlam erupted in the Comunale! A deep-throated roar tinged with Neapolitan dialect rose like a crescendo across the terraces. The great and good of Turin shifted uneasily in their plush seats. This was so much more than just a simple game of football. Lose this match and the genie could well be out of the lamp and free. A shift of power tilting towards a city like Naples was unthinkable for the Northern aristocrats, for whom then would they be able to look down upon?

The blue shirts continued to storm forward. With sheer trickery and pace Diego Maradona ripped past Juve players causing havoc. They wanted more: to win was not sufficient, the weight of history between these two teams demanded a true cleansing of the pain. It came on ninety minutes when the galloping left full-back Giuseppe Volpecina charged upfield to smash the ball low past a forlorn Tacconi to ignite incredible scenes of rejoicing amongst the Napoli supporters. It was a momentous victory. But for Steffano Tacconi, Juve's humiliation could well have been on a scale unthinkable for the final scoreline of 3-1 saw them escape lightly. Not that it mattered to those who ventured to Turin fearing the worse, for in this most unlikely inhospitable and hostile of venues, Neapolitans found paradise. Many stood with tears streaming down their faces, unable to take in the enormity of the victory, one that would live forever in the history of SSC Napoli, and perhaps more importantly, in the hearts of their devoted *tifosi* who were fortunate enough to witness it live. In the eyes of their beloved city they were all heroes for a day.

The Stadio Comunale was theirs alone as the Juventus fans slid away red-faced. They had no desire to witness the gloating and jubilation of the arch-enemy taking place in their midst. An enduring memory of the game was the sight of a track-suited Juve ball boy leaping with delight every time a Napoli goal hit the back of the net, celebrating for all his worth. Lest to say he was later found to be of Neapolitan origin and was not on duty for the next home match in Turin! In a typically sporting gesture a gallant Michel Platini made a point of shaking Maradona's hand before trooping dismally of the pitch. In spite of the gut-churning hatred between their respected cities both men shared a healthy friendship and respect. Platini was struggling with long-term injuries and this proved to be the final season for one of the greatest footballers ever to grace the world scene. He would be missed, but not in Naples! For a changing wind had blown up from the South.

The following day saw the hugely influential *Corriere dello Sport* newspaper jubilantly declare, '*Il Napoli in trionfo!*' ('Naples triumphant!'). The equally prestigious *Gazetta dello Sport* hummed a similar tune, '*Maradona canta Volare!*' ('Maradona sings Volare!'). But this was still a championship fight in its infancy. Napoli were only two points clear of the chasing pack and half a world away from the finishing line. History had taught Neapolitans many things, but none more than that the championship was never won until the final whistle of the season sounded, when your enemy runs out of options and the power to corrupt no longer matters. And yet there was real fear in the North that Napoli would take the title. In Turin and Milan they had already begun to steady themselves for what was slowly becoming the inevitable. For so long Naples had been like a tempestuous, unruly younger brother who though truly talented, was never going to possess the necessary drive and ambition to make anything of his life. But as Diego Maradona conjured up miracles almost on a weekly basis, the question had to be asked. With Juventus struggling and the Milanese unable to mount a serious challenge, just who the hell was going to stop them?

After a welcomed two-week grace for international fixtures, battle recommenced in Serie A on 23rd November when lowly Empoli travelled to Naples fearing a beating, and ultimately receiving one. Waiting for them was a Napoli side fired up to ensure they consolidated their position as league leaders. On a horrendous, damp, rain-lashed Sunday afternoon, with dark clouds hovering gloomily over the bay, Empoli walked into the eye of a Neapolitan storm. Not deterred by the miserable conditions, 85,000 gathered at the San Paolo in typically warlike mood. The anthems of the various clans soared high into the sullen skies, electrifying the arena. Rockets whistled precariously in all directions, blue flares engulfed the terraces. This was Naples! Flags adorned with images and tributes to Maradona lay spread in huge numbers across the stadium. Others spat out insults to their dear friends from the north. One such banner claimed '*Odiamo Tutti*' ('We hate everyone'). This was no idle boast. That all outside their city walls despised them mattered nothing to the hardline *tifosi* who revelled in the notoriety.

In what had become an important pre-match ritual Diego Maradona embraced the club physio Salvatore Carmando before joining Andres Carnevale in the centre-circle to begin the contest. What followed was nothing short of a mismatch as the white shirts of Empoli were ripped to pieces by a Napoli team playing like champions-elect. The early stages saw Maradona create a clear chance for Carnevale with a beautiful flick on, only for him to fluff the opportunity when it appeared easier to score. Shortly after Salvatore Bagni swept a ferocious drive against the bar as the pressure mounted. Endless corners hit by Maradona on the left and the impressive Francesco Romano from the right caused mayhem in the Empoli penalty area with their pinpoint accuracy. Then, the most remarkable miss from Andres Carnevale, who only six yards out with an open net to aim at somehow contrived to shoot wide. Yet to score in the league for Napoli, Carnevale hung his head in despair.

Finally on twenty-six minute the *Capitano* took matters into his own hands and calmed the nerves. A free-kick from the edge of the box by Diego Maradona was curled deliciously out of the goalkeeper Julio Drago's reach and into the top left-hand corner to ignite the San Paolo. The defender Allesandro Renica picked the ball out of the goal and smashed it high into the Naples sky in delight. Drago never had a chance. Suddenly it was vintage

Napoli: another free-kick, this time thirty-five-yards out. Maradona fooled all in the arena as instead of letting fly, he passed short to Renica who flashed in a left foot shot that Drago tipped spectacularly round the post. Still they came: a majestic volley from Romano foiled only by an equally remarkable stop from the under siege Julio Drago. Fiesta football!

With the Neapolitans in full cry another goal had to come and on the stroke of half-time Andres Carnevale opened his account when he ran clear to fire the ball past the beleaguered Empoli keeper. It became a question of how many as the second period went much the same as the first. A third came on sixty-eight minutes when Maradona and Bruno Giordano combined beautifully for Carnevale to grab another with a far post header. Minutes later a wonderful pass from the inventive Romano was finished with a touch of class by Bagni who drilled a terrific left shot past a totally fed-up Drago. Four goals to the good, and all that remained before the final curtain closed at the San Paolo on an exhilarating showing, was for Diego Maradona to perform a last encore.

First was an astonishing back flick that bewildered two Empoli players, for he produced it in mid-air! Then came the main event. Maradona dribbled past one white shirted defender, and as another rushed in to challenge, he dragged the ball clear, controlled with his instep before spinning a remarkable pirouette and speeding away downfield. The church of *El Pibe De Oro* rose as one to salute yet another moment of wizardry. These were heady days in Naples. The Napoli *tifosi* prayed this time round that a happy ending awaited, for there had been enough tears shed over the decades. There was only so many times that a city and its people could be made to suffer. Surely if there was a God, he would prove merciful and end Neapolitan torment? '*Dio Fai Miracoli*'('God works wonders'). Another year in Purgatory or the Promised Land?

Naples pondered its fate over the coming months, for if there were a cause likely to unite the warring clans of the mighty North it would be one that meant denying them the honour of a first *Scudetto*. An unholy alliance was forged with regional feuds temporarily forgotten as Milan, Turin, Florence, Verona and others plotted to bring down SSC Napoli. The mere suggestion of Diego Maradona and his ragged band of Southern *Terroni*, bandits and thieves all, disappearing with the title into the badlands of the Mezzogiorno caused shudders in the Northern corridors of power. The cry went forth to return the Neapolitans from where they came. At the heel of Italy's boot. But had the genie already slipped through their fingers?

On Sunday 4th January 1987, hostilities resumed after the shutdown for the Christmas holidays, and even before the decorations had come down in Naples their lead had vanished. The league leaders restarted their campaign in *la citta dei fior* (the city of flowers). There was no more beautiful city in all of Italy then Florence. Here amidst the splendour of this medieval, architectural masterpiece of spellbinding cathedrals and priceless art galleries, Napoli's title dreams were given a vicious jolt of reality with a 3-1 thrashing by Fiorentina. A capacity crowd at the Stadio Artemio Franchi exploded in joy as their beloved *Viola* hit the Neapolitans with a lightning two-goal blast in the opening half hour that left them on the floor.

Strikes from former Napoli player, Argentinian centre forward Ramon Diaz and Florence legend, *L'Angelo Viola*, Giancarlo Antognoni, hero of the Fiorentine terraces, left Ottavio Bianchi's men looking shell-shocked. The shots rained in on Claudio Garella as the Neapolitans somehow survived to half-time without conceding another. The elegant midfield maestro Antognoni had controlled midfield and carved the traumatic visitors apart with an exquisite display. His adoring followers sang in tribute, '*Voi vincente lo Scudetto, ma noi abbiamo Antognoni!*' ('You may win the title, but we have Antognoni!') A fuming Bianchi ripped into his team during the interval for their lacklustre showing, demanding more from his below-par players. If the ultimate prize was to be won they could not afford performances like they had just given.

Five minutes into the second period his harsh words reaped dividends when a revitalised Diego Maradona swooped to end a fine sweeping move with a clever finish at the near post. Eclipsed in the first half by the sublime Giancarlo Antognoni, Maradona suddenly began to play as only he seemed capable. But despite the re-emergence of their *Capitano*, it was the home side who looked more likely to score again. All hopes of gaining a point disappeared in the dying moments when with Napoli throwing everybody forward, including their goalkeeper, Fiorentina's Paolo Monelli broke and hit a wondrous drive from his own half over the head of Claudio Garella to deservedly seal the win. An embarrassed Garella stood red faced as the ball flew into his goal. The fervid celebrations of the Florence *tifosi* behind the goal in the Curva Fiesole verged wildly towards euphoria as they erupted into a passionate rendition of their club anthem *A Lei Fiorentina*.

The downbeat Neapolitans filed out of the stadium, embarrassed at their team's inept showing. Where was their heart for a fight? Maybe they were just like the rest over the years that had kissed the badge, but come the moment of truth failed to deliver. Elsewhere Juventus and a rejuvenated Inter Milan under Trapattoni won to close the two-point gap. The dramatic scenes of their supporters rejoicing on hearing news of Napoli's defeat in the Artemio Franchi, matched easily the ecstatic *Viola* following who danced in delight long after the final whistle had blown. It was a Northern thing! Game on! So began from that moment a race to the finishing line. Along the way Napoli would be pushed, elbowed and knocked from their stride, but could they remain standing? For their many enemies were after them with a vengeance.

In a post-match press conference Ottavio Bianchi issued a war cry by claiming that his players possessed the necessary 'courage and heart' to bounce back from this defeat, '*ll corragio, ll cuore*'. Seven days later Napoli responded to their manager's comments in the best possible fashion as they hammered relegation haunted Ascoli 3-0 in the San Paolo. After intense pressure the goals finally came in the second half with twenty-three-year-old local boy Ciro Muro breaking the deadlock on the hour. Fellow midfielders Romano and a late strike from Salvatore Bagni once more put Napoli two points clear as Inter crashed at Verona. So much for Northern brotherhood, as sometimes the urge to bash your neighbour proved just that little bit too tempting! How the Neapolitans laughed as maybe, just maybe Diego Maradona's promise to Giuseppe Bruscolotti to deliver the *Scudetto* was set to be realised. But then a history littered with heartache and disasters meant nothing was taken for granted. They had blown it before and few would have been surprised if it happened again.

CHAPTER 14

TOUCHING HEAVEN

But still they feared to dream! In Naples many of the elder and most hard-bitten supporters of SSC Napoli refused to even contemplate the idea of their team winning the championship. Their lives had been full of endless torment, the scars of disappointment and betrayal suffered over torturous seasons past. An epic saga of heartache and tears that if ever put to music would have graced the most tragic of Italian operas. A living nightmare, but one that they were agonisingly close to being awoken from. Touching Heaven? Night would soon turn to day in Naples in a most extraordinary way.

'When Maradona drank the grass'. Spring came and as March showed its sunny face Sampdoria travelled south to Naples eager to throw a rusty spanner in Neapolitan title hopes. A full house in a hostile San Paolo raged with passion and furore. Some indulged themselves by burning an Inter Milan flag for the benefit of television cameras. However they were shocked into silence on thirty minutes when the visitors, through their whiplash forward Lorenzo, had the temerity to take the lead. Lorenzo smashed home past Napoli keeper Claudio Garella from eight yards. Moments later he should have scored again, only to blaze wide when faced with just Garella to beat. The home side appeared fraught with nerves, never had the stakes been higher. The game restarted and immediately Diego Maradona in typically mesmerising fashion received possession, a jink, a turn, look up, pass, then in the blink of an eye he was gone, marauding. The fanatical *tifosi* of Napoli watched his every move, their eyes forever upon him. He was their world, every waking hour, Maradona, their food and drink, lust for life. Nothing mattered but *El Rei* (The King). How had they survived so long without him? Diego Maradona once claimed that with the ball at his feet he had the power to dim the sun. Few in Naples at the time who watched him ply his remarkable talents would have disagreed.

Six minutes later the long legs of Napoli's adventurous full-back Giuseppe Volpecina tore menacingly down the left touchline. Glancing up Volpecina clipped a fine cross into the Sampdoria penalty area that screamed out for a blue shirt to attack it. As the San Paolo held its breath Maradona broke like lightning from his marker and hurtled himself low to the ground to thunder a wonderfully-placed driven header past keeper Pellegrini into the net. How the Argentinian ever reached the ball with it being so close to the turf, never mind score, was itself miraculous. *El Pibe De Oro* had once more cast a spell to bewitch his followers and make them dance like madmen on the grand old steeped tiers of this footballing cathedral.

Where their *Grande Protagonist* (Great Hero) was concerned Neapolitans had grown accustomed to Maradona's sublime genius and wizardry illuminating every Sunday afternoon at the San Paolo; maybe even a little blasé. But on the 1st March 1987 it became apparent that strange powers were at work under the all-seeing eye of great Grandfather Vesuvius. A goal to be forever cherished and immortalised in Neapolitan folklore as the time 'Maradona drank the grass!' In this captivating city of extremes that gave birth to the legendary child puppet Pulcinella, later to become famous as a lovelorn accomplice to the *femme fatale* Judy, Diego Maradona had again proved there was never a show without Punch! A 1-1 draw was earned and the Neapolitans remained four clear.

Next stop yet another perilous trek up-country, this time to the region of Lombardia and the city of Bergamo to take on relegation-threatened Atalanta. The *tifosi* of Atalanta viewed the Neapolitans with the same sneering contempt as the followers of Milan, Turin and Verona. Sat in indignant isolation on the far northern Italian border the people of Bergamo had little time for its own pompous near-neighbours, but even less for the Southern rabble who trampled across the length of Italy plundering highway supermarkets and arriving on their precious streets not scared to pick a fight. And how they would always get one! The black and blue brigade of the Atalanta hardcore forever willing to show the Neapolitans some true Northern hospitality.

At the Stadio Atleti Azzurri d'Italia, in front of a packed house of 27,000, set against a dramatic, if disturbing background of wailing police sirens, baton charges, choking tear gas and violent scenes of all-out tribal warfare erupting on the terraces, Bruno Giordano kept his nerve to hand SSC Napoli a priceless 1-0 win. A mesmeric dribble by Maradona left three Atalanta players for dead before he crossed for Giordano to crash the ball high into the net at the near post. The thousands who had endured the treacherous journey to roar their teams on were doubly ecstatic when news filtered through that sworn enemy Juventus had been held to a shock draw at home to Ascoli and Inter had been thrashed 3-1 in Genoa against Sampdoria. Though hardly out of sight, they were well clear as the win in Bergamo stretched Napoli's lead to five points. The chasing wolf pack gnashed their teeth, spitting blood. The Southerners stood on the verge of a monumental achievement, for barring a collapse of biblical proportions, the *Scudetto* was going south. Though not yet won, the title was for the first time ever harder to lose. Then again no one in Naples required a history lesson.

Beware the Ides of March: With each week the title becoming more of a reality Neapolitans from across the globe were drawn back to their blood country. For the game against Inter Milan at the San Siro a huge Napoli banner bearing the words, '*Forza Napoli New York*' flew high and proud. In a ferocious encounter against the wily Giovanni Trapattoni's Inter, the game ended in despair for Napoli five minutes from time when Milanese defender Guiseppe Bergomi smashed home from five yards out to hand the *Neazzurri* a crucial 1-0 win. Terrible marking in the visitors' defence was punished in the cruellest manner possible. But in a fascinating battle of wits between *Il Trap* and Ottavio Bianchi, the Neapolitans looked to have saved a point with the last kick of the game when Diego Maradona's flick-on found Bruno Giordano, only to see his header magnificently tipped over the bar at close range by Inter keeper Ferri. The final whistle blew. Amidst rabid abuse and smouldering smoke bombs, the Southerners lead was reduced back to three points. Suddenly with eight games remaining, and Juventus along with the rapidly-emerging Roma winning to pile intense pressure on Maradona and his team, all was still to play for. Before the gates of Heaven were entered an unholy trilogy of matches against three of their most despised rivals awaited the Neapolitans. Juventus, Hellas Verona and AC Milan. There lay their fate. First up was a date with an 'Old Lady' in Naples.

It had been a dismal first season for Juve coach Rino Marchesi. The former Napoli man was hardly helped by the unusually insipid form of his flamboyant midfield maestro Michel Platini, who had struggled throughout the campaign. The thirty-two-year-old Platini still possessed all his characteristic flair, but physically he was on the wane. A succession of bad injuries had gradually taken their toll. For five seasons the Frenchman graced the footballing arenas of Serie A with breathtaking artistry in the black and white, winning a treasure chest of medals and trophies. Two *Scudetto*s, a European Cup, the Cup Winners' Cup, Supercup, the Intercontinental Cup and the *Coppa Italia*. A remarkable record.

A unique treble haul of European Footballer of the Year awards and also three-times top scorer in the Italian league meant Michel Platini would be forever remembered in Turin as a true legend. Sadly for Juve, as the showdown in Naples dawned, the swashbuckling Platini's fire was in its dying embers. Only a flicker of the spark remained. The heart and mind were willing but the body said no. The owner of Juventus and self-styled king of Turin, Gianni Agnelli once said of Platini with whom he became close friends that 'We bought him for the price of a bread loaf but Michel was like caviar.' The *tifosi* of *La Vecchia Signora* prayed that their beloved number ten had enough left for a final swansong in Naples. But the days of wine and roses were over.

The *Bianconeri's* reign as champions hung by the most slender of threads. For the mighty Juventus to relinquish the crown in of all places, Naples, was considered to be an *aberrazione* (aberration). Unthinkable. A humiliation to compare with the ragged bloodthirsty peasants of the French Revolution staging public executions of the aristocracy. The Neapolitans sharpened their guillotine, they had waited a long time for such a mouthwatering scenario. A win for Napoli would enhance their dreams of glory and finish off the challenge of a team who had tortured them since the dawn of time.

As if lit by a rush of electrical current, a rain-lashed San Paolo hissed, fizzed and crackled with nervous anticipation, its wide-open terraces awash with blue and white as smoke bombs the colour of Naples erupted like thunder, engulfing both ends of the stadium. Then from the bowels of the arena the sides appeared to do battle in Serie A's match of the season. As the teams warmed up the ever-likeable Marchesi, in a long trenchcoat, chatted amicably to the Neapolitan groundstaff who appeared genuinely happy to meet up again and shake the hand of their former manager. In comparison a grim-faced Ottavio Bianchi, in a grey bubble jacket, wore his normal hound dog expression as he took his seat on the home bench. Bianchi's stern features were etched in concentration for the task ahead. For him, smiling was a rarity that only showed itself when he grimaced.

Rino Marchesi chose to man-mark Diego Maradona with the experienced, tough defender Luciano Favero. The twenty-nine-year-old Favero carried on his broad shoulders the hopes of the majority outside Naples' walls in his task to tame the Argentinian. Immediately Napoli went on the attack with local boy Luigi Cafferelli roaring down the right wing and raiding full-back Volpecina rampaging on the left. Juve were forced back in the early stages as the Neapolitans swarmed all over them with swift, incisive attacking play. Whenever they attempted to keep possession a cacophony of wolf whistles and a hail of boos swept down from the terraces. To the delight of the home crowd Michel Platini's attempts to break the siege failed when two of his normally accurate long passes went astray. It would be a long and weary day for the Frenchman.

On fourteen minutes Juventus defender Manfredonia hacked down Napoli's bustling centre-forward Bruno Giordano thirty yards from goal and found himself fiercely lectured by teammate Caricola for giving away a free-kick in such a dangerous position. For this was *Pibe De Oro* territory. Taking up his predictable place, Maradona fooled all and tapped the ball sideways for sweeper Allessandro Renica to fire a shot, skidding low under a woefully blundering Steffano Tacconi that sneaked like a thief in the night over the line. On a rain-sodden surface the keeper's mistake was perhaps understandable, if not appreciated by his seething Juve teammates who lambasted him. It was an error unacceptable in games of this magnitude with so much at stake. As the huge San Paolo electric scoreboard flashed up 'goal, goal, goal, goal, goal', a red-faced Steffano Tacconi hung his head in shame, praying for the ground to open and swallow him up. Naples was unforgiving on being handed the opportunity to taunt their fiercest tormentors, for it happened so rarely.

The game belonged to Napoli as Bagni, De Napoli and Romano in midfield outclassed their Turin counterparts. A scheming Maradona probed in typically menacing fashion on the edge of danger, threatening a killer pass or a scything one-two. Forever a second away from causing a riot, lurking ominously, patiently, stalking his prey. Everytime a Juve move broke down the Neapolitans sped away on fearful counter-attacks. The blue of Napoli sprang forward and the striped shirts of Juve trailed in their wake like chasing rabbits! On the touchline Rino Marchesi's pre-match, happy-go-lucky demeanour was replaced by that of a man watching his house burn down. The nightmare continued as a ridiculously sloppy back pass from an out-of-sorts Platini was latched onto by Giordano whose rasping drive was turned away for a corner by Tacconi. Michel Platini tried desperately to make amends for his own below-par showing when he skipped past three tackles, but could only watch in despair as his shot flew hopelessly high over Claudio Garella's goal. An animated Marchesi screamed instructions to his inspirational Captain Gaetano Scirea as Juventus earned a much-needed respite with a corner kick. From this Aldo Serena missed by a whisker from eight yards out as he turned and lashed a shot inches wide of Garella's goal. Given the chance they were still dangerous.

As the half-time whistle dawned Platini produced a sprinkling of magic to make space and deliver a wonderful cross into the Neapolitan area for Serena. With time to spare the much-lauded Turin marksman miskicked and was forced to watch in abject horror as the ball bobbled horribly away from him to be cleared by a Napoli defender's relieved boot. Showing full vent to his troubled state of mind, Michel Platini launched a tirade of abuse at his young colleague who looked on non-plussed. The San Paolo was no stage for a Juventus legend such as he to show his frustration as the laughter and mirth that greeted the Frenchman's tirade confirmed. The second period began with the slavishly incessant Neapolitan war cry of 'Diego, Diego' resonating in passionate tones over the vast open terraces and beyond. Maradona as ever responded immediately to this call to arms by slashing through a bevy of Juve shirts to lay off a pass for Francesco Romano to let fly a vicious twenty-yard strike, saved spectacularly by Tacconi. The keeper leapt somewhat dramatically through mid-air to grasp the shot to his midriff as if to show the mocking Naples crowd what he was truly capable of. Sadly for him they already had his measure and simply responded to such histrionics with ironic cheers and sarcastic applause. Steffano Tacconi's card was already marked.

With the normally so cool Marchesi caught up in the frenetic atmosphere of the occasion and reduced to a fraught figure frantically shouting orders from the dug-out, Juventus showed only remnants of their true class. But they were not champions for nothing and Platini strode elegantly forward to lash a fine long-range effort tipped inches wide of the post by Garella. To howls of derision around the ground the Old Lady regained albeit, for a short time, her normally regal composure. The seventeen-year-old Juve prodigy Sergio Buso produced a wonderful dragback on the edge of the Napoli penalty area to create space and play in an advancing Michel Platini on the right wing. Platini's inch-perfect cross towards the near post was met superbly by the glancing head of Serena who stooped to head past Claudio Garella with true flourish. 1-1.

Aldo Serena soared jubilantly over the advertising boards, only to find himself surrounded by hordes of angry Neapolitan officials, photographers and policemen appearing less than pleased with his antics on Naples' soil. Behind that same goal in the Curva South, many of Napoli's hardcore *tifosi*, (the South Boys) stood ready to greet the Juve player into their midst with a frightful relish. Realising immediately he had overstayed his welcome, Serena wisely skipped back onto the pitch to continue celebrations with delighted teammates who shrewdly had not followed him beyond the relative safety of the white line. The South Boys shrugged their shoulders. A close shave for Aldo Serena.

Just when all in the San Paolo expected Juventus to take control of the match it was Napoli who shrugged off their disappointment to lift themselves and pin back the visitors with a barrage of frenzied assaults. Ottavio Bianchi had acted fast in bringing on Andres Carnevale to link with Giordano and Maradona. The coach's intent was clear, to attack and seize back the initiative. Sensing panic amongst the ranks, Juve *Capitano* Scirea raged at his fellow defenders, imploring them not to lose concentration as the home blue shirts swarmed, darted and dashed with increasing menace. As the pressure mounted, it was inevitably Diego Maradona who engineered a route through. His beautifully clipped cross was flicked on by the powerful Giordano to the far post, where substitute Carnevale pounced to scramble the ball back across goal for Francesco Romano to smash home. Naples went mad! Bianchi again moved fast as he made another tactical switch. Off came Giordano to a rapturous reception from the Napoli faithful, and to tumultuous acclaim around the stadium Napoli stalwart Giuseppe Bruscolotti came off the bench to enter the fray and add fire and fury to the Napoli backline. The mean-faced Bruscolotti sprinted towards his position, an ominous proposition for any Juve attacker faced with the gruesome task of beating him.

The remainder of the game was played out in a fervid atmosphere of desperation as SSC Napoli fought tenaciously to protect their slender lead. The tension dipped and rose alarmingly as Juve roused themselves for a last ditch attempt to save their season. Neapolitan hearts were placed firmly in mouths when a reckless Renica foolishly gave away a free-kick on the edge of his own area that allowed Michel Platini the opportunity to save face for Juventus. An unholy silence gripped the San Paolo as Platini lashed in a shot that rebounded off the Napoli wall, only to deflect back and awarding him a second chance. This time the Frenchman let fly a fierce low drive that flew inches wide of the post. Naples took a huge gasp of air, a collective sigh of relief. So often in the past this man had broken their hearts. Secretly they admired Platini; Neapolitans knew their football, but that wasn't to say they did not hate him with a vengeance also.

In the closing moments a poignant, maybe even tragic incident in the centre circle occurred that confirmed Michel Platini's star had finally fallen from the skies. Receiving possession, Platini found himself literally mugged by a blaze of blue shirts that left him slumped unceremoniously on his backside as they sped away with the ball. The Frenchman remained on the turf with his head between his knees. Surely at that instance, this once great footballer decided the time had come to say *au revoir*, leave them wanting more: the roar of the crowds, bathed in magical memories and adulation. A legend of *La Vecchia Signora*. To vacate the arena, kicking and screaming, dragged off, embarrassed, red-faced, was unacceptable. Platini did exit stage right at the end of that season in the same manner he played his football, with typical class and poise. But all mattered little on that long gone day in Naples. For to all present it had become blatantly obvious that *Il Francese* (The Frenchman) Michel Platini was yesterday's news.

Off soared Napoli on a lightning counter-attack with the lung bursting Giuseppe Volpecina careering away down the wing in full, spectacular, looping stride. With Juventus defenders left chasing in his wake the exciting Volpecina looked up and hit a magnificent ball for Diego Maradona to launch himself through the air with a diving header at the far post, only to be foiled by a remarkable reflex save by Tacconi at the last. A breathtaking slice of football by all! The dying seconds of the game saw Juve camped inside the Napoli half, but it was not to be their day. A sea of exploding blue and white at the final whistle swept over the San Paolo. News elsewhere that championship rivals Inter Milan had been held to a draw by Torino and that Roma had lost at Udinese meant the lead was stretched to five points with just six games remaining. The hero of the hour, Francesco Romano, found himself mobbed at the end by his fellow players and a colourful array of Neapolitan characters that found their way onto the pitch to join in the revelry. Napoli President Corrado Ferlaino had watched the game unfold from the touchline, he himself near to nervous exhaustion as *Lo Scudetto* grew so close it could almost be smelt.

The whiff of success drifted through the Naples air. The President stood on the verge of immortality as the man who stood at the helm when Napoli conquered all. His ego was such that he could simply not let such an opportunity pass. As the cameras rolled and photographers clicked away, President Ferlaino lapped up the limelight. After the legendary 3-1 win in Turin a historic double was achieved over the Old Lady that itself demanded celebrations of previously unheard of magnitude. But uncharacteristically the city failed to soar into carnival mood, for there remained a haunting reluctance to indulge whole-heartedly when the nightmare scenario of everything being lost at the last still existed. Of the games left to play for SSC Napoli an arduous journey north to Verona taking on the despised Hellas stood out by far as the most difficult. But with their team in such fine form the Napoli *tifosi* felt convinced of returning home with a decent result to all but clinch the *Scudetto*. But disaster once more was set to befall them.

To the disgust of their manager and supporters SSC Napoli went meekly like lambs to the slaughter at Verona. A shambolic first half performance littered with slack passing and frightful defensive errors were seized upon and punished lethally by a rampant home team that scored three times without reply. In a hair-raising atmosphere of unrelenting hatred and vitriol at the Stadio Bentegodi, Osvaldo Bagnoli's Veronese ripped through the nervy Neapolitans with bloodcurdling relish. Ottavio Bianchi watched on horrified as his side, to the sheer delight of a yellow and blue-drenched Bentegodi arena found themselves put to the sword like Christians of old in the Coliseum. Could it have been that fate had decided they were born to suffer? A murderous rout ensued. Amidst countless close shaves and near misses in the Napoli area, a bullet header from Verona midfielder Pacione, allied to a wicked deflection off Allesandro Renica for a second goal, stunned the Neapolitans. A penalty converted in clinical manner past Garella five minutes from half-time by Verona legend Preben Elkjaer, put the game well beyond the away side. A second period was made worse by news of Inter going in front at Avellino through Allesandro Altobelli to hand them a 1-0 win and cut the Southerners lead back again to just two points. A bad day had by all of Neapolitan persuasion.

The Veronese hardcore of the Brigate Gialloblu taunted their rivals with a song hated by the Southerners, '*Senta che puzza, scappano anchi i cani. Sono arrivati i Napoletani*' ('Get that smell, even the dogs are running. The Neapolitans are coming'). Hitting back in archetypal fashion the travelling Napoli *ultras* unfurled a banner to warm Naples' hearts and to enrage their hosts ('Veronese, Guinea pigs from laboratory!') And so as their team laid down and died on the pitch, Neapolitan honour was seen to be served as all-out war ensued off it, on the terraces and outside the stadium. Following the match horrific scenes of violence erupted on the streets of Verona with thirty-eight of Napoli persuasion arrested. Luckily as the fighting raged no one was killed, but it was not for the want of trying on both sides. Two cities, two tribes, two worlds apart.

As the season drew towards its dramatic finale the humiliation endured in Verona caused many Napoli *tifosi* to question the team's mental toughness in being able to hold their nerve. Even Diego Maradona, *El Rei*, was not immune from the finger pointing and criticism as feeling ran high in Naples following the unacceptable surrender against the Veronese. Doubts were raised regarding where Maradona's priorities lay as he flitted constantly between Naples and Buenos Aires to be at the side of his heavily pregnant girlfriend. The Argentinian refused point blank all orders to remain in Italy and on the 11th April 1987 Diego Armando Maradona and Claudia Villafane were blessed with a baby daughter whom they named Dalma. Whilst Maradona was in Argentina, intoxicated with the joy of playing happy families, back on his adopted soil Neapolitans fretted about their King's state of mind. There loomed large one of the most important matches in Napoli's history against AC Milan at the San Paolo. It was a game they had to win, anything other than two points could well have proved disastrous with Trapattoni's Inter smelling Neapolitan fear and moving in for the kill. Never had they been so near, yet frustratingly so far away. The city of Naples needed *El Rei* like never before.

Coming into land at Naples International Airport, the luxurious private jet carrying Diego Maradona and his entourage back to Southern Italy from Argentina veered low over Mount Vesuvius and all aboard gazed down into the hypnotic, mysterious, foreboding crater of the volcano's dark heart. The legendary poet Goethe once wrote of Vesuvius, 'a peak of hell rising out of paradise'. A terrifying black abyss that one day, nobody yet knows when, would erupt and destroy all who lived their lives in its deadly shadow. The Argentinian was not in the best of moods. Well aware of the mudslinging hurled towards him by non-believers during his absence, Maradona viewed such talk as a slap in the face and a blatant lack of respect after all he had given for the Neapolitan cause.

In an interview for a British television company working on a documentary of Napoli's title challenge, he let his tormentors have it with both barrels. Stung and hurt, Maradona opened his heart. 'Naples is a beautiful city but it has lots of negative aspects too. I don't like Neapolitans worshipping me more than they would their own mother or God. I honestly don't understand that attitude. I also think they are wrong in claiming Naples is the most beautiful city in the world. I just disagree. Naples could be far more pleasant if its inhabitants were more disciplined but, Neapolitans will be Neapolitans. Maradona has not travelled fourteen thousand miles to come and correct their faults. I simply have to accept this way of life. It is not up to me to say anything; okay, every Sunday I do my bit to make them as happy as possible, but that is all.' So much for unrequited love?

The sacred church of San Paolo was agitated as a strange sense of foreboding gripped its packed nerve-wrecked congregation. A full house of tortured souls feared the worse. *Déjà vu*, they had been here before. So many times in the past SSC Napoli had been dealt a decent hand only for them to play the wrong card and lose all. The *tifosi* prayed, pleading with the Holy Saints for it not to happen again. Come the Sunday morning of the game and churches across the city heaved with Neapolitans desperate to gain an edge. Naples eternal twelfth man, San Gennaro, was forced to work overtime as the fantasy of *Lo Scudetto* loomed ever closer. The sides led by their two great Captains Diego Maradona and the regal figure of Milanese sweeper Franco Baresi entered the arena. Amidst scenes of bedlam Maradona cut a fraught sight, full of nervous energy as he limbered up with a rapid succession of feverish quick sprints. Surrounded as ever by hustling crowds of snapping cameramen and photographers *El Pibe De Oro* bore the look of a man with a point to prove, his face etched in total concentration for the job ahead. How dare they doubt him, for he was Maradona and he would show them all.

On forty-three minutes Diego Armando once more had the Neapolitans claiming they were not worthy and falling in worship at his feet. Napoli were already one up with a goal scored by the head of Andres Carnevale, when the *Capitano* produced yet another beguiling moment of genius. Showing wonderful skill and technique, Maradona swept past Baresi and his defenders before exquisitely rounding Galli in the Milan goal to fire into the net. Crowds who had gathered to watch on television in the alleyways, houses, bars and cafés across the bay erupted as *El Rei* raced towards his adoring subjects in the stadium to receive their acclaim. Speaking later after the game, one

135

Neapolitan trying desperately to sum up the magnitude of the Argentinian's worth to Naples claimed, 'We should have known better. You cannot criticize Maradona for in doing so you criticize God. And you cannot criticize God because he is above all else.'

Napoli's Giordano should have wrapped the points up when his header from close range flashed against the bar. Then, what had appeared a comfortable victory suddenly turned into total panic when, with eleven minutes remaining, Milan's centre-forward Pietro Virdis beat Garella from a wide angle to silence the San Paolo rigid. As the scoreboard flashed up news of Inter going in front at home to Fiorentina, the atmosphere on the terraces became increasingly tense. If the *rossoneri* managed an equaliser in Naples and Trapattoni's men managed to win then SSC Napoli's lead would have been cut to a single point with just three games left to play. With nothing to lose AC Milan threw caution to the wind and swept forward in droves. How sweet for them to watch the Southern *Terroni* sweat buckets of fear as their team struggled under the Milanese onslaught. It was considered the lesser of two great evils in helping their fierce local rivals win the championship. With many hardly able to watch happenings on the pitch, there was great relief for a home crowd verging on nervous exhaustion as the final whistle blew. A situation had arisen that meant in just a week's time Napoli would be crowned champions if they won at Como and results elsewhere went their way. In Naples the red, green and white of the *Scudetto* badge was being etched onto thousands of decorative souvenirs ready for this moment of ultimate triumph. Neapolitan confidence was at an all time high that the title was finally coming south and the biggest celebration in their city's history was imminent.

Close to ten thousand Napoli *tifosi* descended like a plague of blue locust upon the idyllic mountainous surroundings of the northern lakes. From first light the massed ragged hordes reached the beautifully picturesque Como. Many took the opportunity to rest on the tree-lined banks of the lakes and catch up on some much needed sleep after an exhausting twelve-hour journey from Naples. The tranquillity and clean air of Como was a stark contrast for lads used to the noise and humdrum of their own city. Appalling poverty, the backstreet stench of rotting garbage, choking pollution from car exhausts of the never-ending traffic jams. The *Camorra*.

The seemingly never-ending lines of cars and coaches entering Como from the south, laden deep with singing, unwanted so-called *Terroni*, began to cause concern to the local authorities who realised this was no ordinary travelling entourage of football fans. It was an invasion: Naples North! Extra

Carabinieri special units were drafted in from surrounding areas to ensure the visitors were kept in hand. *Polizia* helicopters buzzed constantly above the town, watching for the slightest hint of unrest. An almighty Southern army from the badlands of the Mezzogiorno on the march and in every Northerner's face. Armed to the teeth with weapons of faith, hope and Diego Armando Maradona, the Neapolitans came, saw and conquered, the songs anthemic, memorable and tragic. Many *tifosi* in quiet moments found time to call on their Patron for divine inspiration. As kick-off drew agonisingly near, sirens wailed and tensions reached fever pitch an ancient silent prayer was whispered, '*San Gennaro aiutaci tu!*' ('San Gennaro please help us!'). This was a club like no other. Touching heaven.

Molte Grazie Carnevale! On the lakeside in the small but electrifying surroundings of the Stadio Guiseppe Sinigaglia, SSC Napoli fought out a priceless 1-1 draw to ensure only a point was needed to win the championship on home ground in seven days' time. But it had been a gruelling afternoon for the away team when after a determined but nervy showing they found themselves a goal down on the hour and facing disaster. But inspired by a fired-up Maradona, Napoli drew a veil over the disgrace of Verona to lash back. The Argentinan had foraged throughout, kicked and slashed at senseless but never yielding. From the occupied terraces of the Sinigaglia the *tifosi* laid true their feelings as 'Diego, Diego, Diego' thundered out over the stadium and across the vast Lake Como.

Only fourteen minutes remained to play when history was made and Andres Carnevale controlled the ball on his thigh six yards out to lash the ball into the net and send the sweating, praying but forever vocal Southern legions delirious. In that instant the dream became real and all of Italy prepared for the inevitable. The home fans watched on incredulous at the antics and mad hysteria breaking out amongst the followers from Naples. Outside the ground thousands of Napoli *tifosi* without tickets and denied access exploded in joy. Even President Ferlaino received a kiss off an ecstatic Neapolitan as celebrations raged. But it was surely understandable, for never had a goal by SSC Napoli been greeted in such fashion as that of Carnevale's. Heaven on Earth loomed large, so why not go mad? Even the eternally dismal features of Ottavio Bianchi, whom it was said never even smiled on his own wedding photographs, leapt high in delight at seeing the ball hit the net. Come the final whistle Bianchi punched the air, for he knew! Nobody would beat them in Naples, not now. Back in their home city mayhem reigned! With no television coverage of the game crowds stood together huddled round rigged-up radios on every street corner, listening with eyes shut, imagining the action and fingers crossed.

Elsewhere, to make the day beyond reproach, Inter were humiliated 1-0 at relegation-battling Ascoli to all but end their title challenge. In a blinding thick mist of flares igniting high above the Como skyline, Diego Maradona, Captain of Napoli led his teammates over to thank their supporters for what had been a remarkable turnout. Maradona appeared overwhelmed by the emotion of the occasion, his eyes welling with tears. The quest for *Lo Scudetto* was almost at an end, *El Pibe De Oro* was set to lead the Neapolitans into the Promised Land. Everything would be decided in the San Paolo.

MARADONA IS BETTER THAN PELÉ:
Napoli tifosi

This team has bought this one,
this team has bought that one,
but this man is a small devil,
and you need more than one hundred men to stop him.
Maradona is better than Pelé,
They made us such a big ass to let us hold him!
Maradona, let us dream,
take a Scudetto to this city,
Maradona, has it and he gives it,
He strikes you, inebriates you, and then he scores...
Maradona, you are already of Naples,
You are the water that lets us live.
Maradona, now that you are here,
Please erase all the shame about this city.
Maradona, you can't fail,
For us you are a brother, father and mother.
Maradona we are in your hands.
If it does not happen now, it won't happen in the future,
We can't wait anymore,
Finally we can revenge,
We can't wait anymore
...We can't wait anymore.'

CHAPTER 15

BELLA GIORNATA
(BEAUTIFUL DAY)

Sunday 10th May 1987: Never had a night passed so agonisingly slow for Neapolitans. Finally, as a blazing sun rose on the far horizon, illuminating fishing boats lost only seconds before on a black sea, the most beautiful morning dawned in Naples to begin a day unlike any in the history of this most put-upon, vilified, but always charismatic city. In churches and cathedrals, services began early with priests rushing through sermons, knowing well the hearts and minds of normally subservient congregations lay for once elsewhere. Outside sacred walls the noise and furore of Napoli tifosi bellowed loudly, forcing devoted men of the cloth into shouting out the word of God over Naples' own Earth-bound saviour. Maradona!

Hiding their precious blue Napoli shirts beneath angelic white flowing gowns, pensive altar boys glanced nervously at watches as the mass rumbled eternally on. Spluttered coughs from a clearly agitated audience, shuffling uneasily with prayer books, made it apparent that the urge to pray was overtaken by the overwhelming desire to indulge in more earthly pleasures. Sometimes even the Almighty had to be put in his place. SSC Napoli were calling, it was time to head for the San Paolo, as for once the harvest had responded well and not reaped a bitter crop. There would be music, dancing, song and wine as every Neapolitan was handed the indeniable right to go crazy for a day. That they did so with such gusto and energy surprised few as the city partied like it was the end of the world.

Bakers set up stalls under lemon groves to shelter from the sun. They gave away *spaghetti allo Scudetto*! White and green pasta with red sauce. The back streets of Naples were awash with expectation, her ancient monuments, statues, crumbling tenements and churches festooned with swaggering displays of Napoli colours draped proudly. Naples' narrow, poverty-stricken sunless alleys splashed with joyful masses of light blue bunting and flags as the city prepared to self-explode. Every building anointed, nothing was missed, for this was a carnival the likes of Naples had never before experienced. Sixty-one torturous years of being pilloried, laughed at, cheated, abused and mocked. The festival rolled and revenge was sweet on those who had indulged so wholeheartedly in Napoli's misery. Riotous scenes of unheralded revelry descended upon a people whose spontaneity, passion and happy-go-lucky approach to life had helped them survive the despairing hardships of their every waking hour. The time came to unlock the chains and go mad!

Of the chasing pack only Inter Milan were left to offer a challenge, though even they clung by the most slender of threads. Inter trailed by three points with only two games remaining. It would have taken a catastrophe of biblical proportions for the Neapolitans to be dragged back into sight. A single point was all Napoli needed against Fiorentina to take the title. No one in the city dared doubt that the most momentous time in their history was just a few hours away. To even hint all would not be well was viewed as treacherous talk by locals who refused to consider such a dreadful, dark scenario. Napoli's trials and tribulations, her despair, joy and aspirations, touched with heartfelt emotions every house, doorway, window and laundry-strewn balcony of the city. The Neapolitans' all-enduring, romantic attachment with their football club had finally reached its rainbow's end. A love affair unconsummated, until now. Unbeaten all season at the San Paolo there appeared little reason to worry, but woe betide Ottavio Bianchi's team if by some devilish turn of fate they threw all away at the last. The world would not be a big enough place to hide.

Well before midday the *Spaccanapoli* fell into a wildly delightful, chaotic melee. For once the traffic jams that plagued the city failed to irk as a deafening crescendo of blazing car horns drifted high over the bay echoing far across the Peninsula. The *centro storico* (Old town), the cradle of the city, Naples' ancient heart, from the Forcella to the seaport flooded with *tifosi* pouring onto the streets. Traffic policemen, *La vigile*, on horseback with the black uniforms, red braid and dashing white bands across their chests, smiled at the euphoria erupting around them, laughing as fellow Neapolitans wrapped Napoli scarves around the necks of their horses. They even joined in the songs and chants by blowing on whistles adding enthusiastically if rather tunelessly to the endless choruses. An unofficial truce was declared as the polizia joined forces with the many *sicari* (cutthroats), *Spacciatore* (drug dealers), and *scippiatori* (motorcycle menaces), as well as the countless thousands of honest decent Neapolitans, in the shared hope that their football team prevailed. For one day only they would be as one.

The Neapolitans' inherited fascination with fireworks and love of unnerving loud explosions would soon become apparent as they prepared to light up the Naples skyline with all manner of apocalyptic concoctions. Some legal, most not and more suited to a battlefield than for celebratory purposes. Many cast serious misgivings on the city surviving in one piece as the nightmarish, fearsome array of garish looking rockets were revealed. The more worried inhabitants crossed themselves as they prayed for protection from what was set to rain down upon them. There was even an attempt by some enthusiastic, most possibly crazed, Neapolitans to place large amounts of dynamite in the crater of Mount Vesuvius and ignite it when the festival was in full swing. Luckily at the last moment sense prevailed, and it was decided not to provoke the raging fires that burned eternally in the mouth of the volcano. It would have been the ultimate irony and so typical of Neapolitan ill fortune, to be wiped out in a firestorm of death and destruction in their finest hour by Vesuvius blowing its top.

City walls lay plastered with pictures and tributes to those responsible for bringing joy to Naples, their names lovingly scrawled in letters ten feet tall. Garella, Bruscolotti, Ferrara, Bagni, Ferrario, Renica, Carnevale, Di Napoli, Romano, Volpecina, Caffarelli and the *allenatore* (trainer) Bianchi. Though all were admired and loved, none came even close to matching the adoration showered on the *Capitano*, Diego Armando Maradona. For this had become his city and people. Maradona's features were smeared on every house and shop window. Life-size mosaics of *Pibe De Oro* decorated major vantage points around Naples, none more eye-catching than that which covered the main entrance of Stazione Circumvesuviana, a railway station linking the capital with the devastated if captivating ruins of Pompeii and Herculaneum. Here Maradona shone in all his pomp, a glorious technicolour effort that showed him arched over the ball, about to wreak havoc against his opponents. The more fanatical of Neapolitan *tifosi* carved small, beautifully formed chapels out of stonewalls to worship their idol. Because of his exploits on the football field, Diego Maradona had in many Neapolitan's eyes become even more important than the city's Patron San Gennaro and the Virgin Mary. It was a mantle he was hardly worthy of, but though never a saint, Diego Maradona had proved a saviour for a people who invested their dreams in him. None more than he brought about this day of wonder.

Between the palm trees of the Piazzale Tecchio they came in their hordes towards the San Paolo. To illustrate their all-consuming desire to be seen as a separate state, if not country, from the despised, faraway despot regimes of Turin, Milan and all points northern, the Neapolitans adopted the flags and traditional dress code of the American Confederacy dating back to the Civil War between North and South. A mighty Southern army of Johnny Rebs dancing like madmen in the Naples sun, forever the underdog, '*solo contro tutti*' ('alone against everyone'), but at last jubilant after handing the enemy one almighty knockout blow. Payback time on those who had given them hell since the dawn of time.

Four hours before kick-off the ground was already packed. The official capacity of 86,000 was boosted by streetwise Neapolitans whose *furbo* (cunning) saw them entering by all manner of untoward means. They came in disguised as policemen, mascots, first aiders, even priests and nuns. Never had the home of SSC Napoli been graced by so many members of the Holy Faith. For who on this day when the Almighty had never been needed more would refuse entry to a servant of God? To have a ticket for the San Paolo was regarded in Naples as a day pass to heaven, a heartsoaring glimpse into paradise. That the grim foreboding peaks of Mount Vesuvius had vanished in the misty aftermath of erupting fireworks was seen as a good omen by superstitious Neapolitans who feared greatly their volcano's evil eye. They chanted the monster's pet name of *La Buonanima* (the Good Soul), in an unveiled attempt to appease Vesuvius's good nature. But still it maintained an aura of impending doom, the menacing glare. *Il Grande cono* (The Great Cone').

For Gennaro Montuori, the acknowledged leader of Napoli's most well known Ultras, the CUCB, this was a day he had waited for all his life. On the eve of the showdown against Fiorentina, Montuori spoke of his hopes for all to go well both on and off the pitch. 'For eight, nine, ten years I have been leader of the Ultras. I have always been against violence and disorder in the stadia. It is too absurd. The stadium is a theatre where you experiment in folklore. This is a stage for true supporters, for friendship. And above all to express your love of the game. We must not let football waste away. Why turn a party into a tragedy? This is an appeal we ourselves make to the rest of the Napoli fans. When we win tomorrow and claim the title the San Paolo must explode, but with joy.'

Bloodied, battered and scarred from countless confrontations with their northern foes, the foot soldiers of the CUCB intended to stamp their own indelible mark on the day's events. For many weeks Gennaro Montuori's boys had secretly planned a spectacular display of devotion to SSC Napoli and their birthplace. They had with great care designed a banner of previously unseen size and stature bearing the green, white and red of *Lo Scudetto*. Montuori was determined his Ultras would command centre stage at the San Paolo by unfurling their masterpiece which would be talked about and envied by rivals for years to come. In the eyes of Gennaro Montuori, on this *bella giornata* for Naples, no one deserved some long overdue recognition more than his lads from Commando Ultra B.

The plane carrying the Fiorentina team landed at Naples International Airport to be greeted with the same warmth a backstreet Neapolitan butcher shows the neck of a lamb as he slits its throat. Theirs was a mission to bring an entire city to its knees and keep the championship alive for at least another week until the final game of the season. The opportunity to complete a historic double over the champions-elect after thrashing Napoli on home ground was a mouth-watering prospect for the visitors. As Naples and its inhabitants drowned in a raging sea of overwhelming euphoria, the *Viola* prepared to pull the plug and leave the Neapolitans looking foolish. The immeasurable weight of a bitter rivalry down the years meant the men from Florence would never lie down in the San Paolo. Naples would not be given the title on a silver platter; the war may have been won, but there remained one last battle still to be fought.

In the Fiorentine team was a handsomely, gifted, precocious twenty-year-old called Roberto Baggio. This scraggly young kid who arrived in Florence from lowly Vicenza, looking in need of a good meal would in little time set *la Citta dei fiori* ablaze with his unerring sleight of foot, wonderful vision and a devastating ability from set pieces to either blast or bend the ball into the net. He enchanted the *Viola tifosi* who immediately took him to their hearts. A true *fantasista*. Few doubted that Baggio possessed the natural ability to one day walk with kings of Maradona's ilk. Comparisons with Naples finest proved inevitable, He like *Pibe De Oro* wore the number ten shirt, the most coveted in Italian football, and both were kings of their domain. If the Argentinian was the Southern Star, then Roberto Baggio was undoubtedly the brightest of Northern Lights. Sporting a stylish ponytail and a flamboyant image both on the pitch and off, the nickname of *Il Divino Codino* ('the Divine Ponytail') proved remarkably apt for this outrageously talented footballer. Baggio was all set to embark on an illustrious career that would hold more than its fair share of triumph and despair. But first Naples had to be dealt with.

With red lights blaring and sirens wailing, a *polizia* motorcycle cavalcade escorted the Fiorentina coach, bumping and bullying through the hellish turmoil of Neapolitan traffic to the San Paolo. Alongside them, Napoli *tifosi* rode with a suicidal bravura on motorbikes, gesturing the two-fingered salute before roaring off, chased by enraged *Carabinieri*. Nothing could ever compare to the utter confusion and chaos of Naples roads. In certain parts of the city there even existed traffic lights with the colour orange. They held no purpose, except that Neapolitans felt it helped to brighten the place up! Equally, pedestrian crossings were regarded with contempt by locals, who tended to use them only to scare the living daylights out of tourists! Old men would plant their chairs on the pavements to play cards while eagerly anticipating scenes of carnage and mayhem. It was felt the best way to cross a road in Naples was to simply step out into the traffic and stare the driver down, daring them to hit you! Sometimes it worked, sometimes..?

As kick-off grew near *polizia* and Napoli security staff turned rough in their desperate attempts to clear the pitch. Matters were hardly helped when a parachutist adorning the Napoli emblem on his chute dropped from the sky into the centre circle to rapturous applause. This was the signal for the CUCB to unravel their *tour de force*. Soon to enter the *Guinness Book of Records*, this badge of *Scudetto* against a striking blue *azzurra* background cut a magnificent spectacle. Appreciative gasps from across the stadium rang out as its sheer scope became apparent. Entire segments of the heaving terraces disappeared beneath it. In salute fellow Neapolitans unleashed yet another devastating salvo of rockets upon the unsuspecting heavens. The stadium shuddered, many glanced worryingly skywards, convinced they were about to be blown off the face of the Earth. Gennaro Montuori watched from the running track encircling the pitch with tears streaming down his face. For these were his boys. It was from here that Montuori rallied the troops by loudspeaker, leading the chants, songs and organising the legendary choreography of which the Napoli *tifosi* were famed for, their banners expressing with typical eloquence, biting satire and ironic humour the feelings of all Neapolitans on that day of days.

*'Napoli, the Immensity of the Heavens is not enough
to express our love for you!'*

'The Blues, you're Beethoven's Tenth!'

'Maradona illuminates like the sun our once sad Sundays!'

'After God, Diego and Napoli, long live the south!'

*'Children of the sun snatch the championship
from the children of the cold!'*

*'Naples has three beautiful things.
The Bay, Vesuvius and Maradona!'*

*'In the sky of Naples there are many stars,
but Maradona's shines the brightest!'*

'May 87, A New Empire is Born!'

Finally, the gloriously short and sweet, *'Excuse the delay!'*

To a tumultuous reception worthy of their divine San Gennaro, Diego Armando Maradona led his team into the Naples sunlight. A city wept tears of joy. Maradona ducked, weaved and sprinted between the congested hordes of photographers that pursued him, their cameras flashing only inches away from his face. The Argentinian caught sight of Napoli's physio Salvatore Carmando and in what had become a legendary, albeit theatrical, pre-match ritual rushed to embrace him. Despite being surrounded by a brawling circus of excitable Neapolitans, all exaggerated mannerisms, flailing bodies and utter confusion, the highly superstitious Maradona made sure he and Carmando shared their quiet moment before battle commenced. Salvatore Carmando was in tears. Being Neapolitan meant the overwhelming emotions of the day took their toll upon him. He more than any knew the suffering Maradona endured with cortisone injections that had increasingly threatened to curtail his career. As the needle pierced the skin, causing his entire body to writhe in agony, Maradona simply gritted his teeth and took the pain.

Carmando witnessed the affection in which teammates held Diego Maradona. Away from the prying lens of the paparazzi he was capable of remarkable, spontaneous acts of generosity and great kindness. How he risked injury on the many dustbowl surface/football pitches across Naples playing in charity matches, much to the chagrin of his club. The hospital visits to sick children weighed down with gifts. Their faces lighting up on seeing *El Pibe De Oro* in the flesh. Maradona paying for an operation on a young girl whose face was horribly disfigured, insisting it not be made public. These were not the actions of a man with horns. But then there was the tail to the head, the flipside of the coin, an enigma.

Those outside Naples who tended to regard him as nothing more than a creature from the gutter were always guaranteed ample ammunition to fire the bullets. Maradona moved as if nothing ever stood in his way. An inherent hatred of all things authoritarian saw him spark and rage against any who blocked his path. Whether it be a referee, politician, policeman or President, Diego Maradona treated all with equal contempt. He would do whatever he wanted whenever he pleased, the outrageously decadent lifestyle away from football with nightly excesses of cocaine, whoring and drink, hardly the preparation required for a top sportsman. But who was he hurting more than himself? The road to self-destruction lay in the mind of the beholder. Salvatore Carmando always felt he had no right to judge. Diego Maradona had more than any earned the right to follow his own path. That he still held the power to enrapture on a football pitch amazed nobody more than he. It was a sad miracle. But a miracle nonetheless.

'Perhaps now they will love me?' The President of SSC Napoli Corrado Ferlaino bathed in the fawning adulation of his fellow Neapolitans as they queued to pay homage. There was little chance of a car bomb ruining his evening on this May day. Only three years previous Ferlaino had been the most vilified man in the entire city. Now they stood in line to kiss his hand. From sinner to saint, the man who brought Maradona to Naples, who oversaw the *Scudetto* finally head south. Those same faces that once wished him dead now declared undying love. For eighteen torturous years the embittered President endured savage abuse from Napoli *tifosi* who viewed his handling of their club with suspicion. Many were convinced Ferlaino was bleeding Napoli's finances dry to pay for his ailing construction businesses.

They knew well of his rumoured connections with the *Camorra*, but in a city where football and more importantly SSC Napoli mattered so much, this was not sufficient to save him from the wrath of the mob. Corrado Ferlaino had to deliver; to be forever on the brink of extinction and continually having to sell their best players in spite of being amongst the best-supported clubs in Italy was not good enough. Timely remainders were delivered forthwith to Ferlaino in the manner of a succession of car bombs and explosive devices detonating outside the San Paolo. Then, like magic came Maradona! And so as the President blew kisses to his adoring followers on that unforgettable, fine Neapolitan afternoon in May, all was forgotten, if not altogether forgiven. A story set to have a fairytale ending. This was Naples on the early afternoon of Sunday 10th May 1987.

The Match: The rollercoaster that was SSC Napoli rolled slowly upwards before freefalling gloriously into the biggest party ever seen in southern Italy. As Neapolitan mass hysteria threatened to soar out of control in a tidal wave of fluttering flags, ear-piercing whistles and banging drums sweeping over the San Paolo, the game began. A first half hour littered with petty fouls and slack passing was illuminated only by a flashing Diego Maradona free-kick that flew inches wide of the Fiorentina goal. As was expected the *Viola* sat back and dug in, seemingly content with just the occasional foray into Neapolitan territory. But as the roar from the delirious terraces continued unabated, almost demanding a breakthrough, it inevitably occurred.

Dropping deep to the centre circle Maradona eyed Andres Carnevale with a wonderful through-ball that sliced apart the Florentine rearguard. As all Naples roared him on Carnevale raced into the penalty box and clipped a fine shot past the grasping hands of *Viola* goalkeeper Landucci to set the stadium ablaze. If there had been doubts, they vanished forever in the fateful moment that net bulged. As ever Neapolitan celebrations swelled to hugely exotic proportions. Carnevale sprinted across the running track with arms outstretched to share his joy with the blue *tifosi*, whilst Maradona fell dramatically to his knees, thanking God, kissing the turf. Tears were plenty: Gennaro Montuori sobbed uncontrollably on the sidelines, lifetime devotion to his team finally reaping rich dividends after so much misery and despair. Behind him the Napoli ultras danced away the heartache and humiliation of yesteryear.

146

BELLA GIORNATA (BEAUTIFUL DAY)

Determined to provide a fitting spectacle for such a grand occasion, Napoli blazed forward in search of more goals. The nerves disappeared, in its place came swagger and pomp, championship football! News reaching Naples by radio of Inter going a goal down at lowly Atalanta only further increased the euphoric mood sweeping across the stadium. Chants of 'Atalanta, Atalanta' bellowed loud. It was left to the pony-tailed hero of all Florence to bring them down to Earth with a bang, when on thirty-nine minutes Roberto Baggio curled a delicious twenty-five-yard free-kick past the Napoli goalkeeper Claudio Garella. Suddenly it had become interesting again! Garella raged at his defensive wall that appeared to dissolve in the face of Baggio's shot, the first of many in Serie A for *Il Divino Codino*. As the half-time whistle sounded, the restless murmurings of the assembled hordes hinted as to the uncertainty of their fate. A disturbing quiet fell upon the San Paolo; though the flags still waved, it was with a sense of apprehension. 1-1, it was enough, but just.

The re-emergence of the two teams for the second period sparked the crowd back to life, but there remained an uncertainty that wasn't present earlier in the day. Cheers came laced with the nagging doubt that all Neapolitans had tried so hard to block from their thoughts, that all would not go well. Naples' obsession with fatalism once more came to the fore. With nothing to lose Fiorentina opened up to cause consternation on the terraces. The Napoli *tifosi* watched with hearts in mouths as their team was forced to retreat. It was akin to a drunkard turning up at a christening and drowning the baby. Roberto Baggio was magnificent, all silky skills, probing, looking for the killer pass. *Il Divino* appeared to be enjoying himself tormenting the home defence, the raging torrents of abuse hurled upon him from all corners of the stadium seemingly inspiring Baggio to tease them a little more.

The clock ticked down, slowly seconds turned achingly into minutes, hails of derision from the Neapolitans each time a *Viola* player touched the ball and made with deadly intent for their half. The last fifteen minutes dawned and the sixty-one-year wait was agonisingly close to being over. By now most in the San Paolo could barely watch matters on the pitch. The dying moments of the contest saw Napoli playing keep-ball in an effort to wind down time. With 86,000 souls begging the referee to end their misery and the noise level rising to unheard of proportions, at 17.47, the *arbitro*, Pairetto, duly obliged. For a fleeting second older *tifosi* found themselves thinking back to seasons past, when all was black and Naples' dreams of glory were ridiculed. The insults screamed out: '*Lavense*', 'Wash the steps before leaving', 'Vesuvius we are counting on you' and '*Mafiosi*'. None no longer mattered or hurt as the final whistle blew and through the golden gates of heaven Neapolitans poured. How sweet a moment for a people and a city that had wished for nothing more. Held forever in contempt, scorned and laughed at, Naples now possessed the biggest putdown in Italian football history, 'Champions!'

In a blinding, swirling mist of smoke bombs, igniting red flares and earth, shattering firecrackers, the fanatical hordes of blue *tifosi* commenced their long overdue victory festivities. For the first time ever the pride of Naples, SSC Napoli had earned the right to wear upon their shirt the esteemed badge of *Lo Scudetto*. The best of the best, the championship insignia of all Italy. On the pitch a beaming Diego Maradona gestured to his adoring subjects with a raised two-fisted salute, before vanishing beneath a mad flurry of backslapping ecstatic well-wishers. First amongst them was Maradona's younger brother Hugo who had rushed to embrace his older sibling, almost choking him in an all-clasping bearhug. It was a truly emotional moment for the man who though adopted and adored by Naples, always remained in his heart a *Porteno* (native of Buenos Aires). As much that Argentina's victory in the 1986 World Cup was viewed in Naples as a triumph for Neapolitans, so the poor people of Villa Fiorito back in Buenos Aires equally celebrated SSC Napoli's achievements, for Diego Maradona was one of their own.

Glancing up, Maradona caught sight of teammate Giuseppe Bruscolotti making his way towards him through the adoring crowds. If the Argentinian was the talisman in the title finally coming to Naples, then Bruscolotti was undoubtedly the rock on which such foundations were built. A living legend in these parts long before Diego Maradona ever touched ground at the San Paolo, Bruscolotti had led from the front throughout the lean years, a pillar of strength for Neapolitans who despaired as their football club were repeatedly outgunned by Juventus and the Milan clubs. Or as had happened one too many times, shot down by their own hand.

The veteran defender bore the scars of past battles fighting Naples cause, both physically and mentally. His haggard, war-weary features visible for all to see, but the sickness in his heart at seeing his beloved Napoli humiliated by their many enemies not so, except to those closest to him. The courageous decision to hand *El Pibe De Oro* the Captain's armband in exchange for his promise to bring the *Scudetto* south had come to fruition. As the two came together to share a warm embrace the most hardened Neapolitans wept like babies. The heart-rending sight of this ferocious old warrior shedding tears of joy whilst clinging tightly to Maradona meant all the pain and frustration suffered over the decades was a price worth paying to witness such a moment. The young king had delivered on his word to the old master.

With Diego Maradona proudly at their helm, Napoli began a luxuriously swamping lap of honour around the San Paolo, but as hundreds joined in alongside them it resembled more a joyful stampede. A Neapolitan cavalry charged, tinged with blue and heavy doses of delirium. Supporters, photographers and reporters jostled amongst themselves in an attempt to get close to their idols. Maradona picked up a Napoli scarf from the running track and waved it above his head in the direction of the crowd, soaking up the adulation. A banner exclaimed, 'You are as one, San Gennaromaradona!' The entire Maradona clan were present in the stadium to witness their boy's moment of triumph. His Mother watched embarrassed as *tifosi* bowed before her, falling to their knees, thanking Tota for giving birth to the great 'curly one'.

On reaching the relative sanctuary of the dressing room, the *Capitano* led all the team in a rousing rendition of the 'Oh Mama, Mama' tribute song. The Argentinian changed the verses dedicated to himself to ensure each player was serenaded individually by the others. Maradona grabbed a microphone off a television crew and began a series of comic interviews with all of his teammates. But when it came to Guiseppe Bruscolotti, he showed only glowing respect for El Pepe, acclaiming him the true *Capitano* of Napoli. Amidst such wonderful scenes of camaraderie and friendship the men who brought about the greatest day in the history of SSC Napoli danced, sang and laughed. All except one. Despite the grateful handshakes, bearhugs and celebratory kisses planted upon him, the coach Ottavio Bianchi refused to partake, keeping a distance, alone in a crowd. In this, his moment of absolute triumph, he remained stonefaced, only ever hinting at a smile.

But the dour features of Bianchi misled many, for inside burned a footballing heart that lived for SSC Napoli and the city she represented. Deep down none enjoyed winning the *Scudetto* more than he. Already his mind was racing ahead to the following season. Bianchi knew well the northern arisitocracy would come after them with an almighty vengeance. They would not take kindly to being humbled at the hands of Naples. It was a humiliation beyond words and could never be allowed to happen again. But Ottavio Bianchi already had a plan in mind to counteract the mighty forces being lined up against the Neapolitans. Instead of waiting for the inevitable, all-out assault, SSC Napoli would attack from the off! Why wait for the enemy when you can hit them hard, early and blow them away?

Such was the noise and furore created in the San Paolo on that fateful day, Mount Vesuvius could well have blown its mighty top and no one would have noticed or even cared. A poet once wrote of the Bay of Naples, 'I want to bring you to a place where the winter is sweet and the summer is fresh. Where the sea lightly touches the land with lazy waves.' This evoked vivid images of tranquillity, serenity and calm. But not on this day when the title finally came south! For though Naples could never claim to be the sanest of cities, in the early

149

evening of 10/5/87, she truly fell into a state of madness. Nowhere was this more so than the backstreet labyrinths of the Forcella, as open trucks and cars inched bumper to bumper in slow, triumphant procession through the winding, narrow streets of the city's ancient, beating heart. Around them flitting and buzzing like fireflies, hundreds of Vespas sped manically, their drivers hooting and hollering in celebration of the greatest day any had ever experienced. All the pent-up frustrations of living life under the thumb of their alleged betters in the North poured out and the Forcella went wild. Many present swore a witch's spell was cast over its inhabitants, such was the crazed glint in their eyes. Courtesy of the Giuliano clan, the best wine and food was made freely available in abundance as the self-styled 'protectors of the poor' moved heaven and earth to be seen in a good light on this most special of occasions. It was after all their boy who more than any brought the *Scudetto* south, and besides, they could easily afford it.

Unsuspecting nearby towns and villages across the Gulf of Naples found themselves under siege as joyful convoys of Napoli followers swept through their streets in a victory procession. San Francesco, Vico Equense and nearby Sorrento were all treated to a characteristic show of Neapolitan high spirits. Famed for their beautiful sunsets, lemon groves and rose gardens, the highbrow residents of Sorrento watched in utter disdain the antics of the city dwellers as ramshackle trucks crammed tight with cheering *tifosi* roared through Piazza Tasso, their historic town centre. They were to be pitied, like the lunatics of an asylum allowed out for the day. Laughed at, derided, and ultimately told to just go away. Back to their garbage-strewn alleyways in the Forcella. Out of sight and mind.

Let them have their moment in the sun, for tomorrow normality would once more rear itself and again Neapolitans would be left with nothing but aching heads and empty lives. But they would have something far more important, the memories of a day set to go down in Naples' history as amongst its most glorious ever. A song echoed for hours, and later days, weeks and years throughout the city. An ageless *Canzone* called *O Surdato 'Nnammurato* (The Soldier's Song) that somehow captured such a special time for all concerned, '*E mme diciste si na sera e maggio*' ('And she said yes to me on a May evening'). This more than any was the soundtrack of *bella giornata*, and even today it is regarded as the defining song of those heady times.' You were my first love, oh first you'll be for me. Oh sweet life of mine.'

Napoli's historic triumph appeared to stretch far, wide and even beyond this mortal coil. On a graveyard wall, *tifosi* daubed the words '*E che ve site perz!?*' ('What did you miss!?'). The next morning, written in chilling reply beneath was '*E chi ve l'ha ditt?*' ('How do you know we missed it?). Dogs covered in Maradona wigs barked manically at the bedlam around them. Baying donkeys roamed free around the city with the names of Naples most hated enemies placed on placards around their necks. Napoli's unofficial club emblem, the sad-eyed, downtrodden, but always loveable *O Ciuccio*, being used to poke fun against all who had mocked. As the evening drew in and night fell like a cloak of darkness over the Bay of Naples, hundred of Neapolitans gathered on the seafront to participate in what at first appeared a mass funeral service. To signify the end of Northern dominance a temporary chapel had been erected housing wooden coffins bearing the names of SSC Napoli's sworn enemies, Turin, Verona and Milan foremost amongst those.

After a short charade of mock grieving, huge cheers erupted from the shoreline as the hated *Bianconeri*, Veronese and Milanese were dragged into the ocean before being set alight by flaming, handheld torches and cast off into the darkness. As the coffins burned, drifting out on the high tide, the sky above blazed in a tumultuous kaleidoscope of vivid colour. For the Neapolitans had let fly everything at their disposal that went bang! Bengal Bombs, Roman Candles and the wonderfully named, potentially devastating Maradona Ball were amongst those honoured with a San Gennaro blessing, then launched towards the southern stars. It began with a *culpo scuro* (detonation in the dark) and ended with all hell breaking loose! An almighty ensemble of firepower illuminating the heavens, exploding in a glorious cascade above the Tyrrhenian Sea. Blazing red rings of fire glowed, sizzled, then faded, falling away. Fireworks that crashed, fizzed, sparked and thundered before detonating into a thousand pieces, leaving spilt in their wake glistening trails of lingering sulphur lining the black sky. Below Neapolitans roared in delight at their handy work, drunk in body and spirit, totally oblivious to the dangers posed to themselves. What the hell! 'To Vesuvius, sooner or later he'll get us all!' As once forecast, night had turned to day in Naples.

Fire engines raced through the streets, dousing rubbish piles before roaring off at breakneck speed to the next emergency. Never had they experienced such a night, as their fellow Neapolitans appeared insistent on burning the city to the ground. Those who witnessed this remarkable show of near-suicidal, amateur pyrotechnics from a safe distance on nearby Ishia and the Isle of Capri shook their heads in disbelief and no less wonder at the mad antics of their lunatic neighbours from across the water. Typically, Naples appeared on the verge of being the first city in history to self-inflict total destruction on itself from the air! But on Ishia and Capri they at least looked on the bright side, for life might prove just a little more tranquil.

But where was *El Rei*? Away from the madding crowds that chanted his name incessantly amidst the hysterical atmosphere of downtown Naples, it was widely rumoured Diego Maradona spent the night amongst friends at a party hosted in his honour by the Giuliano clan in the discreet surroundings of the village of Nola, on the city outskirts. So as not to alert the paparazzi or unwanted government attention, the venue was kept secret until the last moment. The guests arrived in sleek, black, stretch limousines, surrounded by mean-faced bodyguards and most prized, beautiful mistresses clinging to their arms. It was said to have been a lavish affair, even by *Camorra* standards. Against a backdrop of Maradona's finest goals for Napoli being replayed endlessly on large video screens, the finest women, wine and white powder money could buy was on offer to those lucky enough to be present by special invitation.

All took advantage of the Giuliano's generosity, none more than Diego Maradona who partied equally hard as the most drunken, delighted Neapolitan, enjoying the forbidden fruits of his hard-earned labour. Live for today, as tomorrow is a distant dream! Many of the gangs had gambled heavily on the back of Maradona's leading Napoli to success, earning themselves huge fortunes. Neapolitans had always tended to bet with their hearts, not heads, when it came to their football team. Strange those whose daily existence centred on murder and extortion should act like fawning *tifosi* when faced with Maradona, tipping their glasses in salute, hanging on to his every word. For this man not only earned them fortunes, the genius of *El Pibe De Oro* made their childhood dreams come true.

Morning came and Naples grabbed some much needed rest before throwing itself once more into Samba mood. As a new day broke only the most fanatical *tifosi* remained, bleary eyed, but steadfastly refusing to let go of the moment, grasping it in their hand like a gust of wind, only to watch sadly as it slipped free, blown away on the ocean breeze. The last of the rockets were fired almost half-heartedly, lacking the thunderous impact of the previous night's extravaganza. A lone thud spat and spluttered over the bay, whilst sporadic crackles of fireworks echoed rather wearily in the distance. The city that never slept fell for once into serene slumber. Where the dark blue ocean melted into the sky, a red sun lazily rose, and Neapolitans bade a fond farewell to what had truly been *bella giornata*. A most beautiful day. They would never see its like again.

Winning trophies was becoming a habit. One month later with Naples still drunk on success, SSC Napoli completed a momentous season by thrashing Atalanta 4-0 on aggregate to clinch the *Coppa Italia*. As Diego Maradona lifted high the impressive looking goblet in Bergamo, his adopted city partied on. It promised to be a wonderful Neapolitan summer.

CHAPTER 16

MAGICA

There was a blue moon over Naples! Diego Maradona had led Napoli to a peak so high, there remained only one way left to go. The Holy Grail to claim the Scudetto was achieved, but there were those who desperately wanted it back, at any price. Huge face was lost in the North. A new enemy emerged, stronger and more deadly than any that had gone before. In the highest corridors of power the decision was taken to bring Naples to heel. The Neapolitans had to be brought down. Plans were underway to make this so. A man for whom money was no concern busied himself in bringing together a majestic array of the world's best players in Milan. It would be a team like no other, rivalling any of the past great sides. For make no mistake, the exalted red and black of the Rossoneri were coming!

Totonero: (football pools). It was an open secret in Naples that the formidable Giuliano family ran a clandestine betting syndicate from their territory in the Forcella. Though well aware of its existence the authorities never moved to shut it down. Any attempt to do so may well have ended in a bloodbath such was the Giuliano's hold over their fortress kingdom. Neapolitans poured millions of lira into the *Camorra* coffers on a weekly basis. Its advantages for punters included tax-free payouts and the opportunities to play on credit, though woe betide any who fell behind with payments. With a turnover estimated to be that well in excess of the Italian state pools, this alternate back-alley *totonero* received special attention from none other than the notorious *Il Lione*, Carmine Giuliano. Unlike the vast majority of gangsters who loathed the spotlight, Giuliano loved the public adulation of those in the Forcella who regarded him with respect, as an *uomo d'onore*, a man of honour. One who held the power to give life and take with just as much ease. For respect read fear.

He also loved to flaunt his close friendship with Diego Maradona. Countless photographs exist of him arm-in-arm alongside *El Pibe De Oro* at various clubs and parties. Everybody knew that Don Carmine and Diego were like brothers. He was admired, adored, but always feared. The one letter difference between scared and sacred was never more so than in the case of Carmine Giuliano, for when his temper was roused Carmine would fly into a murderous rage, the equal of any *Camorristi* this city had seen. Ferocious on matters of family business, he ran the gambling rackets with an iron fist. Only those with a death wish dared to tangle or attempt to cross The Lion.

Terno Secco, hitting the jackpot. It was every Neapolitans' dream to crack thirteen results in the Italian football pools and earn for themselves a fortune. It came as little surprise in a highly superstitious city like Naples, where people carried with them blessed amulets to ward off evil spirits, that there were those convinced *totonero* numbers came in dreams, placed there by deceased relatives. It was all just a question of translation. For example, if Diego Maradona appeared, he obviously represented number ten. It was said that with the aid of an ancient, medieval practice of numerology called *Cabala*, believers could try for themselves to pick their own numbers, but to do so was beset with unearthly difficulties. For it was claimed that prickly, troubled souls in the afterlife, who sought only to prevent and spoil, would simply play games with any ungainly, amateurish efforts to make sense of dreams.

To counteract such an unreasonable, unholy foe, Neapolitans were forced to enlist the help of a spiritualist guide known as a *Santoni* (an interpreter of dreams). These self-proclaimed psychics claimed to possess special powers allowing them to snuff out those who led the living astray. Once paid they consulted their required bible, the Smorfia, a mythical book of dreams, that was claimed only *Santoni* could properly translate. Sadly, in desperate attempts to escape from a poverty-stricken existence, Neapolitans handed over these spurious characters their cash. Supernatural powers or total fakes? It mattered little, for to outwit mischievous spirits in the next world was one thing, to second-guess the *Camorra* was something else. No *Cabala*, *Santoni* or even Nostradamus himself could have predicted what was set to occur in Naples. That they would all but destroy the heart and spirit of their birth city meant nothing. From heaven to hell in the blink of an eye.

For Neapolitans, Silvio Berlusconi was nothing less than Nero reborn, a despised modern day Roman Emperor. Born 29th September 1936 to middle class parents in Milan, a bank clerk and housewife, his early days gave rise to unique moneymaking qualities. As a child young Silvio put on puppet shows, charging entrance fees to fellow students at primary school. To pay for his law degree at Milan University, Berlusconi sang as a crooner of ballads on ocean liners, worked as a stand-up comic and even sold vacuum cleaners. Once enrolled he ghost-wrote essays for those willing to pay a hefty sum for his literary skills. Forever scheming, looking forward, a young Berlusconi, wise beyond his tender years, always made a point of mixing in the right circles. Amongst those he made it his business to befriend was future Italian Prime Minister Bettino Craxi, later to be Godfather to his daughter and a loyal ally over the years in dire times of need.

In the 1960s Berlusconi took out huge loans guaranteed by favourable politicians (old school friends,) to create a firm of contractors that went on to build Milano 2. A giant suburban area near Italy's second largest city consisting of ten thousand luxury homes, all supplied with cable television. Two similar suburbs followed as this brave venture proved a huge success. Berlusconi's business empire Fininvest went from strength to strength. As the insatiable desire for money and power grew over the years he went for broke by splashing outright to buy three of the country's main television stations. Such was Berlusconi's bold and brash manner of doing business, the aptly-titled nickname of *Il Cavaliere* (The Cavalier) was bestowed upon him. He also bought up major food chains, newspaper and publishing markets. Building tycoon, media mogul, there appeared no end to Silvio Berlusconi's ambitions. He was a phenomenon. Italy had never seen a man of this ilk before. His was the Midas touch. A new word came into the Italian language, Berlusconism. People lived in houses built by Berlusconi, watched television controlled by Berlusconi and even shopped at supermarkets owned by Berlusconi.

Worried by so much power in one man's hands, the Italian Parliament issued a court order to try and prevent a total monopoly. But Berlusconi's old school tie relationships again came to the rescue when the by-then Prime Minister Bettino Craxi overruled the judges. Silvio Berlusconi, who once had to sing for his breakfast and tell jokes for his supper, had all of Italy dancing to his tune. He was a king without a crown. As ever with Italian high-powered business dealings, dark tales of Masonic corruption and underworld connections were never far away. Berlusconi was no exception. His was a hand in so many pies that almost inevitably the word *Mafiosi* would come to be whispered. In time these rumours would return to haunt him. Years later he was investigated for alleged involvement in the car bombing of an anti-Mafia judge. But in the mid-Eighties none dared to air such damning allegations.

In March 1986 Silvio Berlusconi made his long expected move into *Calcio*, by becoming President of his boyhood team AC Milan. With the debt-crippled *Rossoneri* verging on the brink of bankruptcy, the cunning Berlusconi bided his time to arrive in their darkest hour, riding a tide of Milanese public euphoria. He vowed to make them the number one club not just in Italy but the world. Always with an eye for the adventurous, Berlusconi astonished all by hiring little known coach Arrigo Sacchi from Serie B club Parma to take the reins. Born the modest son of a Parma shoe cobbler, and only a footballer of modest talent, Sacchi had caught the President's eye the previous season when his team, playing football well beyond their lowly position sensationally knocked AC Milan out of the *Coppa Italia*. The stubborn, abrasive but extremely astute Sacchi was entrusted with making real Silvio Berlusconi's vision of a dream team. With a little prompting from above he acted instantly in the transfer market by bringing from Holland two of the world's great emerging talents.

Firstly, for a world record fee the towering, mercurial skills and speed of the dreadlocked midfield maestro Ruud Gullit went to Milan. Then, shortly after for the bargain price of £1.5 million, the imperial, imposing figure of Marco van Basten arrived from Ajax, a prodigy of the great Johann Cruyff and a striker unmatched in the modern game. The best of his generation. Tall, powerful, lightning fast, sublime technique and blessed with a wondrous gift to score goals from any angle. In this audacious double swoop Sacchi had unknowingly initiated a significant shift of power back towards the North, for he had bought gold. President Berlusconi also ordered work to begin on an ultra-modern training complex to be called Milanello. Here no expense was spared to provide his players with the most sophisticated medical and conditional facilities money could buy. The Milan supremo had only one instruction for his coach, to take the *Scudetto* back from the Southern peasants and return it to its rightful home in the San Siro. Only then would Berlusconi feel he had his crown.

In the deep South events in Milan hardly raised an eyebrow. The sun-drenched summer of 1987 was a glorious time in Naples as Neapolitans basked in their newly-crowned mantle of champions. Everything else could wait. There would be plenty of time to worry when battle re-commenced the following season. But there was one who refused to rest on his laurels. Ottavio Bianchi showed clear intent of how his team intended to play by buying from Brazilian champions Sao Paolo one of the most feared strikers in South America, Antonio De Oliviera Careca. Bianchi's battleplan was already set in stone. The Neapolitans would defend their title by taking the war to their enemies. It would be a three-pronged all-out attack christened *MAGICA* by the Napoli *tifosi*. MA for Maradona, GI for Giordano, CA for Careca. The twenty-seven-year-old Brazilian international bonded instantly with Maradona off pitch and along with the exciting, bustling Giordano this electrifying threesome would wreak havoc amongst Serie A defences.

With the ragtag blue *tifosi* of the Forcella, Spanish quarter, Sanita and Fuogoritta convinced Diego Maradona walked on water, and his star in its highest ascendancy, the Argentinian's street-wise guru, Guillermo Coppola struck while the iron was hot to squeeze Napoli for every lira in their bank account. Coppola reacted fast to secure for his illustrious client a further five-year extension to his present contract worth a staggering $23 million. Strong rumours of Silvio Berlusconi planning to steal Diego Maradona away to Milan swept through Naples like the plague. Quickly they gathered momentum, causing rumblings in the city and people were worried. What was it all about? Such talk only helped to serve Coppola's cause and President Ferlaino had little option but to cave in. Though unsure of whether Napoli could even afford it, Corrado Ferlaino knew the alternative of refusing and allowing the player to move north was akin to signing his own death warrant.

The President had finally resigned himself to the fact that it was not he who ran the football club, but the jumped-up *Sudaca*, Maradona and his Argentinian sidekick, playboy manager. Weary of fighting a losing battle and being everybody's fall guy, Ferlaino reluctantly agreed to Coppola's outrageous demands. When the club announced news of Diego's decision to extend his contract, wild celebrations once more erupted in the city neighbourhoods. Any excuse for another party, fire a few rockets! Could life have possibly got any sweeter for the Neapolitans? The flamboyant Coppola poured himself a huge drink on the veranda of his favourite haunt, the Hotel Paradiso on Naples waterfront, and sat back to work out his cut of the deal. What was it to him where the tall tales of Berlusconi's interest in Maradona originated? Chinese whispers? Finally on 11th December 1987 Diego Armando Maradona signed a six-year contract worth $16 million. Coppola's cut was substantial. He declared that 'Maradona's children would eat caviar for the rest of their lives'. Welcome to Naples!

On Sunday 13th September 1987, SSC Napoli, with the badge of *Lo Scudetto* proudly ensconced upon their shirts, went north to the foot of the Apennine Mountains to begin defending the Serie A title. Newly-promoted Cesena bore the nickname of 'Home of the Popes' due to the remarkable coincidence of three Holy Fathers hailing from the town. But even such a divine background failed to help their cause when in a hard-fought contest Napoli scraped home 1-0 with a goal from the redoubtable warrior Salvatore Bagni. Elsewhere Berlusconi's revamped AC Milan lay down a marker, winning 3-1 in consummate ease at Pisa, Dutch stars Gullit and van Basten both on the scoreline to signal a significant show of intent southwards.

Seven days on the champions took the field in Naples receiving a reception worthy of their illustrious achievements. Onto the sacred turf of the San Paolo strode the footballing kings of all Italy to face Ascoli, yet another team fresh up from Serie B. The visitors included in their line-up a young man who in name and appearance was rather familiar to the gathered 86,000 crowd. Maradona! Stories persisted that it was Maradona Senior who put up money to help cash-strapped Ascoli purchase his younger sibling from Argentinos Junior. It was an emotional occasion for the Maradona clan and all were present in the stands to cheer both on. Diego had spent the week building up Hugo's confidence by claiming he possessed the potential to be equally as good if not better than he. Sadly it was just a case of brotherly love. Hugo Maradona was attempting the impossible in trying to do justice his ridiculously demanding surname.

The *Capitano* of SSC Napoli had only one, maybe two challengers to the title of the greatest ever. Comparisons, if only even jovial between the brothers were beyond cruel. For if *El Pibe De Oro* was cut from diamonds, then Hugo as a footballer was moulded from clay. Ascoli's Argentinian number ten appeared miserably out of his depth in the cut-throat, if technically brilliant chessboard arena of Serie A. Indeed, handing him that particular shirt only served to highlight Hugo's limitations when compared to his opposing number. With his small stocky frame and black curly hair Hugo was similar to Diego Armando in looks only. Nothing more.

That blood is thicker than water was truly evident in Diego's overwhelming support for his brother. But in footballing terms they evolved from different planets. Napoli won 2-1 with the two brothers paths hardly crossing. Indeed the closest they came was at the final whistle to embrace and swap shirts. Hugo's time with Ascoli would be short and after making only thirteen appearances that one season impressing no one, he disappeared into the sunset. Later he resurfaced in Spain for a brief period with Rayo Valladolid before finally finding his true level in Japan, where the surname alone guaranteed him a decent payday. But there was only one Maradona!

There was great excitement in the city when the draw for the inaugural round of the European Cup were made, for it handed Napoli a glittering start against legendary Spanish champions Real Madrid. The Neapolitans' first venture into this prestigious competition saw them play the opening leg away in the majestic surroundings of Estadio Santiago Bernabeu. None more than Diego Maradona relished the opportunity to put one over Real, for during his brief ill-fated foray at Madrid's fiercest rivals, Barcelona, the Catalans had indoctrinated him into the evils of *Los Madrilenos*, the white-shirted demons. To them Real Madrid were devils on earth.

The European Cup campaign began in surreal surroundings at the Bernabeu when due to crowd disturbance the previous season, Real were forced to play behind closed doors in front of empty, echoing grandstands. In a vain attempt at gaining the merest of home advantage, the Spanish champions placed hundreds of scarves and banners over the terraces. It became known in Madrid folklore as *el partidio del silencio* (the match of silence). Sadly for Napoli it was they, minus new boy Careca who struggled in such a dreadful atmosphere, sliding to a dismal 2-0 defeat. After the game Maradona was furiously upbeat. He declared to hordes of the waiting world's press that 'they would triumph in Naples, even if Puskas and Di Stefano in their pomp were still playing!' Brave if foolhardy words that Diego would bitterly come to regret.

Two weeks later an estimated 100,000 blood-crazed Neapolitans gatecrashed the San Paolo in a concerted attempt to ensure their side received sufficient support to drag back the two goal deficit suffered in Madrid. Every single vantage point was taken. Never in Napoli's turbulent and at times violent history had anything even come close to resembling the inferno that blazed under the volcano on that special night the great Real Madrid came to Naples. When selecting his team Ottavio Bianchi threw caution to the wind by throwing in a host of forward players. Bianchi hoped the rabid atmosphere stoked up on the terraces would unnerve the visitors, leaving them open to his brave, if dangerous, do-or-die strategy. As the *tifosi* roared for Spanish heads on poles, Naples exploded with noise and Diego Maradona led the charge.

From the first whistle they threw themselves upon the Real defence. Neapolitan dreams of European glory flickered briefly when on nine minutes new signing, defender Giovanni Francini from Torino, set the stadium alight when he marauded forward to grab a vital early breakthrough. The stage appeared set for a grand Neapolitan comeback of epic proportions, only to be cruelly snuffed out by the lethal, Madrid centre forward Emilio Butragueno, *El Buitre* (the vulture), who swooped to kill the tie dead a minute before half-time. Though hardly the outrageously gifted team of old, the Spanish champions had enough in their locker to hold off frantic Napoli efforts in the second period to get back in the game. It finished 1-1. At the final whistle home players walked sullenly off, heads down, whilst the *Madrilenos* celebrated their battling backs-to-the-wall performance. Maradona had been well held, Napoli were out. The *tifosi* went home deflated, for so many years they had waited to see their team in this tournament, taking on Europe's elite, only to see them crash and burn before ever taking off.

President Ferlaino watched on in fury from the stands. The result was a disaster for the club not only in football terms but, perhaps more importantly, financially also. A pirate's fortune was earned in gate receipts for the visit of Real, but after everybody had received their cut, there was little left in the pot. SSC Napoli was like a cow to be milked for all its worth, then discarded when sucked dry. Players, agents and the ever-present invisible black hand of the

Camorra hung like a noose over the San Paolo. Even at such a young stage of the season it became apparent that a second *Scudetto* was required just to make the books balance. With Diego Maradona and the title on board Napoli was an oil tanker that, although leaking, was sufficiently patched up not to sink. But what if the title was lost and the Argentinian abandoned ship? All bets were off. There were no lifeboats, just hopes and prayer.

The stinging, bitter taste of defeat at the hands of Real Madrid was swiftly cast aside as SSC Napoli roared back, exploding into a sensational rich vein of league form, Top spot was quickly claimed with their opening five Serie A games won. It was breathtaking, swaggering football, highlighted by a ruthless 6-0 demolition in Naples of poor unsuspecting Pescara. Only 2-0 at the break, the away side suffered humiliation in the second half. A full house paid homage to the blessed Neapolitan holy trio of Maradona, Giordano and Careca, who opened his account as Napoli went goal crazy. *Magica*! Though only lowly Pescara, a message was sent north to those intending to take the title away from Naples; 'You know where we are. Do your worst!'

The week following at the Stadio Olympico in Rome, AS Roma ended Napoli's run holding them to a draw. On the ancient, historic banks of the Tiber, yet another goal from impressive new full-back Francini earned the champions a share of the spoils. Come the final whistle and the Roma *tifosi* celebrated the 1-1 result like they had won the game, giving rise to just how much SSC Napoli was now respected, if hardly loved. Brushing off their close shave in the capital the Neapolitans remained unbeaten till Christmas, opening up a four-point gap at the top. Juventus were also beaten in Naples with a last minute penalty from Diego Maradona. A draw looked on the cards after veteran defender Antonio Cabrini smashed home an equaliser to level a Fernando De Napoli strike in the first half. But as the crowd hushed in nervous expectation, *El Pibe De Oro*, with unnerving ease scored to send the San Paolo delirious. For the third game running *La Vecchia Signora* were beaten. Words could never describe the feeling of sheer elation and satisfaction that swept through the city as the black and white stripes were sent packing with tails between their precious legs. It was a great time to be alive in the place they claimed you had to see before you died.

Lesser teams than the loathed *Bianconeri* were not just beaten, they were hammered out of sight, collapsing under the sheer ferocity of the champions' firepower. The despised Hellas Verona suffered a 4-1 mauling under the volcano with Maradona, Bagni and two from Giordano all on target as the Napoli forwards tortured the Veronese defence. The goals flew. A magician's potion brewed in Naples, its mystical ingredients brought from afar but soaked in Neapolitan passion. Bianchi's inspired signing of Antonio Careca, who could not stop scoring, proved a masterstroke. It was Salsa football! Especially at the San Paolo, where Careca found himself swiftly granted hero status and serenaded with his own tribute song: '*Care, Care, Care. Tira la bomba, tira la bomba!*' ('Come on Careca, Careca, Careca. Throw the bomb, throw the bomb!'). This was not an honour given lightly. If Maradona was undisputed king of Naples, then Antonio Careca was its *Principe Azzurro* (Prince charming). The beating drums of Napoli *tifosi* set the tempo and rhythm for *Magica* to come alive! The craft and lightning pace of *La Bomba* was a perfect foil for the genius of Maradona, whose unerring eye to deliver a killer pass whilst in full flight was heaven sent for the fleet-footed Brazilian. With Bruno Giordano all strength, poise and presence, Naples was in dreamland.

The much-vaunted challenge from Silvio Berlusconi's bankrolled AC Milan had so far failed to materialise as they were left trailing in the wake of SSC Napoli's blistering start. The two would go head to head in the first week following the Christmas shutdown. All roads lead to the San Siro as Italy waited with bated breath this clash of giants. The Milanese desperately needed to win, it had become imperative the champions were dragged back in sight. Any other result and such was Napoli's form it was odds-on a consecutive *Scudetto* would be heading to Naples. The sheer quality of their football meant only those with an inbred hatred of Neapolitans or a simple-minded fool would have bet against them retaining their title. But already it was whispered the decision had been taken that this would not be allowed to happen. That those ruling from the shadows who with one hand gave, and the other took, were ready to break the hearts of their own.

In Naples the power of the *Camorra* meant everything and anyone could be bought. Politicians, policemen, judges, priests, God forbid even footballers. All came with a price. Affairs of the heart mattered little, it was all just business, nothing personal. Deep in the Forcella stood a masterpiece of early sixteenth-century architecture, the classic domed church of Santa Caterina. On her blessed walls a picture of Napoli's championship-winning team lay pasted. In normal circumstances the much-feared wrath of the local *prete* (priest) meant this would never have been tolerated, but such was the love and esteem in which these men were held the poster was left to hang. Scrawled across it was the word *sacro*, meaning sacred. For the unsuspecting city of Naples the irony of this would in a short time become almost too painful to bear.

CHAPTER 17

FATTACCIO (FOUL DEED)

Amidst the flowers and beauty of Naples beat a rancid dark heart. Carmine Giuliano was concerned for Lo Camorra was not in the business of losing money. Plans were made. Il Lione knew he would have to act fast and with great discretion. He would offer the legendary hand of Giuliano persuasion. 'Be my friend, for you do not want me as an enemy.' When the time came nothing was more certain that everything would be ready. To their eternal shame it was alleged the traitors sold their soul in Vesuvius's shade. The four whose names were whispered, vehemently denied betrayal, presumably to avoid being lynched. It was a fattacio beyond contempt. The heavenly blue skies had turned a ghastly black over the bay. Sadly it appeared that even those who gave redemption were ultimately not beyond temptation. For in Naples even the angels had dirt under their wings.

On Sunday 3rd January 1988 a new empire came of age in the north. 80,000 Milanese *tifosi* awash in red and black bayed with unrestrained joy as a Ruud Gullit inspired AC Milan wiped the floor with Serie A champions SSC Napoli. In a consummate performance, the guile and craft of the tall, slender, explosive Gullit destroyed the Neapolitans, leading Milan to a momentous 4-1 triumph. In doing so he totally overshadowed Naples' own lauded world superstar Diego Maradona in a much-hyped personal duel between the two number tens. The twenty-six-year-old charismatic Dutchman's laidback approach to life off the pitch was in stark contrast to his attitude once he crossed that white line. With more tricks up his sleeve than a bar-room card shark, the deceptively casual Gullit handed the Southerners a heady dose of their own medicine.

And yet it had all started so well for the champions as they began the game full of confidence, passing the ball around with supreme ease. On eleven minutes their reward came when Francesco Romano fed his Captain, and an exquisite Maradona chipped pass left even the accomplished Baresi flat-footed as Antonio Careca raced clear to chest down and volley with marvellous aplomb past Milan's goalkeeper Giovanni Galli. With arms outstretched Napoli's Brazilian number seven ran to salute the thousands of travelling Neapolitans going mad behind the goal. But instead of going for that killer second, Napoli uncharacteristically sat back, playing right into Milan's hands. What followed was an unmitigated disaster for Ottavio Bianchi's team and a historic victory for Arrigo Sacchi's mean, moody and ultimately magnificent *Rossoneri*.

The San Siro rocked on its grand heels as the home side awoke with a frightful vengeance. Ruud Gullit's magical twist and turn enabled him to cross for Milan forward Pietro Virdis, only for Virdis to slash the ball horribly over from just six yards. The tide of battle swept back in Milan's favour. Sacchi's innovative, high intensity, attacking British style, performed with huge finesse and technique, saw his players incessantly pressing the opponents across the field. Napoli buckled as red and black shirts came at them from all angles. Evani, Donadoni, Ancelotti, aided by attacking full-backs Tassotti and Maldini, rampaged forward, pinning the Southerners back in their own penalty area.

With the *Rossoneri libero* Franco Baresi marshalling operations in front of a well-drilled back four, Arrigo Sacchi's team passed immaculately, cutting their opponents to shreds. Whenever Napoli had the ball, Milan fought furiously to win back possession. On nineteen minutes attacking defender Mauro Tassotti played in Gullit, whose precise pass back into the box found all-action midfielder Angelo Colombo to smash home low from eight yards out past a despairing Claudio Garella. The long blond locks of Colombo disappeared beneath a pile of Milan shirts. It was hard running football played at great pace but with poise and wonderful finesse. On the touchline Arrigo Sacchi in a long black trenchcoat danced a jig of joy. This game mattered. Still Milan raged: Evani's header was saved spectacularly by Garella as the onslaught continued unabated.

Again the thick moustachioed Virdis faltered as he shot haplessly over with an open net at his mercy. But such was the overwhelming superiority of the home team another goal had to come and it was Pietro Virdis who at last found his shooting boots. The Milan number eight's weaving run through the Napoli defence finished with him blasting past the keeper to ignite the stadium once more. Again the baldheaded Sacchi could not restrain himself and ran onto the pitch punching the air. The Neapolitans were run ragged. On thirty-two minutes a breathtaking move involving six Milan players that swept the entire length of the pitch ended with Gullit's flying header crashing against Claudio Garella's post and rebounding to safety. Harassed, bothered and ultimately overrun the champions staggered like a punch drunk fighter to the half-time break. But it would be just a brief respite.

The second half saw no let up in the action as the *Rossoneri* tortured their opponents, hitting passes long and short with equally devastating accuracy. At the fore was the mercurial Dutchman Ruud Gullit, leading the Neapolitans a merry dance, tearing constantly down the right wing wreaking havoc. One incident saw three Napoli players left in a blue, bedraggled heap as Gullit cast his own particular Dutch black magic over the champions. Diego Maradona was not so much upstaged as blown off stage. Indeed the great *Pibe De Oro* was even forced on the defensive, hoofing clear from his own penalty area as the pressure remained unyielding. Fifteen minutes from time a scything through-ball from the dynamic midfielder Ancelotti put Gullit clear and he rounded Garella with ease before placing the ball into an empty net. That made it 3-1 and game over. With the Neapolitans having given up the ghost and simply praying for full-time, Roberto Donadoni compounded their misery by beating Claudio Garella with alarming ease from fully twenty-five-yards. A terrible bobble deceived Garella who watched in horror as the ball sneaked horribly over the line. Finally the famed Italian referee Luigi Agnolin took pity on the Southerners and called time on Napoli's agony. The San Siro rose to salute their glorious heroes. Knowing there could be no argument with the result, Diego Maradona and his team left the field with heads bowed. For on that memorable Milan afternoon there was only only one number ten that mattered, and he wore red and black.

High above in the Presidential box, Silvio Berlusconi, dressed divinely by Italy's finest tailors, took the acclaim of an adoring crowd. Wearing a suit the price of a Third World country's national debt, Berlusconi, with beaming smile etched on permanent suntanned features, believed he cut a *Bella Figura*. This was a man who felt nothing of landing his personal helicopter on the training pitch at Milanello in the midst of a training session. How Berlusconi loved the open-mouthed expressions of the players as he made his typically grand entrance. For one whose giant ego was matched only by a bank balance, this mattered. Resembling in his exalted mannerisms a Roman Emperor of old, acknowledging saluting gladiators before deciding the fate of their felled opponents, Berlusconi bathed delightfully in fawning adulation. The dramatic gesture of thumbs down, no mercy to his team, as they twisted the sword deep into Napoli was greeted emphatically by the fanatical 15,000 Milan hardcore support of the *Fossa dei leoni*. To them their President was God on Earth, returning to purge Italy of this plague that had swept up from the south. For Neapolitans he was a despot and big trouble. It was all a timely, if unwanted reminder for Napoli that in January the championship was there to be lost, not won.

Embarrassed by their feeble surrender at the hands of a revitalised AC Milan, Ottavio Bianchi's men returned home shamefaced to Naples. Bianchi was hugely critical in private of the team, whilst remaining totally supportive in public, always adamant his players possessed the necessary character to bounce back. But inside he seethed, for what happened in the San Siro was unforgivable. Losing to one of their great rivals was bad enough but to be utterly annihilated in the process could not be tolerated. Then, seven days later and in typical fashion, with their pride badly stung by the Milan debacle, Napoli thrashed the living daylights out of an unsuspecting Fiorentina in the San Paolo, who must have wondered what they had done to deserve such a mauling. Eager to rid minds of the previous week's humiliation, the Neapolitans put four past the *Viola* without reply. A typically, swerving Maradona free-kick that flew like a rocket into the top corner, two from Giordano and *La Bomba*, Antonio Careca, helped ease the pain. After being drowned out in Milan the Samba drum once more found its beat.

Elsewhere, at the Stadio Comunale, AC Milan ended a fourteen-year losing streak in Turin against Juventus winning 1-0, courtesy of Ruud Gullit. Before the match Silvio Berlusconi entered the Milan dressing room and delivered a rousing speech to his players. He pleaded with them to prove the victory over Napoli was no fluke, but a clear show of intent in their quest to win the title. Berlusconi's inspirational words had the desired effect. Gullit, christened *Il Tulipo Nero* (the black Tulip) by his adoring fans, was magnificent. The larger than life Dutchman had already in his short time in Italy earned cult status amongst the red and black *tifosi*. Indeed the confident Gullit showed he possessed more than one string to his bow by performing live with his reggae band Revelation to a 3,000 crowd at an open-air concert in Milan. But it was on the football pitch where Gullit's true talents shone, as he looked every inch a worthy contender for Diego Maradona's world crown.

Born to Surinam and Dutch parents in Amsterdam, this was a player unique on the world scene, not only in looks with his extravagant Afro dreadlocks but, more importantly, his footballing talent. Two-footed, deadly from free-kicks, forever on the move, arriving unseen in the box causing mayhem. Despite playing centre midfield for Holland, Sacchi preferred playing him wide right, with the electrifying pace of Sardinian Virdis on the left and van Basten through the middle. But like so many of the great Dutch players, Gullit possessed a high measure of versatility that saw him capable of performing anywhere to equally devastating effect. Whilst *Il Tulipo* appeared worth every single lira of the record fee paid to PSV Eindhoven securing his services, Marco van Basten found himself on the sidelines for long periods of his first season in Milan colours. A troublesome and ultimately crippling ankle injury saw Van Basten reduced to performing just a cameo role in the *Rossoneri's* title charge, though ultimately it was one that proved spectacular. For when the return match in Naples came round, van Basten would all but decide the destination of *Lo Scudetto*.

In the distance, kicking up dust, the thundering hoofs of AC Milan pounded in close pursuit of the champions. Everytime the Neapolitans looked over their shoulder Milan were forever in sight and earshot. Like a dog with a bone Arrigo Sacchi's never-say die team refused to let go. Yet another epic confrontation between North and South sprang from its roots into full bloom. Insults hurled back and forth from both cities. The Milanese mocked the lowlife *terroni* of Naples that they had neither the heart nor strength to retain their one lucky, measly *Scudetto*. Soon they would be back in the gutter, to be squashed like bugs under the well-polished heel of Milan's boot. The Napoli *tifosi* retaliated with unreserved venom by claiming the *Rossoneri* were nothing more than a Berlusconi plaything to be discarded when he got bored. A prostitute, all grateful and indulging to her filthy, rich pimp of a sugar daddy. It became clear to all that AC Milan had leapfrogged Juventus to become public enemy number one in Naples, a mantle regarded by many in the north as a backhanded compliment. *La Vecchia Signora* were old news. Banners were prepared, new songs penned. Each week saw hearts soar and hopes dashed. No love lost, no quarter given or asked by either side... Game on.

A ruthless 5-0 massacre of Como at the San Siro with Gullit scoring twice looked to have cut Napoli's lead back even further, only for Diego Maradona to grab a last-gasp goal in Genoa against Sampdoria. With time almost up on a swamp of a pitch at the Luigi Ferraris stadium, Maradona latched onto a sloppy defensive clearance, dug the ball out of the mud and crashed home from the edge of the box to steal the points for Napoli. Off he slid, diving headfirst in delight with his compadres on a rain-drenched surface, arms raised in triumph. The Neapolitans left it late, but once again when all looked lost *Pibe De Oro* saved the day. So it continued with Milan continuing to stalk Napoli's every move. Almost inevitably nerves took hold and points were dropped. But whenever the champions faltered, AC also tripped up. On 6th March Napoli went down 2-1 at home to Roma. Two goals adrift with just ten minutes left Careca pulled one back and all hell broke loose in the visitors' penalty area. The dying seconds saw the Roma players almost on their knees as they came under intense pressure, only to be saved by the referee's full-time whistle. As the home *tifosi* stood forlorn, news reached them of Milan only drawing 0-0 with Verona. The almost beautiful irony of this was not lost on the Neapolitans who laughed their heads off at this unexpected helping hand from the despised Veronese.

166

But such was the wealth of firepower employed by the champions, almost inevitably they pulled away from the *Rossoneri*, and by mid-April they had a healthy four points lead. A 1-0 win earned at the San Paolo against Inter with a stupendous Diego Maradona free kick was deemed exceptional by even his standards. *Perfezione*! (Perfection!) Such was the ridiculously pin-point accuracy of Maradona, Inter's *Azzuri* goalkeeper Walter Zenga simply shrugged his shoulders as if to suggest, 'How do you expect me to stop that? Maradona's flashy Samba dance routine with Antonio Careca at the corner flag celebrated a five-point advantage over Milan. The championship once more looked safe. Appearing hopelessly outgunned, the hopes of Arrigo Sacchi's men was left in the hands of others. On 17th April 1988, SSC Napoli travelled to Turin to deal with an old thorn that forever pained them. It would prove a defining weekend in the battle for *Lo Scudetto*, for no other team in Italy relished more the opportunity to knock Napoli off their pedestal. *La Vecchia Signora*, the deposed grand old lady of Serie A stood ready to wreak revenge. Beware a proud woman scorned?

By their own exceptionally high standards Juve's season had been spectacularly mediocre. Lying haplessly adrift in seventh place, Rino Marchesi's team was in a state of readjustment following the retirement of the exalted Platini. Unfortunately there was no such phrase as 'transitional period' in the *Bianconeri* dictionary and the same sense of unease that dogged Marchesi's last years in Naples returned to haunt him. His signing of Liverpool's prolific goalscoring centre forward Ian Rush proved nothing short of calamitous with Rush appearing to lack even the basic technique and tactical nous required to operate in the highest echelon of Serie A. The Welshman's struggle to learn Italian was all too obvious as teammates grew increasing agitated at his ineffectual performances. It became beyond embarrassing with Rush looking incapable of trapping a medicine ball, let alone being allowed to lead the line of the great Juventus. That he would later infamously claim that his time in Italy 'was like being in another country' perhaps said it all.

The Neapolitan hordes descended on Turin in typically vast numbers, but alas for them the sweet memory of the previous season's fixture was not to be repeated as Juve upset the odds to beat Napoli 3-1 and blow the title race wide open. At the same time beyond the Seven Hills of Rome, AC Milan overcame Roma 2-0 to go just two points behind the champions, with a game against Napoli still to come. Leading 1-0 at the break, a fired-up Juventus playing easily their best football of the season tore into Ottavio Bianchi's side, which to their supporters horror appeared to lack heart for a fight. Defeat against their Turin foes could be tolerated, God knows they had enough experience over the years, but to lie down before them? Napoli appeared to have blown a gasket, *Magica's* spell was broken.

On sixty-seven minutes to rub further salt into their seeping wounds, the heavily derided Rush earned himself some much needed breathing space with the Juve Ultras when he pounced to double their lead. The Neapolitan *tifosi* hardly knew whether to laugh or cry on seeing Rush of all people score against them. He the object of their jokes and scorn, had lashed back to leave them choking on their venom. This had proved a bad day in the North. As sweet their last visit to Turin was, so this time round it had fallen sour. A penalty driven home by Juventus midfielder Di Agostini was the final nail in their coffin.

A late effort finished with fine aplomb by Antonio Careca merely papered over an insipid, scandalous surrender by the Southerners. Something was wrong. The thousands of miserable, downbeat Neapolitans who stood crestfallen on the terraces of the Stadio Comunale smelt a rat. But none felt more betrayed than Ottavio Bianchi. The *allenatore's* bewildered, shocked expression at the full time whistle gave rise to the notion that the battle for *Lo Scudetto* was already over. For Bianchi the shocking realisation that certain players wearing Napoli colours had thrown in the towel left him sick to the stomach. To lose by bad play was galling enough but to sell your soul and betray a city and its people who had nothing else was a *Fattacio* beyond words. Bianchi could only pray his suspicions were unfounded. Here was a man desperately seeking answers but at the same time dreading to be proved wrong.

Before the *Rossoneri* trod a fateful path to Naples for their title decider against Napoli, both sides had potential banana skins to overcome. Milan faced city rivals Internazionale at the San Siro, whilst the champions endured yet another perilous journey up-country to take on Hellas Verona. Neapolitans joked that William Shakespeare must have been in ironic mood when he penned his legendary description of Verona as the 'city of lovers'. Outnumbered in a strange land inhabited by even stranger people, many times they were left battered, bloodstained by murderous hordes of the Brigate Gialloblu, and the outrageously biased local polizia who viewed Southerners with sneering disdain. But the visitors could hardly complain for when the northerners went south the abuse was returned with interest. They found to their bloody cost that Naples was not all romantic splendour, singing mandolins and haunting *Canzone*. Choking chaos, stifling heat, the heavy smell of volcanic sulphur forever lingering. Paradise with an edge. This was the true home of SSC Napoli. Take liberties and their title if you dare! Welcome to Naples!

FATTACCIO (FOUL DEED)

On the pitch a win for Napoli and defeat for Milan would all but seal the *Scudetto*, however it was not to be. For as Maradona's brilliant first half strike from the edge of the box guaranteed his team a hard earned point in Verona, Sacchi's men triumphed gloriously over Inter with goals from Gullit and Virdis. The points difference was down to one, as the *Scudetto* suddenly became theirs to touch. All eyes fell upon the San Paolo. Three games remained for each side but there was only one that mattered. Both cities braced themselves for one almighty clash. A loss for either in Naples would surely end their challenge. Diego Maradona called on his team and supporters for one last great effort. *El Pibe De Oro* urged Napoli *tifosi* to shake the foundations of their stadium with noise and rouse Vesuvius from its slumber. Let them all go together as kings of Italy, top of the pile. For it would have been a scenario much preferable to them being dethroned at the *Rossoneri's* hands. Neapolitans prayed that the days of Northern bullies coming to their city laying down the law, all pomp and arrogant swagger, was just a distant nightmare. They were damned if they would let it happen again. The people of Naples were ready to play a part, determined not to let their Captain down.

Ottavio Bianchi experienced a horrific time in the week leading up to the Milan showdown. His fraught state of mind meant everywhere he looked conspiracies loomed. A chasm of mistrust, bordering on hatred, had grown wide between the coach and many of his senior players. But surprisingly one spared criticism was Diego Maradona. Though neither would ever claim to be remotely close in any way, Bianchi had no reason to doubt Maradona's sheer will to win, for there had been too many times he had single-handedly saved Napoli with a piece of individual brilliance, when it would have been so easy for him not to do so. Though the Argentinian's off-pitch antics repeatedly reduced his coach to despair, even to the point where he considered selling him, there was no doubt whatsoever in Bianchi's mind of his Captain being on the take. Diego Maradona may have taken many things in his time, drink, drugs, but money to throw matches? Ottavio Bianchi thought not.

Of the other *artista* (performers) he could not be so certain. There were reasons that Bianchi did not sleep well at night, for amongst his line-up there were some whose pasts were tarnished by allegations they would rather forget. Though living legends of *Lo Scudetto* and beloved folk heroes of the *tifosi*, could these leopards have ever truly changed their spots? Bianchi's mind remained racked with doubts. Was the gallant performance at Verona in a most intimidating atmosphere a positive sign that his team's heart for battle had returned? Or was it all simply part of a cruel charade to allow the leading characters in this dreadful masquerade to deliver the final *coup de grace* in the San Paolo? On Naples' sacred turf upon which their dream was consecrated, this disturbing tale would unfold for the entire world to witness. For if the dark rumours that emanated from the southern capital were of any true substance, then Arrigo Sacchi was leading the *Rossoneri* into a supposed bearpit to fight a lame toothless animal wishing only to lay down and die.

Like all his Milan brethren Silvio Berlusconi trusted Neapolitans only as far as he could throw them! With this in mind a paranoid Berlusconi decided on extraordinary measures of security, for if any city in the world could concoct a devious plot to blight his team's preparation it was Naples. This unholy place where the Devil needed a bodyguard, where snake charmers and voodoo witches earned a good living sat on blankets outside fancy boutiques and antique bookshops, where double-dealing, intrigue and corruption were part of everyday life. The President was convinced an attempt would be made to bring them down. In order to avert such a scenario he hired two planes for the journey to Naples, one for the team and the other to carry food, drink and medicine supplies. For the danger that these dastardly Neapolitans would poison his superstars by sprinkling something extremely nasty on the food or spiking their water was deemed a real danger by the Milan President.

To such an extent he brought along his own personal chef and private legion of bodyguards to supervise all meals served, with no local hotel staff allowed anywhere near. Purposely waiting until the last possible minute, AC Milan went south only on the eve of the game. On landing at Naples International Airport, the two planes were immediately surrounded by an armed ring of *polizia* and army vehicles. Amidst ridiculously over-the-top, indeed surreal security measures for a mere visiting football team, the bemused players were ushered swiftly across the deserted runway and onto a waiting bus. Then with a formidable escort in place, including a *Carabinieri* helicopter buzzing their every move, they sped off with dramatic red sirens wailing on a specially pre-arranged route meant to avoid the Neapolitan lynch mobs supposedly lying in ambush across the bay. Through veiled curtains Ruud Gullit and co dared to sneak a look and gaze in utter bewilderment at an entire city draped in Napoli colours. Every roof, balcony and doorway lay covered in blue. It appeared beyond fanaticism. An old lady looking to cross the road happened to catch Gullit's eye as the coach became struck at traffic lights. Her wickedly insulting gesture to the Dutchman, delivered with heartfelt meaning left all who witnessed it rather shocked, such was the look of sheer hatred ensconced in her cragged features.

As the coach made its wary way on the seafront, Via Partone, past the dock, it was if everyone had just up and gone! The harbour's giant lifting cranes left abandoned, precious cargo lying stacked high on pallets untouched. Hulking freight ships stood silent, their goods unloaded. But

170

unknown to the visitors, prying eyes reported their every move to a huge welcoming reception of Napoli *tifosi* waiting to greet them outside their temporary residence of the inaptly named Hotel Jolly! Men, women, children, all armed to the teeth with rocks and rotten fruit, took aim. On the final lap of their journey the Milanese felt the full warmth of Naples' greeting, for as they entered the city centre the bombardment began! What appeared like the entire population had turned out to vent their hatred against these northerners who dared to take their *Scudetto* away. Security barriers manned by lines of *polizia*, erected to keep out the baying crowds, came under fire. All hell let loose as from nowhere thousands pounced, hurling stones, broken bottles, coins, spitting, screaming abuse. Sheltered by a ring of steel the beleaguered Milan players ran for their lives through this gauntlet of hate into the relative safety of the hotel foyer.

There they watched the scenes outside of Neapolitans serenading them with their legendary collection of derisory chants, insulting songs and vitriolic insults. It was a day where nothing was sacred. Even parentage was questioned. Fathers and Mothers, either bastards or whores. This was war, nothing more or less. In a concerted attempt to ensure none of the Milan squad slept a wink that night, the locals set up camp outside the hotel and began indulging in a raging sea of noise. The despised Silvio Berlusconi already owned their shops, television stations and newspapers. His triumphal talk of a new dawn scared and irritated them beyond words. History had always shown Neapolitans eager to embrace new conquerors, if only to bathe in the misery of the former. But times had changed, they were now kings of their own castle, and Berlusconi with his *Milanisti Puppazi* (puppets) would not be allowed to break Naples' hearts.

Fanatical Neapolitans beat drums, crashed bin lids, set off firecrackers, indeed anything that banged was put to use. With typical foresight Berlusconi had already made plans to counteract by renting the entire 25th floor of the towering Jolly. There the jeering and cat-calls could still be heard but at least they were out of firing range as catapults and all manner of improvised homemade siege weapons fell short, crashing to earth. As evening drew in and the Naples black sky became drenched with stars, the frenzied enthusiasm of the Napoli *tifosi* refused to be curtailed by minor irritants such as tiredness or fatigue. Theirs was a holy mission, undertaken by the fanatically loyal foot-soldiers of Maradona, blessed by San Gennaro. Thou shalt not sleep! It was almost as if the Neapolitans feared their team was not capable of beating AC Milan unless they themselves gave all till morning came.

But they had sadly misjudged the fierce resilience of Arrigo Sacchi's men. No amount of wailing, hollering, cursing or hooting car horns would rattle the ice cool Baresi and the chilled-out Gullit. For if any team in the world possessed the class and character to overcome such an overwhelming atmosphere of rancid hostility, it was they. The *Rossoneri* would give their reply in the San Paolo. Finally a reluctant dawn broke and Naples woke with nervous trepidation. Churches as ever rapidly filled, though this time round congregations felt no fervid obligation to rush off to their football stadium. Suddenly it had become more important to pray. The unspoken rumours drifting like a rotten smell throughout the city appeared to have left its indelible mark. Nobody wanted or even dared to believe, but such was the doom-laden nature of Neapolitans they feared the worse.

So the most infamous game in the history of SSC Napoli unfolded. Laced with heady doses of drama, passion, tears and despair. For when they struck it was through those loved and least suspected. After over-estimating Napoli's odds at 5/1, the Giulianos would have lost billions in revenue if they retained their crown, such was the vast amount of cash bet by loyal Neapolitans on their heroes. *Lo Camorra* operated along the lines that the meek and mild may go on to be saints in the afterlife, but in this world they were quite simply fools and there to be exploited. It would prove the ultimate betrayal. The assassins were at the gate. The Endgame loomed and Ottavio Bianchi could do nothing about it. For sadly in Naples, even angels had dirt under their wings.

CHAPTER 18

ENDGAME

All dreams end. On Sunday 1st May 1988, amidst haunting flares and a crying sea of tears, Naples died a thousand deaths. AC Milan went south to conquer in exhilarating style. Though sick at heart in losing, 86,000 Neapolitans rose as one to acclaim Milan as worthy winners. This in itself was an achievement beyond words for many reporters and journalists present that day in the San Paolo stadium, for such a spontaneous act of sportsmanship by a normally rabid, fanatical support was unprecedented. But if the truth were known it was the lesser of two evils to be seen as magnanimous in defeat. For the alternative in having to acknowledge being undone by the treacherous acts of their own was simply too horrible to comprehend. The Napoli hordes watched in dismay. Just who were these pitiful strangers adorning the colours of their beloved club? The endgame loomed, Armageddon was at hand.

The cobbler's son had an ace up the sleeve to surprise all. Unknown to any except those in his inner sanctum Marco van Basten stood on the verge of a sensational comeback from long-term ankle injury. After a lengthy consultation with Milan's medical team Arrigo Sacchi felt it a worthwhile gamble risking having the brilliant Dutch centre-forward on the bench in the San Paolo. Who better than van Basten to call on if the need arose for a goal? With the Neapolitans threatening to self-implode through suspicion and unrest, the *Rossoneri* intended to clinch an eleventh *Scudetto* badge by winning in Naples, leaving the champions spent. The Milan party had remained wholly unaffected by the hatred and animosity shown towards them by their inhospitable southern hosts. Several of their players even had the temerity to wave at their baiters as they once more came under fire, making the short but perilous journey from the Hotel Jolly to the San Paolo.

The relaxed demeanour of Ruud Gullit spoke volumes, not just for himself but all his teammates. There was a wry smile on the face of Gullit as he watched incredulously through his window at Napoli *tifosi* on scooters racing at death-defying speed alongside them, faces etched in blood boiling fury, spitting venom at the detested Northerners. From the sideways, balconies and open windows the coach was battered ignominiously with rotten fruit. On arrival at the stadium a Neapolitan lynch mob intent on doing them serious harm fought with their own baton-wielding police in near-suicide attempts to reach the Milan team. Feelings were running out of control under the volcano. Finally the *tifosi*, their faces hidden by blue scarves, retreated, they could do no more. The sword of battle was passed on to those trusted in carrying the fight onto the pitch.

Diego Maradona led the defence of their most coveted crown. But little did Maradona realise the overwhelming odds stacked against him. *El Pibe De Oro* would find himself hopelessly outgunned. No matter how much courage and determination was shown, some games were not meant to be won. As the late afternoon sun cast towering shadows over the wide-open terraces of the San Paolo, a surreal atmosphere fell upon the stadium. An entire city braced itself for either triumph or more likely despair, for Neapolitans had already been blessed with one fairytale ending. Few doubted whether another *bella giornata* would be allowed to occur. Maybe God was forever merciful, but sadly it wasn't the Almighty on that Mayday in Naples calling the tune. The strings were tugged and the puppets danced.

Napoli began looking fraught, full of nerves and scared of their own shadows. Such obvious unease spread quickly onto the terraces, and in the early stages it was Milan who impressed as they sought to dominate possession, frustrating both the home team and supporters. Against an ear-piercing, deafening soundtrack of boos and whistles Arrigo Sacchi's superbly-drilled outfit passed the ball in supreme manner. The much-vaunted *Magica* trio of Maradona, Giordano and Careca found itself isolated and cut off as their midfield concerned themselves more in resisting the *Rossoneri* onslaught. Di Napoli, Bagni and Romano ran like madmen in a vain attempt to win the ball back from the swaggering, strutting red and black. But it was clear that Napoli, who only one year previously had swept all before them in swashbuckling fashion, were up against a side that in both style and players were just a little too good.

Whilst the champions continued to give the ball away carelessly, the movement, pace and technique of Milan caused gasps of astonishment around the stadium. The Naples clans howled in displeasure, they feared the worse. Maradona tried in vain to kickstart his team by dropping deep but found himself swamped by the seemingly rocket-fuelled midfield of AC Milan who fell upon him like a pack of wolves. Sacchi's men sparked and fizzed before finally exploding on thirty-six minutes when veteran striker Pietro Virdis pounced on a deflected free-kick to fire a vicious drive past a flailing Claudio

Garella high into the Napoli net from close range. A delighted Virdis wheeled away in triumph, though immensely careful to stay on the pitch and avoid the Neapolitan photographers and officials who stood encamped, grim faced and in murderous mood, behind the goal. An exuberant Arrigo Sacchi raced characteristically onto the field and embraced Virdis. The *Rossoneri* had cut deep, Naples was bleeding.

On the stroke of half-time Maradona broke free from his Milanese shackles, beat one man then two, only to be brought crashing to earth by Paolo Maldini on the edge of Milan's penalty area. The San Paolo soared into life on seeing its favourite son at last show a flash of his true self. Who else but *Pibe De Oro* to stem the blood flow when his perfectly flighted twenty-five-yard free-kick left Milan goalkeeper Giovanni Galli looking leaden-footed as the ball soared gloriously into the top left hand corner. It was a goal hardly deserved for the Neapolitans who had been outplayed until then. As celebrations raged inside the stadium a visibly distressed Galli fell to his knees and lent forlornly against the post. His team had gone to Naples and played the champions off the park on their own turf. As the Argentinian danced an exuberant Samba with Brazilian teammate Careca at the corner flag in front of an ecstatic crowd, Galli watched on in dismay. His shocked features bore the expression of a man wondering just how Maradona had contrived to bend the ball over the Milan defensive wall and into the net when all angles appeared to have been covered. Composers compose memorable symphonies, painters paint masterpieces, authors write magnificent epics and Diego Armando played his football. Pure unadulterated genius. It was a goal that typified Maradona's time in Naples. 1-1.

The thin dividing line between joy and despair was never more evident as suddenly the San Paolo became convinced Maradona's wonder strike would spur their team on to greater effort. But come the second period Milan again carried on carving up the Neapolitans at will. None more than Ruud Gullit whose trickery and speed down the right wing made life hell for the Napoli defenders, and especially the left full-back Giovanni Francini who was exposed constantly and with great ease by the tantalising skills of the flying Dutchman. He appeared unstoppable. Finally fed up of being made to look foolish, Francini hacked his haunting tormentor down and was booked by the referee. Taking full advantage, the wily Gullit taunted his opponent, goading him into another reckless challenge that would see him dismissed. As the Naples crowd screamed vitriol in his direction, Gullit simply laughed in Francini's face, baiting him into retaliating.

On sixty-eight minutes Ruud Gullit cast a spell once more on a despairing Francini, twisting him one way then another, before firing in a cross that was finished expertly by the head of Pietro Virdis. Claudia Garella was left helpless as scandalous marking in the Napoli defence by their sleepwalking centre-half Moreno Ferrara left Virdis with acres of space to pick his spot and grab a second goal. That Garella stood with hands outstretched in disbelief at the apparent half-hearted efforts of his defender to stop the Milan forward, fooled few in the San Paolo. Such theatrical gestures and mannerisms were viewed daily on every street corner in the city by conmen and hustlers plying their trades. Napoli stormed right back and Bruno Giordano crossed for Maradona to stab a low shot whilst off balance straight at Galli. Immediately the Milan keeper threw the ball out to Paolo Maldini who quickly fed Ruud Gullit to begin yet another lightning counter-attack for this breathtaking team. Throughout the afternoon Milan's number ten had caused palpitations amongst the home crowd everytime he received possession. And there was still more to come.

Fourteen minutes remained in Naples when the striding, elegant figure of Gullit, with his Rastafarian dreadlocks flowing, raced with deadly intent over the halfway line bearing down on the retreating Napoli defence. Across the emotionally-charged, tortured, massed terraces, Neapolitans squirmed and sweated as their defenders shuffled backwards, looking petrified, caught in the eye of this Milanese onslaught. Gullit soared with outrageous ease into the penalty box before crossing perfectly for the Milan substitute Marco van Basten, standing totally unmarked eight yards from goal. His precise sidefoot effort beat a flailing Garella to make it 3-1. Sacchi's gamble had paid off. Van Basten had been on the pitch for only minutes but had returned to make his mark in inimitable manner. A deafening silence heard continents away gripped the San Paolo. The time and space which the Dutchman was given again caused disgust and alarm amongst the blue *tifosi*. Amidst haunting flares and a sea of tears, the city of Naples died a thousand deaths. Rumours like fresh air were free to spread. But how was it possible for a team that had so spectacularly won the Italian championship only a season previous to fall so low?

Two minutes later Antonio Careca pounced from close range to cut the deficit. Suddenly the gloomy air of resignation that had settled over the stadium melted away to be replaced by newfound hopes a point could still be had. Both managers looked close to a breakdown as they raged on the touchline barking out orders. Whilst Bianchi threw his arms manically upwards, urging his team to attack, attack, attack, Sacchi with eyes almost popping out of his head, cut a near-hysterical figure as he ranted, raved, implored and pleaded with his players not to concede an equaliser. He need not have worried, for with his *Capitano* Franco Baresi in typically commanding form at the back, Milan were ferocious, yet calm in defence.

Napoli swept forward in a last-gasp attempt to save face. The dying seconds saw a corner earned and a final chance to score. Marco van Basten received an ear bashing of monumental proportion from his coach for staying on the halfway line in expectation of a breakout, instead of running back to defend. But it was not to be. Neapolitan prayers to their patron San Gennaro for divine intervention fell on deaf ears. The referee Carlo Longhi blew for full-time and Milan led Serie A by a point with just two games left to play. Diego Maradona finished the contest lying slumped on the floor, his efforts in vain. As for Ottavio Bianchi, the ninety minutes left him with despair in his heart. His team had performed as if drunk on fatigue. Heavy legged, listless and disinterested, a *disgracia* (disgrace). A white flag had been raised over the San Paolo. A city held its head in shame.

As the beaten Napoli players slid sullenly away, embarrassed with heads sunk, the visitors, to their utter disbelief, were handed a wonderful standing ovation. From a ripple to a tidal wave the applause grew. Milan gathered in the centre-circle to acknowledge this remarkable, spontaneous display of sportsmanship from a crowd that would have gladly torn them limb from limb before the game began. Such behaviour showed clearly in Naples that they appreciated good football. Alas, the truth may have been darker, for many secretly feared something ghastly had occurred before their eyes. But for the time being such a scenario was best unspoken of. Better to be seen in a good light. Show the world they knew how to lose with grace. For the *Rossoneri* had been magnificent. Not for Sacchi's team the defensively minded, drab and dreary Northern tactic of *catenaccio* in order to steal a result on Neapolitan soil. AC Milan had gone south and exploded in all hell and fury, playing in a composed and thrilling style. With their bravura showing in the San Paolo, Milan achieved something no other side from up-country had ever managed to attain *rispettare* (respect).

It was like seven days on Death Row for the Neapolitans before the title was finally dragged from their grasp. In faraway Florence, against a fired up Fiorentina side enjoying their moment in the limelight, and the eyes of all Italy upon them, the dream died. But in all reality the thousands of loyal blue *tifosi* who ventured north to witness Napoli's last stand travelled more in blind faith than actual belief. Deep down they knew it was a hopeléss task. Before the game President Ferlaino reportedly paid Napoli's dressing room a visit in order to wish them luck, only to leave hastily after experiencing an atmosphere that he referred to rather disturbingly as '*inenarrabili*' ('an unutterable thing'). What Ferlaino actually witnessed has never truly come to light, but it was clear by that time Ottavio Bianchi had lost his players, Bianchi's anger at what occurred over the final months of the season obviously leaving him close to breaking point. He was not the type to let matters lie. It is not beyond comprehension to believe that the President walked into a hornet's nest as his coach told certain individuals exactly what he thought of them, and they he.

Amidst fire and fury a gloating *Viola* administered with unreserved joy the last rites to SSC Napoli. For Neapolitans it came as little surprise that the man who delivered the final nail into their coffin was a former Napoli player. Argentinian centre forward Ramon Diaz delighted at scoring twice in a 3-2 win and breaking the heart of his old club. With ghostly echoes of Jose Altafini, *Core Ngrato*, many years before, Diaz finished off the Southerners to leave their supporters despairing and the Artemio Franchi stadium bathed in euphoria. As news of Napoli's defeat reached Milan, 80,000 Milanese in the San Siro erupted. The Rossoneri's 0-0 draw with Juventus meant the title would return north. A triumph wholly deserved. The old order had once more been established, the way of things. But at what price this was achieved will probably always remain shrouded in controversy.

The fallout from this devastating loss fell like acid rain in Naples. Strange tales abounded in the backstreets of the city that the *Camorra* had bribed a number of players to lose the Milan match and make a huge killing on their illegal *Totonero*. Others claimed that Silvio Berlusconi, with the establishment backing and his countless millions, had simply bought the *Scudetto* off Napoli. All was hearsay, heresy even, but in the immediate aftermath of such a shocking defeat many Neapolitans, still bitter at their loss, believed anything they were told. Wild, weird and wounding, the accusations flew like spears. Only Maradona and Careca appeared to emerge from the debacle with reputations intact. On the rest the jury was out. Both had been undermined by a spurious lack of fight amongst others in blue shirts that simply proved too heavy a burden for even a genius of Maradona's ilk to carry. To make matters worse a civil war broke out inside the club. Fed up with Ottavio Bianchi's authoritarian attitude and well aware of the feelings towards them in the city at that time, an attempt was made to shift the blame of losing the *Scudetto* onto the head of their coach.

Bianchi had finally exploded in all his pent-up fury at those he was convinced betrayed him. For the accused it was the final straw and a number of Napoli players approached Corrado Ferlaino to inform him they were prepared to go on strike if their coach was not dismissed. They had all signed a letter to such effect demanding action be taken. In Naples such a dramatic event could not stay secret for long and very quickly it became common knowledge. An entire city held its breath and pondered the inexorable question. The eyes of the *tifosi* fell on one man. Just where did Diego Maradona's loyalties lie?

Although not one of the original perpetrators it was no surprise that the Argentinian sided with his teammates by letting it be known to the Napoli hierarchy that he supported their actions. That one of Maradona's closest friends, Salvatore Bagni, was foremost amongst the protesters who wanted rid of the Iron Sergeant, and the small matter that the *Capitano's* own relationship with Bianchi was at best tolerable meant there would be few tears shed by *Pibe De Oro* if he was sacked. But an indignant Ferlaino blew a gasket at the sheer arrogance of those he considered still mere employees. As for Diego Maradona, he was told to behave and keep his mouth shut. Napoli's star player was reminded of the recently signed lucrative contract and who paid his wages. Such talk was like a red rag to a raging bull for the Argentinian, as he in archetypal manner launched a blistering attack on his Neapolitan paymasters by declaring publicly that the President would have to choose between him and Bianchi. A line in the sand was dug. This southern empire that only a short time before had appeared impregnable, now lay in flames. By their own hand the fires had been lit. *Il sogno esperito* (The miracle had vanished). Naples was burning.

Diego Maradona's rabid hatred of authority in any manner or form surfaced with a vengeance and he went to war, for nobody told *El Pibe De Oro* what to do. In a fit of self-righteousness, Maradona flew home to Buenos Aires vowing never to return unless Ottavio Bianchi was removed. The Napoli supremo's situation was desperate. Never in all his years at the club's helm had he faced such turmoil. In backing Bianchi, Ferlaino risked far more than just his job. The President's neck was very much on the line. He had experienced before just what the hardcore Napoli support were capable of if pushed. But luckily for him, the stories at the time which swept Naples regarding a supposed Fattacio occurring against AC Milan, that was neither his nor more importantly their idol Maradona's doing, saw the pressure ease. Others were deemed far more worthy of the *tifosi's* wrath. For in the Forcella and beyond the secret was already out. Somebody, somewhere had talked and whether it was out of disgust or simple, Neapolitan mischief-making, it had the desired effect for all hell let loose across the Bay.

The names of those said to have brought shame to the south were spat out in the city as gossip turned ever increasingly to believable fact. The four accused were goalkeeper Claudio Garella, defender Moreno Ferrario, midfielder Salvatore Bagni and centre forward Bruno Giordano. In Naples sunshine or night's shadow they could not hide. All kept an uneasy silence, but privately contact was made with *tifosi* organisations such as the CUCB to plead their innocence. Of the four only Moreno Ferrario's career appeared clear of any misdemeanours. But of the other three? Rumours that Claudia

Garella threw matches whilst playing for Lazio were long known, if never proved. Even a twice-former Napoli coach Luis Vinicio, who managed Garella in the late Seventies when both were employed in Rome, spoke out regarding past alleged wrongdoings of the keeper.

Salvatore Bagni found himself involved in a mysterious incident during his time at Inter Milan. Five years previous, whilst playing away at Genoa, Bagni set up a last minute winner for Milan striker Graziano Bini in a 3-2 victory. However instead of being applauded by the rest of their colleagues, both were snubbed and later in the dressing room attacked by teammates furious with them for ruining an alleged fix. A Milan newspaper got wind of the story and published it, thus prompting the Italian Football Association to order an investigation. However Inter were found not guilty on the grounds of 'insufficient evidence' As for Bruno Giordano, he was caught hands down in the infamous *Totonero* match-fixing scandal of 1980.

Italians still to this day shake their heads at the sheer scale of the conspiracy. Giordano was one of thirty-three Serie A footballers who became involved with a corrupt Rome betting syndicate, that after being double-crossed by certain players reneging on their side of the deal, took revenge by blowing the lid on the entire sting. On Sunday 23rd March 1980, in stadiums nationwide, the whistle was blown on the largest match-fixing scam the country had ever witnessed. All Italy watched horrified on live television as police officers walked onto football pitches to execute arrests. As the darkest chapter in Italian football history unfolded and sentences were passed, Bruno Giordano was shown little leniency in being handed a two-year ban. Armed with such proof of what these individuals were capable of, was it so surprising that all who loved SSC Napoli doubted their honesty when donning the blue shirt?

Many Neapolitans found themselves gripped with feelings of betrayal and paranoia. Everything they had was gone. Then there was *Il Lione*. For with Neapolitans betting billions of liras on their side retaining the title, a Milan triumph left *Camorra* families such as the Giulianos sitting on a mountain of cash once they failed. And maybe here is where the answer lay. The first line of Mario Puzo's epic novel *The Godfather* claimed, 'Behind every great fortune lay a crime.' It would have been against the very nature of these men to let such a once in a lifetime business proposition pass them by. A childish obsession with football could easily be tossed aside and surpassed by an overwhelming, burning passion for money. Carmine Giuliano's close friendship with Diego Maradona meant easy access, if ever required, to the rest of his teammates. Not that someone of Don Carmine's standing in Naples needed such an invitation. The Giuliano name alone guaranteed an audience.

It was obvious to all that the *Camorra* possessed the power to bring SSC Napoli to heel. All it required was the will to do so. And yet despite all the talk, rumours and gossip, there remained no definite proof! Typical Naples!

A promise from his President that he would not be fired saw Ottavio Bianchi feel confident enough to go on the offensive and sack in merciless fashion those who had called for his head. The coach lived up to his ruthless reputation by ripping apart the title winning team, ridding Naples of those he felt guilty of betrayal and of others deemed simply surplus to requirement. But what would they do with Diego Maradona, for Bianchi knew only too well that to even hint at selling Napoli's golden boy would see his life expectancy, never mind job security, dramatically shortened. In Naples at that time such a decision was literally life and death. Personal opinions and grudges faded into comparison. For in plotting the removal of Maradona, Ferlaino and Bianchi were attempting to depose a king, whom, despite many human failings, retained fierce backing amongst his subjects. *El Pibe De Oro* held the power in his dancing feet to bring this football club and the city she represented to its knees. There had to be another way?

Corrado Ferlaino roared out in defiance. 'He was President of SSC Napoli and would not be held to ransom.' Ferlaino gave interviews to all who would listen that he was prepared to hold Maradona to his contract, thus denying him the chance to play elsewhere. From Argentina counter-threats hurled back across the ocean. It was all a game, bluff and bluster. Who would break first? Both sides made noise about never backing down, but behind the scenes great efforts were under way to end the stalemate and ensure all emerged from this mess with pride intact. Despite what was aired for public consumption Diego Maradona was not yet ready to abdicate. As for President Ferlaino and Bianchi, they knew well that when fully fit and firing on all cylinders, their *Capitano* was undoubtedly the finest player of not just his era, but arguably of all time. It would have been the act of a madman to sell him.

Although Brazilians and all football purists would fiercely disagree about such a point of view, Diego Armando had, with his stupendous performances in leading Argentina to victory in the 1986 World Cup and taking Napoli to previously unscaled heights, placed a marker that could simply not be ignored. Any attempt to argue the heaven sent prowess of both men would prove an enjoyable, passionate but ultimately pointless debate. Pelé's immense contribution to Brazil's three World Cup triumphs saw him rightly hailed as a true genius, superhuman even. Argentina's finest, despite his many off-pitch frailties, that at any time threatened to overwhelm him, made miracles too. In footballing terms there was little to choose between them, but as men they differed like night and day.

Once retired, Pelé, who loved a dollar equally as he enjoyed a goal earned a fine living as football's official greatest player ever. The Brazilian travelled the globe shaking hands, patting the heads of wide-eyed little children, whilst all the time smiling amiably, talking in clichés. This fatherly figure who appealed to football fans of all ages proved perfect for corporation giants such as Coca-Cola who paid him vast sums to advertise their goods. Pelé was turned from footballing legend to corporate prostitute almost overnight. If the price was right he would perform. The good guy extraordinaire! Pure as the driven snow. As for Diego? The general media perception of Maradona was that of an ogre, the bad guy who stood for all that was wrong in the game. Indeed whilst Pelé, the kindly politician and preacher was happy to simply turn wine to water, Maradona excelled at turning water to wine. Some of the Argentinian's most outrageous tendencies had yet to become public knowledge, but a habit of saying whatever was on his mind meant he was never far from a headline. Maradona had a favourite saying that he never tired of quoting; 'I speak what I feel.' Everybody from lambasted referees to FIFA and the Pope felt his wrath at some stage. Maybe there was only one ever Pelé. But also, there was only one Maradona.

As *Pibe De Oro* sat sulking in Argentina, a strife-torn Naples remained unsure of whether their king would ever again see the sun rise over Mount Vesuvius. For the *Scudetto*, despite its fleeting beauty, was just a mere dream, one from which all Neapolitans would eventually wake. But Maradona was life itself, the air they breathed. Prayers were said for him to see sense but most were resigned to the notion that their sacred *Dieco* had gone forever. But they would be wrong, for not even on his native soil had Maradona experienced the adoration bestowed upon him by his adopted people. For him their love was a craving he simply could not live without. Could you ever imagine Romeo leaving Juliet? *El Rei* was not about to desert the Neapolitans in their most desperate hour of need. And the money was also a consideration as Guillermo Coppola convinced his client that the Italians were good yet for a few dollars more. DIARMA Productions spent like every day was their last. The old adage that the best things in life were free proved untrue in Maradona and Coppola's case as their insatiable, lustful appetite for fast cars, cocaine and beautiful women saw fortunes made and lost on an almost weekly basis. Why ruin a good thing?

So a deal was struck. A charade, a cheap act, a simple marriage of convenience. A press conference was called in Naples. Television news crews, photographers and journalists rushed to Napoli's training ground. Word as ever spread swiftly over the bay and hundreds of *tifosi* descended on Soccavo, laying siege to the complex. In an unreserved showing of loyalty to their king

182

they sang his name loud and proud. As Ferlaino stood ready to address the audience, a familiar chant reached his ears. The Napoli anthem of 'Diego Diego Diego' resonated loudly through the walls. It was, if needed, a final reminder to their President to do the right thing. Or else? As photographers snapped and cameras rolled, a smiling though distinctly nervous President Corrado Ferlaino paused for great dramatical effect before declaring in grandiose fashion, 'People of Naples, Diego Maradona is coming home!'

A last, sad epitaph of this depressing, Neapolitan tragic farce was the sudden, unexpected departure that summer of Napoli stalwart and club legend Guiseppe Bruscolotti. Only twelve months previously in the joyous aftermath of the *Scudetto* triumph *El Pepe* was proclaimed by Diego Maradona as, 'The true *Capitano* of SSC Napoli.' His decision to call time on a fifteen year career at the San Paolo caused many to shake their heads. Especially as he was not included in the Bianchi purge. It was claimed by those closest to him that Bruscolotti left a broken man after learning the extent of the treachery within.

Whilst adorning the blue shirt, nobody ever fought harder for the Neapolitan cause on the pitch than he, sometimes with a ferociousness verging on fanatical. But what about when your enemies lurk in dark shadows, undermining a lifetime's work, when they stand beside you in the same colours, only to possess the sole intent of not trying? Then it became a battle that even a warrior such as Bruscolotti could never win. The infamous events of Sunday 1st May 1988 caused him a terrible sadness, one to this day *El Pepe* refuses to discuss, preferring instead to keep his own counsel on what he saw and heard. But in saying nothing he says everything. Neapolitans did not deserve what befell them on that fateful day.

That same summer the miracle of San Gennaro failed to transpire. Few in Naples were surprised.

CHAPTER 19

STATE OF GRACE

SSC Napoli 8 Pescara 2! It appeared the demise of Maradona and his southern hordes had been greatly exaggerated. On Sunday 23rd October 1988, regenerated by an exhilarating, life saving transfusion of fresh blood, Ottavio Bianchi's revamped Napoli slaughtered a hapless Pescara, who experienced for the second year running a humiliating defeat in Naples. One of the most sensational scorelines in Serie A history sent shockwaves through Italian football. Amongst the goal-glut were old heroes joined by the new. Maradona, Carnevale, Careca and Alemao. Many outsiders regarded the tragic loss of Lo Scudetto to the Milanese as the final nail hammered into the coffin of Napoli's brief if illuminating reign as champions. But there was to be many a twist and turn of fortune both ill and good before they, as ever cut their own throats. The epic saga of Diego Maradona's time in Naples was set to hail in even more heady doses of triumph and despair. And yet, during the Neapolitan summer of 1988, few would ever have bet on him being around for so long. For the best of times had suddenly become the worst.

It was a sullen, unshaven Diego Maradona who returned from self-inflicted exile in Buenos Aires to once more take up his Naples crown of thorns. But all was still not well with the King. Despite what was aired for public consumption there remained rivers of bad blood between himself and the club hierarchy. The Argentinian had always been bigger than SSC Napoli, the difference now arose that he acted like it. The prickly small acorns that had niggled him since arriving from Barcelona suddenly became jagged spears. His accommodation in Posilippo, despite being amongst the finest in the city, was deemed by a foul mood Diego Maradona 'a cage without bars'. Every time he set foot upon his balcony, *tifosi* below would scream his name. There was nowhere to hide, privacy was impossible. The adoration suddenly threatened to strangle Maradona. The Naples nights still echoed with the joyful sounds of partying, samba music and laughter. Cocaine and wine flowed free as ever but it had become more a necessity to relieve the pain and anger rather than enjoyment. The magic vanished, he could no longer stay faithful. Amidst great secrecy a fed-up Maradona instructed his manager Coppola to find him another club.

Also the brutal manner in which Ottavio Bianchi dismembered the title-winning side irked Diego. It very swiftly became clear that Diego Maradona had no intention of making up with Bianchi. The animosity between the two proved overwhelming and the utter contempt each held for the other was such that no matter what deal Coppola and Ferlaino tried to conceive, it became blatantly obvious they could never again work together on a daily basis. A compromise was suggested in which the player would be allowed to train alone, away from the hawk eyes and barking voice of the Iron Sergeant. Hardly a perfect scenario, but one deemed preferable for Neapolitans to *El Pibe De Oro* plying his trade elsewhere. Say Milan, or, God forbid. . . Turin?

The Napoli coach consented only through gritted teeth to such an absurd arrangement. Only in Naples could this madcap charade have been concocted. But when it came to Diego Maradona, normal rules did simply not apply. That he appeared hellbent on doing all in his considerable power to undermine Bianchi, only fuelled what was an already intolerable situation. For even a hardnosed veteran like he was not immune from the extreme pressure managing a club like Napoli brought. There were those who due to his historic triumph in bringing them the long-awaited *Scudetto*, still remained wholly loyal to Maradona with a blind faith tottering on fanaticism. The enemies of *Pibe De Oro* were their own. If needed many of these young *tifosi* would have gladly sided with *El Rei* against God or the Devil himself. What chance an unloveable character like the sourfaced Bianchi?

He was on borrowed time. Only the momentous achievement in realizing every Neapolitans' fantasy prevented the axe from falling. To take on a king, two weapons are needed in your armoury; the love of the people and a preferable alternative. Ottavio Bianchi had neither and had resigned himself to the only possible outcome, the sack. But Corrado Ferlaino had no intentions of firing Bianchi. After all the riches brought to the table by his beleaguered coach, he believed it a matter of honour to stand by him. The President sought a meeting with Diego Maradona to end this nonsense and ensure peace broke out in Naples. In this city anything untoward that affected his football club never stayed secret long and Ferlaino quickly became aware of the Argentinian's expressed desire to go elsewhere. He proposed a deal to suit all. Call a truce with Ottavio Bianchi, play one more year, then, and only then, would he be released from his contract. There would be nothing in writing, a simple promise, a handshake. A Neapolitan State of Grace. But the understanding was clear. Maradona would be free to leave. An olive branch that pricked when you least expected. As *Pibe De Oro*, in time, discovered to his cost.

Diego Maradona had suffered enough the endless painkilling injections, so many more than were good for him. His battered ankles and leg muscles had become almost permanently inflamed. Before matches he could hardly walk, only to be 'helped', albeit temporarily, by a club surgeon's jab that allowed him to play. Once a year in an attempt to lift the searing pain, Maradona put himself under the surgeon's knife to have bits of unwanted, leftover cortisone quite literally scraped off his joints with a scalpel. This was the unseen world, the true reality of Neapolitan legend, *El Pibe De Oro*. Away from the adoring crowds, the player both in body and mind was close to collapse. But such was Maradona's ultimate box office appeal, the pressure was on the coaching and medical staff to ensure their *Capitano* took to the field every week. For how do you replace genius? To take Diego Maradona out of the Napoli line-up was akin to removing a bullet from a gun. That every Sunday in Serie A he was ruthlessly hacked down, mauled, punched and spat at by opposing defenders under instructions to stop him playing at all cost, meant little to those at his football club who cared all about money, and nothing about the Argentinian's health. He was a commodity, nothing more, to be milked until there was nothing left. And God help Maradona if he dared complain. Or even worse, leave before they had bled him dry.

With the President's word that his position was secure, and the bribed, rogue genius of Diego Maradona available for selection, Ottavio Bianchi began the task of rebuilding a team good enough to win back the title. Despite all, Bianchi's enduring love affair with Naples and her football team still thrived with a passion rivalling any young *tifosi* from the Forcella, Sanita or Spanish Quarter. Though not a native, the blue blood of this fair city ran fierce through his veins. The coach understood those chosen to wear the Napoli shirt had to possess special qualities. Neapolitans demanded an air of *fantasista* about their footballers. To satisfy this fanatical support Bianchi proved once more a shrewd operator in the transfer market by bringing in players of such flair and imagination to replace those sold during his summer bloodletting.

Foremost amongst them was Brazilian international playmaker Rogerio Ricardo de Brito, otherwise known as Alemao. Bought specifically from Athletico Madrid to supply ammunition for fellow countryman Antonio Careca and Diego Maradona, the twenty-seven-year-old Alemao quickly felt at home in the footballing cathedral of San Paolo. Wonderful dribbling skills and an eye for the killer pass saw this tall, languid *median* (left half/midfielder), who played with just the right touch of arrogance and with socks rolled permanently around his ankles, tailormade to make a huge impression in Naples. To replace his discarded number one, Claudia Garella, Bianchi turned once more to Verona, signing the experienced goalkeeper Giuliano Giuliani. Also in a double swoop on Turin, the Torino winger Massimo Crippa and highly rated full-back Giancarlo Corradini were snapped up. From Ascoli came another dogged defender, Antonio Carannante. Finally the coach wrapped up his spending of President Ferlaino's money by buying Sampdoria's strong-running midfielder Luca Fusi. A new Napoli was born.

Ottavio Bianchi readied himself for yet another helter-skelter ride aboard the Neapolitan rollercoaster, aka SSC Napoli. As ever there would be no seatbelt or parachute. Instead he would ride in the lap of the Gods. San Gennaro willing, Bianchi could only pray he be allowed the chance to reclaim *Lo Scudetto*, before freefalling and going the way of so many before him. The early signs were hardly promising, for after an opening last gasp win over Atalanta in Naples, the Neapolitans suffered a humiliating 1-0 loss at unfancied Lecce. Then, just when the critics looked set to unsheath their slings and arrows upon Bianchi's head, a Maradona-inspired Napoli exploded in truly spectacular manner. On 23rd October, all came together when little Pescara went south with some trepidation after being thrashed 6-0 the season before. Never ones to go along with the general consensus that lightning never stuck the same place twice, Neapolitans proved otherwise and dished up yet another merciless drubbing for the unfortunate visitors. This time by 8-2!

A stunned San Paolo watched in disbelief as *El Pibe De Oro* led the line in glorious style with a bewitching, understated, but sensational performance nonetheless. It was a rampant orgy of rip-roaring attacking football. Two goals each for the *Capitano*, Careca, Carnevale, and new boy Alemao sliced apart a Pescara team, whose faces with the tally steadily mounting turned equally red as their shirts. The highlight of a 4-0 lead at half-time was a typically wicked, swerving thirty-yard free-kick from Diego Maradona that flew like a rocket into the top right hand corner to set the stadium ablaze. Further mayhem followed, but again it was Maradona who stole the show when from fully forty yards he cut inside from the touchline, feinted to pass, only then, with the outside of his left foot, clip an outrageous shot that missed only by a whisker. It was a magnificent effort by Maradona, still the finest exponent of his trade on the planet.

Blessed spontaneity: a bewildering sleight of footwork, miraculous in the making and exemplifying the magic that set apart those touched by angels. The stadium stood as one to applaud. Neapolitans had grown increasingly weary of the constant bickering between Guillermo Coppola and Corrado Ferlaino as the battle to own Maradona's soul raged. They had no interest in two such mere mortals. Who bothered listening to the carpings of a contemptible Salieri whilst Mozart plied his own heavenly gift? For the countless thousands of Napoli *tifosi* who basked gloriously in his diminutive shadow, only one thing truly mattered. *El Rei* was back doing what he did best, making their dreams come true. Despite alleged rumoured longings for pastures new, in the back alleys of Naples the popularity of Maradona showed little sign of waning, as he remained to Neapolitans a living God. Woe betide any who suggested otherwise.

Three weeks later SSC Napoli topped even their crue, massacre of Pescara with a ridiculously swashbuckling 5-3 defeat of eternal enemy Juventus in Turin. A home side under a new coach, former Napoli and Juve great Dino Zoff, found themselves blitzed in an opening period that saw the Southerners roar deservedly into a 3-0 lead. Two from a rapacious Careca and a third from a rejuvenated back-in-favour Andres Carnevale (after the selling of Bruno Giordano) saw the massed blue hordes ecstatic. As always in Turin between these two bitter adversaries, southern banners and flags lay drenched en masse over Stadio Comunale terraces. Three minutes into the second half the home side pulled a goal back for what appeared merely scant consolation from midfielder Roberto Galia. Then, shortly after, Juve's sublime Russian international Zavarov shot home past Napoli goalkeeper Giuliani to make it 3-2 and game on. Turin was alight! Sadly for the Old Lady, the fire was swiftly extinguished when Antonio Careca (*La Bomba*) struck once more to complete a memorable hat-trick. Thirteen minutes from the end, Juventus rallied one last time through wide man Luis Di Agostini, only for Napoli defender Allesandro Renica to wrap the points up with a late penalty. 5-3, and yet another superb showing by Ottavio Bianchi's restructured team.

But just when Neapolitans thought life could not get any sweeter, champions AC Milan re-entered their sights. On Sunday 27th November, Arrigo Sacchi's *Lo Rossoneri* returned to the San Paolo. For the blue *tifosi*, red and black shirts back in their midst conjured up disturbing reminders of the last time they crossed swords under southern skies. The controversial events which devastated SSC Napoli on that soiled, May, Sunday afternoon still caused sleepless nights in Naples. Many remained confused as to what actually took place. Others refused simply to believe, for nothing had ever been proven. All was rumour, secondhand gossip. But Neapolitan belief that the bigger the conspiracy, the easier it was to hide meant serious misgivings remained.

The San Paolo held its breath as these two great rivals prepared once more to do battle. From the kick-off both sides appeared pensive, reluctant to open up, preferring instead to rely and wait for their opportunity. For forty minutes it was typical Italian cat and mouse. Then, a lofted pass was hoisted over an unsuspecting Milan rearguard that to Milan's infernal horror was latched onto by an unmarked Diego Maradona. Out came Giovanni Galli to confront the Argentinian, only for Napoli's number ten to leap high and head the ball over the stranded keeper into an open goal from twenty-yards out. The San Paolo erupted as Maradona raced across the running track to celebrate his fifth strike of the season with the *tifosi* hordes. Neapolitans rose to salute their beloved *Capitano, El Pibe De Oro*. '*Il sangue azzuro dalla nascita*' ('Blue blood since birth'). One of their own.

With the referee Luigi Agnolin ready to blow for half-time, a long goal-kick from Giuliani was misjudged for once by the normally impeccable *libero* Franco Baresi, and Antonio Careca sprinted through to shoot past a despairing Galli, sending the stadium once more into raptures. Shortly after the second half began two became three, when with Milan pressing forward, the home side broke. Sprinting clear into the *Rossoneri* penalty area, Andres Carnevale's low shot was half-saved, only for the rebound to fall at the feet of the raiding Napoli full-back Giovanni Franchini, who from close range gleefully sidefooted the ball into the net. A crazed melee ensued behind the goal. Naples had waited long for this moment of redemption, a cleansing of the soul. The Milanese appeared close to collapse: Careca let fly a thunderbolt from thirty-five yards that the overworked Galli somehow managed to tip miraculously over the bar. *Lo Rossoneri* were being run ragged. Arrigo Sacchi showed clear his frustration on the bench, angrily waving away a television crew filming his animated features, politely informing them in no uncertain manner to clear off!

Repeatedly Napoli launched swift, incisive counter-attacks that many times threatened to increase their lead. The San Paolo throbbed with furore and excitement. As he led yet another breakout from a Milan corner, the time came for Diego Maradona to add his own brand of magic to this Naples carnival. Surrounded by red and black shirts, Maradona bewitched them all with an outrageous back-flick to teammate Allessandro Renica that left Baresi, Maldini, Costacurta and Tassotti wondering where the ball had gone. Though Pietro Virdis converted a late penalty to grab his customary goal against Napoli, it was just a consolation for Milan, and twelve minutes from time the unstoppable Careca set the seal on a memorable day for the Neapolitans when he pounced to make it 4-1. Any other season in Serie A the Southerners would have been clear favourites to win back their title. But not that year, for Milan's other great empire had awoken from its slumber, the famed blue and black stripes of Internazionale. *La Grande Inter*!

Powered by the thunderous, Teutonic heartbeat of twenty-seven year old Lothar Matthaus, the *Nerazurri* had begun the campaign in explosive style. Matthaus was lured that same summer along with another established German international, defender Andres Brehme from Bayern Munich. The highly-regarded Inter coach Giovanni Trapattoni, *Il Trap*, had built a powerful team brimming with technical expertise, creativity and experience. Up front *Azzurri* forward Aldo Serena and the much-travelled Argentinian hitman Ramon Diaz proved a lethal combination. A water-tight rearguard, marshalled superbly by goalkeeper Walter Zenga and defensive stalwart Guiseppe Bergomi, allied with the fire power and lung bursting Lothar Matthaus in midfield, meant the *Nerazzurri* were an awesome proposition for any team in Serie A. As the months rolled on Trapattoni's relentless, all-conquering Inter remained unbeaten, crushing opponents both at the San Siro and beyond in ruthless manner. In order to just hang on to their coat tails Ottavio Bianchi's side found themselves in the almost impossible situation of having to win every week. Inevitably the Southerners faltered and when they did Inter slipped that little further out of reach. But though Napoli clung on, desperate to claw them back, their dreams of glory instead turned abroad, to foreign fields and the UEFA Cup.

Come New Year the Neapolitans had advanced to the quarter final stage of that competition to draw, of all teams, Juventus! The sighs of disappointment could be heard loud in both cities. Neither wanted the ignominy of being knocked out by the other, for bragging stakes were just too high. On Wednesday 1st March 1988, the first leg took place in Turin, with Juve gaining a 2-0 advantage to take south. Napoli *tifosi* were despondent, for their team had not performed in the Stadio Comunale. Many feared the deficit would not be turned round in the San Paolo. But as had been shown in the past, once under the volcano, with San Gennaro's blessing, anything was possible. Two weeks later Naples welcomed *La Vecchia Signora* with a hospitality befitting the generations of hatred that had existed between them since time immortal.

Juve coach Dino Zoff, who many years before left the southern capital to take Turin gold, knew his team faced a difficult task, despite the two-goal lead. So it proved as the Neapolitans ripped into them from the first whistle. An early penalty from Diego Maradona and a second from Andres Carnevale before half-time levelled the tie on aggregate. Only the great pride of the *Bianconeri* players who refused to bow down in the face of this Southern onslaught upon their heads saw them survive till extra-time. But just as a penalty shoot-out loomed large, on 119 minutes a Maradona corner was met by Allessandro Renica, whose bullet header flashed past Stefano Tacconi into the Juve goal. A courageous stand by the Old Lady had been broken at the last. A nerve shattered San Paolo erupted in sheer joy and relief. As the Juventus players lay distraught on the turf, all of Naples wallowed in their despair. A loathing supreme. At the full-time whistle Renica was lifted shoulder-high by his ecstatic teammates and chaired around the running track to take the acclaim of a delirious crowd.

For SSC Napoli a semi-final against crack West German side Bayern Munich lay in wait. Revenge for Dino Zoff's side came swift, a fortnight later when they returned south to inflict a devastating 4-2 defeat on the Neapolitans and all but end their *Scudetto* challenge. For on that same Sunday, Inter Milan thrashed Como 4-0 in the San Siro to go six points clear of Napoli. Ottavio Bianchi gave up all hope of catching Inter and turned his concentration fully on the UEFA Cup. Four days on from their savaging at home by Juventus, Diego Maradona led his team out to face Bayern Munich in front of 79,950 screaming blue *tifosi* in Naples. In an all-red kit, Bayern proved typically tough and resilient German opponents. It was Bavarian efficiency against Neapolitan flair. Played in driving rain, Bayern Munich were in control for the vast majority of the first half, looking by far the better team. A snap shot by Bayern forward Olaf Thon almost handed them the lead, only to be saved superbly by Giuliani. Cruel then, they dropped their guard for a split second and paid the ultimate price.

Five minutes before the interval, a deft touch from an unusually subdued Maradona let in Carnevale, who fired home from twelve yards. Munich continued to impress in the second period as they forced the Neapolitans back with some neat, inventive football. Again the Germans enjoyed plenty of possession, only for Napoli to strike back on the break. From one such move the home side should have doubled their lead when Diego Maradona fed Antonio Careca wide on the left, and his precise pass was met by Andres Carnevale's diving header that thumped loudly against the post. With all Naples still bemoaning their ill-fortune, Maradona popped up once more to hit a dipping cross into the Bayern penalty area for Carnevale, whose glancing flick soared gloriously into the net. This time there was no mistake. Game over.

Two weeks later, armed with their 2-0 advantage, Bianchi's men travelled to Germany as huge favourites to get through. But in the daunting atmosphere of Munich's Olympiastadion, with an uproariously passionate Bavarian 65,000 crowd behind them, a ferociously committed Bayern gave all to try and pull back the deficit. Though nowhere near the calibre of past great Munich teams that possessed such world superstars as Beckenbauer, Muller and Rummenigge, the modern class of 89 remained a potent threat on home territory. Sadly for them, Napoli were just that little better. With Maradona pulling the strings and the lethal Brazilian, Careca, in the form of his life, scoring two more goals, the Neapolitans fought out a thrilling 2-2 draw that eased them into the UEFA Cup final.

There they faced yet another German team, VFB Stuttgart. Never had the Neapolitans won anything of note in European competition. For Diego Maradona, winning this tournament presented the perfect opportunity for him to leave Naples, hopefully with the cheers of Napoli *tifosi* ringing in his ears, wishing him well. For Maradona's mind was made up. Make no mistake, win or lose against Stuttgart, he was off! President Corrado Ferlaino's personal pledge that he be allowed to leave, meant contact with top French side Olympique Marseilles had already taken place. All had gone well, the abdication appeared imminent. Guillermo Coppola had met secretly with Marseilles' controversial chairman Bernard Tapie, who promised to double whatever the player was earning. And more! It was the deal of a lifetime. For nigh on five years Diego Maradona had been centre-stage as the leading actor in a dramatic Neapolitan opera, played out every Sunday in football theatres across Italy. Loved and despised in equal measures, booed, hissed, cheered and adored, villain, demon, hero and saviour. It had all got out of hand. Had he not given them what they craved for? The time had finally come when Maradona just wanted to be human again. He wanted out. Once Upon A Time In Naples: The fairytale was close to being over.

Wednesday 3rd May 1988: UEFA Cup Final First Leg: Diego Maradona's supposed Neapolitan swansong began in the worst possible manner when after just seventeen minutes in Naples, the Germans took a shock lead through their exciting, long-haired young forward, Maurizio Gaudino. His twenty-five-yard free-kick, hit low, was horribly fumbled by Napoli keeper Giuliani, who watched in abject horror as the ball fell from his grasp and rolled agonisingly over the line. The deafening barrage of noise that had roared like thunder from the 81,000 *tifosi* on the San Paolo terraces from the first whistle fell silent. As the white shirts of Stuttgart celebrated, Giuliani sat hunched with head in hands. After dominating the early stages with Antonio Careca missing two glorious opportunities, Napoli appeared stung by Gaudino's unexpected, if fortunate, strike. VFB's coach, former Dutch international Arie Haan, gesticulated madly on the touchline as he screamed instructions to his team, imploring them to concentrate. Be prepared. For Haan was sufficiently astute to realise that the Neapolitans were about to hit them with everything they had.

Inevitably a siege ensued with a scheming Maradona working overtime, searching for that elusive equaliser. Chances were made only to be woefully wasted. Foremost amongst the guilty was Careca, who appeared for once to have put his boots on the wrong feet. The second half saw no respite and with the screw turned ever tighter, they finally got a break. On sixty-eight minutes, a scramble in the Stuttgart area ended when a volleyed shot on goal by Diego Maradona was deemed blocked by a German hand and Greek referee Germanakos awarded a penalty. The cheers from San Paolo that swept over the bay were of more relief than joy. Maradona appeared the calmest man in Naples as he stepped forward to beat Stuttgart's keeper Eike Immel with delightful ease and level the tie. Napoli's *Capitano* grabbed the ball out of the net and raced back to the halfway line. There he kissed the one true love of his life before placing it gently on the centre spot to re-start the game.

Now they went for the kill. The visitors' goal led a charmed existence as the ball bounced, whizzed and flew everywhere, except where Napoli forwards desired it. Close shaves, bad luck, catastrophic finishing, all conspired to drive the Naples clans mad with frustration. German luck appeared to be holding; then, three minutes from time, it finally ran out. Again, it was the wizardry of Maradona saving the day as he dribbled past desperate, lunging, Stuttgart defenders, before crossing from the byline for Antonio Careca to slot home from eight yards and win the game. But it had been close. Ottavio Bianchi appeared content at the final whistle. The 2-1 scoreline meant that VFB on home soil would be forced out of their defensive shell to attack. With this in mind, Bianchi was confident his team possessed enough pace and skill to wreak mayhem and hit on the break. All would be decided in two week's time at Stuttgart's Neckerstadion.

Just when all appeared calm and serene in Naples' waters, Diego Maradona surfaced in inimitable style to rock the boat and once more cause an eruption worthy of their volcano. Four days on from the UEFA first leg, Napoli travelled to Bologna minus their esteemed number ten, who claimed to be suffering chronic back pain. Bianchi fumed; genuine or not, he had finally grown exhausted of the Argentinian's every whim and need being pandered to. This was no God, just a greedy, selfish, arrogant, peasant boy from the backside of Buenos Aires, who cared for no one but himself. And yet his teammates and fans adored him. Could Neapolitans not see, like he, that the myth of *El Pibe De Oro* was just that, pure illusion? If this was truly a King why did he not act like one? A crown of thorns that cut so deep they affected his brain and he couldn't think straight. Why fake injury to save himself for the game in Stuttgart when there remained a chance, slim maybe, of winning the championship?

Ottavio Bianchi's men lay six points adrift of the all-conquering Inter Milan. With Inter away at Juventus, and the Neapolitans still to play at the San Siro, it became essential they won at Bologna. But without Maradona it wasn't to be, and a disappointing 1-1 scoreline proved insufficient as the *Nerazzurri* also claimed a vital point in Turin. The title was gone. Bianchi was appalled at his *Capitano's* non-appearance, but by this time he had adopted the attitude, 'If he plays he plays'. He knew only too well that Diego Maradona was a law unto himself and interested just in staying fit for the second leg in Germany. The Iron Sergeant also was set to call time on his historic stay in Naples. Like Maradona, Bianchi hoped Stuttgart would provide him with a fitting farewell. That he never shouted from the rooftops about his passion for the Neapolitan cause did not mean the fire burned any less within. SSC Napoli *allenatore* Ottavio Bianchi had already earned his place in Naples' folklore. Now all that remained was to provide the most magnificent finale.

Wednesday 17th May 1988: Broadcast live on *Raiuno*, the opening titles screamed out:

VFB STOCCARDA - SSC NAPOLI
FINALE COPPA UEFA
1' TEMPO

The rich, dulcet tones of *Rai's* acclaimed, legendary, television football commentator Bruno Pizzul welcomed Neapolitans and all of Italy to the Neckerstadion. By plane, car and train, the *tifosi* had travelled in their many thousands over the Alps, through Switzerland and into Southern Germany to follow their team. Across Stuttgart's impressive stadium, huge smatterings of blue lay drenched on the terraces. Even the home dugout was covered in a Napoli flag, put there by mischievous Neapolitans who were enjoying teasing the annoyed Germans from their seats behind! Looking pumped-up and ready for battle, both sides appeared from the tunnel. Many of the Napoli players gazed around in total astonishment at the enormity of support for them around the stadium. The banners were everywhere. 'Blue Tigers', 'CUCB', 'Napoli Platoon', 'Ultra Napoli', 'Sorrento Napoli' and 'South Boys', amongst many more. A Union Jack flag was also visible, brought along with the sole intention to wind-up the home supporters! The 'fit again' Diego Maradona even swapped high fives with *tifosi*, who using typical Neapolitan ingenuity had managed to infiltrate down onto the running track, posing as cameramen and photographers. Before kick-off Maradona sought out Napoli's physio, Salvatore Carmando, to plant the ritual kiss on his forehead. It was the manner in which the Argentinian looked worryingly around, before he finally glimpsed Carmando, that showed just how important this little superstition had become. Not just to both men, but the entire team.

Boosted immeasurably by the return from injury of their twenty-three-year-old rising superstar Jurgen Klinsmann, the home side began brightly, brimming with confidence and attacking from the off. With the dashing, blond-haired, golden boy of German football adding much needed pace, skill and strength to Stuttgart's forward line, the Napoli defence came under tremendous pressure in the opening stages. The lightning Klinsmann showed a devastating turn of pace down the left flank, only to be sent crashing to earth by full back Giovanni Franchini, who appeared in no mood to be chasing shadows. The fight for midfield superiority proved no place for the faint hearted, as tackles and challenges flew high and dangerous. Stuttgart's tall, gangling, Yugoslav defender Srecko Katanec gave the impression of having ate raw, red meat before kick-off as he attempted to start fights with all and any in a blue shirt.

On the touchline home coach Arie Haan raged each time a decision went against his team. He claimed the Neapolitans were overly-theatrical in falling to the floor at every opportunity. Each time Diego Maradona received the ball, Haan's face turned a worrying purple, barking out instructions for the Argentinian maestro to be closed down. That Maradona was picked out for special treatment by the Germans surprised few, for they feared him greatly, knowing that given the slightest inch, he could destroy them. But the Neapolitans were quick to fight fire with fire and retribution was swift when required. On nineteen minutes Maradona was scythed down brutally in the centre circle by the fired up Katanec, only for the referee to wave play on when Alemao came away with possession. The Brazilian broke forward to play a one-two with his countryman Careca, before racing into the penalty box and stabbing the ball past keeper Immel into the net. With arms outstretched Alemao sped across the running track to salute the fanatical hordes of San Gennaro.

The sheer extent of Napoli's support suddenly became apparent as half the Neckerstadion erupted in a wild sea of blue/white flags. Only one man of Neapolitan persuasion appeared unmoved by it all. Ottavio Bianchi sat motionless as around him bedlam raged in the Napoli dugout. With the overall score now 3-1, the Germans threw caution to the wind and in typical fashion came roaring back. From a corner, Klinsmann levelled with a brave header through a mass of bodies to make it 1-1. On scoring he turned to the crowd, imploring them to make more noise and out-sing their Neapolitan visitors, who for once had fallen silent. For what remained of the opening period it was Stuttgart who had the edge, as Jurgen Klinsmann and Maurizio Gaudino left the Napoli defence repeatedly stretched with their fearsome pace and intelligent link play.

So it was a relief that with only moments left on the clock before the break, the Neapolitans broke out to earn some respite with a corner up the other end. Maradona's initial effort was easily cleared, only to bounce high and rebound towards him. This time the Argentinian headed back into the six-yard box where waiting to pounce was the unlikely figure of defender Ciro Ferrara. Arriving unmarked, the Neapolitan lashed home with great delight a right foot volley past Eike Immel that flashed into the net. Born and raised in Naples, it was a moment that meant everything to Ciro Ferrara. As a teenager he proudly captained Napoli's youth team to a national championship. The man who presented him that trophy was none other than Diego Armando Maradona. Now the Argentinian had given him yet another precious memory to treasure, one he would never forget. The look on Ferrara's face as he ran back to retake up his defensive position was one of total incredulity. Back in Naples the wine tasted increasingly sweeter, and many a glass was raised to 'Our Ciro!'

The second half began with the Germans still pressing relentlessly forward. But Napoli were holding, and on the hour '*FINALE COPPA UEFA*' was finally won. A long clearance was flicked on by Antonio Careca to Diego Maradona who, after bewitching two Stuttgart defenders, played a beautifully measured pass back to the Brazilian who had raced to support him. Sprinting at great pace Careca took the ball in his stride before finishing immaculately with a masterful shot into Immel's bottom left-hand corner. *Raiuno's* commentator, the famed Bruno Pizzul, roared in delight, '*Gol Di Napoli! Grandissimo!*' Though Bruno Giordano was gone and three had become two, they still had it. *Magica*! A witch's potion brewed in South America but enjoyed most heartily in Naples. An emotional Careca sank to his knees. He appeared momentarily distraught, overcome with emotion. Napoli's beloved *La Bomba* screamed out loud, 'Diegooo!', as his *compadre* raced to congratulate him. The two friends shared a special embrace, before disappearing beneath a joyful mass of blue.

With thirty minutes left to play, jubilant *tifosi* began their victory celebrations around the stadium. Smoke bombs engulfed the terraces. Rockets shrieked high into the Stuttgart heavens, lighting up the skies. Amidst amazing scenes of Neapolitan revelry, the home side refused point blank to believe all was lost and continued to attack. But the forlorn features of coach Arie Haan spoke volumes. Looking resigned to the inevitable, Haan had retreated to the dugout, his earlier fire as he blazed on the touchline apparently snuffed out. A slight glimmer of hope appeared for the Germans when Gaudino's twenty-five-yard shot brushed off Fernando Di Napoli to beat Giuliani, making it 3-2, though still 5-3 on aggregate. Scant consolation. As the dying moments ebbed away, large swathes of German police mounted a human shield around the stadium's running track to prevent any excitable *tifosi* reaching the pitch. A Neapolitan fervour/madness had taken hold in the Neckerstadion. A minute into injury-time a horrendous backpass by Di Napoli was intercepted and headed powerfully past a helpless Giuliani by Schaler, making it 3-3. Insignificant, but soothing to German egos nonetheless.

Finally ending Stuttgart's misery, Spanish referee Armenio called time and a carnival began in Southern Germany! Miracles were common in Naples, but Ottavio Bianchi breaking into a half smile at the full-time whistle was deemed by many of Neapolitan persuasion, reason itself to party! However the coach quickly resorted to type when he disappeared down the tunnel, leaving his players to bask in the glory. That away from the crowds Bianchi shed a quiet tear said more about the man than any book could ever aspire to. His time amongst the Neapolitans was almost up. Sometimes heroes just disappear through a side door. Ottavio Bianchi was such a man, but how in years to come SSC Napoli missed their Iron Sergeant. On the pitch Diego Maradona found himself alone, cut off by an incessant barrage of microphones and cameras thrust within inches of his face. Pushed, shoved and manhandled, it became a dangerous farce as he struggled to retain his footing amidst such relentless attention. It was only the intervention of Napoli goalkeeper Giuliano Giuliani, grabbing Maradona away from the paparazzi circus, that allowed him to rejoin his adoring teammates. Immediately the *Capitano* was lifted high, for they like all Napoli *tifosi* worshipped the air he breathed and the ground that *El Rei* chose to walk on.

Still the Stuttgart flags waved as, defiant to the very end, many of the locals stayed behind long after the final whistle to salute their brave side. A host of white shirts, Klinsmann and Gaudino foremost amongst them, remained slumped on the turf, devastated in defeat. Showing great sportsmanship, home supporters applauded the all-singing/dancing Neapolitan clans rejoicing in their midst. Not familiar to being shown such respect, the *tifosi* responded in equally good fashion, a novelty indeed for the visitors. At 22.07, set against a deathly black sky, the giant electronic scoreboard in the Neckerstadion flashed up a huge neon-blue Napoli badge. This proved too much for the Stuttgart fans, who at last admitted defeat and left to drown their sorrows in the many, nearby, drinking holes.

To the victors went the spoils, as the time came for the trophy to be handed over. Fighting through a frenzied mass of hollering reporters, cameramen and photographers, all desperate for a soundbite, Diego Maradona finally made his way to the presentation table. Wearing a beaming, wide grin, he suddenly found himself confronted by Corrado Ferlaino, who stepped forward from the crowds to whisper into the player's ear, 'We are going to see the contract out, aren't we Diego?' For just a mere second the Argentinian appeared shocked by what he had heard, but recovered instantly. With a wry smile on his face the President moved back into the shadows, leaving the way clear for his *Capitano* to be handed the trophy. In the blinding glare of a thousand flashlights, Maradona raised the UEFA Cup high. A city and its people unashamedly wept tears of joy.

As for their King? The realisation that Ferlaino had double-crossed him hit home like a bullet crashing into his chest. So much for the promise of just 'One more season'. A supposed State of Grace? He vowed to make his President pay for such treachery. Fuming at this betrayal, the Argentinian plotted revenge. But even though Diego Maradona considered himself wise to the ways of his adopted city, little could he have known the terrifying powers set to be unleashed upon his head. As *El Pibe De Oro* schemed to escape Napoli chains, a decision was taken to teach him a lesson in respect. For in Naples, even kings did as ordered. No exceptions. Their strings were tugged and they would dance to whatever tune was required. Maradona's misguided/dangerous sense of self-delusion meant he walked unsuspectingly into a viper's nest. To beat the world with a ball at your feet was one thing. Taking on the Neapolitans in their own backyard, armed with nothing but wounded pride,` was akin to an act of madness. For it was no longer just a game. No rules, no referees, no mercy. And ultimately no contest.

CHAPTER 20

ENCORE

Naples awaited with trepidation the coming storm. The abdication of their king appeared imminent, for Diego Maradona's crown of thorns had pricked so deep the wounds were now visible for all to see. As he sought solace far across the ocean on another continent, it became clear there was to be no happy ending. But just maybe, God willing, before the tragic drop into the abyss they would be allowed a final great triumph. Prayers were said for the salvation of El Pibe De Oro's footballing soul to help cast away the demons and bring Lo Scudetto home. Together, one last time with Maradona back to lead them, Neapolitans raged against the light. Encore!

With the sole aim to engineer a one-way ticket out of Naples and into the welcoming embrace of Marseille chairman Bernard Tapie's idyllic, southern French paradise, Diego Maradona stumbled unknowingly into a Neapolitan minefield. In the closing weeks of the season he withdrew without warning from a game at Ascoli, claiming to be suffering from a stomach upset. Cynics however believed it was all a charade, with Maradona's non-appearance a less than subtle show of support for Ascoli and former Napoli folk hero Bruno Giordano. Following the infamous events of 1st May 1988, and the controversial defeat by AC Milan at the San Paolo, Giordano found himself tossed like garbage into the dustbin by Ottavio Bianchi's ruthless purge of alleged offenders. The Rome-born player's past crimes saw him cast amongst the chief villains of this particular, sordid Neapolitan drama. Stones were hurled in Giordano's direction with no shred of evidence, hard or otherwise. But his tainted history meant mud stuck. Blinded by a deep sense of injustice, Diego Maradona's refusal to play against his old friend surprised none who knew something of his true character, for he showed towards those he considered *compadres* a remarkable loyalty. That Bruno Giordano scored in a 2-0 win to play an integral role in beating the Southerners helped only to fuel a powderkeg situation.

Rumours were already rife that Diego wanted out. A deep sadness coloured by a sense of betrayal saw for the first time doubts emerge in the

Forcella and beyond by those who loved *El Rei* unconditionally. An incessant desire and passion for their football club meant the *tifosi* had been taken for fools before. Maybe this latest saviour was just cleverer in hiding his true face? A slow fuse simmered, for in Naples as love soured and tempers were roused, blood inevitably was spilt. Standing by a former teammate was to be admired, betraying your adopted people with a self-centred arrogance was not. Diego Maradona's rabid desire to be rid of Neapolitan shackles could no longer be hidden, and a week later it became clear for everyone to see when all hell broke loose in Naples. After just twenty minutes of a home match versus Pisa, and to the rising fury of a 70,000 crowd, the Argentinian signalled to the Napoli bench, demanding to be substituted. Limping theatrically, Maradona's exaggerated gestures pointed to a supposed leg strain. But those present knew different and as he made his way off the field, apparently in severe pain, the San Paolo made its true feelings known.

This incident proved the final straw for a fraught *tifosi*, who vented their frustration at his girlfriend Claudia and business manager Guillermo Coppola, both watching on stonefaced in the Presidential Box. As plastic bottles and coins were hurled in their direction, Maradona stared daggers from the touchline. His own ears rang with the deafening crescendo of boos and catcalls raining down upon him. Memories of *Lo Scudetto* and the recent triumph in Stuttgart were swiftly forgotten. It is said that the greatest of love affairs end only through death or betrayal. This was to be no exception. Hails of displeasure poured out from all corners of this crumbling pit of a concrete bowl, though still a consecrated ground for Neapolitans. The legendary terraces of the Curva Sud that hosted the blue/white hordes of the CUCB howled in derision as SSC Napoli, without their inspirational *Capitano* slumped miserably to a 0-0 draw against the already relegated Pisa. Reeling from this monstrous display of public humiliation, an indignant Diego Maradona, blazing with anger, lashed out at the detractors. Furious at the manner in which Napoli *tifosi* had turned violently on his girlfriend and manager, he launched a post-match tirade against his tormentors.

By accusing them of insulting his family honour and declaring that he was prepared to leave Naples there and then, Diego Maradona set about burning all his bridges. In an atmosphere dripping in bitterness and acrimony, he let fly at all and sundry against his enemies, both real and imagined. In what appeared a concerted attempt to anger everyone in Naples, Maradona continued to wage war against all in his fiefdom. The Argentinian's television programme, broadcast live every Thursday evening on local station Channel 21, was used solely as a platform for the player to fire broadsides at Corrado Ferlaino and other foes, mainly journalists who had the temerity to question his actions. A show that was once a simple half-hour love-fest between *El Rei* and Napoli *tifosi* became nothing more than a weekly tirade of vitriol and venom. Such increasingly manic behaviour and a refusal to accept the merest criticism hinted heavily of someone out of control.

The incident when an incensed Diego Maradona visited the local newspaper offices of *Il Mattino* to confront the unsuspecting reporter who dared to award him only a measly three out of ten performance entered Napoli footballing folklore. Armed only with a copy of that same paper Maradona sought out the shocked scribe and stuffed it into his mouth with a promise that any more similar pieces and he would be back! With pride duly satisfied the Argentinian did nothing more than turn on his heels and swagger out, leaving behind a bewildered audience of onlookers, A stony silence gripped the building as people were unsure whether to laugh or be utterly disgusted at what they had just witnessed.

So when Maradona flew home to Buenos Aires for the summer threatening never to return, few in Naples were hardly surprised as they had heard it all before. The difference now that feelings towards him had changed so profoundly many Neapolitans couldn't care less. But there remained those who kept the faith. A newspaper poll in the Forcella, undertaken by *Il Mattino*, showed that strength of feeling towards the Argentinian remained split. There were no neutrals. Whilst there were those who swore a blood vendetta against *Pibe De Oro*, others claimed they were willing to travel to Argentina and beg their hero to return. In order to try and defuse the situation, Coppola proposed that they speak out to appease the doubters. But feeling safe back on home soil and wholly unaware of just how volatile emotions in Naples had become regarding Diego Maradona's absence, the statement issued on the player's behalf proved a disastrous piece of public relations. That he complained about the treatment meted out to Claudia and Coppola in the match against Pisa was sufficient enough to alienate him further, but what Maradona went on to further claim shocked even the most hardened of *tifosi*.

'I will not report back to training for Napoli because I am convinced there is a plot against me, my wife, daughters, brothers and parents which places us in real danger. As a man and father I bear the responsibility of defending the greatest treasure I possess. My family.' He went on to rage about threatening phone calls, the mysterious vandalising of a Mercedes car, and most seriously a break-in at his sister's apartment in which nothing was stolen, but certain objects were simply tampered with. Furniture was re-arranged; spirits in the night? At this last allegation Neapolitans gasped, for it was well known in Naples that the *Camorra* favoured such action as a warning to those said to have displeased them, a last chance before it got bloody. Without actually saying, the player was seen to be accusing the mobsters of intimidation in their efforts to stop him going to Marseille. It was unheard of and simply not done. The Napoli police were fully aware of Maradona's close relationship with the Giulianos, but showed little interest in such allegations. For them the player was reaping what he sowed. Without a shred of proof they claimed it would be a waste of time investigating. Play with fire and you risked getting burnt by the flames.

Dropping hints like grenades that the Naples underworld had threatened his family made many think Maradona bore some kind of death wish as that could be the only possible, logical explanation for such madness. Neapolitans shook their heads. Five years under the volcano and still he did not understand the way of things? It was a most obvious slap in the face for the feared Giuliano clan, and the dark Princes of Forcella could ill afford to let such a blatant show of disrespect go unpunished. There would be an answer, but it was not to be with a bomb, knife or gun. The Giulianos, if challenged, could unleash a small army of footsoldiers numbering 500 from their territory by simply snapping their fingers. A more ruthless band of cutthroats it would have been difficult to find. Loyal to the point of fanatical, all orders were carried out with religious zeal. This was the frightening power of Maradona's true paymasters. Luckily for the Argentinian, it would instead be a more subtle strategy used to teach him a lesson in manners. For *El Pibe De Oro*, an Irreversible Sunrise was set to break and all but destroy him.

Less than a week after the catastrophically-worded statement was released to the world's press, a picture appeared on the front cover of *Il Mattino* showing Diego Maradona alongside the Giulianos, toasting champagne with a huge grin ensconced upon his face. It was a photograph taken years before at a party laid on in the player's honour, and was one of countless snapped on many family occasions when he was present. Whilst Maradona appeared totally relaxed in the photo, enjoying the legendary hospitality of the *Camorra* and all that entailed, the notorious brothers Carmine, Rafaele and Ermine stood each side of him with fixed, steely-eyed expressions, finding it desperately hard to raise even a half-smile. With hindsight it is clear to see that they were desperate to capture that first image of the player in their midst, an anxiety lost on Maradona who believed, naively, that he was amongst blood brothers, men who understood him. But to the Giulianos, he was simply a licence to print money.

It was blatantly obvious to all who understood how the Naples underworld operated that the picture was only printed with the consent of the gangsters. *Il Mattino* may well have had access to such material for years, but would never have been able to publish for fear of dreadful retribution by *Lo*

Camorra. They had let it be known in typically conspiratorial manner that Maradona was a 'friend', a word that in Naples carried sinister undertones. This opening, enduring glimpse of the Argentinian at play with his mad, bad, Neapolitan *amigos* was carefully calculated to cause most damage to the player's reputation. The caption alongside read, 'It is absurd to think that anyone would want to challenge the *Camorra* by threatening its idol.' The meaning was clear, Diego Armando was one of them. It was crazy to suggest they would hurt him, and he they. With one slight nudge, tremendous pressure was placed on Maradona, for it had become clear that a drip-drip policy was about to be put into use by the Giulianos in order to make him see sense and return to Naples. There would be, if required, infinitely much worse to follow. But as all eyes and ears turned towards Argentina the silence was deafening, for *Pibe De Oro* had disappeared off the map.

To escape the rising furore his actions had provoked, Maradona fled Buenos Aires in secret with his father and travelled 400 miles by car up the Rio Parano to Diego Senior's birthplace, the little fishing village of Esquina. There he was guaranteed anonymity and time to think. Whilst some in Naples would have gladly seen the Argentinian sleep with the fishes, away from the prying lens of the paparazzi both men spent hours relaxing on the river banks reminiscing about childhood days, when life was so much more simple. It was left to Guillermo Coppola to stave off the arrows hurtling over the ocean towards them. Realising just how bad the situation had become and how that infernal statement had blown up in their face, he contacted Napoli's President Ferlaino and expressed a wish for peace talks. For once Corrado Ferlaino rejoiced at holding the upper hand over this cocky Argentinian whom had caused him so much heartache in the past. Wallowing in Coppola's obvious discomfort, the President enjoyed making him sweat, before agreeing to a meeting. He sent to Buenos Aires one of his most trusted aids, Luciano Moggi. A man in his middle forties, with lizard features and skilled in the art of Neapolitan street politics, he was more than a match for the slick, cunning, if for once, clearly on the back foot, Guillermo Coppola.

The formidable Moggi flew immediately to Argentina where he wasted little time seeking out Coppola. He informed him in no uncertain terms that Napoli still held Maradona's signature and were not prepared to waive it for any amount of money. Not standing on ceremony, Moggi also let it be known that on returning to Naples the player would have to train, travel and rest with his teammates. No more special privileges such as arriving at away games by private plane, which had so infuriated club officials in the past. As Coppola tried in vain to make a point and fight his corner, Moggi's revelation that

Napoli intended to begin proceedings on a civil lawsuit against Diego Maradona for breach of contract if he did not tow the line in the future completely floored the Argentinian, for they were assuming there was to be one. Was it simply arrogance by the Neapolitan, or were there other forces at work in the shadows pulling his strings? It hardly took a genius to work it out. A rare day indeed when Guillermo Coppola was stuck for words. But the time Luciano Moggi went to Buenos Aires, it duly occurred. He detected in his voice and mannerisms an utter confidence that could only stem from the fact Moggi was speaking not just on President Ferlaino's behalf, but for others of more dubious distinction. Three things had suddenly become crystal clear. 1: Napoli's tough stance could only have been taken with the backing of the *Camorra*. 2: Financially, they were shot without Neapolitan dollars. 3: Whether he liked it or not, Diego Maradona was Naples-bound. They were going back. It was with little enthusiasm that Coppola journeyed to Esquina to inform his young master of their predicament.

As expected, Maradona exploded with rage on being told. It appeared he was forever destined to be a prisoner of a city that with equal measures shackled him in chains of love and hate. But after much thought, soul-searching, tears, tantrums and threats of retirement, he accepted the wise counselling of his father and reluctantly gave up. This was the only man alive capable of making Diego Maradona see sense. A striking resemblance to his boy in looks, if not temperament, was uncanny. Diego Senior's reasoning was that his son desperately needed to play football, for it was the water that gave him life. The Neapolitans had made it clear they would rather see Maradona rot in the wilderness than released from a five-year contract. It might as well have been written in blood, such was Napoli's determination to win out. Also there was his problem in fighting off the pounds. Since his early teenage years, Diego was pumped full of cortisone, steroids, painkillers and all manner of injections to ensure he kept playing. If abused these possessed crippling long-term side effects and as time rolled on they took their toll, none more than a worrying capacity to pile on weight, for without a strict training regime Diego Armando's physical condition tended to see him blow up alarmingly. An unhealthy tendency to gorge wildly on junk food whilst embarking on alcoholic marathons, interrupted only by cocaine binges, caused a dramatic effect in his appearance.

To cover up Maradona grew a beard to hide his double chin and took to wearing baggy clothes in an effort to disguise the excess fat gained around the midriff. When pictures of him looking dreadfully out of shape appeared on Italian television, Neapolitans watched in disbelief. What on earth had happened to *El Pibe De Oro*? Despite great disillusionment with their

Capitano, Naples heaved a heavy sigh. This wasn't right. Just who was this impostor on their screens? Finally, his father's selling point to Diego Junior was the fact that a World Cup loomed large on the horizon. Argentina's crown, won so spectacularly four years previous in Mexico would have to be defended in of all places, Italy. That his country so wholly depended on him was all the immensely patriotic Maradona needed to hear. Playing for *La Nacionale* in hostile cities such as Milan, Turin and, God forbid, maybe even Naples, was an opportunity worth eating a little humble pie for. But he would make the Neapolitans wait before finally heading back.

Playing his foolish games, Diego Maradona had yet to arrive from Argentina when the Napoli team returned for pre-season training in August, where a new face was there to greet them. As expected Ottavio Bianchi had vacated his post to take a well-earned sabbatical, safe in the knowledge he would be forever immortalised as a Neapolitan legend who led them to their first ever *Scudetto*, admired, respected but sadly never truly loved by Napoli *tifosi* who struggled in warming to Bianchi's rather outwardly dour persona. But history would prove a more astute judge of Ottavio Bianchi's achievements. In time Neapolitans would come to regret treating their greatest ever coach with such little love. To replace him Corrado Ferlaino swooped for a man rated amongst the best tactical minds in Serie A, Cesena coach Albertino Bigon. The forty-two-year-old Bigon had enjoyed a wonderful playing career at AC Milan where he made his name as an attacking midfielder of some style and repute. Once retired he took up coaching with equal panache and won promotion with little-fancied Cesena into the top flight, keeping them there against all odds for two seasons. In the cutthroat world of Italian football he learned good and fast, so much so that the Neapolitans took note and came calling. It was an opportunity the ambitious Bigon could ill afford to refuse.

With his dashing good looks, confident manner and a remarkable resemblance to a youthful Charlton Heston, Albertino Bigon cut an impressive figure when introduced at one of Napoli's legendary press conferences/riots. The expert handling of the baying press pack as he fended off questions regarding a certain Argentinian in a calm, polite but always articulate, fashion was a performance that delighted his President for it confirmed to Corrado Ferlaino he had chosen well. SSC Napoli was in safe hands with this man. The new coach was wise enough to realise that despite their present spat, Diego Maradona remained a saint on Earth to the majority of Neapolitans, a Prodigal Son who would be instantly forgiven if he showed the slightest hint of remorse or, more importantly, a return to form on the pitch. It would have been foolish to rule out reconciliation. But

Bigon was also a realist. Maradona's debauched lifestyle and unfortunate habits meant that he was close to becoming a spent force, verging on meltdown. Already the physical aspects of his game that at one time made him untouchable had gone forever. The quick brain and breathtaking skills remained, but the body had become an unwilling vehicle to carry out the required tasks.

A great player was still to be had, but now the effort needed would have to be tenfold anything he had ever produced before. With good grace Albertino Bigon left the door open for *El Pibe De Oro* to return. Whether he could be bothered to walk through it was doubtful. On September 1st 1989, Diego Maradona and his eternal entourage of loved ones and bloodsucking leeches boarded a plane to carry them to Naples, when the player once more blew a fuse on learning that Guillermo Coppola had been refused permission to sit with him in first class due to lack of space. Taking this as a personal insult, he stormed off. This happened time and again as the player, with his pride pricked, seemed hellbent on making the Neapolitans and all around him sweat by acting like a petulant child. Over thirty provisional bookings were made, only then to be cancelled as Maradona refused at the last to travel. Finally on the 6th September, amidst a mass human barrage of paparazzi, he took flight back to Italy.

Diego Maradona's ill perceived notion that he would be welcomed back onto Neapolitan soil with open arms was horribly misjudged. Local newspapers loyal to the President continued to wage war; 'MARADONA ARRIVES BUT NAPOLI MAY SNUB HIM!'

Determined to show all that he had won the battle of wills with his least favourite, surly Argentinian, President Ferlaino organised a press conference at the Soccavo training centre in which only an invited audience of journalists sympathetic to himself were present. It was in all but name a victory parade. 'Maradona is the greatest player in the world,' he exclaimed loudly, 'but precisely because of this he has greater duties than others. A fine of $24,000 has been imposed and now he must get in shape and stop skipping training. No more.' This scathing, public criticism by the Napoli supremo left all Naples waiting for Diego's reply. Maradona's ego was such, it was felt impossible for him not to lash back. Instead, in typically mischievous fashion he issued a statement that from now on a $10,000 fee would be charged for all interviews, cash to be paid up front. Beaten but unbowed, they had still to truly break him. Such arrogance helped only to infuriate the press who prepared to wreak revenge. With the *Camorra* clans withdrawing their protective shield Maradona was stalked day and night, his every move snapped by a prying lens and blazed across the front pages.

By this time Napoli's campaign was already underway. An opening 1-0 win away to Ascoli and at home to Udinese saw them top the table. Albertine Bigon had proved a shrewd character in the transfer market. Lacking the funds previous managers had enjoyed, Bigon showed a good eye for bargains. From Juventus the experienced midfielder Massimo Mauro and the powerful, robust Lecce defender Marco Baroni arrived to bolster the squad. Whilst both were good solid Serie A professional players and proved fine additions, neither set the Napoli *tifosi* hearts beating. The turmoil felt over Diego Maradona cast dark shadows over their morning, noon and night. Every waking day was met with sunken hearts and spirits desperately needed lifting. Hope sprang from a most unlikely source. Deep in the murky, hidden depths of lowly Serie C, a young man by the name of Gianfranco Zola plied his remarkable trade to small, but still wonderfully receptive audiences. It was almost if his talents were such that those lucky enough to view it every week made a deal not to inform strangers of this genius in their midst. The vast gulf in both talent and finances between the backwaters of the Italian Third Division and the millionaire, world-class footballers of Italy's upper echelon meant Serie A may as well have existed on the moon.

But this kid who still played with great passion for his hometown club Torres in Sardinia was that rare exception, a precious gem in a sea awash with mediocrity. With club scouts from the mainland rarely visiting the island, the twenty-two-year-old Zola's world-class potential remained criminally unexploited at the top level. Only through the kind act of a Torres director, Nello Barbanera, who personally contacted Napoli pleading with them to come view their boy, was he given a chance. After listening to Barbanera lauding huge praise on the player, Luciano Moggi travelled to Sardinia to see for himself what all the fuss was about. After witnessing Zola in action Moggi was blown away and wasted little time signing him up. On return Luciano Moggi's words to his President were, 'I can assure you we have discovered another Maradona.' It was said Ferlaino did not know whether to laugh or cry!

The happy-go-lucky Sardinian's small, stocky build, deft sleight of foot, strength and devastating forward play demanded comparison to a young Diego. Such talk at one time would have been construed in Naples as heresy. Not anymore. When Gianfranco Zola eventually arrived, an Italian journalist in the know wrote, 'He was not just "a mysterious object", but "a very mysterious object".' He would not remain secret for long. Deputising for Maradona, Zola made his Serie A debut in the San Paolo against Udinese and impressed from the off with a wonderful all-round display, including a wickedly-hit free-kick that smashed into the crossbar. The little man enchanted the Napoli faithful who instantly christened him 'Zoladona'. High praise indeed and a sure sign Zola had been adopted as one of their own.

As for Diego Maradona, he had come to understand that only on the pitch could he win back Naples' heart and once more earn the right to walk between Neapolitan raindrops. It was time to get back to what Maradona did best, playing football like no other. His Trojanesque effort to regain match fitness saw the new *allenatore* warm to him enormously, so much that with Napoli defending an unbeaten four-match opening sequence and sharing top spot with Juventus, Bigon named the Argentinian as substitute for an upcoming home game against Fiorentina. The coach was prepared to wipe the slate clean and start afresh. Looking like a sea pirate with his dazzling, gold earring, long hair and bushy beard, Maradona strode across the turf to take up a place on the bench, a first, faltering step on the road to redemption.

The reaction to him from home *tifosi* was warm if not wholly overwhelming. Support rang out from the Naples tribes of Carmando Montuori's CUCB. High in the heavens, the second section of Curva Sud, a huge banner was unravelled over the advertising boards, '*Diego, El Emperadur Del Mundo!*' ('Diego Emperor of the World!'). Thousands of Maradona's foot-soldiers, drunk on blind faith and cheap Neapolitan wine paid homage to *El Rei*. In their eyes he could do no wrong. But there remained those in the 80,000 crowd still to be convinced of their former *Capitano's* loyalty to the cause. For them it would take an act of forgiveness rare in these parts to accept Diego Maradona back into the fold. A rekindling of Naples' most passionate, enduring love affair was made infinitely more difficult because of hurtful and damning claims by both sides. Accusations that cut deep. Their legendary stubborn Neapolitan pride meant something extraordinary was required to help change minds. That such a scenario happened so quickly surprised all.

For in a disastrous first half against Fiorentina, Napoli were given a footballing masterclass by a young man already being hailed as heir apparent to Maradona's world crown, Florence's own golden boy Roberto Baggio. A two-goal lead was handed the visitors by the *Viola's* number 10, who though viewed by Napoli *tifosi* as a dandy boy because of his trademark ponytail, secretly held their grudging admiration, a respect tinged with jealousy for *Il Divino's* wondrous sorcery on the ball, this maker of dreams. For they too were once blessed with one of similar ilk who produced Neapolitan miracles. The man in question was relegated to watching on animated from the sidelines, roaring encouragement to his teammates, showing a passion sadly bereft in their performance. Roberto Baggio's first goal caused gasps of admiration from all corners of the stadium as he dropped his shoulder, jinxed, dummied and left the entire Napoli defence for dead before rounding the keeper Guiliani to slot home with ridiculous ease. Across the San Paolo a smattering of applause was heard as the most hardened of blue *tifosi* saluted this moment of wizardry.

His second produced only cries of derision from the terraces as the Divine Ponytail's darting run was stopped at the last by the lunging tackle of Ciro Ferrera to concede a penalty. To a crescendo of boos, Baggio got up, dusted himself down, before calmly scoring to hand Fiorentina a 2-0 half-time lead. Baggio had been nothing short of sensational. He had shown all the hype over him being the *Azzurri's* great hope for the forthcoming World Cup Finals on Italian soil held real substance. Roberto Baggio was in the process of single-handedly taking Napoli apart on their own patch. It appeared game over for the Neapolitans, as in Serie A no team came back from such a deficit. So went the logic. But then again, this was Naples and here when the mood arose, anything was possible. As the spot-kick hit the back of Napoli's net a familiar chant began to resonate loud from the terraces. It began as a whisper and swiftly rose to a crescendo, 'DIEGO, DIEGO, DIEGO!' Nothing like a family crisis to focus Naples' hearts and minds, to heal old rifts and let sleeping dogs lie.

With nothing to lose, Bigon instructed his exalted Argentinian to warm up in preparation for the second half. Maradona took to the stage determined to prove there was life yet in the old seadog! With the leading man set to once more tread the boards at his hometown theatre, events were about to be turned on their head. He gestured to all corners of the stadium with clenched fist and was greeted with a deafening response. *El Rei* retained the power to have Napoli *tifosi* eating out of his hand. Though forced to adorn the number 16 shirt instead of his legendary 10, and still showing signs of an obvious weight problem, the sheer presence of Diego Armando had an immediate galvanizing effect on the home team. Players like Careca, Alemao, Crippa and Carnevale, who had struggled miserably in the first half suddenly came to life with their former *Capitano* back alongside them.

El Pibe De Oro orchestrated the onslaught from deep, probing, hitting passes both long and short. With Napoli attacking incessantly, rewards came swiftly when a dubious penalty for handball was awarded. The San Paolo held its breath as eyes turned towards one man. A Hollywood movie script would surely have had the returning hero stepping forward and blasting the ball into the net. The credits roll, everybody goes home, happy ever after. But the story of Diego Maradona was never meant to be the stuff of fairytales and to the horror of all Naples, Fiorentina keeper Marco Landucci saved his weakly-hit effort easily. Maradona berated himself, cursing, annoyed, but there was scant time for self-pity. A shrug of the shoulders and it was back to work. Still Napoli came, roared on by a crowd seemingly possessed. It was on the hour when after unrelenting pressure the Neapolitans finally got a goal back. A Carnevale cross fired in from the left wing was deflected by luckless defender Pioli past a helpless Landucci at his near post to set the stadium ablaze. 2-1 and game on.

A burning desire to make amends for his wretched penalty drove Maradona on. There were moments when he appeared back to his devilish best, creating with ridiculous ease countless opportunities for the Napoli forwards. But there was no after-thrust, that frightening acceleration of pace which once enabled him to leave opponents for dead had gone. Instead his unerring ability to spot a killer pass and bewildering footwork proved equally effective in torturing the besieged visitors. Chances were made and missed, all foiled by the courageous Landucci who at times appeared to be playing Napoli on his own. Maradona also went close, letting fly from twenty-five-yards, only to see his low, swerving shot flash past the post. Fifteen minutes remained when a terrible lapse in the tiring Fiorentina defence enabled Antonio Careca to sneak unnoticed behind them, before poking a shot under Landucci's body that rolled agonisingly over the goalline and into the net. As the Neapolitans went wild, even *Rai's* television cameras showing the match live across Italy visibly shook as the foundations of the stadium rocked. It had been a comeback inspired by Maradona's introduction and the little man was not yet finished with the visitors from '*la Citta dei fiori*'.

With just three minutes left and the *Viola* hanging on grimly for a point, the Argentinian delivered an inch-perfect cross onto the head of attacking full-back Giancarlo Corradini, whose diving header won the day as it flew like a bullet past the forlorn Marco Landucci. Naples celebrated a famous comeback. The ecstatic Corradini ran straight into the arms of Diego Armando to thank him for his magnificent assist. Albertine Bigon watched on with a look of incredulity at those around him celebrating, old and young like madmen! So this was Naples? Such passion! Around the San Paolo, cries of 'Maradoona, Maradoona' rang loud. It appeared some things never changed. It was love again, *amore*! And it had always been so.

The full-time whistle saw Florence's beloved Prince Regent, Roberto Baggio, share an embrace with Naples' own royalty, Diego Maradona, in the centre circle. After a superb opening showing, *Il Divino* and his team found themselves overwhelmed by Napoli's blistering second-half display. He had ventured south, deep into enemy territory, determined to dethrone Maradona on home soil and take his world crown. But *El Pibe De Oro* was not yet ready to relinquish the title. The young pretender blessed by the footballing Gods was sent packing in typical, uncompromising Neapolitan fashion. Naples did not take kindly to those who dared to doubt the divinity of their own *El Rei*. To no ones real surprise Diego Armando was reunited with his number ten shirt after the game! And, together for the final time, Maradona and his brethren raged against the coming light. One last great battle with the Northern powers remained. There would be no rules, encore!

CHAPTER 21

NAPLES' LAST STAND

With heart-wrenching resignation, Napoli tifosi understood they were on borrowed time. All roads spiritually and financially for their club pointed tragically to self-made oblivion. But with Maradona back in the fold and still the measure of Neapolitan dreams, hopes remained high for one final fling with immortality. Whereas once their only concern was Vesuvius spilling molten lava upon their heads, a new fear now gripped. For after being blessed with a taste of greatness, a return to being mere also-rans filled them with dread. In order to survive what lay ahead something was needed to grasp onto, to take into this impending eternity of doom and despair. A glorious reminder of when they were king of kings. As the curtains closed on SSC Napoli's most glorious era, a final battle dawned. Naples' last stand.

It was Carnival time in Naples! Goals from striker Andres Carnevale, both made by Diego Maradona, gave Napoli an unassailable 2-0 lead against arch rivals AC Milan. Carnevale: a man blessed with the perfect name for such a grand occasion. Caught up in the fiesta-like atmosphere, the electronic scoreboard in the San Paolo flashed up images of smiling faces. With the contest clearly won, 80,000 Neapolitans reacted with delight when their heroes on the pitch indulged in showboating. Cries of '*Ole*' rang out from the crowd as the home side mocked their opponents with a spell of keepball that had Silvio Berlusconi's recently crowned European champions looking decidedly second-rate. Foremost amongst the tormentors was Maradona who had proved to be the difference between two evenly-matched sides.

Only a fortnight on from the miraculous comeback against Fiorentina, *El Pibe De Oro* continued to confound his critics. After scoring a vital, late equaliser at Cremonese seven days previous, he was looking fitter by the week and, having got rid of the hideous beard, appeared to have acquired a new lease of life. Only six minutes remained against the *Rossoneri* when Maradona raced clear of the Milan offside trap to beat keeper Giovanni Galli with a sublime chip of such genius that for a moment the stadium appeared to momentarily hold its breath and ask, 'Did he really do that?'

When questioned afterwards on how marking Diego Maradona compared with other Serie A superstar forwards, Milan defender Paolo Maldini remarked, 'When you have played against Maradona, all the others are small fry!' On their most hated foes' soil the Milanese were humiliated 3-0. And love, loathe, hate or admire him, there could be no argument. Those Northerners who hoped they had seen the back of this Southern, turbulent priest shook their heads in dismay for Maradona was back!

This second honeymoon period between player and club failed to last. On 1st November, Napoli were due to play a UEFA Cup second round tie against unfancied Swiss side Wittingen at the San Paolo. A first leg 0-0 draw in Zurich ensured the holders were clear favourites to qualify, only for Albertine Bigon's meticulous pre-match preparations to be thrown into chaos an hour before kick-off when Diego Maradona was sensationally declared unfit to play. Bigon knew well the reasons for this, as it was an open secret around the city that he had returned to the ways of old. In the days leading up to the match, Diego Armando had been conspicuous by his absence from the training ground at Soccavo. The Neapolitan grapevine overflowed with dark and crazed rumours, some beyond belief, others, knowing the characters involved, quite possible. A joyful reunion had occurred. Maradona's recent spectacular renaissance saw old 'friends' welcome him with open arms back into the fold. He was family again and Naples' forbidden fruits were offered up in abundance.

Aware of a city's eye upon him, the *allenatore* moved fast. Knowing he could not afford to be seen as weak, Bigon showed a ruthless streak by suspending Maradona until further notice. For the first time he realised just what previous managers were up against when dealing with *Pibe De Oro*, of the thorns beneath the surface. With a talent like Gianfranco Zola now available to call on, it was no longer the nightmare of old and a battle this impressive Napoli coach felt he could win. But the opening skirmishes proved traumatic at a nervy San Paolo. With the *tifosi* pining unashamedly for their idol, the Swiss minnows took full advantage to lead 1-0 at the interval. However, disaster was averted in the second half when Bigon's revamped side roared back with goals from new boys Baroni and Massimo Mauro's late penalty saving the day. But it had been close. As for Maradona, blessed with a little time on his hands, he found himself with a most unexpected date at the altar.

Just when Neapolitans thought their *Dieco* could never again surprise them, he announced his decision to make an honest woman of long-time suffering girlfriend Claudia Villafane. The sound of female hearts breaking was heard loud across Naples Bay, none more than Cristina Singrita, the mother of his son. Never one for half measures and determined to show Argentinian high society that the kid from the backstreet slums was now their equal, and more, Maradona instructed Guillermo Coppola no expense was to be spared. It was jokingly claimed that Claudia's spectacular wedding gown alone, laden deep with pearls, gold braid and specially-imported lace from Switzerland, could well have wiped out Argentina's national debt. With money no object Coppola moved heaven and earth to acquire for the big day nothing less than Buenos Aires Cathedral! 1,200 invitations were sent out for what became the hottest ticket in town. It was a guest list unlike any other, consisting of the great, good and notorious. An extraordinary cross-section of characters.

From the dirt and dust beginnings of Villa Fiorito, old friends pulled on their Sunday best, unable to believe their *compadre* had remembered them. Equally in Naples, *tifosi* such as CUCB leader Gennaro Montuori were rewarded for their loyalty. A 747 jumbo jet was hired by Maradona to ferry over the 250 Italian entourage that included, amongst others, all his teammates and various Napoli staff and directors. They, alongside a heady mix of family, close friends, Argentinian television celebrities, popstars and politicians, filled the pulpits to await the arrival of Diego Armando and Claudia. *Camorra* chiefs were also present, a peace offering by Maradona gladly accepted by the Giulianos. From every background, far and wide, all came to pay their respect to the beloved *El Pibe De Oro* for he made dreams come true. A rare gift.

Not since Eva Peron's wedding had Argentina witnessed such lavish scenes of pomp and circumstance. On the day the bridegroom's obvious foul mood was clear to all, his pre-nuptial nerves never more apparent than when he punched one of the hundreds of paparazzi photographers outside the Cathedral who had dared to block his path. Both he and the bride appeared anxious throughout the service, their forced smiles a giveaway to an undercurrent of tension. Maradona cut a fraught figure as last minute doubts looked to have overwhelmed him. But with a preening best man Coppola alongside, pretending all was well, and preventing him dropping his shoulder, throwing a dummy, and disappearing into the sunset, the glittering ceremony unfolded. Not a dry eye remained in the building as the happy couple were officially declared man and wife. Wild applause accompanied the newly-weds back down the aisle as they made for a rented Rolls Royce Phantom 111, said once to be owned by a certain visitor to these parts, Nazi war criminal Joseph Goebbels. The short journey from the Cathedral to the reception saw thousands of cheering Argentinians lining the surrounding streets to wish the Maradonas well. Escorted by a police motorcycle cavalcade, the Rolls made its way to a local boxing arena call Luna Park, one of Diego Armando's childhood haunts. There 1,500 guests prepared to party away the evening in unforgettable fashion.

A famed Buenos Aires eighty-piece Tango Orchestra ensured events went along with a real swing. As the music blasted out nothing was denied those present. A hundred solid gold rings lay hidden inside a huge wedding cake for the lucky guests. Masquerading as waiters, an undercover journalist managed to slip past the tight security barriers to make astonishing claims as to what occurred that night away from the public eye. They told of fully paid-up prostitutes posing as international interpreters, offering their unique services. Along with the finest champagne and cigars, in sugar bowls on every table cocaine was said to have been openly available to those who wished to indulge themselves. Nothing was left to chance in order that the 'chosen' had the time of their lives. Whether true or just blatantly falsified, all added to the legend of Diego Maradona and the world he had come to inherit. Behind all the self-indulgence, decadence and sheer excess lay one man's all-consuming desire to prove he had arrived. The poverty-stricken childhood of Villa Fiorito remained in his heart, but those times had gone forever. The message was sent loud and clear; 'I'm Maradona, and I can do what the hell I like!' But back in Naples there was one who had his measure.

The courageous decision to drop Maradona for the match against Wittingen showed Albertine Bigon possessed the necessary bravery to take on and even, if the need arose, sell him. With Italia '90 on the near horizon the Argentinian realised this was not a man to be messed with. Any lengthy spell out on the sidelines could have proved disastrous. As in Mexico, Argentina's World Cup hopes again rested almost entirely on the shoulders of their beloved *Capitano* as the cupboard was relatively bare and Maradona's footballing talents had never been needed more by his country. It had become essential he played regularly to ensure being in prime condition for the tournament. Even cutting out the dreaded cortisone injections and deciding instead to simply play through any pain barrier over the coming months. Whilst the many critics felt they had good reason to question his errant lifestyle, Maradona's courage and sheer desire to play football was never doubted. It was beyond reproach.

With Napoli's *allenatore* not one to bear a grudge, and impressed with the giant efforts made by a seemingly remorseful Maradona in training to amend for his latest misdemeanours, Bigon handed Diego yet another lifeline. But woe betide if he let him down again, for waiting in the wings was Gianfranco Zola. A most unlikely vulture, but one who, though counting himself amongst Diego Maradona's most fervid admirers, stood ready, if needed, to come and replace the most revered of Neapolitan heroes. But typically Maradona surprised all in his attitude towards the fledgling Zola. Naples watched in amazement as the Argentinian took the young Sardinian under his wing, sheltering him from those who threatened to lead him astray. A master and pupil relationship developed, one that quickly blossomed into a close friendship. After every training session at Soccavo, the two remained behind. Watched by admiring crowds of Neapolitan players, journalists and *tifosi*, they performed acts of sorcery that defied belief. Maradona would stand in the centre circle, flick the ball up and purposely smash it time and again against the crossbar. Bang! Astonishingly he never missed! Zola followed suit and though succeeding many times, failed to match *Pibe De Oro's* unerring eye. Maradona would strike the ball twenty yards, only for it to then curl in mid air and fly back towards him. This he would do repeatedly across the pitch, each time the same outcome. Zola's efforts to match often ended in frustration, only for his master to wrap a consoling arm around his shoulders, whispering advice. And on they would go, one striving for perfection, the other already there.

With Diego Maradona back in the team Napoli's attempts to win back the Serie A title intensified. A much-deserved 2-0 victory over Inter Milan in Naples offered growing proof that the Neapolitans meant business. Both goals came in the last fifteen minutes when the champions' fierce resistance finally cracked. Firstly wonderful skills by Maradona enabled him to find Alemao on the edge of Inter's penalty area. The fleet-footed Brazilian played a sublime through-pass to countryman Antonio Careca, who twelve yards out turned and smashed a terrific low shot into the net. Spearheaded by new signing Jurgen Klinsmann the visitor threw caution to the wind, only to be suckered by the ultimate counterpunch. Six minutes remained when Napoli broke out. With the entire stadium on their feet, roaring them on, Alemao stayed calm to feed Maradona a wonderfully weighted ball that the Argentinian controlled delightfully, then with ridiculous ease side-footed past goalkeeper Walter Zenga. Game over and as the San Paolo rocked one man suddenly realised that he had possibly the best job in the world. Albertine Bigon had that special look in his eyes of a man who knew he was onto something good.

In yet another rousing contest at the Stadio Comunale in Turin against Juventus, a draw earned saw them go three points clear at the top. An early strike by winger Massimo Crippa electrified the tens of thousands of blue *tifosi* present to give Napoli a perfect start. But in a storming second half the *Bianconeri* roared back. Inspired by their clever, tenacious Sicilian born centre forward Salvatore Schillaci (soon to be immortalised in Italian World Cup folklore) a deserved late equaliser arrived when Juve defender Bonetti came upfield to level with a powerful header from a corner. Points shared between two fierce, old foes whose bitter feud from generations past only increased in venom as the years went by. It was a blood thing. From father to son: the eternal battle, North versus South. For Neapolitans, rivals came and went over the seasons. Verona were loathed, Milan despised, but there remained only one true adversary. No respect, no love, just sheer unadulterated hatred. *La Vecchia Signora*, the accursed Old Lady of Turin.

Napoli continued to set a scintillating pace. However, disaster befell them in Europe when in just the third round, their brief reign as UEFA Cup holders was brought to a crashing end by German side Werder Bremen. In the first leg the home side found themselves two down at the San Paolo. But in a gallant second-half fightback, goals from Brazilians Careca and Alemao looked to have saved face, only for the Germans to snatch a last minute winner. Where the Neapolitans could have claimed to be slightly unlucky on home soil, the return leg in Germany left them shamefaced and reeling. For the striking green/white-striped shirts of Bremen handed out a 5-1 mauling. A full house of 38,000 at the Weserstadion raised the roof as their team ran riot. Total humiliation. It was without doubt the Neapolitans worst thrashing for years and was received with rancid indignation in Naples. The overall aggregate scoreline of 8-3 to Bremen hardly did them justice, such was the manner in which they outclassed the Italians.

But Bigon showed his true worth and quickly rallied the troops. SSC Napoli, minus an injured Maradona on the bench, returned to form and thrashed Atalanta 3-1 in the San Paolo. Gianfranco Zola was simply divine, a playing style reminiscent of *Pibe De Oro* in so many ways. Full of bewildering sorcery, teasing, twisting, turning, a swerve of the hips leaving defenders trailing. Then to cap a perfect day in Naples, scoring a truly memorable goal, letting fly a magnificent twenty-five yard shot that screamed into the net. Maradonesque! He had been taught well. Nine minutes from time Zola departed from the fray to be replaced by the great man himself. As the stadium rose to acclaim their new hero 'Zoladona', a smiling Diego Maradona warmly embraced his friend on the touchline and the two swapped high fives. These were heady days once more in the south.

He just couldn't help himself! Diego Maradona's God-given talent to arouse controversy whenever he opened his mouth showed itself again in early December. Convinced that the footballing hierarchy had fixed the World Cup draw to ensure Argentina received the toughest group possible, he went public to suggest it was all a pre-arranged farce. An outraged FIFA President Joseph Sepp Blatter lashed back, labelling the Argentinian's comments 'a very grave offence'. He warned that 'Maradona could well be banned from

Italia '90 for his actions'. Blatter claimed 'It is idiocy beyond belief. Either he is stupid or he is plain bad.' Not that Maradona appeared too perturbed. In reply he said, 'I will apologize, but I am not going to recant anything.' Surprisingly he received huge support from inside footballing circles, for it was long rumoured previous competitions had been rigged in similar ways. And those who called for Maradona's head on a plate after his outburst found themselves facing much unexpected criticism as many rushed to the Argentinian's side. Questions were asked. Hardly used to being put in his place by the petulant ravings of a semi-literate, streetwise urchin from the backside of Buenos Aires, Sepp Blatter plotted revenge. When asked his opinion of the finest players to emerge from Argentina, he retorted spitefully, 'I know of only one great Argentinian footballer, Alfredo di Stefano.' Maradona had made himself an enemy for life in upsetting the cushy world of FIFA's President/dictator. In time he would pay a heavy price. Blatter would have his day.

On the 10th of December Napoli travelled the short distance to fellow Southerners Bari. Determined to put one over their big city neighbours, the home side set about their task with a passion. They defended an early goal from their exciting forward Monelli with a passion verging on fanatical. Leading 1-0 with only nine minutes remaining, a shock appeared on the cards, only for Maradona to mastermind a piece of magic that produced a cross from which Andres Carnevale saved Neapolitan necks. Suddenly with the vast support of Napoli's away following evident, scenes of violence erupted across the entire San Nicola terraces. Soon a full-scale riot exploded. The local *Carabinieri* displayed little neutrality as they charged the visiting *tifosi* with batons and shields. After being beaten back, in went the tear gas. Carnage ensued. The final whistle saw Maradona rushing across the pitch pleading for his supporters to be shown a little leniency, but as the fighting raged it became apparent that the lads from Forcella and the Spanish Quarter were holding their own! With closest rivals Inter and AC Milan both drawing, the gap remained three points. As the Christmas break dawned and footballing hostilities ceased for a brief respite, it became clear that Albertine Bigon had rebuilt and instilled such confidence in his side that a second *Scudetto* in four years was within reach. But this was a journey Neapolitans had undertaken many times before and only once had they succeeded. Aware of the pitfalls that lay ahead, no one in Naples was getting too excited.

When battle recommenced late December in Rome, Southern hopes of further glories received a horrific dose of reality. Playing in all white Napoli went down 3-0 at the Stadio Olimpico against Lazio. Inspired by one of their own, twenty-one-year-old Paolo di Canio, the home side delighted the fanatical

Lazio Ultras with an all-out attacking display. Hard to believe that only a year previous he himself stood on the terraces as a member of the feared *Irriducibili*, on the Curva Nord. Full of devilish skill and pace, di Canio ripped the Neapolitans to shreds everytime he received the ball. Indeed the *Biancocelesti* were unfortunate not to win by many more, such was their superiority over the visitors. After the match Diego Maradona, with a shrug of his shoulders and a wry smile, was painfully honest. 'We deserved nothing, congratulations to Lazio, they were the better team.' One to forget for all Neapolitans.

Seven days later Napoli played host to relegation-haunted Ascoli. A demanding San Paolo, still feeling the bitter taste of defeat in their mouths from the Lazio debacle, cried out for a bloodfest. But it was not forthcoming as Bigon's men struggled woefully against an Ascoli side intent only on defending for a point. Andres Carnevale suffered the kind of afternoon forwards dread as the ball appeared determined to make him look ridiculous. Napoli's performance was so poor that the crowd vented their frustration onto a distraught Carnevale, who visibly wilted under the hail of abuse. He had now reached the point where *'No n chi resta che piangere'* ('There is nothing left to do but cry') when, on sixty-six minutes, redemption arrived. A Maradona cross found the leaping Carnevale and his towering header finally broke the deadlock. Once more how they loved Andres Carnevale! Such was Naples!

One week on further humiliation dawned away at lowly Udinese. Already a goal down, an 86th minute thunderbolt from home striker Mattei looked to have won the day for the struggling Northerners, who were managed by former Napoli coach Rino Marchesi. Then a footballing miracle of San Gennaro proportions occurred. Though far from home, their Patron showed that he had not forgotten his troublesome flock when for some unknown reason the *arbitiro* Pairetto awarded the visitors a dubious penalty. With time almost up Diego Maradona swiftly rushed to place the ball before reducing the deficit and giving his team a glimmer of hope. Surrounded by six black/white-striped shirts *El Pibe De Oro* set off on a last run. Deep into injury-time the game turned on its head. With the Neapolitans throwing everything they had left at a panicking Udinese rearguard, salvation arrived as so many times before in Maradona, the closest thing to San Gennaro available for Neapolitans here on Earth. Somehow the magical little Argentinian squeezed a pass through to the far post, where rampaging full-back Giovanni Francini stabbed home an astonishing equaliser.

The final whistle saw the Napoli players celebrate like they had already won the *Scudetto*. A somewhat shell-shocked Albertine Bigon shook hands with his Udinese counterpart. Though deeply entrenched in the relegation struggle, a rueful Marchesi shared a quiet word with the Naples coach. He knew more than most that when it came to this club, it was always best to expect the unexpected! They left the arena deep in conversation, each with vastly different problems, but both forever cursed/blessed with having SSC Napoli in their heart. To their grave, once in never out. The Neapolitans remarkable comeback against Udinese kept the Milan clubs at bay, albeit by a single point. But with fifteen games still remaining and the Milanese approaching top form another classic North/South championship race was on.

A narrow 1-0 home win against Bigon's old club Cesena came courtesy of a goal immaculately conceived by Diego Maradona for Massino Crippa, who with great technique smashed a wonderful shot past the Cesena keeper from ten yards. But it was the eye-catching, instant lay-off from the *Capitano* that caused eyebrows to be raised around the San Paolo. A strict fitness regime designed to have the Argentinian in peak condition for the forthcoming World Cup had kicked in and the Neapolitans were reaping the benefit. Both physically and mentally Maradona appeared almost back to his best. Next to suffer were a side genuinely detested in Naples for matters hardly relating to football, a club and its supporters that regarded themselves as infinitely superior to Neapolitans. From the far reaches of Italy's Northern regions, the hated Hellas Verona went south.

Bottom of Serie A and looking certainties to go down, fortunes had changed dramatically for the once feared Verona. It appeared unthinkable as they stood on the brink of humiliation that only six years previous the championship badge of *Scudetto* had flown proudly over the Comunale Bentegodi. Coach Osvaldo Bagnoli remained at the helm, but even this master tactician had been unable to prevent the drop into the abyss. The players Bagnoli now possessed bore no comparison to those who once graced the blue/yellow shirts of Hellas. How he yearned for a Briegel or an Elkjaer. Sadly for all Veronese those days had gone as the Napoli *tifosi* were swift to remind the derisory number of Brigate Giaboblu who had braved the perilous journey, standing huddled together for safety, in one small, heavily protected section of the San Paolo. The CUCB had arranged a very special surprise for those who once dared torment them with banners such as 'Stench from the South' and the infamous '*Lavatevi!*' ('Have a wash!').

The appearance of the two teams was the cue for an immense, perfectly choreographed yellow banana to appear like magic upon the terraces. A typical example of Neapolitan, gallows humour, aimed at the large racist elements amongst the Verona following that indulged in monkey chants and waving swastikas everytime Napoli played at the Bentegodi. Recently on their terraces the mocking Giaboblu had taken to wearing surgical masks in games against the Southerners. Payback came with Maradona who appeared determined to put on a performance worthy of what had occurred pre-match. Playing with all his old swagger, enjoyment and enthusiasm, the mesmerising Argentinian set about bringing the arrogant Northerners to their knees. Every darting run came laced with torturous menace. Time and again the San Paolo lay enraptured by their king's dagger like thrusts into the heart of Verona's defence. A day to remember for those who put their faith in Naples' most holy saints, San Gennaro and Maradona!

At one stage, such was his burning desire to entertain the Neapolitan masses, Maradona appeared to be laughing whilst running amok amongst a terrified flurry of yellow shirts. He was at his mischievous best. Every so often he waved at the crowd, even picking out a familiar face! It was personal: every trick, flick and deft sleight of pass was used to inflict wanton humiliation on those who dared once to disrespect *El Rei*. Perhaps deep down Diego Armando already knew his time with Napoli was drawing near and therefore was hellbent on giving Verona something to remember him by? A deflection off Hellas midfielder Giacomarro opened the scoring, but the moment all Naples craved arrived two minutes before half-time. Racing clear of three defenders Maradona tore into the penalty box before rounding the keeper Peruzzi and making it 2-0. Off he sprinted over the running track to be as one with his adopted people. Delirium gripped the San Paolo terraces. That strange, fervid atmosphere which only this crazed city and its inhabitants could generate had again taken hold. The second period simply offered further opportunities to tease and torment the bedraggled visitors. The referee's whistle for full time ended the Northerners' plight. Diego Armando Maradona's honour had been satisified. Though still to have a vital say in the destination of the *Scudetto*, it was to be a long time before Hellas Verona recovered from their eventful journey south to Naples.

February began well with further victories away at Fiorentina 1-0, and yet another barnstorming performance from their *Capitano* against Cremonese on home soil. Maradona weaved ghost-like through the red/white-striped defence to score twice and wreak havoc throughout the entire ninety minutes. His finest moment came with a thirty-yard free-kick that he curled with consummate ease past Cremonese keeper Rampulla into the net. Due to renovation work for the World Cup this game was played out in an eerie, echoing, half-filled San Paolo. Naples had been picked to host a semi final venue. A tale soon to unfold. As for Napoli, their true test was still to come, for Milan and Inter lay in wait over the coming weeks. With both matches at the San Siro, the Neapolitans faced their most crucial spell of the season. On Sunday 11th February 1990, they failed miserably against Arrigo Sacchi's European champions, losing 3-0.

With AC Milan's superstars threatening a massacre, Napoli survived a first half only with the blessed luck of San Gennaro. But the pressure was such that a goal had to come, and shortly after half-time winger Daniel Massaro struck from close range. A thundering header from Paolo Maldini and a late strike from the glorious Marco van Basten gave the scoreline a more realistic look as the *Rossoneri* blasted Napoli out of sight. The Neapolitans' lead had vanished and it was Milan who now topped Serie A. The Red Devils had *O Ciuccio* by the tail. Few thought they would let it go.

A week later further misery descended on Naples after just four minutes when Roma defender Nela hit an unsuspected rocket of a free-kick leaving Giuliani standing. The San Paolo was silenced, all seemed to be falling apart. Bigon watched with increasing alarm as his team repeatedly fell down in their attempts to equalise. Only Maradona looked up for the challenge, singlehandedly taking on AS Roma. But as the jeering and boos rang out from the terraces, even he appeared to lose heart. However, a fifteen minute respite from the pressure at half-time worked wonders, for after the interval Napoli came out a team possessed. It was like a light being switched on in the San Paolo! The players who had earlier performed like strangers, failing to string two passes together, suddenly woke up to what was at stake. Alemao came alive: it was the Brazilian's precise pass that put Crippa clean through, only for the lightning winger to be sent crashing in the penalty area.

Striding purposefully forward *Pibe De Oro* made no mistake with the spot-kick, placing his shot into the bottom right-hand corner. After being on cruise control for almost an hour, Roma suddenly found themselves with a real game on their hands. For ten minutes a blue wave surged forward. Then Carnevale played a superb through ball that sent Antonio Careca roaring unmarked into the box. What followed was one of the finest goals ever seen at the San Paolo. Forced wide onto the goalline by the keeper's challenge, Careca somehow produced an amazing shot that flew into the net from what appeared an impossible angle. Already ensconced in *tifosi* hearts, that instance saw *La Bomba* enter the esteemed realms of Neapolitan legend.

With the taste of Roman blood sweet in their nostrils, Napoli turned up the heat. The on-fire Massimo Crippa was again sent sprawling for yet another penalty. This time round Diego Maradona placed the ball in the opposite side of the goal. So easy! Still not satisfied, the San Paolo roared out for more. Attempting to appease their rapacious appetite, Maradona flicked the ball up on the edge of the box and let fly with an outrageous overhead bicycle kick that if successful would have surpassed even Careca's earlier monumental effort. Unfortunately for the Argentinian, Roma keeper Cervone leapt high and produced an outstanding save, tipping the ball over the bar. Sportingly

Maradona applauded his opponent. After the AC Milan debacle, Albertine Bigon's extravagant if wholly unpredictable side recovered some pride. And how they had needed it, for next on the agenda was a return date at the San Siro against Serie A champions Inter. And it was one they were forced to face without Diego Maradona.

To celebrate the 3-1 victory over Roma, a partying Maradona vanished ominously into the Naples night. When time came to return for training at Soccavo he never showed. The rumours began. A frustrated Albertine Bigon held a meeting with his President as to the Argentinian's whereabouts, but even the all-seeing, knowing Corrado Ferlaino was at a loss to explain his absence. Word was received by phone that Diego Armando was at home looking after his sick daughter, but this cut no ice with Bigon, for more reliable sources allegedly informed him that Maradona lay wasted in a notorious Forcella brothel. The *allenatore's* preparation for Napoli's most important match of the season, one that could well decide whether *Lo Scudetto* was returning south, had been thrown into chaos due to the selfish behaviour of Maradona, a man who claimed endlessly Naples was in his heart.

Prior to the game, travelling *tifosi* scaled the gigantic heights of the San Siro to unravel a huge Napoli banner that was visible across the city. Nothing could have inflamed Inter followers more than seeing the Southern colours flying high over their territory, and they sought retribution. Unbelievable scenes of mayhem erupted in the stadium as the two tribes, masked by scarves across their faces, clashed. Chains, bottles, flares and knives flashed and were hurled before the Milan *Carabinieri* finally calmed the situation. On the pitch SSC Napoli were handed the perfect start when after just seven minutes Antonio Careca dribbled past half the Inter team as he ran from the halfway line before rounding keeper Walter Zenga and scoring. The Brazilian delighted his *tifosi* as he danced the Samba routine in front of them, whilst at the same time infuriating the baying Milanese. It would be one of the few times they made it out of their half, for the remainder of the opening period saw them pinned back by Trapattoni's powerful, hard-running, skilful side. Jurgen Klinsmann was a nightmare for the Neapolitan defenders. His long legs eating up the turf, always harassing, forever waiting to pounce. With Aldo Serena alongside him, Klinsmann caused the visitors endless problems. Added to the fearful midfield surges of Lothar Matthaus exploding amongst them, Napoli held on for grim life.

Klinsmann was unlucky to see a goal disallowed for offside, whilst Matthaus smashed a vicious free-kick against the post. Plenty of luck and courageous defending saw the Neapolitans reach half-time still leading. But shortly after the break their walls were finally breached when Matthaus crossed perfectly for his countryman Klinsmann to power a fine header past the besieged Giuliani. What followed was nothing less than a siege as the champions went for the winner. From a corner Klinsmann again rose high to grab his second and leave the Napoli keeper pounding the turf. With Inter hitting them from all angles the Neapolitans were run ragged and a final goal came when the tormenting Klinsmann once more crashed in a shot that Giuliani failed to hold and forward Allesandro Bianchi swooped to make it 3-1. The day deservedly belonged to *La Grande Inter!* Come the final whistle blue/black smoke bombs engulfed the San Siro pitch. Elsewhere the *Rossoneri* had gone to Rome and thrashed Lazio 4-0 in the Stadio Olimpico, with the inestimable poaching talents of van Basten grabbing a brace. Sacchi's men had opened a two-point gap. The loss of their influential *Capitano* had taken its toll on Napoli and suddenly Diego Maradona had a lot to answer for.

Pibe De Oro surfaced to find himself in hot water with Albertine Bigon. For Maradona had simply pushed him too far. The atmosphere at Soccavo could have been cut with a knife as the two men locked horns. The *allenatore* refused to consider the Argentinian for selection, instead he chose Gianfranco Zola for the upcoming home game against Genoa, one Napoli could not afford to lose. Journalists confronted General Manager Luciano Moggi about the stand-off, but Moggi just shrugged his shoulders, claiming in a resigned manner, 'I walk on eggs round here!' As expected the match with Genoa was a taut affair. In a tense, stifling atmosphere at the San Paolo with the *tifosi* still singing for Maradona, Napoli looked to be heading for a calamitous 1-1 draw, a result probably enough to finish off their challenge. But once more Zola proved his own weight in gold. Keeping cool when all around were looking edgy, Zoladona took aim and cracked a last-minute winner to keep the nervy Neapolitans in touch with AC Milan. Gianfranco was already in danger of becoming a legend in these parts. Seven games remained to play. Many in Naples feared they could not take much more.

With the stakes so high Albertine Bigon decided it was in the best interests of all to forgive and he recalled Maradona. The city of Lecce sits deep in the south boot of Italy and on 11th March 1990, played host to Napoli. Lecce were fighting for their lives at the opposite end of Serie A and promised their big city rivals a southern battle royal. They remained true to their words and it was not until the second half that they managed to edge in front through a Carnevale header. The situation improved even further for the visitors when news filtered through from Turin by radio that Juventus were beating Milan. On hearing, the travelling blue army exploded with joy! Once more they dared to dream. Could it really happen again? Reality did not take long to slap

Neapolitans in the face. The yellow/red-striped shirts of Lecce refused to lie down and twenty minutes remained when their flying winger Pasculi levelled. Overcome with relief, the charismatic Lecce manager Carlo Mazzone raced along the touchline dancing a jig of unrestrained delight to celebrate the goal. Mazzone's celebrations took him within range of the Napoli faithful. Luckily their attempts to lynch him narrowly failed and the game finished 1-1! Despite the disappointment for Bigon's team of not being able to hold on for a win, Juve's 3-0 shock hammering of the *Rossoneri* meant the points deficit was reduced to just one. All considered, a good day for the South.

A city divided: AC versus Inter. Neither club desired such a potentially high-octane occasion so late in the season, for there could be only one winner. But events in Milan were put to the back of Neapolitan minds as they had enough on their plate away to Sampdoria. Napoli found themselves under pressure from the off by a home team still grasping on tight to an outside chance of the title. All be slender. Their explosive pairing of Roberto Mancini and Atillio Lombardo wasted little time testing out whether the Southerners were up for a scrap so far away from home. A stirring contest ensued with both sides creating and missing a hatful of chances. It wasn't until thirty seven minutes that a breakthrough occurred when the creative Mancini cut inside the Napoli box and laid the ball off for his teammate Dossena to smash a flashing drive past Giuliano Giuliani into the top corner.

Shortly after the interval it was the eye-catching Careca who let Neapolitans breathe a little easier when he played a stupendous one-two with Carnevale, before finishing with some aplomb to equalise. A draw suited neither side so there was no let-up as both continued to attack with little thought of defending. It was end-to-end football that left the crowd breathless and the managers speechless! Just when the visitors looked to be getting on top, a Mancini corner found the balding Lombardo whose header beat Giuliani all ends up to make it 2-1. Napoli's last opportunity to save themselves came with a Diego Maradona free-kick twenty-five yards from goal. Many Neapolitans would have put their hard-earned life savings on their hero saving the day, but alas for them he struck a disappointing effort wide of the post.

By his own exceptional standards Maradona had not played well, and there were even rumblings amongst his most fervid supporters that maybe *El Pibe De Oro* was not the force of old. Many wondered just what he had left? The apprentice had learned fast. If needed, though with heavy heart, Zola was ready to answer the call from Albertine Bigon. The final whistle signalled great celebration in the Stadio Luigi Ferrari, and not just from the home crowd. For word came from the San Siro that Inter had beaten AC Milan 3-1.

225

Amazingly with only five games left to play, Milan, Napoli, Inter, Juventus and Sampdoria remained in with a chance of the title. In the most open championship for years the dream of winning *Lo Scudetto* was causing heart attacks across the length and breadth of Italy!

Juve were in town! If ever there was a game tailor-made for Diego Maradona to silence the doubters and put Napoli's challenge back on track, it was *La Vecchia Signora* in Naples. In the tunnel shortly before kick off, Maradona walked along the line shaking the hand of all his teammates. He and they knew it was make or break time. Lose this game and there was no coming back. Opposite, the eleven men in black/white-striped shirts appeared pensive, knowing full well what awaited those who dared to wear the Juventus colours in this most sacred of Neapolitan shrines. An inferno! Together the two sides made the short walk up the stone stairway, each step seeing the noise level reach higher decibels before the sunlight dazzled their eyes and 86,000 blood-curdling voices greeted their entry into the inner sanctum of the San Paolo. Beat us if you dare! Welcome to Naples!

Diego Maradona began the match looking more like his old self, demanding the ball, explosive, full of guile and zest. It took him just thirteen minutes to set the stadium on fire. A thunderous drive by Andres Carnevale crashed against the Juve bar, pinged around, before finally falling to Maradona who swivelled and hit a classic shot that Steffano Tacconi never saw as it ripped past him. How many times would he prove them wrong? On the half hour Maradona brought the house down once more with an archetypal swerving twenty-five-yard free-kick that Tacconi could not even dream about preventing. On the terraces and across the city, Neapolitans fell in homage, pleading forgiveness. Never again would they take his name in vain. A crown of thorns so bloodied, yet still the miracles occurred? All his many enemies cursed loud as the Argentinian maestro shoved a million words of criticism back down their throats for daring to suggest his star was on the wane. Maradona's was a story that if written as a novel would have been shelved as being too fanciful for words.

As the game wore on Napoli toyed with Juventus, content to just keep possession, torment and humiliate. A dangerous tactic and one that irritated their coach no end as he screamed at them from the touchline to go for a killer third. Bigon had been right to worry, for with a whole half hour still left to play the exhilarating Salvatore Schillaci was hacked down in the penalty box and De Agostini fired home to make it 2-1. Suddenly those of local persuasion were no longer laughing. Their team's over-confidence had left them vulnerable in a way unimaginable only a short time before. With spirits raised the *Bianconeri* began to play in a manner that scared the hell out of the home *tifosi*. But Neapolitan nerves were finally soothed when an in-swinging Maradona corner found Giovanni Francini and the defender, in a mad scramble at the far post, stabbed the ball over the line. Game won. Come full-time the San Paolo erupted with delight at not only winning and keeping Milan within their sights, but also ending any faint hope Juve had of the title. What gave them more joy could never be certain!

Tavolino: a Serie A season was never complete without one notorious incident of Neapolitan skulduggery causing national uproar across Italy. On Sunday 8th April 1990, in the far Northern city of Bergamo, to no great surprise it duly occurred. Napoli were involved in a dour struggle against an Atalanta team fighting to save face after a recent humiliating 7-2 thrashing by Inter Milan. Playing in a rare change strip of red shirts, the Southerners came under relentless pressure on and off the pitch as hails of objects from a hostile home crowd rained down upon them. Twelve minutes remained and a game seemingly fated to end scoreless exploded in truly controversial fashion. After going to take a throw-in, Alemao suddenly fell to his knees, claiming to have been hit by something thrown from the terraces. Television replays showed that a coin appeared to have dropped short, but such was his apparent discomfort it was originally thought that another had struck him off camera.

Napoli physio Salvatore Carmando immediately raced to usher the player off pitch, gesturing wildly to the bench for assistance. Carmando was picked up on a nearby microphone imploring Alemao to, 'Stay down, stay down!' In what looked a rather overtly theatrical act to shelter him from further assault, his teammates crowded round, pleading with the highly experienced referee Carlo Longhi for protection. Gianfranco Zola replaced the stricken Brazilian for the final stages, but still Napoli failed to break the stalemate and despite late pressure the game finished 0-0. Full-time saw tempers overflow in the stands as rival *tifosi* attempted to settle the day with their own version of extra-time. As the fighting raged only yards away, Diego Maradona embraced fellow countryman, Atalanta winger Claudia Caniggia in the tunnel area and the two swapped shirts. The wailing of sirens mattered little to either Maradona or Cannigia, for to them this was merely a petty, insular, Italian squabble. More importantly to all of Argentinian persuasion was that Italia '90 drew increasingly near and both would play an integral role in the defence of their coveted World Cup trophy.

A still seemingly 'dazed' Alemao was taken with great haste to a Bergamo hospital where later that night he was visited by club President Corrado Ferlaino. After spending a little time at the player's bedside, Ferlaino emerged to face the waiting press. Wearing his most doom-laden expression, the President, when asked on 'Alemao's condition', replied in all seriousness, 'He did not recognise me.' Ferlaino went on to demand the same kind of of justice be handed out to Atalanta that so often was shown his club over the years in similar circumstances. The President was swift in claiming that he expected nothing less than to be given the points. Three days later the Italian Football Federation shocked all by coming down in Naples favour, awarding them a 2-0 win. They were left with little option when the *arbitro*, Longhi, submitted his report in favour of Napoli and through grinding teeth and pounding fists the Federation adjusted the Serie A table to place them level alongside AC Milan with only three games remaining. *Tavolino*: a mathematical rescheduling of the result. A paltry hundred lira coin had blown the championship race wide open. In the elegant surroundings of the city's countless coffee houses and bars, Milanese seethed with disdain at these 'cheating Africanos' from the Mezzogiorno. But not only they cast aspersions south, followers of every club north of Rome did likewise. Local rivalries mattered little in such circumstances for everybody hated Napoli! No neutrals.

Not surprisingly *Rossoneri* supremo Silvio Berlusconi led the moral outrage campaign. Berlusconi was in the early throes of a political career that in time would lead to the Italian Presidency. *Il Cavaliere* realised nothing pleased the masses more than some good old-fashioned Neapolitan baiting. So he duly obliged, telling of his disgust at what occurred in Bergamo. Condemned by all except those of Napoli persuasion, the newspapers, television and radio stations vented fury upon Southerners' heads. An overreaction bordering on hysterical took hold, every half-baked insult and cliché regarding Neapolitans was dug up and hurled in their direction. Again those who hailed from beneath Mount Vesuvius had contrived to almost ignite civil war against their fellow countrymen. Not that they were too concerned for when *Lo Scudetto* was at stake there could be only one tactic. Whether by Diego's 'Hand of God' or Alemao's dramatic, dying swan routine, to win was all that mattered. *Scopa!* Thirteen years later in an astonishing interview given to *Il Mattino* (Naples' largest-selling local newspaper), Corrado Ferlaino cleansed his soul and confessed it had all been a set-up. In his own words, 'It was Salvatore Carmando who came up with the idea. The player was actually struck by a coin, but we extended the episode to make a little scene.' Ferlaino went on, 'At the beginning Alemao did not understand what we were up to. It was only after Salvatore whispered into his ear that he played along. Later after visiting Ricardo in hospital, the game continued when I informed the press that he did not recognize me! Afterwards when alone I fell about laughing, for Alemao was perfectly well. We fooled them all!

As the accusations flew there came only typical defiance from Naples. They had longed ceased worrying about the opinions of outsiders. Despite endless attempts over the centuries to grind them into the dirt, fires continued to rage wild in rebellious Southern bellies. With a snarling vitriol and utter contempt Neapolitans spat back, refusing to cower under the well-polished heel of northern Italy's aristocratic boot. For all except one there were no regrets. The main *attore* (actor) at the centre of this Machiavellian-style plot. Ricardo Alemao's decision to go along with this charade was claimed to have haunted the highly religious Brazilian for years. So much that a later decision to become an Evangelist priest was said partly due to the guilt he still felt regarding his actions. In Naples it is claimed behind every man of the cloth a dark secret lurks, a past indiscretion. In such circumstances *prete* were treated with great respect, but also secretly with a crude suspicion. How else explain their decision to refrain from humanly desires? But not Alemao, his fall from grace was well known and richly appreciated by Neapolitans. Nobody ever threw stones (or indeed coins) in his direction. Except that is in Milan and Bergamo!

While the vast majority of Italians prayed feverishly for SSC Napoli to fall flat on their face, they returned to action taking on Bari in the San Paolo. Fired by the overwhelming tirade of abuse and criticism in previous days, Albertine Bigon's team proved irresistible and dismissed their sadly outclassed Southern cousins with a merciless display of attacking football. Maradona, Carnevale and Careca excelled as they indulged in shooting practice. A first-half penalty made and converted by *Pibe De Oro* was scant reward for the Neapolitans' scintillating play. Performing to the gantry Napoli showed off to a watching Italy! Second-half goals by their twin striking duo, both taken in breathtaking style made the final score 3-0, laying down the gauntlet to Milan. Far away in the San Siro, a Daniel Massaro header handed *Lo Rossoneri* victory against Sampdoria to place them on forty-nine points with just two games remaining. On Sunday 22nd April 1990, all roads led north for a fateful double-header that would ultimately decided the destiny of *Lo Scudetto*.

Whilst Albertine Bigon's men were forced to endure a last, perilous journey up-country to Bologna, AC Milan faced a Hellas Verona side fighting for their lives to stave off relegation. The footballing Gods were in mischief-making mood, for a Hellas win in the Stadio Bentegodi over Milan would almost certainly hand the title to their arch enemy, should they triumph in Bologna, the ultimate irony for the Giaboblu hordes, but one deemed wholly acceptable if it enabled them to survive in Serie A. In times past Bologna had prided itself on showing wonderful hospitality to all outsiders except Neapolitans, and after being greeted with the warmth of a freezing snowstorm, Napoli took swift revenge on their unwelcoming host, roaring into a 3-0 lead at the Stadio Renato Dell'ara. Antonio Careca began the rout in the third minute. In one movement the lethal Brazilian chested the ball down before letting fly an unstoppable drive into the top corner from fifteen yards to cause unbridled celebrations amongst the 5,000 travelling Neapolitans. Careca's stupendous effort was met with dismay by the Milan *tifosi* in Verona who listened intently on radio to unfolding events in the Dell'ara.

The gloom doubled moments later when Diego Maradona cut in from the left hand touchline to hit a tremendous shot low past home keeper Cusin from the edge of the penalty area. Maradona was proving back to his devilish best as Napoli continued to sweep forward. On fifteen minutes Carnevale played in swashbuckling defender Francini to finish with sumptuous ease past Cusin. On enemy territory Neapolitan songs resonated loud as they stood on the brink of a potentially historical victory. With their game already looking over, all thoughts turned to what was unravelling in the Bentegodi. On the half hour Naples fervour temporarily dampened when Milan grabbed a lifeline with Marco Simone's deflected free-kick giving them an undeserved lead over a ferociously battling Verona. With both contenders winning and each having their final game at home, a play-off to decide the title suddenly became increasingly likely. But it would not be required for in Verona the second period brought a drama and excitement unmatched in Serie A history, as Arrigo Sacchi's much-lauded superstars self-exploded in incredulous style with, it was later claimed in true Neapolitan conspiratorial fashion, more than a helping hand from a friend of Naples.

Immediately after the break Bologna grabbed a goal back to help ease wounded pride after their first half mauling. But the Southerners reply was instantaneous. Who else but a ravaging Maradona crashed in a wondrous thirty-yard effort, forcing Cusin into a miraculous save as he leapt high to punch over the bar. As Napoli went all out for a fourth they were boosted immeasurably on sixty-three minutes when news arrived that Hellas defender Sotomayor had smashed in a header to equalise for Verona. Bedlam exploded in the Bentegodi as the home *tifosi* wept tears of joy and relief. The *Rossoneri* swept back and shortly after, Arrigo Sacchi went crazy on the touchline when Marco van Basten was refused what looked a sure-fire penalty by referee Rosario Lo Bello (a name soon to become demonised in Milanese folklore). He completely lost his cool, charging onto the pitch to confront Lo Bello, only to be swiftly shown a red card by the official and dismissed from the bench. Off trudged a scowling Sacchi to the safety of the tunnel, where surrounded by armed riot police he continued to watch as outraged Giaboblu attempted to reach him with a hail of coins from the surrounding terraces.

With the clock speeding incessantly onwards Milan tempers frayed and frustrations overflowed. None more than their imperial centre-forward Marco van Basten who repeatedly found himself hacked and slashed down by defenders, only for the referee to ignore his many pleas for protection. The normally well-oiled footballing machine that was AC Milan stuttered badly. Disaster loomed. Unless they scored again a win the following week for Napoli against Lazio at the San Paolo would see a second *Scudetto* in four years head south into the badlands of Mezzogiorno and Naples. As for the Southerners, the old adage of 'The enemy of my enemy is my friend' had never been more apt as Verona gave everything. Even in their wildest dreams no self-respecting Neapolitan could ever have believed such a scenario possible. A thought equally shared by the Veronese.

After being felled for the umpteenth time van Basten cracked and got himself booked for simply complaining. But worse followed when fellow Dutchman Frank Rijkaard remonstrated on his behalf, only to receive a ridiculous red for daring to do so. A melee ensued as an irate, dumbfounded Rijkaard refused to leave the field before being allowed a potentially explosive last confrontation with the remarkably calm Lo Bello, who clearly appeared to have lost the plot. Or had he? That he looked to be shamelessly enjoying himself hardly helped to calm tempers. Lo Bello's inept display at times bordered on the ridiculous, such was his seemingly one-sided bias. It was only the wise actions of Franco Baresi and Ruud Guillit ushering their teammate out of harm's way that temporarily calmed the situation. Just when it was thought the day could not get any worse for the beleaguered Red Devils, more gut-wrenching news came from Bologna.

Five minutes remained in the Dell'ara when Diego Maradona fed a delicious pass through for a quick thinking Alemao to beat the offside trap. The so-called 'Villain of Atalanta' surged on, rounded the goalkeeper and made the score 4-1. The Brazilian looked to have fully recovered from recent events as he lapped up the adulation of the vast travelling support. A miracle recovery? San Gennaro moved in mysterious ways! Whilst Neapolitans danced in jubilation, Milan misery increased tenfold in Verona when an infuriated van Basten finally reached the end of his tether. After yet another decision went against him, the forward took off his shirt and threw it at Lo Bello. Cue the exit. With almost indignant haste, out came the card to signal expulsion. Off he went, joining a worryingly ashen-faced Arrigo Sacchi and Frank Rijkaard in the tunnel area. Driven to despair by the alleged injustices being meted out to them, *Rossoneri* fury with the referee was such, many swore he performed as if wearing the Napoli blue under his supposedly neutral black shirt. Something stunk to high heaven that day in Verona and if the Milanese thought rock bottom had been reached with the departure of Marco van Basten they were sadly wrong. For what happened next left them reeling on the floor.

With time slipping like sand through their hands, Arrigo Sacchi's nine men continued to press and carry the battle forward. All shape and method had vanished to be replaced by wanton panic. On eighty-eight minutes the final nail was hammered into their coffin. A lightning break saw the darting, swift little winger Pellegrini chased all the way by a desperately tired and depleted Milan defence. As the Bentegodi held its collective breath the scraggly, long-haired Pellegrini took aim and executed a wonderful chip over keeper Giovanni Galli into an empty net. Convinced Pellegrini was offside the Milan players once more surrounded the referee, only to be given short shrift. Costacurta refused to be silenced and as went the script found himself flashed a red by Lo Bello. With just eight men left on the field *Lo Rossoneri* finally threw in the towel. Hellas were still alive! Scores across Italy meant a weeks' grace and the opportunity to fight on. But in the end they would go down, much to Naples' delight!

As for Senor Rosario Lo Bello? Due to Berlusconi's insistence and his own safety he was never again allowed to referee a game that Milan were involved in. Many years later when the dust had finally settled and tempers relatively calmed, Napoli President Corrado Ferlaino hinted heavily in an interview to Naples' *Il Mattino* that he was at the time 'very close' to Lo Bello. Ferlaino spoke of 'good relations'. Comments really that hardly needed interpreting. Hopefully the president was simply attempting to wind-up further Naples' many enemies in the north and elsewhere.

Game, set and championship point! Verona and Naples. Two cities, a world apart in so many ways, spontaneously combusted! The full-time whistle in Bologna saw chaos on the pitch as the Neapolitans waited with bated breath confirmation of Milan's fate. Then it came and the sudden realisation of a second *Scudetto* heading to Naples hit home. A familiar song broke out amongst Napoli *tifosi* that belonged exclusively to their fair city. Sung with huge gusto and a heartfelt passion the words drifted high into miserable, grey, northern skies; 'Oh my first love, oh first you'll be for me, Oh sweet life of mine.' Barring a disaster of catastrophic proportions the title was returning south. The Napoli players found themselves mobbed by hordes of reporters. Their main target was inevitably Diego Maradona who, faced with a barrage of microphones shoved within inches of his face, spoke only in gushing terms of his teammates. A great victory had been won in the north and a further point against Lazio on home soil would guarantee festivities fit to signal the end of the world. Alas for Neapolitans, such a dreaded scenario was at hand. The good times were drawing to an end, but not before one last helluva party!

Sunday 29th April 1990. Seven days later the inevitable duly occurred and uproarious scenes of revelry descended upon Naples. The 86,000 fanatical congregation in the San Paolo witnessed a lone header from defender Marco Baroni secure the required win against a lame Lazio side that came, saw and did not dare attempt to conquer. Against a breathtaking sea of blue/white flags SSC Napoli were crowned champions. Speaking in the immediate aftermath of the game an emotional Diego Maradona dedicated the title to his father, '*Dedicato a mio Padre.*' *El Pibe* had again proved how dangerous it was to write him off. In just a short time Maradona would be back playing on Naples soil, only in Argentina's colours. Amidst the rising euphoria, the man that delivered the ultimate prize, Albertine Bigon remained the same composed figure who attended his opening press conference only nine months previous, fending off with effortless ease searching questions about Maradona. Bigon's epic achievement meant he entered with full honours the realms of Napoli folklore. A treasured place in Neapolitan hearts forever assured.

The entire city spilled out onto the streets. On every corner vendors sold bottles of sea water labelled 'Berlusconi tears' to joyful revellers who snapped them up as mementoes. Baying mules roamed loose with pictures of Milan's hated President pinned to their asses! A 4-0 win for Sacchi's team over Bari played out in a funeral-like atmosphere at the San Siro meant nothing, for the Donkeys had truly bolted! Across the bay a sense of disbelief took hold. It had happened again! Against all odds Naples had won the day. Yet where the first *Scudetto* was greeted with utter joy and a great feeling of relief, this second came etched with an overwhelming sense of desperation. An almost painful longing. As night fell, southern skies once more filled with all manner of breathtaking rockets and flares. The partying went on long and hard, too hard. Three years previous it was perceived as the start of the fairytale. Somehow this time round it felt like the end. Naples last stand.

CHAPTER 22

REBELLION

Only Diego would have the nerve to attempt such a trick. Never in World Cup history had a similar, torturous choice been forced upon a city. Surely this time Maradona had gone too far? For what right anyone, a king even, to demand a people turn against their own? Neapolitans riled in horror, why them? Had they not suffered enough? A banner on that fateful evening in the San Paolo spoke succinctly of their plight; 'Diego, you are always in our hearts, but Italy is our blood.' Naples was split: at a time when they should have been basking in the joy of a second historic Scudetto, El Pibe De Oro had once more tipped them over the edge. A nation held its breath, rebellion was in the air. Surely not even Neapolitans would stoop so low?

Italia '90 produced little in terms of spectacular football but more than redeemed itself with drama and controversy aplenty. It began on Friday 8th June at Milan's San Siro stadium with an almighty upset when unfancied Cameroon stunned the world champions Argentina. In a courageous performance full of guts and guile, wholly appreciated by a fiercely pro-Cameroon, 74,000 majority, Milanese crowd, the African minnows outclassed, bullied and ultimately battered the reigning holders into submission. Argentina's one great hope, Diego Maradona, was anonymous throughout, his every move tracked and ruthlessly dealt with by huge green-shirted defenders who cared little for the great man's health or reputation. From the kick-off it became apparent that a pre-tournament injury to his divine left foot, sustained during a warm-up match against Israel, had left *Pibe De Oro* all but spent and in constant pain. But desperate measures called. Without their legendary number ten the Argentines were bereft of both quality and hope. So once more the *Capitano* relented and underwent the torturous stab of a cortisone needle to ensure he played against the Cameroon.

Maradona's frustration began before kick-off when his country's national anthem was heckled throughout. Against a background of howling derision the Argentinian's face was of thunder as he listened to his nation's honour being ridiculed, its flag mocked. All this whilst the African's was cheered to the rafters and greeted with rapturous applause at its finale. The recent infamous events in Verona and the controversial loss of *Lo Scudetto* remained an open wound amongst the Milanese, ensuring a special welcome was reserved for the southern barbarian king who had dared to wrestle their title away. Never had this famous old footballing cathedral heard such vitriol directed towards one man, this despised Neapolitan despot. With Pavarotti's *Nessun Dorma* supplying Italia '90 a wonderful soundtrack all that was required in this grand Italian opera was a larger than life villain. Diego Armando fitted the bill to perfection. Maradona's appearance meant that an occasion normally noted for bringing nations together for once resembled a hate-fest.

Appearing oblivious to the hail of abuse raining down upon him, Diego Maradona showed off before battle commenced. Gently he coaxed the ball with his left foot onto the shoulder, juggled four times, back down to the knee, before finally flicking it off to an admiring teammate. All with such absolute nonchalance. Sadly for Maradona and his *compadres*, the day from that moment on took an inexorable turn for the worse. After an opening fifteen minutes in which a nervous Cameroon appeared intimidated by their more illustrious opponents, the fourteenth World Cup exploded into life. Awoken to the surprising notion that Argentina was nothing special, the Indomitable Lions came out of their defensive shell and went for them with ferociousness verging on brutality. None more than the toweringly, fearsome centre half Benjamin Massing, who introduced himself to Maradona with a horrific stamp on his ankle, for which he was rightly booked. The South Americans were hardly shrinking violets when it came to the game's darker aspects and a niggly, violent contest ensued with no quarter given by either team.

Cameroon were swiftly opportunistic up front, brimming with energy and skill in midfield, whilst breathtakingly savage at the rear. As for the champions, they looked dire. Their vastly outnumbered supporters in the stadium refused to be intimidated by what appeared the entire world wishing them ill-fortune. An enthusiastic Argentinian band tried with impressive if foolhardy bravado to pretend all was well, but secretly they must have feared the worst as their team's showing begged loudly to differ. Diego Maradona was misfiring badly. Relieved of possession with worrying regularity, he became increasingly infuriated at his own inability to grab hold and make things happen. There remained the odd flicker of wizardry to remind them he was still around, but nothing more. The brain was willing but his much abused body was finally saying no. An exhausting, albeit successful Serie A campaign with Napoli had taken its toll both physically and mentally on Maradona. There appeared nothing left in the tank. On the touchline Carlos

Bilardo looked close to a heart attack watching his team being mercilessly overrun by an African team showing little respect for either name or stature.

The half-time whistle offered brief respite from what had been nothing short of a mauling for the champions. In an attempt to ease the pressure Bilardo introduced lightning-fast Verona winger Claudio Caniggia. The tall, blond, long-haired Caniggia was good friends with Maradona off the pitch. There were many similarities between the two. Each hailed from similar backgrounds, plied their trade in Italy and most disturbingly, shared an unfortunate cocaine habit. Caniggia was only allowed to play in the competition at the last moment, after being the subject of a police investigation in Italy involving drug trafficking. Once cleared he was allow to join up with the national team, though great doubts remained over his complete innocence. But on the field, when focused, he remained a potent weapon in Argentina's less than impressive armoury.

With a devastating turn of pace and unerring ability to ride a tackle, allied with great skill and finishing, Claudio Caniggia on his day was a world beater. But he also possessed a truly annoying trait of falling over whenever an opponent looked at him. In the early stages of the second half this quickly irritated the Cameroon players no end, and they made certain that if he did go to ground it was for a good reason. Diego Maradona's total frustration at being unable to influence events around him showed itself. Not the type to find fault with fellow teammates, he instead vented his anger at the highly-respected French referee, Mr Michel Vautrot. Pleading with typically Maradonesque dramatical gestures, Diego Armando argued every decision, praying it would help stem the green tide.

But it was to no avail for the Cameroon, with nothing to lose, simply overwhelmed them as they attacked incessantly. Only bad luck and fine goalkeeping by Neri Pumpido kept the holders alive. Thunderous cheers greeted every African foray over the halfway line as the rabidly biased Milanese roared them on. But events took an unexpected turn on sixty-two minutes when the Lions' patience finally snapped with the antics of Claudio Caniggia and justice, Cameroon-style, was meted out. Breaking clear from his own penalty area, Caniggia accelerated away at great pace through a host of green shirts before being stopped ignominiously in full flight by an outrageously high tackle from Kana Biyik. Left with little option the referee flashed a red card and Biyik received a standing ovation from all corners of the stadium as he left the pitch.

Rather than being deflated this helped only to spur on Cameroon and astonishingly five minutes later they took a deserved lead. From a deflected free-kick Omam Biyik (brother of the dismissed Kana) rose to crash a header straight at Pumpido, only for him to watch in horror as the ball slipped out of his grasp and over the goalline. Huge celebrations followed as the Cameroon players cavorted wildly next to the corner flag with all manner of crazed high-jinks and death-defying forward rolls. African smiles had lit up the San Siro. The expected onslaught from the world champions failed to transpire and much to the despair of their ashen-faced Russian coach, Valeri Nepomniachi, the Indomitable Lions continued to carry the fight to Argentina. Defending stoutly and breaking with great menace, a most unlikely upset appeared on the cards. With Maradona reduced to mere mortal status, the South Americans, try as they might, lacked the necessary firepower to trouble their opponents' goal. Eight minutes remained to play when Nepomniachi played his ace and brought on the legendarily mystical Cameroon figure of the ageless Roger Milla. Officially said to be thirty-eight, many scoffed, putting his true age in the mid-forties. All mattered little, for in this short cameo Milla terrified the Argentinian defenders whenever in possession with his alarming mastery of the ball and devastating shooting.

As time ran down and utter humiliation loomed large, all Milan prepared to bask wonderfully in Argentina's and particularly Maradona's misery. Then, with only moments remaining, Claudio Caniggia awoke from slumber to race with deadly intent into the Cameroon half. With his blond locks flowing, Caniggia cut a dashing sight as he soared onwards, leaving in his wake a trail of despairing green shirts. Suddenly, arriving in mid-air and at high speed came the man-mountain Massinga, who with what appeared measured foresight seemed intent on slicing the Argentinian in two. As Caniggia rolled around in an apparent death throe on the turf, Massinga did not even wait to discover his fate as he began the long walk to the touchline. In a remarkable display of support the San Siro rose to acclaim the defender, who in turn waved to his new-found Italian friends. '*Forza Cameroon*' resonated loudly over the terraces. Left with nine men, the Africans steadfastly refused to buckle and reward came with the sound of Monsieur Vautrot's whistle. Their Captain apart, the Argentinians made a subdued exit, leaving the stage clear for African jubilation. Diego Maradona sportingly went round shaking the hands of his elated opponents.

Later, after being rather predictably chosen to partake in a random drugs test, Maradona attended the post-match press conference. In an attempt to win back some much needed face, and still seething at his maltreatment by the Milanese, the Argentinian was at his mischievous best when he declared to a waiting audience, 'I am proud to have played a part in the people of Milan putting aside their racism for a day to cheer on Cameroon.' The irony of these well chosen words was not lost on all present. But the fact remained the holders had been defeated and victory in the next match against Russia suddenly became essential. Safe in the knowledge this time round they would be amongst friends, the world champions headed south, to Naples. With Neapolitans still in seventh heaven after clinching their second championship title, it was with great joy they welcomed home their sacred *El Dieco*. The king had returned and a city rejoiced. Argentina was in safe hands.

Despite only a half-filled San Paolo, Maradona's name was sung with tremendous gusto by Argentinian and Italian alike. On the pitch the red shirts of Russia began brightly with a touch, technique and swift incisive passing that made their opponents appear leaden footed. On thirteen minutes drama occurred when Argentinian keeper Pumpido was stretchered off with a broken leg following a collision with his own defender Olarticoechea. On came substitute Sergio Goycochea whose first action was to palm away a Russian corner. From the resulting kick a fantastic header from Oleg Kuznetsov was stopped on the goalline by Maradona's hand. At first it appeared to be a shoulder, but television replays showed clearly it was the same right arm that felled the English in Mexico. All hell let loose as the Russians pleaded with the referee for a penalty, but the Swede Erik Fredriksson, as Ali Ben Nasser four years before, were up against an artist schooled in the dark art of *Scopa*, Neapolitan black magic. It was no contest.

Stunned by such a blatant act of injustice the Russians became dispirited and their stomach for battle waned. It came as no surprise on the half hour when forward Pedro Troglia headed the Argentinians in front. In a low key affair, with neither side overtly impressive, victory was sealed twelve minutes from time when the man who scored the winning goal in Mexico, Jose Burruchaga, latched onto a sloppy backpass by the unfortunate Kuznetsov to make it 2-0 and game over. In between Argentina had again flattered to deceive. Diego Maradona remained a sad shadow of past glories, though sheer presence alone appeared sufficient to inspire a vital win for his countrymen. Throughout the contest Maradona bickered constantly with the referee, appearing more interested in diving and winning free kicks than actually creating opportunities. Hardly the behaviour of a man named recently by his President, Carlos Menem, as Argentina's Official Consultant ambassador for sport. This was not the magician who had cast a spell over all who crossed his path in times gone by. Age, injuries and a destructive, self-indulgent, decadent lifestyle had finally taken its toll. It was desperation, the acts of one who had come to realise he was human after all.

Argentina's final group match was again in Naples where a 1-1 draw with an impressive Romania eased both nations into the second round. Maradona was insipid once more. If Italia '90 was proving witness to the sad demise of arguably the greatest player of all time, it also hailed the arrival of a new world superstar from Eastern Europe. The man known as the 'Maradona of the Balkans', the pride of the Carpathian Mountains, Romanian Captain Gheorghe Hagi. Against the Argentinians Hagi was magnificent, a wonderfully sublime left foot ripping apart the South Americans at will. Playing in a manner so reminiscent of *Pibe De Oro* in his pomp the Romanian was awe-inspiring, totally overshadowing the real thing. After yet another turgid performance by the champions even the most fanatical Argentinian supporter did not hold out much hope of them retaining the title.

Drab, dreary and little more than average with their Captain hopelessly off form, it was felt only a miracle would see them overcome their opponents in the second round knock-out phase for waiting in Turin were deadliest rivals Brazil. Though not possessing the heavenly talent of past great sides, the Brazilians remained a potent force and were being hailed as clear favourites along with Italy to win the competition. This city, home to one of Italy's most sacred relics, the Turin Shroud, prepared to play host to the greatest grudge match of them all, Argentina v Brazil. For most it was already a foregone conclusion, a mismatch. The Argentinians were not given a prayer. But in this place where Christ chose to return, another also was hell-bent on showing his true face. Diego Maradona was determined to prove that he too performed miracles, and the whole world would bear witness to his second coming.

On 24th June 1990, at the remarkable, newly-constructed Stadio Delle Alpi, 61,381 gathered to watch the showdown between these two giants of international football. On a swelteringly hot Turin afternoon, vast swathes of yellow/gold shirts and flags stretched out in breathtaking style across this space-age stadium. The Rio Carnival had for a day been transferred to Turin. Support for Brazil on the terraces was overwhelming as watching neutrals got behind them with the same fervid passion as a street kid from the *favelas* (slums). Everybody apart from their small if fanatical support wanted this irritant, boorish bunch of Argentinians removed from the tournament so that the partying could continue right up until the final. Even their own Football Association feared the worse, for unknown to the players they were already booked on a provisional flight back home the following day. As expected Maradona's name was greeted with a deafening barrage of whistles when read out over the tannoy. It had become par the course. The Samba drum beat thundered loud, the beautiful girls danced, the band played. Against this spectacular backdrop of passion, noise and colour Brazil began in whirlwind fashion. Stung by terrible criticism from their nation's media that they were by far the most defensive side ever to leave Brazilian shores, Sebastian Lazaroni's men appeared on a mission, for in the opening period they blitzed

Argentina's goal. With players such as Napoli's Antonio Careca and Ricardo Alemao in full flow, Brazil stormed forward. Neapolitan blood kinship appeared to have evaporated with Careca's pre-match labelling of Diego Maradona, his supposed good friend, as an 'Argentinian Pygmy'!

It was the man nicknamed *Lo Bomba* by the Naples *tifosi* who in the first sixty seconds burst though to fire a shot that Sergio Goycochea just managed to block. In what was a typically tempestuous, fiery, encounter between these aged old adversaries, the Argentinians battled through the first half without conceding. Though heavily outclassed the holders were not going down without a fight. Last ditch defending laced with a tenaciousness verging on fanaticism saw them survive, though in all but the scoreline it had been a massacre. Brazil created sufficient opportunities to win a dozen games. Their Captain, Dunga, came closest when he rattled the woodwork with a powerful header whilst Alemao saw a fierce shot palmed away by the heroic Goycochea who at times was all that stood between his nation and total humiliation.

As the second half unfolded, further gilt-edged chances were created and missed. Amongst Brazilian supporters a muttering of discomfort for the first time could be heard. When Antonio Careca once more shot against the post and Alemao followed up with a drive that cracked the opposite side, a terrifying sense of foreboding grabbed hold. Maybe it was not to be Brazil's day? Throughout the entire game Diego Maradona had been like a ghost at his own funeral, desperate to help ease the torment of his loved ones but utterly helpless to do so. As the battle raged and yellow shirts pinged the ball to each other, ripping through Argentina with effortless aplomb, he was simply invisible. Even the Brazilian fans had lost the urge to boo, such was Maradona's apparent utter inability to hurt them.

Eight minutes remained of this epic contest when *El Pibe De Oro*, Captain of Argentina, King of Naples, loved, hated, feared and adored, roared back to life. With both sets of supporters stricken by the unbearable tension prevalent in the stadium, the idea of extra time and even the awful possibility of a penalty shoot-out was deemed preferable to experiencing a goal at the last. Agony or ecstasy, it mattered little, for the shock could well have been fatal. Games between these two were often decided by moments of sheer genius that caused eyes to blink and the heart to soar. It would happen again. With his back to goal in the centre-circle, Diego Maradona picked the ball up, turned and accelerated past his marker. A momentary shudder rocked the Stadio Delle Alpi. Suddenly Maradona was clear, and the yards as did the years fell away. Fear gripped Brazilian souls: their worse nightmare realised. He was back!

240

Yellow shirts chased in desperation, slashing, hacking, out of mortal terror. But somehow an unerring ability to ride the most ferocious of challenges enabled him to keep possession. As if carried by angels Diego Maradona soared past three more defenders before laying off an exquisite pass for the unmarked Claudio Caniggia. With the Brazilians concentrating solely on Maradona they forgot totally about the Argentinian winger and, with space inside the penalty area to pick his spot, Caniggia flashed a superb drive past Taffarel into the top corner. With his Captain alongside him the goalscorer raced over to the corner flag where he fell flat with arms outstretched, before being mobbed by ecstatic, disbelieving teammates. Maradona punched the air, he bore the look of a man reborn. As for Brazil, both their team and followers gave the impression of being mugged!

A last chance in the dying moments to save themselves came through Muller who lashed over when it appeared easier to score. But it was not to be and the final whistle signalled Argentina's first victory over Brazil in four World Cup meetings. In Buenos Aires the celebrating began as they set about proving that not only Rio could party like it was the end of the world! The champions had stolen it. A quarter-final in Florence against Yugoslavia loomed large. But already many were doing their maths. If the skilful but unpredictable Slavs could be overcome, the mother of all semi-finals waited in Naples. Surely the Gods of football were having a private joke, Italy against Maradona's Argentina in the San Paolo? Neapolitans said their prayers and hoped beyond hope it would not come to pass. But somehow they already knew. *Dieco* was coming home to break their hearts.

After having disposed of the real thing, the Argentinians now found themselves against a nation widely regarded as the 'Brazilians of Europe'. When such wonderful ballplayers as Robert Prosinecki and Dejan Savicevic were in the mood, Yugoslavia were a match for any team in the tournament. But the highly-fuelled concoction of Croats, Serbs and Macedonians that made up their team meant they were often more likely to beat themselves, a nationalistic self-destruct button pressed on many occasions and one that returned to haunt them again in Fiorentina's Comunale stadium when it mattered most. After outplaying Argentina for 120 minutes, this bitterly fought quarter-final went down to penalty kicks. During the contest Diego Maradona had fell back into anonymity, his *tour de force* against the Brazilians appearing now just a sad drunkard's rendition of classic poetry. Sluggish and frustrated, Maradona looked a busted flush, no more than when he scuffed a spot-kick in the shootout that would have put his nation 3-1 up.

241

Taking advantage the ice cool Savicevic stepped forward and blasted a shot past Sergio Goycochea, making it 2-2. When Troglio hit a post for Argentina next time round it really did seem as if they were going home. But then events turned on their head as Yugoslavia missed the next one, Dezotti netted for Argentina and to the dismay of neutrals Goycochea saved once more, this time from Hadzibegic to win the tie. With the luck of the devil Carlos Bilardo's team had made it to the semi-finals. An emotional Bilardo joined his players as they took the salute of their small boisterous following. That nobody liked them was wholly irrelevant, for the holders were through and hanging on to their trophy for dear life.

Later that same day in Rome, Italy set up the ultimate showdown at the San Paolo when they beat the Republic of Ireland with a lone Salvatore Schillaci goal. No one slept in the Eternal City that evening as the car horns blazed away in triumph. Few were worried that for the first time Italy were now forced to leave the capital and play away from the electric atmosphere of the Stadio Olimpico, where they had been guaranteed incredible support throughout the competition. None believed that a mischievous, even downright rebellious city as Naples would fail to give vociferous backing to the beloved *Azzurri*. Neapolitans were, after all, though it begrudged Northerners to admit it, Italian. Their loyalty to the blood country unquestionable, surely? And so all eyes turned south, for in just four days' time, with the world watching on, Naples would be forced to bare its soul.

The *Azzurri* were on the march! Under the astute management of an experienced coach, fifty-seven-year-old Azeglio Vicini, they had cast away their defensive shackles of decades past in favour of a more attacking style. With fifty million Italians constantly giving him advice on who to pick, Vicini remained focused on the job in hand to mould together a side capable of withstanding the pressures that competing for a World Cup on home soil brought. On the eve of their opening game against Austria one paper carried the headline 'Failure will not be tolerated'. His was an Italian team brimming with skill, power and pace. A magnificent defensive stalwart to organise the rear in AC Milan sweeper Baresi, midfield guile from Giannini, Donadoni and De Napoli, whilst in attack a marvellous array of strikers from which to choose in Serena, Carnevale, Vialli, Baggio and 'Toto' Schillaci, this son of a Palermo bricklayer whose mad, staring Sicilian eyes lit up Italia '90.

The coach's one true Achilles heel lay with an absurd reluctance to acknowledge the rare genius of Roberto Baggio, choosing instead to select the more solid, hardworking Gianluca Vialli. In a first round match Baggio scored the goal of the tournament when from the halfway line he took on and beat the entire Czechoslovakian defence. But Vicini was far from impressed and insisted that *Il Divino* lacked the required mental toughness to play in every game. However, just when the Italian press were building up a head of steam in their clamouring for the golden boy Baggio to start against Argentina, up popped Diego Maradona to lob a verbal grenade that not only rocked Italia '90 on its head, but threatened to spark open civil war between North and South; 'The Italians are asking Neapolitans to be Italians for a day, yet for the other 364 days in the year they forget all about Naples. The people do not forget this.'

In an unveiled attempt to propel Napoli *tifosi* onto Argentina's side, Maradona spoke directly to his people, urging them to cheer for their king. 'What has Italy ever done for you?' he asked. Naples reeled: *El Pibe De Oro* had issued a call to arms. Opinion was split, a Pandora's Box had been opened. Bitter feelings that Neapolitans had tried desperately to bury whilst the tournament ran its course returned to immeasurably haunt them. The actions of their *Dieco* never failed to arouse the deepest passions and this blatantly cynical ploy to divide and conquer caused even them to consider whether he had finally gone too far. One Neapolitan man when questioned on local television reacted angrily to the suggestion that he should even consider going against his country: 'Neapolitans are more Italian than Italians,' he retorted. 'We are Italians and we support Italy.'

Whilst there were many who were genuinely horrified at Maradona's remarks, the more fanatical in the Forcella welcomed their hero's words as yet another opportunity to goad their good friends in the North. What better weapon than worldwide humiliation? *Tifosi* made ready their '*Forza Argentina*' banners. On the eve of the game, with emotions spiralling wildly out of control, the Argentinian flag was torn to shreds outside their training camp at Trigoria, near Rome. Speaking on *Raiuno* an outraged Maradona pledged to avenge his nation's besmirched honour in the San Paolo by knocking out the Italians. Though most regarded such talk as more mischief-making, there was something in the eyes that caused Neapolitans to sit up and take notice. They had seen that look before, he was serious.

On that fateful morning of 3rd July, Naples awoke in anticipation of the coming storm. Its people pondered their heart-rending choice, Italy or Maradona? Throughout the day Argentinians had begun arriving, their numbers swelling dramatically since the smash-and-grab raid against Brazil. Embraced warmly by the locals, spontaneous parties broke out along the Spaccanapoli. Hopes for an unlikely victory over Italy were high, for was this not the City of Miracles? Many took the opportunity to visit churches where they whispered quiet prayers to their host's Patron. Others partook in a different kind of holy pilgrimage, to *El Diego's* home in the hills of Posilippo, though perhaps most poignantly a blue/white Argentine scarf was placed with great discretion around a statue of San Gennaro. In this greatest hour of need all straws were to be clutched at. Secretly in more quiet moments supporters feared wanton humiliation at the hands of an exhilarating *Azzurri*. But their new found Neapolitan friends were quick to remind them that all was far from lost, for they would be playing under Vesuvius' shadow, and there anything was deemed possible. Anything.

As kick-off drew near and the San Paolo bathed gloriously in the red/green/white of the Italian tricolour, it appeared Maradona's call for Rebellion had fallen on deaf ears. Naples' plight was reflected in the words of one succinct banner, '*Diego nei cori, Italia nel cuore*'. Diego in our chants, Italy in our hearts.' But the night was still in its infancy and as a tremendous roar greeted the teams' entrance, those Napoli *tifosi* who had broken ranks with the vast majority were clearly visible amongst the Argentinians, joining in with their singing. Other Neapolitans decided simply not to cheer for either side. It was a strange atmosphere, restrained even. Make no mistake this was a city at war with itself. As the players' names were read out over the tannoy all the South Americans were roundly booed until it came to their Captain, who received a cheer that echoed far over the stadium and across the city. Maradona applauded the crowd, that they still loved him was not in question. *El Pibe De Oro* came from the sky and made their dreams come true, but this was blood. Those who did choose to side with the *Azzurri* did so in the hope that here on sacred turf, their *Dieco* could take care of himself.

The game began as expected with Italy quickly finding their rhythm and pinning Argentina back. Once again Vicini risked the vengeful wrath of his countrymen by leaving out Roberto Baggio, but as the host nation tormented the holders with their movement and pace in the early stage, he was hardly missed. In danger of being overrun the Argentinians mercilessly hacked down their opponents. Throughout the tournament they had attempted to make up for their dearth of class by displaying an almost savage determination to defend their crown at any cost. But this was Italy, it was sheer folly to believe they could ever be bullied or intimidated. As tackles flew the *Azzurri* replied with a bloodcurdling, bone-shattering interest. On seventeen minutes Toto Schillaci drew first blood when he pounced upon a Goycochea block from Vialli's shot to lash a ferocious drive into the top corner from eight yards. Off he soared with arms outstretched, eyes bulging from the sockets! No matter what became of him afterwards, Schillaci remains to this day the defining image of Italia '90. A shooting star maybe, but a legend forever.

Diego Maradona fished the ball out of the net and sprinted back to restart the game. He appeared to have found a semblance of his old form, probing and prompting in centre midfield. But it was still Italy who looked by far the better side, their rapier-like incisive passing cutting a swathe through the Argentine defence. Though enlightened every so often by moments of pure skill, the remainder of the first half was a cruel tense affair, with the French referee Vautrot requiring eyes in the back of his head as flare-ups raged. Much to the disgust of Baresi, Maldini and Bergomi, Claudio Caniggia spent most of the time collapsing like he had been felled by a sniper's rifle. It was a grim, brutal but still fascinating encounter between two nations with so much at stake. Finding it hard to resist their natural tendency to defend a lead, Italy came under increasing pressure and just before the break a rejuvenated of sorts Maradona let fly a rocket that was saved spectacularly by keeper Walter Zenga. It must have been the Naples air for Diego Armando had found from somewhere a new lease of life!

Half-time passed quickly and Italians everywhere suddenly realised their so far glorious rush to the final had turned into a crawl. Even the great Franco Baresi was displaying signs of nerves as his usual immaculate distribution went awry. With an hour gone Argentina had opened up and for the first time in the tournament began to play in a manner befitting their status as world champions. The South Americans attacked incessantly, Carlos Bilardo screamed out instructions from the touchline for his players at every opportunity to 'find Maradona'. By this time Italy had retreated *en masse*. Vicini looked close to a coronary as he implored his team to push up the pitch, but a combination of nerves and traditional old habits meant they were unable to break out. As the clock ticked down tension inside the San Paolo became unbearable. Individual errors in the Italian defence saw supporters closing their eyes in horror. On sixty-seven minutes, with a full moon shining bright in the black Neapolitan heavens, their worse fears were realised.

Almost inevitably it was Diego Maradona who orchestrated the move, as he received possession in midfield and laid a pass out wide to the attacking full-back Jose Olarticoechea. Blessed with a little time the defender's cross found Caniggia, whose glancing header dipped over a badly flailing Zenga with ease to land in an unguarded net. Suddenly with a ragged Italy looking vulnerable and ripe for the kill all bets were off! Someone had not read the script. Not only Argentinians celebrated in the San Paolo that infamous evening, a minority of Neapolitans also could not resist such temptation. Joy in Buenos Aires, abject misery in Rome, Milan, Turin, Florence and beyond. Maradona blew kisses to his adoring followers. From the beginning of the competition he had been jeered, whistled, heckled, his anthem abused. Loathed, hated and detested, who was laughing now? 1-1, welcome to Naples!

With extra-time looming Vicini gambled and threw on his joker in Roberto Baggio. *Il Divino* found himself an immediate target for defender Ricardo Giusti, who was booked for leaving a stud mark up the back of his leg, an induction course Argentinian-style! The seconds ticked down, Monsieur Vautrot's whistle was greeted by both sides with relief, a brief respite from the overwhelming tension of battle. All inside the San Paolo took a sharp intake of breath before being plunged again into emotional turmoil. The match resumed with the fresh legs of Baggio tormenting the weary, South American rearguard, his silky skills leaving opponents two options, either look foolish or bring him to ground.

Giusti was of such mind, for after being left in an embarrassed heap by the Divine One, he extracted revenge by punching the exalted Italian in the face. Vautrot immediately flashed the red card, reducing Argentina to ten men. An incensed Maradona harangued the French official. His hands bound in prayer, the Captain pleaded Giusti's case but the referee simply waved him away. With the Argentinians defending for their very lives and the Italians almost paralysed by nerves, the game inevitably fell into stalemate. Vautrot's decision to call time on proceedings cut like a knife across Italy, for the horrible charade of penalties would be called upon to decide the winner of this searing drama in the San Paolo. On a sweltering, dripping hot Naples evening, Franco Baresi, *Capitano* of *Lo Rossoneri*, loyal stalwart to the *Azzurri* stepped out of the centre-circle to begin proceedings.

Baresi, Baggio and Di Agostini all scored, as did Serrizuela, Burruchaga and Olarticoechea for Argentina. Then, at 3-3, the night took its inexorable twist when Milan's Roberto Donadoni made his wary way forward. He walked in the doom-laden manner of a man heading for the gallows. It came as little surprise when Donadoni hit a weak shot straight at Goycochea, the line was broken. The spotlight fell on one man and, not for the first time in his remarkable career, Diego Armando Maradona entered centre-stage. If he scored the Italians would have to convert their next effort or face the ignobility of being eliminated from their own World Cup, and to make matters worse, by a man whom they had treated with total disdain from the opening match of Italia '90.

With a ridiculous par-nonchalance that beggared belief, Maradona simply rolled the ball into the bottom left-hand corner, whilst Zenga went in the opposite direction. As Diego wheeled away in triumph, Italy stood on the brink. Only Aldo Serena stood between them and utter desolation. Carrying a nation's hopes, the Inter striker stepped forward and hit a woeful penalty straight at Goycochea. With tears streaming down his face Serena collapsed to the floor. In that moment a dream died. Later he wept live on television begging forgiveness for the miss; 'I wear the sadness of fifty million people on my back.' The *Azzurri* were out. On screens throughout the land Italians watched in horror as Maradona led his team on a celebratory lap of honour around the San Paolo. The King of Naples saluted those who had joined with his countrymen in support of Argentina, for it was not only Argentinians who laughed, danced and sung under Vesuvius's shadow; there were others also who celebrated with glee the unfortunate exit of their Northern brethren.

It did not take long for the recriminations to begin. Maradona's post-match comment of 'I hate to enjoy the sadness of my friends' was not appreciated with emotions running so high as that night his house was stoned by grieving *tifosi*. An angry Azeglio Vicini slammed the level of support Italy experienced in the San Paolo, claiming it was nowhere near what they had received in Rome. Many Northerners cast treacherous glances towards Naples and accusations of betrayal raged. But all were vehemently denied by its inhabitants. However, the facts remained that those triumphant war cries of '*Dieco*' and 'Argentina' echoing over the bay, way past midnight on that fateful evening, came tinged with a local dialect. Maradona's cunning plan to exploit Neapolitan resentment had worked to perfection. His words had been heeded by some, if not all. On 3rd July 1990 Italians cried themselves to sleep, for a rebellion had occurred in the South that broke their hearts.

CHAPTER 23

SNAKEBITE

In the early spring of March 1991, a lone figure walked warily into the grand marble surroundings of Naples Palace of Justice, demanding to see the city's chief magistrate. He looked nervous, clutching tight on a cigarette, fully aware of the magnitude his actions were about to cause. The man's name was Piero Pugliese, a shadowy figure from the Neapolitan underworld. Pugliese claimed to possess intimate knowledge of a famous Napoli footballer linking him with drug trafficking and match-fixing. He wished to cut a deal, total immunity from prosecution for past misdemeanours, in return promising the authorities a prize beyond their wildest dreams, to expose the myth of El Pibe De Oro and dish the dirt on the soiled, private world of Diego Armando Maradona, shaking the ground beneath him.

In Rome on 8th July 1990 at the Stadio Olimpico, an Argentinian side decimated by injuries and suspensions went into a World Cup Final against Germany fired up with a nationalistic passion verging on psychotic. After the tumultuous events of the San Paolo five days previous, Maradona was despised like never before by Italians and when caught on the stadium screen mouthing 'sons of bitches' in reaction to the crowd drowning out his nation's anthem in a crescendo of boos, open season was declared on the Argentine Captain. A hailstorm of vitriol rained down that shocked even those who were there to support Franz Beckenbauer's team. What should have been a showcase occasion deteriorated into a horrific, ill-tempered affair with the holders by far the worst offenders. Their battle-plan appeared simply to reach penalties by any means. Argentina had achieved the impossible by making the normally boorish Germans the neutral's favourite.

Bilardo's men spent almost the entire contest hacking down any German player who had the misfortune to go within twenty yards of goal. Reduced to ten men on the hour when half-time substitute Monzon slashed down Jurgen Klinsmann, they went even further into their defensive shell. But with just six minutes remaining Rudi Voeller looked to be tripped by the trailing defender Sensini in the box and the Mexican official, Edgardo Codesal, decided to put

Italia '90 out if its misery, awarding a penalty. It was a highly dubious decision with the theatrical Voeller looking to have dived, but still one much appreciated by a rabid, pro-German crowd. Immediately the referee found himself surrounded by a Diego Maradona-led mob who seemed intent on a lynching if he did not change his mind. But despite the outrageous bullying tactics of the Argentinians as they bumped and pushed him, Codesal kept his cool. Showing equal nerves of steel Inter full-back Andreas Brehme stepped up to fire low past Sergio Goycochea and win the World Cup for his country.

Knowing the cause was hopeless, Argentina became even further enveloped in red mist when Dezotti brought more shame upon his nation by grabbing German defender Jurgen Kohler round the throat as he raced away from him with the ball. Codesal's immediate branding of a red card was a sign that the thuggish South Americans had truly plunged the depths. As the final whistle resonated in the ancient capital, Rome bore witness to a public display of emotional turmoil the likes of which no footballer has ever been subjected to. Maradona sobbed uncontrollably, his face welled in sorrow, all to the sheer joy of the Stadio Olimpico who wallowed wonderfully in such obvious grief. In front of a watching world, with all eyes and cameras upon him he broke down, both physically and mentally wasted. The pressures of carrying Argentina and Napoli over such a long period finally proved too heavy a burden to carry. The tears fell, but here in this footballing-mad country there could be no sympathy for a man who had single-handedly orchestrated Italy's downfall. Diego Armando Maradona's descent into hell had begun.

The Last Act: There was a great sadness on the San Paolo terraces as they watched the slow, bearded, overweight impostor in Napoli's, legendary number ten shirt masquerade as their beloved *El Pibe*. But also there existed much anger, for the cause of his malaise was an open secret amongst the *tifosi*. Diego Maradona was out of control, he no longer trained, preferring instead to spend nights in Naples' red light area, whoring and taking cocaine. His teammates tried desperately to make him see sense, none more than defender Ciro Ferrara, who would go to Diego's house and try to persuade him to attend training sessions at Soccavo. Ferrara recalls: 'I would explain how much we loved and needed him. He'd react and come with me, work the cocaine out of his system and then we'd go off and have a pizza together. Sometimes when I think back now I wish I'd done it more often.' Sadly Ciro Ferrara was fighting a losing battle, because unknown to him cocaine had for the first time overtaken football in the life of Diego Maradona.

But even at his lowest ebb Maradona still produced moments of wizardry. A magnificently executed scissor-kick against Hungarian side Ujpest Dozsa in the European Cup helped the Neapolitans to a 5-0 aggregate win, and reminded people of the player he once was. After the game he declared in typical robust manner, 'I would play for Napoli in a wheelchair if needed.' But whispers across the city were that Maradona's time in Naples was short. Matters were brought to a head before a second round match against Spartak Moscow when the Argentinian claimed, to the astonishment of the club's medical team, of being injured and so could not travel with the squad to Russia. But after being threatened with a huge fine he relented, making his own way at the last. In the end many Neapolitans wondered why he bothered going, for a clearly sulking Maradona appeared totally uninterested in influencing events on the pitch. Bereft of any inspiration and far from home, a stuttering Napoli team were eliminated 5-3 on penalties in the Moscow snow. *Eliminato*. Going out at such an early stage once more, as against Real Madrid two years before, did not go down well with the hierarchy. Much needed revenue had again slipped through their fingers. They, like the most fanatical of *tifosi*, were fast losing patience with the increasingly unpredictable Maradona. It could not go on. For when a magician reaches into his hat and the rabbits refuse to appear, what is there left? A spluttered cough, deafening silence, before a slow embarrassing shuffle off stage. The show was coming to an end.

On the 22nd November SSC Napoli played host to Fiorentina. Albertine Bigon knew victory was essential if his team were to have any chance of retaining *Lo Scudetto*. After a superb 5-1 pre-season massacre of great rivals Juventus in the *Supercoppa Italia* (Italian Super Cup) hopes were high of another successful league campaign. But events off pitch regarding their Captain had an unsettling effect on the team, and one win in the opening seven games left them lying in a miserable tenth position. Also, the coach was growing ever weary of the constant backstabbing, political intrigue and in-fighting that existed in the corridors of powers at Napoli to such an extent that he was already contemplating a move elsewhere. As for Diego Maradona?

A late decision to exclude himself from selection on the day of the *Viola* clash left Bigon almost speechless with rage. The player and his manager Guillermo Coppola had spent the previous evening snorting coke, drinking and partying the hours away with expensive call-girls in a private residence of the Hotel Paradiso. That the home side won 1-0 with a rare Ciro Ferrara goal was for once of secondary importance for it was claimed that same night a meeting took place in which President Corrado Ferlaino finally issued the order to deal with Maradona. The love affair was over. He had outgrown his usefulness and become an embarrassment to the city. Plans were put in place, phone calls made and favours called in. So it began.

SNAKEBITE

The following day an astonishing article appeared on the front page of the prestigious newspaper Gazzetta dello Sport. Generally regarded as pro-Neapolitan, the feature by its well-respected Napoli correspondent Franco Esposito, made virtually unveiled references to Maradona's worsening cocaine addiction. He wrote of 'a dark evil taking hold. A mysterious illness affecting the world's greatest player'. Esposito was a journalist with intimate knowledge of the Naples scene. He'd have been well aware of what was occurring, but wise enough to realise some things were best left unwritten. That he produced such a hardhitting piece slaughtering Maradona meant it was clear the green light had been given by those in authority to do so. For whatever reason, it suited them for it to be published. Normally, on the rare occasions such scathing attacks found their way to print, Napoli officials shouted and screamed, threatening lawsuits and blue murder. But this time there was only a deafening silence from the San Paolo.

That itself spoke more than a thousand words. It became clear the veiled cloak of protection that had shielded Diego Maradona from prying eyes since his arrival in Naples had been swept away. Whilst performing miracles on the pitch, Neapolitan tolerance with their king knew no bounds, all they asked was for him to win them football matches. But when human failings were revealed and the magic touch waned, he was spat out with venom. The sheer ferocity of what happened next caused even the city's most hardbitten to wince. In what could only have been a concerted campaign, a systematic deluge of lowlife pimps, pushers, prostitutes and addicts appeared to denounce Maradona in newspapers across the land as nothing less than a sexually-depraved, drug-crazed maniac. Lurid tabloid headlines screamed out scandalous stories of cocaine-fuelled orgies in Naples backstreet brothels. Italians shook their heads in disbelief; if only a fraction were true, how did he ever find time to play football? Each day brought new revelations. Some were simply ludicrous and obviously fake. They came, sold their story and disappeared. Journalists who attempted to follow-up Diego's more 'interesting' encounters found not only were the characters involved hard to track down, most simply did not exist.

Reeling badly from this almighty onslaught, Diego Maradona's world was rocked even further when an undercover operation by Napoli *polizia* recognised his voice speaking on a wire tap, during a surveillance operation against a Forcella based cocaine and callgirl racket. The Argentinian was caught red-handed asking for 'gear' off a well known local woman called Carmela Cinguerama, who was said to run for the *Camorra* a chain of seedy establishments close by the city's main port. Although cleared of any involvement with the original investigation, it was felt enough information was available for the government to launch a separate legal action against the player for alleged possession and possible distribution of narcotics. A public announcement was made, boosting both egos and personal profiles of those adjudicating. Maradona was a huge, if relatively easy catch in a sea brimming with sharks. Having his head on a pole would prove a coup in the ongoing battle against organised crime. Piero Pugliese to arrive unannounced on their doorstep, desperate to cleanse his soul, was a joy they could hardly have expected.

It was a confession that came drenched in blood. Pugliese owned up to a host of gangland assassinations. He also dropped strong hints to interrogators that he was prepared to spill the beans on those who ruled from the shadows. Suddenly he was entitled to the highest state protection. With such a tempting statement Pugliese immediately became *pentiti* (turncoat) an inhabitant of the dangerous world of *pentismo* (repentance), a living death sentence shown to those whose efforts to expunge their sins left them facing the merciless wrath of former lords and masters that had vowed to make their deaths an excruciating one. Times were desperate, corruption was rife, gangster chiefs were blatantly putting forward their own people as candidates in local elections across Naples, and winning! Any honourable politician who dared to mention ballot-rigging was ruthlessly gunned down. It had become a matter of survival between good and evil. As all-out war was declared on *Lo Camorra*, Piero Pugliese attempted to escape a messy end by telling all.

Prosecutors listened with a mixture of incredulity and suspicion to his tall tale. He claimed to have been a valued member of Diego Maradona's inner circle, with much sought after duties such as being chauffeur and bodyguard to *El Rei*. Life with Diego brought many perks. Wine, women, drugs, all available on tap. It was a pleasurable existence, much preferable to previous employment working part-time as a security guard at the San Paolo, whilst allegedly having to supplement income by moonlighting as a hired gun for the *Camorra*. Piero Pugliese's story begins at Maradona's wedding in November 1989, where he was approached by Guillermo Coppola and asked to oversee a package that needed delivering home. Pugliese understood immediately the parcel was drugs and not wanting to risk the wrath of his paymasters agreed to go along. Through the aid of an unsuspecting courier who believed she was only carrying paper documents, the cocaine was successfully ferried to Naples.

According to Pugliese he was rewarded handsomely for his role in the smuggling, with 20 million lira paid out of DIARMA's bank account, for which only Maradona and Coppola had signature rights to sign off. Unbeknown to the Argentinians, their Neapolitan employee, in fear of being used as a scapegoat if all went wrong, secretly taped meetings between them, a paranoia that stemmed from the Naples streets where trust came only through those related by blood. The allegations were made known to all and as expected were vigorously denied. When confronted Guillermo Coppola could not deny the transaction due to taped evidence and his name on the cheque. But cool as ever, he claimed the money was simply a loan and for the good of Naples' children. The cash was to start a football school with a promise to be paid back within the month. Where other people had blood in their veins, Coppola had ice.

Serious cracks in Piero Pugliese's credibility as a witness appeared when he changed his story on how the cocaine found its way in. An absurd statement that it was brought by the Argentinian squad on their way to play a friendly match against Italy saw officers begin to think they were being led up a blind path. More raised eyebrows occurred when he cast crazed accusations that Maradona had conspired with the *Camorra* to ensure the Neapolitans failed to retain the *Scudetto* in their infamous collapse towards the end of the 1987-88 season. Endgame, that Diego had ensured thousands of Neapolitans, who bet with their hearts on the *Totonero* to win Serie A, would not collect and his gangster friends clean up. Such comments caused despair amongst even those who desperately wanted Pugliese to be proved right. It was outrageous, stupid even, to suggest Diego Maradona had thrown matches. For as Napoli fell away during that fateful time, it was so obviously visible that none fought harder than he. Maybe the blame lay elsewhere? Doubts were aired regarding certain individuals; it is a mystery still to be resolved. But not Maradona, to even suggest such was perceived as the muttering of lunacy.

Experienced members of the elite *Nulceo One*, Naples' finest crime fighting force smelt a rat. They failed to comprehend just what to make of this particular *pentiti*; streetwise *Camorristi* who was willing to say or do anything to save his skin, or a Neapolitan Walter Mitty character with a death wish, unbridled imagination and living in a fantasy world? One frustrated veteran officer of the *Camorra* war was famously said to have remarked about Pugliese that 'he had more faces than dinner time at Snow White's place'! But if enough mud is thrown some inevitably sticks and as Maradona's star hurtled forever downwards, the feelings of resentment were such, many had come to believe he was capable of anything. *Fattacio*, even. For Guillermo Coppola the heat from all sides had become even too hot for someone of his normally chilled persona to handle. Beating a hasty retreat, he fled home to Argentina.

There on safe ground he declared the split from Maradona had been 'purely affable and only temporary'. He simply wished to spend more time with his family in Buenos Aires. A pathetic charade of a public statement, made with the intention of healing what had already become back in Naples a mortal, untreatable wound, ended with, 'Diego Maradona did not and never has taken drugs.' Looking wonderfully tear-stained and quaking with emotion, but superslick to the end, Guillermo Coppola vacates the story. To say this pantomime was greeted with contempt and utter disdain in the Southern capital was the equivalent of calling Mount Vesuvius a teapot. This was the home of street theatre. Neapolitans knew a second-rate, two-bit actor when they saw one. The truth being Coppola had left his so-called *compadre* alone to face the lynch mob, whilst he ran to save his own neck. With friends such as these Diego Maradona had little need for enemies.

As the raging fires of hell engulfed Maradona's adopted city in all its fury he sought shelter on a football pitch. Once it had been a sanctuary, away from the pitfalls and stresses that being a living God to so many involved. But not anymore; where once they came to admire, now it was to stare and poke fun. *El Pibe De Oro*, who skipped beneath the raindrops with the ball tied to his feet by a mystical piece of string, no longer existed. Stolen away, never again to be seen. The pitch was a cage, whilst the stadium a zoo. That Maradona still continued to be picked by Albertine Bigon was for reasons of both pity and the hope that a momentary spark of the old magic might create an opportunity for his badly misfiring side. Amidst the controversy of a horrific season the Neapolitan's title was long gone. All that remained was for the same fate to befall their *Capitano*.

In the end it all came down to pure mathematics. Knowing they could save two years of astronomical wages and escape the nightmare scenario of having to sell him, President Corrado Ferlaino prepared to call time on the once exalted but now disgraced Argentinian's reign in Naples. Years before when an exuberant Maradona swaggered arrogantly into the President's office, laying down the law on who should or should not be bought, Ferlaino thought then that given enough rope he would inevitably hang himself. That day had drawn ever closer. To be treated with so little respect irked Corrado Ferlaino in a way perhaps only other Neapolitans could understand. But they needed him. Despite everything that went on behind the darkened veil, Maradona lit up lives, made dreams come true, banished nightmares, put away old scores and gave Naples back its pride. But there was a curse that lurked constantly, nagging, gradually eating away both at body and soul. It was one opponent *Dieco*, despite all his God-given gifts, could not shake off. And in the end that was why they crucified him.

For seven years Napoli's shadow army of fixers went to extraordinary lengths to ensure Maradona's drug-taking never surfaced at post-match doping tests. His urine was either swapped for a clean sample or, in a ploy so typically Neapolitan in its scheming, the player would use a hidden tube from which he could produce a false specimen. 'Close friends' of Naples who worked in the Italian Football Association always made certain their number ten shirt never appeared in the chosen list at away grounds. On 17th March 1991, Napoli played Bari at the San Paolo. It was one of the rare occasions that Bigon played both Gianfranco Zola and Diego Maradona together. That they won 1-0 with a lone Zola goal was totally irrelevant, for what happened in the immediate aftermath would in a short time cause shockwaves across not just Italy, but the entire world.

Moments after the game finished a shattered Maradona was approached by the club's chief medical officer Arcangelo Pepe who told him he had been selected for testing. Knowing well the safeguards in place the Argentinian went happily along with proceedings, never dreaming that he was cutting his own throat in doing so. There is only so many times you can twist a snake's tail before it turns round and bites you. Seven days later in Genoa, Diego Armando Maradona played his last game for Napoli in a 4-1 drubbing by champions-elect Sampdoria, a sad irony being that it was against these same opponents whom Diego scored his first Serie A goal for the Neapolitans. Now would be the last, a penalty hit with grim conviction into the bottom left-hand corner. Then it happened, like a nuclear explosion ripping across the southern peninsula, news broke that Diego Maradona had failed the drugs test administered the week before. Evidence taken from a Rome laboratory shown traces of cocaine in the player's urine. Sensing blood and seemingly desperate to dance on Maradona's grave, the Italian authorities moved with indecent haste in handing out an immediate suspension. No appeal, no hope, '*Arrivederci* Diego, see you in hell.' His true enemy had at last surfaced, only then did Maradona come to understand the full extent of the conspiracy waged against him. Snakebite!

The lightning speed of events and the cold, calculated manner in which they unfolded bore all the traits of a traditional *Camorra* style sting. Without a blessing from the Giulianos and other influential families, such an audacious *coup d'etat* would never have been undertaken. That it was allowed to occur meant they too had washed their hands of him. What use a lousy cokehead? Diego Maradona was alone, for the first time Naples must have felt like a foreign city. Friends became strangers overnight. Those who once fell at his feet proclaiming, '*Ti amo piu che I miei figli*' ('I love you more than I love my children') now looked at him with nothing but contempt. Aware that this unseen foe would never stop until he was ran out of town, Maradona decided to grant them their wish. The fairytale was over, it was time to go home.

'*Vedi Napoli e scappa*' ('See Naples and run away'). In the early hours of Sunday 1st April 1991, the distant drone of a small jet engine was heard over the beautifully lit up Bay of Naples. On board was Diego Maradona, his family and a small huddle of lifelong Argentinian companions who had remained loyal to the end. He came from the heavens in the blazing glare of the Neapolitan sunshine and left like a thief in the night under cover of dark. Against a sleek black sky glistening with stars, *El Pibe De Oro* made his getaway. It would be eight long years before Maradona again set foot on Italian soil.

The next day at the San Paolo a spontaneous gathering took place of the Napoli players and backroom staff. All were upset, none more than Gianfranco Zola who broke down in tears and had to be consoled by Ciro Ferrara. The young Sardinian had lost not just a teammate, but mentor also. Speaking from the heart Zola claimed that, 'It would be difficult to wear that shirt.' Word spread quickly of the King's abdication. In years to follow, when fathers related to sons incredulous tales of *Dieco's* epic exploits during the glory days, how it all came to end would surely haunt them forever. The realisation that they would never again see him in a blue shirt suddenly hit home.' 'My God,' exclaimed a grief-stricken *tifosi*, 'what have we done?'

CHAPTER 24

EPITAPH

On Monday 2nd August 2004, SSC Napoli were officially declared bankrupt and ceased to exist. It appeared San Gennaro had finally lost patience with his Neapolitan flock. No more deadlines, the club was wound up and the San Paolo gates draped in chains. A door slammed shut on seventy-three years of rich history soaked in passion and unrelenting drama. How could this have been allowed to happen? Only four months previous in Buenos Aires hundreds staged an all-night candle-lit vigil outside the Suizo medical clinic, faces etched in grief, old ladies, children, men, young and old, hoping for a miracle. A priest arrived to administer the last rites, but was ushered away by the crowd. They were not yet ready to give up on their boy. A man received a call on his cellphone and yelled out, 'He is going!' Suddenly all around people fell to their knees and began to pray for the soul of Diego Maradona. Couldn't live together, lost souls apart.

Just six years after Maradona vanished into the Naples night never to return, Napoli were relegated from Serie A for the first time since 1964. Somehow it had all felt so predictable as years of wanton abuse, mis-management and outright corruption left a once proud club in ruins. Still the star players had been bought in a vain attempt to appease their fanatical support. Fonseca, Di Canio, Boksic, all failed in comparison, for the small if monumental shadow of Diego Maradona hung like a colossus over the San Paolo. Those who even dared to dream of following in such footsteps were simply wasting their time, for Maradona's dynasty was beyond compare and out of reach to mere mortals. It was like throwing a bucket of water at a lightning bolt.

As much as Napoli courted trouble on the pitch, behind the scene chaos reigned as the financial status of the club soared out of control. The fortunes earned from the *Pibe De Oro* era were ripped off mercilessly. The club had been nothing more than a moneymaking machine for *Camorra* overlords. But when success dried up they washed their hands of it and looked elsewhere to plunder. The great players who brought such success were sold off to clear ever rising debts. Gianfranco Zola, who carried the hopes and dreams of the next Neapolitan generation, was sacrificed and transferred to Parma. Though not wanting to go, Zoladona was left with little choice when it was explained to him that if he did not leave, Napoli were out of business. Thus reluctantly he packed his bags. Zola's transfer was a move that incensed the already bleeding *tifosi* who, blinded by despair, turned once more with a vengeance on their President. It was time again for Corrado Ferlaino to check under the car each morning!

As expected Albertine Bigon did not hang around and the Neapolitans hired a promising young coach from Caligiari called Claudio Ranieri. With lawyers demanding wages for their clients/players in the dressing room and bankers threatening to pull the plug at any moment, Ranieri fought a courageous firefighting campaign to keep Napoli's head above water. But the President, who still possessed in his head wild delusions of grandeur, deemed this insufficient for a club of their stature and promptly sacked a stunned Ranieri. Marcello Lippi was lured from Atalanta. Lippi was already viewed in Italy as a master tactician, and a marvellous successful season in which against all odds he led them to a UEFA Cup spot saw Juventus pounce to snatch him from Napoli's grasp. From that moment it became a matter of time.

Come the 1997-98 season it turned critical as each week they were beaten almost on a weekly basis. Some of the scorelines were beyond embarrassment. A disgusting 5-0 at Empoli, 0-4 at home to Parma, 6-2 away to Roma, 5-1 at Bologna and 6-3 by Sampdoria in Genoa. It was wretched. Neapolitans spoke of biased refereeing decisions, faceless enemies in the North plotting to bring them down, but this was a Napoli team hardly in need of such conspiracy theories for they were quite capable of doing it themselves. An astonishing three managers and thirty three players were used by a fearful Ferlaino in desperate attempts to find a winning concoction. But it was to no avail as a torrid campaign in which only a measly fourteen points were won meant the outcome became inevitable. The unthinkable had become reality; it was just a question of when and where.

It arrived in Parma on 15th April 1998 and total desolation descended on Naples when a 3-1 defeat confirmed their drop into the uninhabitable backwaters of Serie B. Marooned, a giant blue whale beached alone on a sand teeming with termites, slowly eaten away. Neapolitan sadness was matched only in feeling by the spontaneous outbreaks of partying breaking out in Milan, Turin and Verona. They had longed to witness the back of these Southern *terroni*, watch them squirm in their lowest hour. The hatred was such that celebrations erupted in the North, the likes of which had not been seen for years. *Arriverderci* Napoli! See you in hell!

But they would return, albeit briefly. Two years of footballing misery followed before the Neapolitans finally won promotion, and in May 2000 amidst wonderful scenes of new-found optimism SSC Napoli soared back into Serie A. Horns from ships moored in Naples harbour blared out in triumph. Tragically, after just one season in which old acquaintances were made, with at times gruesome consequences both on and off the pitch, they were again relegated. A heinous lack of funds to pay or even buy players proved too much of a cross to bear. This time it was for keeps, Napoli were dying.

Diego Maradona's harrowing, turbulent journey through the Nineties was an even more self-destructive path than that taken by the Neapolitans. After testing positive for cocaine in his system, FIFA acted swiftly in handing out a fifteen-month ban from all competitive football. Returning home to Buenos Aires, a depressed Maradona fell back into old habits and in an extraordinary incident shown live on Argentine television, he was dragged away in handcuffs by undercover police from a friend's apartment into a waiting mass of cameras. Appearing still in a drug-induced haze and trying desperately to avoid being photographed, he sheltered his eyes from a blinding barrage of paparazzi flashing only inches away. It was a blatant set-up with the media circus receiving a tip-off well in advance of the arrest. Somebody, somewhere wanted him ground into the dust.

The appearance in court was again a sensational news story as this fallen star awaited his fate. A lenient judge, Amelia Berrez De Vidal, ordered Maradona to seek treatment and placed him under medical supervision whilst he quit the drug. For two painstaking years he battled against the addiction and for a time looked to have exorcised his demons to such an extent that when the playing ban expired, a surprising old 'friend' resurfaced asking for help. Unbelievably, SSC Napoli made a last-gasp move to stave off the coming storm by prising him back to Naples. 'Napoli soccer has not forgotten its great champion,' claimed President Corrado Ferlaino. With a remarkable rehashing of recent history Ferlaino attempted to attain the moral high ground by claiming the Argentinian must return and complete his contract.

In Naples the President came under immense pressure from his volatile *tifosi*. He knew more than any of their penchant for unremitting hostility, if the cause required. A notorious reputation had reached ferocious new heights as Napoli struggled against their impending doom. The disaster that had befallen them was blamed entirely on the shoulders of their supremo. For Corrado Ferlaino, if it meant going cap in hand to his greatest enemy to avoid the wrath of his blood clans, so be it. The alternative was unspeakable. But if they thought Maradona had even vague thoughts about returning to a place that nailed him to the cross they were sorely mistaken. The Neapolitans were paid off and for the second time in his career he was Spain-bound.

Famed for its splendid orange groves, the beautiful Southern city of Sevilla became Diego Maradona's showpiece home for a short period whilst he portrayed his God-given gift for wreaking mayhem in foreign ports. It was a disastrous time for all concerned. Convinced by Sevilla coach and former Argentinian guru Carlos Bilardo that it was the right move Maradona crossed the water. But he never settled, indeed Diego's time in Sevilla is remembered more for an infamous incident when he indulged in a spot of team bonding and treated his new *compadres* to a night of debauchery at a notorious local brothel. Also, well-publicised fisticuffs in a nightclub that ended with a wild west-type free-for-all signalled it simply was not meant to be. A paltry four goals in twenty-six appearances was a poor return for a $7 million investment. Both sides were glad to be rid.

Returning home Maradona found himself followed everywhere by eager photographers desperate to capture him up to no good. Buenos Aires became a prison. In order to recharge his batteries he retreated out of sight to a country home in Moreno where for a while peace broke out in the crazy world of Maradona. But they soon found him and Diego, under severe pressure and feeling the strain, finally snapped. A posse of paparazzi had gathered outside the main gates. After asking them to leave and them steadfastly refusing, all hell broke loose, their constant shouts of 'Diego, Diego, Diego, Diegooo' driving him to distraction. The man in question decided enough was enough. Taking cover behind a car with an air rifle he began taking potshots at the unwanted guests. With an aim unerring, Maradona wreaked mayhem, ensuring the next days, weeks and months of headlines on the front of every Argentinian newspaper. Only intervention by an old ally, President Carlos Menem, and massive public support allowed him to escape jail, paying only a large fine for injuries caused. But in reality they would never have dared putting him behind bars, for if you took on *El Diego* in his own backyard you risked revolution.

On 5th September 1993, Argentina suffered the most humiliating defeat in their history. In a vital World Cup qualifier, a 5-0 thrashing by a brilliant Colombian side at their own Monumental stadium left the 77,000 fanatical home crowd stunned. The men from the mountains of Bogota and Medellin administered on their aristocratic neighbours the mother of all beatings and delighted in doing so. It was a result that left them struggling to qualify for the Finals. As Carlos Valderrama and Faustino Asprilla ran riot, a familiar chant resonated across the terraces. The crowd began to call for the return of their hero. 'Maradona, Maradona' thundered loud. It was a desperate plea for help. Only one man could save them from disaster. Forever the patriot, he was unable to ignore such a passionate call to arms. On 17th November, although looking a sad shadow of his former self, Maradona led his nation to an uninspiring 2-1 play-off victory over Australia, clinching their place in USA '94. That the performance was poor mattered little to Argentinians, for their Diego was back!

By that time he was home playing for provincial club Newells Old Boys. Maradona claimed it was a return to his roots, but a $25,000 sum paid monthly into a bank account by Old Boys President Senor Cattaneo no doubt proved a powerful sweetener. But again disturbing whispers emerged regarding Maradona's health. In just a few months his weight plummeted, the excess fat disappearing at an alarming rate, his face gaunt. The official word was that Diego had undertaken a strict diet with the result he was now healthier in both body and spirit. The truth as ever was much darker and that summer in North America Maradona would be found out in front of the entire world.

In Boston on 29th June 1994 Diego Armando Maradona's world was rocked like never before when it was confirmed traces of the banned substance ephedrine had shown up in his urine and he was being thrown out of USA '94. Argentina had just beaten Nigeria to secure qualification for the second round phase of the World Cup. Maradona had played astonishingly well, too well for someone of his ageing thirty-four years. FIFA officials had already chosen him to undergo the post-match drugs testing, a drawing of lots picking out Diego's number ten shirt. Suspicions were aroused after the Argentinians' first game against Greece when their Captain scored a wonderful goal, a typically sublime one-two before shooting devilishly past a stunned Greek goalkeeper. His celebrations caused raised eyebrows around the world as he raced up to a pitchside television camera and with eyes bulging roared out a death-defying yell. Some called it sheer relief, a reaction to those who sneered that he, 'Maradona', was all washed-up. A busted flush. Others claimed he appeared possessed, with demons in his soul, whilst the vast majority of football supporters simply watched on in amazement, mouthing 'What the hell is he on?'

Once again in the world of international football Diego Maradona had become a disgraced figure, his many enemies given fresh ammunition to fire their bullets. At a press conference to give his side of this sad, sordid tale he lashed out saying, 'They have cut off my legs,' a thinly veiled attack on FIFA and its dictatorial style Presidency. Years before in the run up to Italia '90, Maradona had caused Sepp Blatter great embarrassment when he alleged that World Cup draws were pre-arranged. In his mind what happened in the USA was payback time, a theory to this day in Argentina and most of the Third World believed as fact. When news of the ban was announced, tens of thousands took to the streets protesting in far off places such as India's New Delhi.

For Diego Maradona was the idol of an underclass scrubbed off a post-modern American-driven world map. A God to those who lived in shanty towns, bare foot, poverty-stricken, who watched his goals on battered televisions beside open sewers. Victims of changing times where materialism was all that mattered. Their cruise missile against oppressors far too powerful to be hurt by slingshots. From Naples' ancient labyrinth of hidden alleyways to the backstreets of downtown Cairo, these were the people who cried when news broke that Maradona had once again been brought to his knees.

Despite being handed yet another agonising fifteen-month FIFA playing ban, and scribes worldwide penning Maradona-related footballing obituaries, the player himself steadfastly refused to step out of the limelight. The adulation was like a drug which without it he would simply wither and die. To the utter dismay of the Argentinian football hierarchy, Diego decided to try his hand at becoming the greatest manager ever. Fuelled with a burning desire to succeed Maradona failed in truly spectacular fashion, first as coach of lowly, struggling Argentine first division side Deportivo Mandiyu, then in charge of Club Racing. Both terms lasted together no longer than six months, but proved entertaining mayhem as he collected a bevy of touchline bans and fines for speaking his mind in a manner hardly suitable for a living legend.

But this was Maradona, no hidden agenda or banal clichés, everything flowed from the heart. A fierce passion for football that at times, more than was healthy, threatened to explode. One particular discerning rant about a referee he memorably referred to as a 'gutless coward with no balls', was pretty typical of what occurred, as he went down with all guns blazing. As disasters go it took some beating. Frustrated at every turn by the inability of players to carry out set instructions due to the fact that many were overawed by his sheer presence, or mostly just not good enough, Diego simply lost interest and instead vented anger at 'enemies' in the establishment who sought by any means to bring him down. Forever plotting, scheming, waiting for an opportunity to twist the knife deep. Realising football management was not for him, he turned to another field where his particular, persuasive talents might be of better use. Politics!

With him at the helm Maradona dreamt of a worldwide international players' union, one that stretched across oceans, over mountains, for rich and poor. All would have their say, a democratic vote. It would be a mighty stick to fight back against the autocratic heavyhandedness of

FIFA. Take the game back from the faceless ones. Those who forced them to perform like slaves in the blazing heat of Mexico '86 at twelve noon, all for the sake of television companies. The players were the artists who sweated blood and tears, they should set the rules. He sent messages to top footballers across the globe urging them to join him in Paris, where at the elegant surrounds of Hotel Le Meridien, this brave new venture would begin. And come they did, Eric Cantona, Gianluca Vialli, George Weah. Others such as Hristo Stoitchkov and Paul Gascoigne contacted Maradona pledging help.

Those who actually showed up offered moral support for the Argentinian's noble, if somewhat spontaneous idea. None more than Manchester United's Cantona who at the time was serving a nine-month ban for karate-kicking a Crystal Palace supporter who made the dreadful mistake of insulting the volatile Frenchman's mother. Unfortunately events did not go as planned. A press conference hosted jointly by both Maradona and Cantona swiftly became prickly, two egos so large that France itself, never mind the conference suite of the Le Meridien would not have proved large enough. As Cantona spoke in philosophical tones of the grand merits of their scheme, Maradona became bored and asked his new-found *compadre* if he was going to go on all afternoon! Needless to say the atmosphere soured, and well before the moon shone over the Seine, Diego was off enjoying all the hospitality Parisian nightlife had to offer. This footballing utopia for brothers from the Soweto townships to Madrid uniting together never again saw the light of day. For the bright lights of Paris were calling Maradona. Nothing came before a party.

Shortly after, yet another ill-fated but highly emotional comeback occurred, this time with Boca Juniors, the club of Diego Maradona's heart. It proved calamitous, as his ballooning weight saw him reduced to an almost comical figure in the eyes of those whose love was not blind. As a child he wished only to wear the famous blue/yellow shirt of Boca, setting fire to La Bombonera with wonderful goals. He would daydream of receiving the ball, skimming a defender, through the legs of another, before soaring into the penalty area and flashing an unstoppable drive that burst the net. The crowd would rise and chant his name, 'Maradonnna!'This Diego had already experienced, but as his thirty-seventh birthday dawned, he could only once more fantasise about such moments.

A horrendous sequence of missed penalties and truly embarrassing performances stretched the patience of even the most passionate fan. When he again failed a post-match dope test with traces of cocaine found, few were surprised. On 24th August 1997 it was officially announced and as ever the usual tired, dreary excuses were dragged up by the player's entourage, who lived off his back, picking up scraps, stealing a living. But those who really cared about him, who remembered with tears in their eyes the fresh-faced kid from Villa Fiorito casting spells on a football pitch, prayed he finally sorted himself out. Sadly it was not to be. A leading Argentinian specialist Doctor Ricardo Grimson became appalled at his refusal to curb the white powder. In an effort to shock and bring him to his senses Grimson broke the news that 'Maradona could die at any moment if he does not quit'. But sadly a deluded Diego carried on. 'Gods don't die,' they told him, just one more hit, then another, then. . .

Three years later in January 2000 Diego Maradona felt the first larcenous tap of death upon his ever-widening shoulders. As a result of a cocaine binge whilst partying in the Uruguayan holiday resort of Punta Del Este, he suffered what was first feared a fatal heart attack. When the grave news reached Argentina people sobbed openly, for it was feared only hours before they lost their most beloved son. For a short time as doctors fought to revive him, his heart actually stopped for twenty seconds, and legend goes in Naples, at that moment Mount Vesuvius rumbled. Neapolitans were devastated, it appeared their boy was mortal after all. Past grudges were forgotten in an instant, for this was *Dieco*. A treasure of San Gennaro. But remarkably, showing amazing powers of recovery, he came back. This was one bright light Diego refused to go towards. Only a week later he was sat up in bed earning a hundred thousand dollars for giving an interview telling of his close shave with 'The Beard' (Maradona's pet name for God!). After just ten days in a Montevideo hospital, Maradona was deemed well enough to be flown home by private jet and continue his recuperation at the Sacred Heart clinic in Buenos Aires.

Doctor Carlos Alvarez who oversaw the treatment was alarmed at the extent to which his patient's vital arteries had been damaged by cocaine. 'He has flirted with death,' exclaimed an emotional Alvarez, no doubt a football fan. 'Maradona's heartbeat is down to just 38 per cent. It is akin to pouring a kilo of salt down the throat of a person who has hypertension.' But for Diego this was beyond a sickness, the drugs had become a necessity to breathe. He would go to any lengths to acquire them. Matters came to a head when one night a notorious local dealer dressed as a doctor in a white coat was caught redhanded in his private room. Diego claimed he was simply a childhood friend who had come to visit, but the truth was clear to all. His personal physician Alfredo Cahe knew they had to get out of Argentina or Maradona would be dead within months. He recommended Canada, but an unexpected invitation saw them head towards the Caribbean.

Since the Cuban people's revolution of 1959, President, General and founding father of modern day Cuba, Fidel Castro ruled supreme. Even America, Castro's sworn enemy whose mighty fist attempted many times to destroy him, had failed to bring about his downfall. No argument, it was Fidel's island. In the early summer of 1994 a fawning Diego Maradona was first introduced to his life-time idol. Both shared a similar political ideology, and despite being a generation apart, the coming years saw an unlikely but enduring friendship flourish. Any opportunity which arose for Diego to talk up the man he christened with great affection, *Il Commandant* was taken. 'I am proud to be a friend of the greatest man in living history.'

Such kind words were not forgotten by a man like Castro and in Maradona's deepest, darkest hours, he offered his hand. In a blaze of publicity the Argentinian arrived in Cuba looking horribly overweight but still striding defiantly through the airport foyer. He showed off a pride tattoo of Castro's trusted legendary Lieutenant Ernesto Che Guevara emblazoned upon his arm, himself a *porteno*, native of Buenos Aires. Speaking to waiting reporters Diego 'praised the dignity of the revolution'. Then, with tears in his eyes and voice cracking with emotion he opened up. 'Maradona does not want to leave this world. I want to live, watch my kids grow up, I vow to beat this sickness.' Alongside him were parents Dona Dalma, Diego Senior and the ever-faithful, suffering Claudia with their two daughters. All were smiling, for it appeared the penny had finally dropped with their boy. Chances of a happy ending suddenly looked a trite rosier. Welcome to Cuba!

The rehabilitation process began. For a while the wonderfully tranquil, laidback atmosphere of the island and its peaceful lifestyle appealed. Convalescing west of the capital Havana at a health farm, La Pradera, a specialist medical centre that dealt with those deemed untreatable elsewhere, his condition dramatically improved. Under a strictly controlled diet Diego Armando slimmed down, lost two stone and looked to be winning the battle against cocaine addiction. Bizarrely he even hinted at playing again for Argentina. 'It is true I wish to represent my country one last time. No matter what mistakes I have made with drugs, I am still Maradona. I am still *El Diego*.' But it couldn't last. The inner demons returned and a late night head-on car collision with a bus outside Havana was heavily rumoured to have been caused by a coked up Maradona losing control at the wheel. Driving on the wrong side of the road, it was a miracle he was not killed. Two strikes down, one left. Though denied vehemently by those around him the path to redemption appeared further away than ever.

Over in Naples they watched with heavy hearts the tragic demise of *Pibe De Oro*, their one-time demi-god. In the Forcella where Maradona was loved

265

like no other, he never really went away for on every wall his face and name still lay lovingly adorned. Handpainted murals with heartfelt messages placed alongside them, one in particular catching a rare optimistic mood of this troubled but totally charismatic city's caustic outlook on life; 'The Sun always rises'. Neapolitans prayed at night to deliver him from evil and back into their hands, let they be the ones to save his soul. In the name of the father, son and holy Dieco. It would be Naples' greatest victory. Whether it was simple yearnings for glories past or a guilty conscience at how he left them, a feeling existed that the time had come for reconciliation. For as Napoli languished in Serie B, close to extinction, littered with players not fit to clean Maradona's boots, everything became clear. Despite all that had occurred, it was without question a love supreme. Made in heaven, divorced in hell. Loved and hated, but how they missed him so.

Attempts were made to heal old wounds. On 24th August 2000 amidst great pomp and ceremony, SSC Napoli retired their number ten shirt in honour of Diego Maradona. Also they presented a request to Naples city council that the San Paolo stadium be renamed after their greatest ever player. The club acted on the back of daily newspaper *Napolipiu* that ran a huge popular campaign. Under intense pressure local politicians wasted little time passing the motion, before failing in having it officially recognised by central government. Unfortunately an ancient seventy-six-year-old by-law dating back to the Mussolini era prohibited any public building being called after a person until they had been dead ten years, the despot *Il Duce* returning from the grave to haunt them. Desperate to appease an infuriated populace, anxious councillors applied for special dispensation. Sadly Rome was not in the business of helping out a city that viewed state taxes as simply an irritant to be ignored. To Naples' disdain the bill was eventually allowed, but only on the understanding it came into existence a decade after Diego's departure from this mortal coil. Hardly cause for celebrations in Maradona's city.

Later that same year FIFA awarded both Diego Maradona and Pelé a joint award as their best Player of the Millennium. But the embarrassing truth for the authorities was that votes cast by the public had Maradona winning hands down and delivering a crushing victory to his Brazilian nemesis. An official FIFA internet poll showed overwhelming support for the Argentinian. This could not be allowed, as those in power could never live down such humiliation. So arrangements were made. A dubious 'Special Committee' of experts ensured Pelé tied in the final count, thus sharing the mantle.

On the 11th December at a glitzy ceremony in Rome, the footballing establishment announced the results and few were surprised at the final outcome. To the bureaucrats' dismay Diego Maradona travelled from Cuba to accept his prize and the speech had them reaching for the tin hats! 'Grazie to the people who have voted for me. Grazie to FIFA who have listened to the opinions of the public for without them we are nothing. I dedicate this prize to the most famous Argentinian of all time, Ernesto Che Guevara, to the Argentinian people and to my family.' His piece said, Maradona vacated the stage to polite applause from the suits, nothing more. But across the globe in 'Diego's world' they were dancing in the streets!

Though few would ever have dared to admit at the time, there appeared an almighty rush to honour Diego Maradona's achievements whilst he was still around to appreciate it. An onslaught of plaudits ensued from people whose lives were irrevocably touched and enriched by his extraordinary exploits on a football pitch, no more than on Saturday 10th November 001 in Buenos Aires, where 60,000 packed out the Bombonera for the' official Maradona tribute match, '*El dia de Diego*' (Diego day!). It was a fiesta of an occasion at what Maradona himself called, 'the temple of football'. A huge flag draped lovingly over the terraces of Boca Juniors' stadium spoke for millions unable to be present. It simply read, '*Gracias Diego!*' The match itself was a mere sideshow to the lovefest going on around Maradona, with the present Argentine national team lining up against a Rest of the World XI, Higuita, Matthaus, Ferrara, Francescoli, Valderrama, Stoitchkov, Suker, Careca and Cantona. All threw away egos for a day to pay respects to the finest footballer of their or any other generation.

The star of the show played one half apiece for both sides, his every touch cheered to the rafters as players from both sides fell over themselves in a desperate attempt to let Diego score. Though a wretched weight problem was obvious to all, his redoubtable spirit meant he never gave up. This plodding, hapless figure being waved through by opponents, but still unable to produce the moment all in the Bombonera craved. Then late on Maradona managed to convert a penalty past Colombian madcap goalkeeper Rene Higuita, whose well-meaning if rather obvious decision to dive the wrong way set the stadium alight. With tears rolling down his cheeks Diego took off his Argentine top to reveal underneath a Boca shirt. Cue unadulterated scenes of mass hysteria! Everybody cried, even the referee. It was that kind of day. *El dia de Diego*.

A familiar name appeared once more in the colours of SSC Napoli. In 1993 an Italian magistrates court ruled beyond any doubt Diego Maradona was the father of his one-time girlfriend Cristina Sinagra's child. That he turned out to be a talented footballer deemed good enough to be taken on Napoli's books had Neapolitans whispering crazy talk of a messiah, a second coming. Would they ever learn? The enormous hype placed upon his young shoulders was in total contrast to actual playing ability. He was good, but not that good. This was no *Pibe De Oro* Mark II. Diego Senior refused point blank to admit from afar that this 'stranger' was of Maradona blood. He spat insults at any who dared to suggest otherwise. 'I never ever want to talk to anyone about that kid, ever.' On 20th May 2002 he was left with little option when the seventeen-year-old Diego confronted him on the course during a charity golf tournament in Fiuggi near Rome.

Left with nowhere to run Maradona simply stared at this young lad whose features resembled so much his own. Then, whether angry, unimpressed or just simply overwhelmed, he panicked and fled. But the powerful notion of a son, after having been blessed with two daughters, appealed and later that day they did meet up. The two talked alone for an hour before embracing and promising to keep in touch. Whilst an overjoyed Diego Junior returned to Naples, his Pop left for Buenos Aires and a soon-to-be third run-in with 'The Beard'. Once home he returned to type. Despite God granting him precious time to make peace with his boy, still Maradona appeared to have a death wish. Not content with just flying close to the sun, he flew into it, stoking fires, tempting, teasing the Grim Reaper to make his move. Endless white lines of cocaine tapped out and snorted, slowly destroying him. It couldn't go on, for nobody lived forever. Not even *El Diego*.

Epitaffio: the story ends. On Sunday 18th April 2004 a shockingly bloated, heavily sweating, forty-three-year-old Diego Armando Maradona joined in the chants of the crowd for his beloved Boca Juniors from a VIP box in the Bombonera, the animated antics and gestures so typical of a man whose ailing heart continued to be worn outside his enormous dearth of a stomach. So entertaining were Maradona's passionate rants and spontaneous bursting into song that most of the people who sat close by spent more time watching him than the actual match. But the mood changed in an instant from joyful excitement to blind panic when Diego suddenly lost balance and fell to his knees. With prying eyes trying desperately to catch sight of their fallen hero, terror gripped those closest to him. Was this it, the end? As Maradona fought for breath an ambulance was called, and with sirens blazing he was whisked away, swept at full speed through the hectic Buenos Aires traffic to the Suizo Argentina medical clinic.

Amidst scenes of bedlam at the emergency entrance a seemingly dying Diego Maradona was literally thrown into intensive care as concern heightened about his health. He was admitted with blood pressure, a swollen heart and, most worrying of all, acute respiratory failure. A condition officially described as 'critical' by a sombre-faced hospital spokesman who also worryingly related, 'a feverish Maradona has been heavily sedated and placed on a ventilator allowing him to breathe'. As the devastating news swept through the capital, every televison, radio and newspaper hurtled headfirst towards Suizo. Hospital security staff jostled with paparazzi, eager to capture the death throes of a king. Inside doctors fought to stabilise Maradona, but the situation looked grim. His people swore it was not cocaine-related but such words were meaningless considering what had gone before.

Only a ghastly silence came from the clinic, no one was talking. Disturbing rumours he was already dead circulated amongst the mass crowds gathering outside, only to be immediately denied by the authorities. As the evening drew in, the night had never felt so long, dark and cold for Argentina. A nation was in turmoil. In an emotionally tear-stained show of unity hundreds joined hands to form a candle-lit vigil around the building. Together they prayed he would somehow find the strength to triumph once more over adversity and pull through. But this was surely one opponent even Diego's powers could not overcome. The unwanted appearance of a priest to administer the last rites was met with a hail of derision by Maradona's supporters. The man of the cloth was told with all great respect that he was not welcome, for they were not yet ready to give up on their boy.

Monday dawned and as Buenos Aires swung into life, every vehicle of any description that drove past the clinic on Pueyrredon Avenue carried the Argentine flag and honked its horn in a 'good luck' gesture. Banners lay draped over the floor carrying messages of support. One read, 'Diego, Argentina needs and adores you. Don't go away'. Another was from a people who though far away were there in spirit, 'From Naples with Love'. Never was *Scopa* needed more. Further bad news emerged from inside when it was announced that Diego Maradona had developed a serious lung infection, to hamper even further his chances of recovery. Only family and close friends were allowed in to visit the stricken star. Such was the large numbers congregating around Suizo, police officers were forced to cordon off the entire area. His by then ex-wife Claudia Villafane, their two daughters, mother and father and, surprisingly, former business manager Guillermo Coppola, who had somehow wormed his way back into the clan's affections, were escorted through the wailing hordes who chanted constantly Diego's name.

A small chink of light shone mid-morning when personal physician Alfredo Cahe claimed he was responding to treatment, though later that afternoon an official medical update threw cold water on such optimism by saying, 'Maradona remains in a critical condition'. Again hopes waned. Finally, after a torturous three-day wait a heartwarming statement was released saying he was off the danger list, but still faced a long stay in hospital. If what happened next was a miracle then the Almighty worked in mysterious ways, for after just a two-week recuperation, Diego Maradona fought back from the brink to declare himself fit enough to be discharged. It was an extraordinary recovery that left the Suizo medical staff perplexed and also dismayed for they knew there would be no next time. This was the last chance to get clean. When leaving, on asked by a huddle of disbelieving reporters as to his true health, a smiling Diego called out, 'Give me a ball and I'll show you I am well!' Even after everything that Maradona endured, his laughing eyes still hinted at mischief. Once more he had slipped through the Reaper's desperately grasping fingers. Maybe God just didn't fancy sitting at the right hand of Diego Maradona? Who knows where the road will eventually lead? As Maradona bows out, his fate uncertain, few carry hopes of a rainbow's end. For sometimes it is just not meant to be. Three cheers for the bad guy, for chances are we may never see his like again.

As their deposed king simply refused to die, so it was that in true, dramatic Hollywood style SSC Napoli were saved from extinction at the very last by one of their own! Just when it appeared San Gennaro had grown weary of the troubles and strife of his city's football team, a new saviour stepped forward to save their necks. Corrado Ferlaino was long gone, run out of town by irate *tifosi*, only to see those who took control make an even bigger mess. Salvatore Naldo, Giorgio Corbelli, Luciano Gaucci, all wealthy businessmen who promised grand ideas but never delivered. But then came the real thing. Billionaire movie mogul, Aurelio De Laurentiis, the cash-rich son of legendary film producer Dino, received the eternal gratitude of his blood kin by splashing out the equivalent of £20 million to own Napoli outright.

Italian FA rules stipulated that any club in bankruptcy had five days to find a buyer. Also, if support was of sufficient size, they could begin again in Serie C1 (third division) rather than have to scrape through the minefields of amateur leagues. But most importantly banks would be forced to cancel any money owed. With massive debts reaching to over £40 million this was a blessing from heaven. Suddenly, doubting Neapolitans realised their sacred San Gennaro had not forsaken them after all. For as Napoli's luck turned, he too looked to be back on form! One who could tame lions, cure the dead, produce Maradona and bring about the *Scudetto*. What price a few measly bankers? For was this not the City of Miracles? '*San Gennaro aiutaci tu.*' Now and again their Patron liked to remind his flock he was still around. Welcome to Naples!

It was clear De Laurentiis had done his homework. This was the richest owner since Achillo Lauro, and arguably the most astute. Napoli had incredible potential, mouthwatering even. In the age of pay-per-view television and an estimated eight million supporters worldwide, maybe life did exist after Diego? Once more something special was stirring under the volcano. The canny Don Aurelio knew how to play the fiddle of his fellow Neapolitans. 'Naples has always been my heart, and we, my people, have suffered like no other. It is time to put Napoli back on top of the world.' Music to the ears of a city that had all but given up hope. Players were brought in, seasoned veterans, promising local youngsters, all proud to wear that cherished light-blue shirt.

They scraped off the dirt, dusted themselves down and began again! It was a fresh dawn, a clean slate that wiped away past failings. Aurelio De Laurentiis christened his team 'a new Napoli!' An astonishing 55,000 *tifosi* showed up at the San Paolo to witness their first game in the previously uncharted, murky depths of Serie C1. A banner on the Curva Sud ominously declared, 'Juve, we are coming to get you!' This was no idle threat and all in Turin knew it. They shook their heads, would these infernal Neapolitans ever go away?

The epic adventures of this glorious if tragic club goes on, but no matter what unfurls in forthcoming chapters the seven years of Diego Maradona will never be surpassed. For once upon a time in Naples Maradona made dreams come true. What finer epitaph could there possibly be?

FINI